2004

MULTICULTURAL EDUCATION AND HUMAN RELATIONS

Valuing Diversity

DAVID W. JOHNSON

University of Minnesota

ROGER T. JOHNSON

University of Minnesota

ALLYN AND BACON

Boston ■ London ■ Toronto ■ Sydney ■ Tokyo ■ Singapore

Series Editor: *Arnis E. Burvikovs*
Series Editorial Assistant: *Lauren Finn*
Marketing Manager: *Kathleen Morgan*
Editorial-Production Service: *Omegatype Typography, Inc.*
Manufacturing Buyer: *Julie McNeill*
Cover Administrator: *Kristina Mose-Libon*
Electronic Composition: *Omegatype Typography, Inc.*

ISBN: 0-205-32769-9

Printed in the United States of America

10   9   8   7   6   5   4   3   2   1   06   05   04   03   02   01

This book is dedicated to our children,
James, David, Catherine, Margaret, Jeremiah;
Todd, Kristin, Timothy

CONTENTS

CHAPTER SIX
Cooperative Learning   131

CHAPTER SEVEN
Using Cooperative Learning   151

CHAPTER EIGHT
The Conflict-Positive School   185

CHAPTER NINE
Academic Controversy   206

CHAPTER TEN
Teaching Students to Be Peacemakers   232

PREFACE

It has taken us over 35 years to build the theory, research, and practical experience required to write this book. Our roots reach back through Morton Deutsch to Kurt Lewin. We wish to acknowledge our indebtedness to the work of both of these social psychologists. In the 1960s we began reviewing the research, conducting our initial research studies, and training teachers in human relations. Since then our work has proliferated.

Many teachers have contributed suggestions for implementing the procedures in this book and have field tested our ideas in their classrooms with considerable success. We have been in their classrooms and we have sometimes taught beside them. We appreciate their ideas and celebrate their successes. In addition, we have had many talented and productive graduate students who have conducted research studies that have made significant contributions to our understanding of human relations. We feel privileged to have worked with them.

NATURE OF THIS BOOK AND HOW TO USE IT

This is not a book you can read with detachment. It is written to involve you with its contents. Reading this book not only will enable you to learn the theoretical and empirical knowledge now available on human relations, but also will help you learn to apply this knowledge in practical ways within your classroom and school.

Often in the past, practitioners concerned with human relations did not pay attention to the research literature, and human relations researchers neglected to specify how their findings could be applied. Thus, the knowledge about power and potential of diversity was often divided. In this book we directly apply existing theory and research to the learning and application of effective human relations procedures and skills. In other words, this book combines theory, research, and practical application.

In using this book, read the chapters carefully, discuss the relevant theory and research provided, diagnose your present knowledge and skills, actively participate in the exercises, reflect on your experiences, and integrate the information and experiences into your behavioral repertoire. In doing so, you will bridge the gap between theory and practice. You should then plan how to continue your skill- and knowledge-building activities after you have finished this book. Most important of all, you should systematically plan how to implement the material covered in each chapter into your classroom.

We thank Linda M. Johnson for all of her hard work, help, and assistance in completing this book and Thomas Grummett, Nancy Waller, and Tim Johnson for supplying most of the illustrations.

CHAPTER ONE

INTRODUCTION TO MULTICULTURAL EDUCATION AND HUMAN RELATIONS

DIVERSITY: PROMISE OR PROBLEM?

The first duty of society is justice.   —*Alexander Hamilton*

In the story *Beauty and the Beast*, Beauty agrees to live in an enchanted castle with the Beast, to save her father's life. Although initially frightened of the Beast, and horrified by his appearance, she is able to look beyond his monstrous appearance into his heart. Considering his kind and generous nature, her perception of his appearance changes. She no longer is repelled by the way he looks but instead is drawn to his loving nature. The better she gets to know him, the less monstrous he seems. Finally, finding him dying of a broken heart, she reveals her love for him, which transforms the Beast into a handsome prince. Beauty and the Beast not only live happily ever after, but all those in despair who stumble into their domain are changed, finding on their departure that their hearts are now filled with goodness and beauty.

This is an often repeated story. Many times we are repelled by those we do not know. Yet after they have become our friends, we do not understand how once they seemed monstrous to us. Nowhere is the wisdom of the story *Beauty and the Beast* more apparent than in schools and workplaces. For it is within schools and workplaces that diversity among individuals is most often faced and eventually valued. ∎

The diversity of students in U.S. schools is increasing. By 2020 demographers predict minorities will comprise nearly half of school-age students. Such pluralism and diversity creates an opportunity with potentially positive or negative outcomes:

1. **Diversity among individuals can result in beneficial consequences.** Such consequences include increased achievement and productivity, creative problem solving, growth in cognitive and moral reasoning, increased perspective-taking ability, improved relationships, and general sophistication in interacting and working with peers from a variety of cultural and ethnic backgrounds.

2. **Diversity among individuals can result in harmful consequences.** Such consequences include lower achievement and productivity; closed-minded rejection of new information; increased egocentrism; and negative relationships characterized by hostility, rejection, divisiveness, scapegoating, bullying, stereotyping, and prejudice.

Activity 1.1 will help you clarify your own attitudes toward diversity.

To maximize the promise and minimize the dangers of diversity and pluralism, you must (Johnson, 2000; Johnson & F. Johnson, 2000; Johnson & R. Johnson, 1989; 1995a; 1995c):

1. Recognize that diversity exists and is a valuable resource.
2. Seek out relationships with diverse individuals within a cooperative (not competitive or individualistic) context.
3. Build a personal identity that includes
   a. Your historical and cultural heritage and the view of yourself as an individual who respects and values differences among individuals
   b. Respect and appreciation for the historical and cultural heritage of others
   c. A superordinate identity that unites all relevant groups
4. Understand the internal cognitive barriers (such as stereotyping and prejudice) to building positive relationships with diverse individuals, and work to reduce those barriers within yourself.

ACTIVITY **1.1** ■ MY ATTITUDES TOWARD DIVERSITY

List below several things you like about having diverse friends and several things you dislike about having diverse friends.

Benefits of Diverse Friends	Detriments of Diverse Friends

5. Understand the dynamics of intergroup conflict (such as the dynamics of inter-group interaction, high- and low-power groups), and work to establish the conditions for constructive intergroup interaction.
6. Understand the social judgment process and know how to create the process of acceptance while avoiding the process of rejection.
7. Understand how to structure cooperative interaction among diverse individuals.
8. Understand how to resolve conflicts constructively, and skillfully use the following procedures for doing so:
   a. Controversy: Intellectual conflicts that are part of learning and decision-making situations
   b. Peacemaker Program: Conflicts of interests that are resolved by problem-solving negotiations and mediation
9. Learn and internalize pluralistic, democratic values, such as the commitment to the equal worth of all persons and each individual's inalienable right to life, liberty, and the pursuit of happiness.

Box 1.1 provides a brief summary of this list of issues, each of which is discussed in this book.

CULTURE AND MULTICULTURALISM

To understand muticulturalism, it is first necessary to understand culture. There are hundreds of definitions of the term *culture,* but generally *culture* is a shared way of life for a group of socially interacting people. Prior to the 1950s, definitions of culture emphasized patterns of behavior and customs whereas more recently definitions have emphasized shared knowledge, belief systems, symbols, and meanings. Culture consists of tangible elements (such as the artifacts people make, the food they eat, the clothing they wear, and the language they speak) and intangible elements (such as values, attitudes, norms of behaviors, and social roles members adopt). Like an iceberg, culture tends to be 10 percent above water (the tangible aspects) and 90 percent under the surface (the intangible aspects). Culture is transmitted from generation to generation by the processes of enculturation and socialization and continues to exist as long as members are committed to continuing it. It is becoming increasingly rare to hear the word *culture* without the prefix *multi.*

Every person has multiple cultural identities—nationality, ethnicity, religion, gender, and so forth. Every person is thus multicultural. These identities are dynamic, always changing, adapting to changes in environmental circumstances and group associations. In an increasingly interconnected world society, for example, the

---

BOX 1.1

1. Value diversity as a resource.
2. Create a cooperative context.
3. Build a unifying superordinate identity.
4. Reduce cognitive barriers.
5. Reduce intergroup barriers.
6. Create a process of acceptance.
7. Structure cooperative interaction.
8. Manage conflicts constructively.
9. Internalize pluralistic, democratic values.

conception of independent, coherent, and stable cultures is somewhat passé. The processes of globalization draw people from different cultural origins into interaction and close relationships, thus influencing and modifying each other's culture, and in some areas, such as economics, creating a single global culture.

The fact that we are all multicultural does not mean, however, that the cultures are all mixed together. *Multicultural individuals* are people who have internalized several cultures, which then coexist inside them. Many multicultural individuals report that the internalized cultures take turns in guiding their thoughts and feelings (LaFromboise et al., 1993; Phinney & Devich-Navarro, 1997). In discussing the African American experience, for example, DuBois describes movement back and forth between "two souls, two thoughts, two unreconciled strivings, two warring ideals" (1903/1989, p. 5). Asian Americans and Hispanic Americans have described switches for cultures rooted to whether they are at home or at work and to whether they are speaking English or their native language (Padillia, 1994; Shore, 1996). Contradictory or conflicting cultures can be simultaneously possessed by an individual; they simply cannot simultaneously guide thought and behavior. Each may come to the fore in certain situations.

MULTICULTURAL EDUCATION

To foster the intellectual, social, and personal development of all students to their highest potential, it is necessary to provide each student with an equal opportunity to learn. This is the purpose of multicultural education, and it may be achieved through four interrelated activities.

The first activity is ensuring the educational opportunities of all students are fair and equal so that all students, including minority and economically disadvantaged students, can achieve their highest potential. This includes transforming the school environment, especially the hidden curriculum characterized by teacher expectations for student learning; groupings of students; instructional strategies; school disciplinary policies and practices; school and community relations; and classroom climates. Central to creating a fair and equal education for all students is establishing cooperative interaction among diverse students in which conflicts are managed constructively. The cognitive dynamics of prejudice and stereotyping and the dynamics of intergroup hostility must be understood and replaced with processes of acceptance and appreciation. Activity 1.2 has been provided to help you reflect on these dynamics.

ACTIVITY **1.2** ■ REFLECTIONS

1. Think back over your life. Have you ever experienced a hostile or destructive manifestation of intergroup conflict? If so, write down a description of a specific incident. Find a partner. Share your description, listen to your partner's description, and write down your estimate of how often such incidents happen in our society.

2. Reflect on your elementary and high school years. Write down specific incidents in which you (a) were "educated for pluralism" and (b) experienced a salient event (positive or negative) that influenced how you learned to relate to "different others." Find a partner. Share your incidents and experiences, listen to theirs, and write down three conclusions about how you were taught to manage diversity.

The second activity is reforming curricula so that multicultural and global perspectives are studied. The curricula should present the history and contributions of major civilizations in Asia, the Middle East, and Africa as well as Anglo-European civilizations. Curriculum reform is aimed at ensuring students develop multiple historical perspectives that include both minorities within their own society and third-world nations. Past and current world events should be understood from multiple cultural perspectives, and students should learn to consider both minority and majority points of view in interpreting local and national events.

From learning multiple historic and cultural perspectives, students' cultural consciousness should be strengthened. *Cultural consciousness* is (a) recognition that one's cultural perspective is shared by only the members of the culture and that it differs from the perspectives of members of other cultures and (b) understanding how one's culture is viewed by members of other cultures. Closely related to cultural consciousness is cultural identity, which has three important parts: A person's historical and cultural heritage, respect and appreciation for the historical and cultural heritage of others, and a superordinate identity that unites all relevant groups.

The third activity is teaching intercultural competencies to students so that they can interact effectively with members of cultures different from their own. *Intercultural competence* is the ability to behave so the consequences of a person's behavior match his or her intentions when interacting with members of other cultures (Johnson, 2000). This requires both (a) interpreting accurately intentional communications, unconscious cues, and customs from members of cultures different from one's own and (b) presenting intentional communications so they are accurately understood within the frame of reference of the culture of the individuals receiving the messages.

The fourth activity is teaching students the knowledge and social action skills needed to combat prejudice, discrimination, and the other major problems that threaten the future of the planet and the well-being of humanity. Multiculturalism requires an end to prejudice and discrimination. Central to these social action skills are the competencies required to structure multicultural situations with clear cooperative groups and ensure that conflicts are managed constructively.

Engaging in these four activities should result in the inculcation of important values. Students need to learn and internalize pluralistic, democratic values including the commitment to the equal worth of all persons and each individual's inalienable right to life, liberty, and the pursuit of happiness. Other important values are (a) appreciation of cultural diversity, (b) respect for human dignity and universal human rights, and (c) reverence for the interdependence among all human beings and all aspects of the natural environment.

DIVERSITY IS PERVASIVE AND INEVITABLE

In facing the promise or problems of diversity, there should be no doubt that avoiding diversity is not an option. Diversity exists and it is increasing. Diversity is pervasive and inevitable. Acquiring the skills to interact with diverse individuals effectively is not a luxury; it is a necessity.

We Increasingly Live in One World.   The problems facing each person, each community, and each country cannot be solved without global cooperation and joint action. Changes in the world economy, transportation, and communication have resulted in a level of interdependence from which no nation, society, organization, community, or individual in the world is isolated, separate, or apart. Because of technological, economic, ecological, and political interdependence, one individual or country alone cannot achieve the solution to most problems. Problems such as environmental pollution, global warming, unemployment, hunger, and terrorism are not solved by actions taken only at the national level.

These and most other problems have become so internationalized that the international affairs of one country are the internal affairs of other nations and vice versa. The forests that burn in one country can create pollution in neighboring countries and even in countries halfway around the globe. The currency problems of one country can create economic problems for a whole region. With increasing interdependence, diversity cannot be avoided or bypassed. Solving the problems facing each person, community, and country requires the cooperative efforts of diverse individuals and societies.

Business Ventures Are Globalizing.   The globalization of business is an example of worldwide interdependence. It is reflected in the increase in multinational companies, coproduction agreements, and offshore operations. More and more companies are exchanging their local and national perspectives for a worldview. For example, a hand-held calculator most often consists of electronic chips from the United States, is assembled in Singapore or Indonesia, is placed in a steel housing from India, and is stamped with the label Made in Japan on arrival in Yokohama. (The paper and ink in the label are all made and processed from trees and chemicals from elsewhere, and the plastic in the keys and body are also made elsewhere.) For another example, modern hotels in Saudi Arabia are built with room modules made in Brazil, construction labor from South Korea, and management from the United States.

Global economic interdependence is almost beyond imagining. A survey of 408 opinion leaders in business (e.g., executives, consultants, faculty) on the strategic issues that business will face in the future, for example, found that managing a more diverse workforce was the one issue repeatedly mentioned (Sirota, Alpher, & Pfau, 1989). To be competitive in the global market, companies must be staffed by individuals skilled in building relationships with diverse individuals.

Diversity in Most Settings Is Inevitable.   Individuals, therefore, need the skills to interact effectively with people from a wide variety of backgrounds. For 200,000 years humans lived in small hunting and gathering groups, interacting only infrequently with other nearby small groups. It is only with the recent development of worldwide interdependence, communication, and transportation systems that diverse individuals have begun to interact with, work with, and live next to each other. In North America, Europe, and throughout the world, individuals increasingly interact with people who come from different cultures and ethnic backgrounds, speak different languages, and have grown up in markedly different conditions. In addition, interaction between genders and generations is quite different from what it used to be. Such diversity is relatively new. Diversity among acquaintances, classmates, coworkers, neighbors, and friends is increasingly inevitable.

For these and many other reasons, diversity is pervasive and inevitable. Most countries, therefore, are becoming more pluralistic. In the United States, however, diversity is a tradition. (See Activity 1.3 to participate in thinking about the question, How then shall we live?)

Diversity in the United States

Historically, the United States has always been pluralistic (see Table 1.1). Our common culture has been formed by the interaction of subsidiary cultures and has been influenced over time by a wide variety of willing (and sometimes unwilling) European, African, and Asian immigrants as well as Native Americans. American music, art, literature, language, food, and customs all show the effects of the integration of diverse cultures into one nation.

ACTIVITY **1.3** ■ HOW THEN SHALL WE LIVE?

The central theme in Tolstoy's *Confession* is expressed by the question, How then shall we live? Form a pair. Write six answers to this question. Then join with another pair. Explain your answers, listen carefully to their explanations, and create a new set of answers that combines the best reasoning of both pairs. Afterward, form a group of eight. Continue until there is one set of answers for the entire class.

How Then Shall We Live?
1.
2.
3.
4.
5.
6.

The diversity of the United States is still increasing. In the 1980s alone, more than 7.8 million people from more than 150 different countries, and speaking dozens of different languages, immigrated to the United States. In the year 2000, more than one third of the population is expected to be racial or ethnic minorities, and more than 75 percent of the people entering the labor force are racial and ethnic minorities and women (D. Sue, Parham, & Bonilla-Santago, 1998). The Carnegie Foundation (1995) notes that from 1980 to 1990 the number of immigrant children increased by 24 percent and the number of children with limited proficiency in English increased 20 percent, thereby linguistically isolating those children of households where no one over 14 years old speaks English very well. In 1970, 20 percent of students were from minority groups whereas in 1992, 40 percent were. The percentage of students with disabilities, from families in poverty, and suffering from abuse is increasing. There is every reason to expect the diversity of students' cultural and experiential backgrounds, knowledge, abilities, and skills to continue to increase in the future.

Historically, since the founding of the United States, compulsory education has been used as the means for promoting unity among diverse individuals. All children, no matter what their religious, ethnic, or cultural background, have been required to

TABLE 1.1   Waves of Immigration

ORIGIN	PERCENTAGES		
	1820–1860	1901–1921	1970–1986
Northern and western Europe	95	41	6
Southern and eastern Europe		44	9
Latin America			37
Asia		4	41
North America	3	6	3
Other	2	1	4

Sources: Population Reference Bureau, Bureau of the Census, Immigration and Naturalization Service, Washington, DC.

attend a common school. It is within our schools that usually we lay the groundwork for creating *unum* from our *pluribus*.

Diversity and the Law

Three major recent government actions have established equality and improved relationships among diverse individuals:

1. *Brown v. Board of Education* Supreme Court decision was made in 1954 to improve ethnic relations.
2. Title IX was passed in 1972 to improve relations between males and females.
3. Public Law 94-142 was passed in 1974 to improve relations between individuals with and without disabilities.

In the United States, it is illegal to segregate students on the basis of ethnicity, gender, or disabilities. Broadly, it may be illegal to segregate any category of students.

Sources of Diversity

The major sources of diversity are (a) demographic characteristics, (b) personality characteristics, and (c) abilities and skills. *Demographic diversity* includes culture, ethnicity, language, handicapping conditions, age, gender, social class, religion, and regional differences. North America, for example, is becoming more multicultural and multilingual.

In addition to demographic diversity, individuals can have different *personal characteristics*. Groups can be composed of introverts as well as extroverts and of people who approach problems randomly as well as sequentially. Group members also can have different values, attitudes, opinions, lifestyles, styles of interaction, and commitments. Attitudes, values, and beliefs vary systematically with demographic variables. Age cohorts can have different attitudes toward economic conditions and war, males and females can have different attitudes toward interpersonal relationships, and education can be related to attitudes toward innovation and reductions in prejudice.

Finally, individuals differ in the abilities and skills they bring to a group. Experts from a variety of fields, for example, may be brought together to solve a problem or conduct a project. Representatives from design, manufacturing, distribution, and sales may form a team to bring a new product to market. Accountants and creative artists may work together to revitalize a neighborhood. It is difficult, if not impossible, to find a productive group whose members do not have a wide variety of abilities and skills.

THE PROMISE OF DIVERSITY

The more affects we allow to speak about one thing, the more eyes, different eyes we can use to observe one thing, the more complete will our concept of this thing, our objectivity, be.
—Nietzsche

Diversity is desirable. First, interaction among diverse individuals can (a) decrease stereotyping and prejudice and (b) increase positive relationships. It is only through direct contact and interaction with diverse individuals that stereotypes can be disconfirmed, that personal relationships can be built, and that prejudice can be reduced. Positive relationships can lead to acceptance, respect, appreciation, and a commitment to equality. Second, diversity is a source of creativity. The interaction (and conflict) among individuals with diverse perspectives is the source of new forms of music, art, dance, literature, and other aspects of culture. Diverse groups tend to be more creative in their problem solving than homogeneous groups. Third, diversity increases the sophistication of individuals involved. Being sophisticated means that one can see the world, events, and issues from a variety of perspectives. It is through relationships with diverse individuals that sophistication is created. Fourth, diversity highlights the value of American democracy. The values advocated in the Constitution and the Declaration of Independence can best be understood through the protection of minority rights and the ability of minorities to influence the decisions of the majority. Perhaps the most important positive outcomes of diversity, however, involve productivity, cohesion, and constructive conflict.

Diversity and Productivity

How does heterogeneity of group membership affect group performance? Researchers have studied the degree of homogeneity and heterogeneity among members' (a) personal attributes (including demographic, personality, and values and attitudes) and (b) abilities and skills (both technical and social). The impact of these characteristics has been studied on four types of tasks: (a) production tasks that have objective standards for performance evaluation and require the proficient use of perceptual and motor skills, (b) cognitive or intellective tasks that require problem solving and have correct answers, (c) decision-making tasks that involve reaching consensus about the best solution to a problem when the "correct" answer is not known, and (d) creative idea generation tasks (Jackson, 1992; Johnson & Johnson, 1989; McGrath, 1984).

The specific results of the research on group composition and task performance are summarized in Table 1.2. Heterogeneity of membership, both in personal characteristics and abilities and skills, tends to facilitate performance on creative and decision-making tasks. Heterogeneity of abilities and skills seems to be beneficial for performance tasks. There are too few studies on intellectual tasks to make a conclusion. Homogeneity of personal characteristics and abilities does not seem to facilitate performance on any of these types of tasks.

The results of the research are mixed and complex. Generally, however, diversity among group members results in higher productivity and more frequent higher-level reasoning than does homogeneity because diverse groups have a wider range of resources available for completing the task and apply more than one perspective to the issue. (See Table 1.3.)

TABLE 1.2   Group Composition and Types of Tasks

TYPES OF DIVERSITY INVESTIGATED	TYPES OF TASKS
Personal attributes (demographics, personality, attitudes, values)	Performance on clearly defined production tasks
Abilities and skills (technical, social)	Performance on cognitive or intellectual tasks
	Creative idea generation and decision making on ambiguous judgmental tasks

Other Outcomes

Absenteeism, turnover, and satisfaction are nearly as important as group performance to groups and organizations (Nadler, Hackman, & Lawler, 1979; Schmidt, 1974). These outcomes are determined largely by cohesion and conflict. Haythorn (1968) concluded that the effects of *personality heterogeneity–homogeneity* on cohesion depend on a number of factors, including personality characteristics, task characteristics, and extent of interpersonal contact. Bantel and Jackson (1989), in a field study of decision-making teams at 119 banks in six states, found no relationship between team heterogeneity and cohesiveness. Jackson, Brett, Sessa, Cooper, Julin, and Peyronnin (1991) in a follow-up study found that (a) the demographically homogeneous teams had lower turnover and (b) were more likely to fill vacancies with employees from inside the firm, both of which may indicate higher cohesion. *Turnover* tends to be higher in work groups composed of members who are more diverse with respect to their ages and years of organizational tenure (e.g., Jackson et al., 1991; McCain et al., 1983; O'Reilly, Caldwell, & Barnett, 1989; Wagner, Pfeffer, & O'Reilly, 1984) and who are heterogeneous in terms of college alma mater, curriculum studied, and industry experiences (Jackson et al., 1991).

Attitude similarity may be mildly related to group cohesion. People are attracted to others with similar attitudes (Byrne, 1971; Heider, 1958; Newcomb, 1961), and group members tend to become more similar in their attitudes as they interact over time (Newcomb, 1956). Terborg et al. (1976), however, conducted one of the few studies in which attitudes were assessed directly and then used to assemble groups. In their longitudinal investigation of student groups, cohesiveness was assessed at six points in time. At each assessment, cohesiveness was greater in the groups composed

TABLE 1.3   Impact of Group Composition on Outcomes

TYPES OF OUTCOMES	PERSONAL ATTRIBUTES	ABILITIES AND SKILLS
Production Tasks	The few studies found mixed results, so no clear effect of group composition on performance is proved.	The few studies found that heterogeneity of types and levels of ability increase productivity.
Intellectual Tasks	Overall, the number of studies is not sufficient to draw a conclusion. Mixed-sex groups may outperform same-sex groups.	Almost no directly relevant research is available.
Decision-Making Tasks	Heterogeneous groups outperform homogeneous groups.	Heterogeneity of ability levels is beneficial.
Cohesion	Heterogeneous groups are somewhat less cohesive and have higher turnover rates.	Almost no direct research is available.
Conflict	More conflicts tend to occur in heterogeneous groups.	Almost no direct research is available.

of attitudinally similar members, although the magnitude of the effect of attitude similarity on cohesiveness did not approach statistical significance until the last three assessments.

The heterogeneity among group members promotes increased argumentation and conflict (Nijhof & Kommers, 1982). Such conflicts can be beneficial for completing complex problem-solving tasks (Cosier, 1981; Janis, 1972; Johnson & Johnson, 1979; 1989a; 1992; Schweiger, Sandberg, & Rechner, 1989; Schwenk, 1983). There are so many advantages of diversity that one has to feel sorry for those who live in very homogeneous communities and societies.

In an extensive study of affirmative action in college admissions over the past 50 years, the authors, Bowen and Bok (1998), collected data on more than 80,000 students who matriculated at 28 selective colleges and universities in 1951, 1976, and 1989. They concluded that students of all ethnic backgrounds share a favorable impression of the value of diversity in contributing to their education. Astin (1993) surveyed approximately 25,000 students attending 217 four-year colleges and universities between 1985 and 1989. His results indicated that the strongest positive effects of a college emphasis on diversity are cultural awareness and commitment to promoting racial understanding. Gurin (1999), in a study of 187 black and 1,134 white students at the University of Michigan and 9,316 students at other schools (observed between 1985 and 1994), concluded that students in a more diverse environment showed the greatest engagement in active thinking processes, growth in intellectual engagement and motivation, and growth in intellectual and academic skills.

Disadvantages of Homogeneity of Membership

There are a number of disadvantages to members being homogeneous. First, homogeneous groups may lack the controversy and clash of perspectives so essential to high-quality decision making and creative thinking. Too many members who think alike and see the world in the same way make for a dull and mediocre group. Second, homogeneous groups tend to be risk avoidant (Bantel & Jackson, 1989) and may, therefore, miss opportunities to increase their productivity. Third, homogeneous groups more frequently engage in groupthink (Janis, 1972). Fourth, homogeneous groups tend to function best in static situations. They have trouble adapting to changing conditions.

Problems with Group Composition Research

First, in defining heterogeneity, only easily measured attributes are considered important. The research has focused on personal attributes (such as personality, attitudes, gender, ethnicity) and skills and abilities because these qualities can be measured. Other qualities are ignored because of measurement problems.

Second, no one attribute is likely to make much difference in the complexity of real work. Thus, multiattribute research is needed. Instead of studying the impact of gender, ethnicity, age, or cognitive style, studies should simultaneously track composition on all these dimensions.

Third, organizations employ people to perform a wide variety of both simple and complex tasks that involve perceptual and motor performance, intellectual performance, creativity, and judgmental decision making. Groups may be working on a variety of tasks simultaneously, and today's tasks may not be the tasks they work on tomorrow. Because the tasks a team has to do at any given time are unpredictable, the safest thing to do is to maximize member heterogeneity.

Fourth, it is difficult to determine what is and is not diversity. What outsiders may define as heterogeneity may not be perceived as being heterogeneous by insiders. The self-categorizations of group members depend on members perceiving themselves as relatively similar on some attribute(s) and relatively different from the members of other groups. To judge whether a group is heterogeneous or homogeneous on an attribute, therefore, it is important to consider how the attribute is distributed among nongroup members.

Fifth, little is known about precisely how group composition and tasks interact to affect performance. Thus, recommendations cannot be made about the procedures and strategies group members should use to utilize their diversity to improve their productivity. The complexity of the real world makes recommendations about optimal group composition and specific strategies for utilizing particular attributes impossible.

Sixth, group members are simultaneously both heterogeneous and homogeneous. Each person has hundreds of characteristics and abilities. Members that are homogeneous on one or two attributes are heterogeneous with respect to other attributes. Conversely, group members that are heterogeneous with respect to several attributes still share common attributes. Thus, it is impossible to create a homogeneous group.

THE DANGERS OF DIVERSITY

Bringing diverse individuals together does not automatically result in positive outcomes (Johnson & Johnson, 1989). Proximity is a necessary condition for the positive potential of diversity to be realized, but it is not sufficient in and of itself. The promise of diversity is that it will enrich and enhance relationships, productivity, and other important outcomes. There is a risk, however, that diversity will lead to negative rather than positive outcomes. When diverse individuals interact in destructive ways, or when the interaction takes place under competitive or individualistic conditions, diversity can create great problems. The dangers of diversity are outlined next (Johnson & Johnson, 1989).

First, the initial contact among diverse individuals is often characterized by *interaction strain* (individuals feeling discomfort and uncertainty as to how to behave). Interaction strain inhibits interaction, creates ambivalence, and fosters atypical behavior, such as overfriendliness followed by withdrawal and avoidance. Second, interaction can result in negative relationships that confirm stereotypes and increase prejudice. One of the early findings in interpersonal attraction research is what takes place before interaction. We tend to like people we see as similar to ourselves and we dislike people who seem different. Before actual contact takes place, furthermore, only vague impressions of members of other groups may exist. With actual contact, stereotypes can be confirmed and expanded, and prejudice can be strengthened. Direct interaction among diverse individuals in competitive and individualistic situations can create negative relationships characterized by hostility, rejection, divisiveness, scapegoating, bullying, stereotyping, and prejudice.

Third, when diverse individuals work together, productivity can suffer. Under competitive and individualistic conditions, diversity can result in such dynamics as difficulties in communication, coordination, and decision making and in feeling threatened, defensive, and egocentric as well as experiencing closed-minded rejection of new information. These difficulties result in more time being spent trying to find ways to work together productively and less time being spent completing tasks. Fourth, interacting with diverse individuals can require more effort than interacting with similar individuals. The effort is both external (e.g., the more diverse the group is, the more you have to monitor your statements and behavior to ensure that you do not inadvertently insult or hurt someone's feelings) and internal (e.g., being exposed to different and new ways of perceiving the world can create internal conflict, resulting in anxiety that has to be resolved). In comparison, it is easy to relate to similar people. Complete Activity 1.4 to ascertain what competencies you have and those you need to develop to interact effectively with diverse individuals.

ACTIVITY **1.4** ■ COMPETENCIES FOR DIVERSITY

In the chart below list the competencies you now have and the competencies you need to develop for interacting effectively with diverse individuals.

Competencies I Now Have	Competencies I Need to Develop

Diversity is pervasive, inevitable, and increasing. The choice of avoiding diversity does not exist. In school, on the job, and in the community, you interact with people different from you in many ways, whether you want to or not. This does not mean that capitalizing on the promise of diversity is easy. Diversity and pluralism pose a risk. They can result in either positive or negative outcomes, depending on how they are managed. The promise of diversity far outweighs the dangers as long as the individuals involved understand how to capitalize on the benefits while avoiding the pitfalls. The greater the understanding of multicultural education and human relations, for example, the more constructive will be the results of diversity. The next sections of this chapter, therefore, contain a discussion of the goals and history of multicultural education and human relations.

THE GOALS OF HUMAN RELATIONS

There are two goals of human relations: (1) to improve relationships between majority and minority citizens by eliminating prejudice and discrimination, primarily through teaching all subsequent generations to value and respect diversity among individuals; and (2) to increase participants' competencies in interacting effectively with diverse individuals by teaching participants procedures and skills.

THE HISTORY OF HUMAN RELATIONS

Business and Industry

The exact date the human relations movement in business and industry began is difficult to specify. It may be safely said, however, that it was not until the second half of the nineteenth century that (a) workers' needs received broad attention and (b) the relationship between workers' needs and workers' productivity was broadly discussed. Prior to that time, employers and managers viewed the labor force as a commodity to be bought and sold like any other commodity. Long hours, low wages, and miserable working conditions were commonplace.

Early in the twentieth century several interrelated developments highlighted the need for developing human relations. The first was the pioneering development by Henry Ford and others of mass manufacturing with an assembly line. Ford created his assembly line about 1910. Second, at about the same time, Frederick Taylor and others introduced and developed the practice of scientific management. They believed that greater productivity could be achieved by breaking down work into isolated, specific, specialized tasks. Advocates believed that production could be increased through better cost-accounting procedures, premium and incentive payments, time and motion studies, and other related procedures. Taylor, however, had a larger vision.

Taylor believed that the primary objective of scientific management was to have workers and employers work together to increase productivity and profit, thereby reducing the conflict between them and maximizing the prosperity of both. Critics, however, pointed out that the focus on time and motion procedures dehumanizes workers and increases the impersonality of the workplace. Generally, critics pointed out that scientific management paid no attention to the complex social networks created by workers on the job and that it was precisely these social networks that had the greatest influence on production rates.

In 1920, Kurt Lewin wrote an article discussing the Taylor System of eliminating superfluous effort through scientific management. He began by observing that work has a central role in life, as a person's capacity to work gives meaning and substance to his whole existence. Accordingly, every job should sustain or enhance this "life value," and Taylor's emphasis on efficiency, increasing productivity, and decreasing the number of hours a person has to work, ignores the value the worker places on what he is doing and the satisfaction he derives from it. What Lewin believed to be most important is an improvement in the inner value of the work as experienced by the person performing it.

The third influence on the development of human relations was the new view of each worker as a unique, complex human whose individual skills and abilities could be measured, tested, and trained. In the 1920s, the use of testing for job selection became popular. The individual worker was viewed as a combination of various traits that could be measured accurately and improved by appropriate training. Testing was advocated as a way to solve most, if not all, problems related to job selection, placement, and promotion. An unanticipated result of the popularity of testing was the finding that workers' personal motivations influenced test performances, and, therefore, a worker's skills and abilities could not be isolated from a worker's human interests and emotions. In addition, by 1924 the view was growing that just as workers should be tested and trained, so should managers.

The fourth influence on the development of human relations was the increasing power of unions. From 1897 to 1994, membership in trade unions in the United States grew from 400,000 to 2 million. Often with considerable struggle, by the 1920s unions became a powerful force in the workplace.

The fifth influence was the rapidly changing technology of manufacturing and business that continually redefined the role of worker and manager. Increasingly, the worker was viewed as a person with multiple needs and the manager as a person who manages people, not work processes.

Sixth, in the 1920s, the human relations approach to business and industry was advanced by the famous Hawthorne studies conducted by Elton Mayo and his colleagues for the National Research Council and the Massachusetts Institute of Technology. The studies focused on the effects of illumination, ventilation, and fatigue on workers. One study, for example, investigated the impact of levels of illumination on two groups of employees working under similar conditions and doing similar types of work. The intensity of the light under which one group worked was varied systematically while the light was held constant for the second group. The general result was that productivity increased each time the intensity of light was increased. This finding was anticipated. Decreasing the intensity of the light under which employees worked, however, also increased productivity. In fact, one of the highest levels of productivity was recorded during an extremely low level of illumination. When interviewed, employees stated that it was easier to work faster in the test room because it was special and fun and there was little, regular supervisory control. The overall conclusion is that greater freedom and feelings of importance were powering productivity, not the level of illumination.

After a series of such studies, Mayo and his colleagues concluded that group morale and personal motivation factors were so important that they completely obscured the effects of factors such as illumination, ventilation, and fatigue. Normal interactions among workers create a social network, an informal organization, that influences workers' behavioral patterns and productivity, regardless of official orders passed down through the formal organization. As a result of the Hawthorne studies, workers could never again be viewed as mere economic tools or as isolated units in the production process. Instead, workers must be viewed as complex humans whose interactions affect production output, no matter how sophisticated the technological processes used. These studies are a bright light that still shines in the field of human relations.

Interest in human relations in business and industry declined in the 1930s during the Great Depression. In the late 1930s and the industrial expansion during World War II, however, interest revived in the relationship between productivity and worker satisfaction. Social scientists began conducting numerous studies on human relations.

In 1939, for example, Kurt Lewin was invited to visit a new manufacturing plant in a rural community in Virginia by the Harwood Manufacturing Corporation, of which Alfred Marrow was an officer. Although employees were being paid more than they earned on previous jobs and felt good about their jobs, turnover was extremely high. Workers were not producing enough and the plant was suffering heavy losses. All known systems of rewards to increase production had been tried. Pressuring employees to work harder only resulted in a higher turnover rate. Lewin suggested to stop putting pressure on individual employees and to deal with workers as members of small groups. He suggested that some method be found to give the group the feeling that the standard was realistic and could be reached.

Lewin actively encouraged Harwood management to begin a program of research and to employ Alex Bavelas to conduct a series of small-group studies on human factors in factory management. Bavelas conducted studies on group decision making, self-management, leadership training, changing workers' perceptions of certain jobs, and overcoming resistance to change (the Coch and French study). These studies are the second bright light in the field of human relations.

In 1946 Lewin was asked by the Connecticut State Interracial Commission to help in training leaders and conducting research on the most effective means for combating racial and religious prejudice in communities. At the same time, two adult educators, Lee Bradford and Ken Benne approached Kurt Lewin for help in training community leaders in leadership and group decision-making skills. This led to the creation of National Training Laboratories (NTL) and eventually to the establishment of organizational development as a field of study and practice. NTL became a network of social scientists who would engage in (a) consulting and training in human relations and (b) action research. The small group dynamics movement of the 1950s and 1960s began and was fueled by NTL. Sensitivity training, interpersonal and group skills training, and organizational development all came out of NTL's work.

Other important influences on the field of human relations were Douglas McGregor's theorizing (proposing that traditional management be called Theory X and humanistic management be called Theory Y), Abraham Maslow (who proposed a hierarchy of human needs), Carl Rogers (who proposed humanistic relationships in organizations through extensions of his active listening therapy procedure), and others such as Daniel Bell, and C. Wright Mills. By the 1960s, human relations became a body of knowledge that no student of business could ignore. Furthermore, on-the-job democracy became promoted first in the 1960s, through participative management, and later in the 1980s, through quality circles.

As a result of the interest in human relations in business and industry as well as in the society as a whole, several books were published to help social scientists educate a broad range of citizens. Three of the most important of these books were *Reaching Out: Interpersonal Effectiveness and Self-Actualization* (Johnson, 1972), *Joining Together: Group Theory and Group Skills* (Johnson & F. Johnson, 1975), and *Learning Together and Alone: Cooperative, Competitive, and Individualistic Learning* (Johnson & R. Johnson, 1975).

Education

In 1925, Ella Lyman Cabot submitted a curriculum for a course in human relations to the Massachusetts Department of Education. Her stated objective was for students to develop an understanding of human nature so they could increase sympathetic, thoughtful, and loyal relations among people. In 1939 the Delaware State Department of Education funded H. E. Bullis to create a human relations curriculum to be taught statewide. He drew heavily on literature and the humanities in presenting an appeal for fellowship. Bullis (1954) later published a book entitled *Human Relations in Action*, in which he stressed creating stable relationships by increasing psychological adjustment, stability, and understanding of how to meet the psychological needs of others.

Beginning with World War II, the federal government began to address the inequities experienced by minorities in the areas of employment, education, and access to income. One result was the 1954 Supreme Court decision in the *Brown v. Board of Education* ruling that it was not possible to have "separate but equal" educational facilities. This was followed by legislation in 1972 to improve relations between males and females (Title IX) and in 1974 to improve relations between individuals with and without disabilities (Public Law 94-142).

The strong government emphasis on human relations reflected the growing belief that all people in the United States must get along with all other people in the United States as well as with people in the rest of the world. In the 1960s, as a result of the civil rights movement, awareness that minority students might not be taught effectively by majority teachers began to grow. It was concluded that white teachers needed to be trained to interact effectively with minority students to (a) promote their achievement and academic success and (b) reduce ethnic tension. Human relations courses began to appear to provide such training. The major approaches to these courses included information about ethnic groups, sensitivity training, cognitive training, creating promotive situations, creating positive intergroup dynamics, simulations, and skills training. Participating in the exercises in Activity 1.5 will introduce you to these approaches.

ACTIVITY **1.5** ■ APPROACHES TO HUMAN RELATIONS TRAINING IN EDUCATION

The goals of human relations training are (a) to improve relationships between majority and minority citizens and (b) to increase participants' competence in interacting effectively with diverse individuals.

1. Working individually, choose three approaches from the table below that seem to you the most effective for achieving the above two goals and write out the reasons for your choices.

2. Form a pair. Working cooperatively, (a) share your choices and your reasoning, (b) listen carefully to your partner's choices and reasoning, and (c) come to consensus about the three most effective methods for teaching human relations.

3. Repeat the above process for the three least effective approaches for teaching human relations.

APPROACH	ASSUMPTION
Information Approach: Giving majority members information about the nature and experience of minority groups.	Constructive relationships among diverse individuals cannot be built without knowledge about the other groups.
Personal Sensitivity Approach: Having white and minority members confront each other in sensitivity training groups.	Constructive relationships among diverse individuals cannot be built without honest and open personal interchanges.
Psychological (Cognitive) Approach: Teaching the cognitive dynamics involved in prejudice, stereotypes, biases.	Constructive relationships among diverse individuals cannot be built without understanding the cognitive processes involved in stereotyping and prejudice.
Social Psychology (Situational) Approach: Creating situational conditions under which positive relationships are built between majority and minority individuals.	Constructive relationships among diverse individuals cannot be built unless their interaction takes place within certain situational conditions.
Sociology (Intergroup) Approach: Teaching about intergroup relations on a societal and international level.	Constructive relationships among diverse individuals cannot be built without knowledge of intergroup dynamics.
Simulation Approach: Placing majority members in the role of minorities in structured simulations.	Constructive relationships among diverse individuals cannot be built without direct experience of what it is like to be a minority group member.
Skill Training Approach: Teaching the interpersonal and small-group skills required to relate to diverse individuals.	Constructive relationships among diverse individuals cannot be built without the required social skills.

Although most approaches to human relations focused on attempting to change the white majority, a few approaches addressed minority citizens. In the early 1960s, for example, as part of the civil rights movement, Freedom Schools were initiated throughout the country. One of the objectives of most Freedom Schools was to teach African American children African American history to improve their pride in their heritage and their personal self-esteem. Although little research has been done on the effectiveness of Freedom Schools, the two studies that have been done (Johnson, 1966a; 1966b) found that learning African American history improved the African American children's self-esteem, pride in their heritage, more confidence in themselves and their competencies, an increased conviction that African Americans and whites are equal, and more positive attitudes toward the civil rights movement. Johnson (1966b) also investigated the impact of participating in a civil rights group that planned and conducted demonstrations. Actively working for civil rights had very similar effects to learning African American history.

THE MYTH OF HOMOGENEITY

In nature, no two things are the same. No two snowflakes are identical, no two blades of grass are the same, and no two trees are identical. Nature seems to demand variation and differences. This is as true for people as it is for leaves. Each individual person is unique. No two individuals are the same. Thus, individuals are simultaneously both heterogeneous and homogeneous in regard to identifiable attributes. Each person has hundreds of characteristics and abilities. Individuals who are homogeneous on one or two attributes are heterogeneous with respect to other attributes. Conversely, individuals who are heterogeneous with respect to several attributes still share common attributes. Thus, it is impossible to create a homogeneous group. Clearly, it is unrealistic to cope with the diversity of people by attempting to control the extent to which they are similar or different. Instead, efforts should be directed toward capitalizing on the promise of diversity and minimizing the dangers (potential negative consequences) of heterogeneity.

CAPITALIZING ON THE PROMISE OF DIVERSITY

To maximize the promise and minimize the dangers of diversity and pluralism, you must fulfill the following goals.

1. Value diversity as an irreplaceable resource.
2. Integrate diversity into your personal identity:
    a. View yourself as an individual who respects and values differences among individuals and your own historical and cultural heritage.
    b. Respect and appreciate the historical and cultural heritage of others.
    c. Develop a superordinate identity that unites all relevant groups.
3. Work continually to reduce within yourself the cognitive barriers (such as stereotyping and prejudice) to building positive relationships with diverse individuals.
4. Work continually to avoid the pitfalls of interaction among diverse groups (especially high- and low-power groups) and to establish the conditions for constructive intergroup interaction.
5. Create the process of acceptance in making social judgments and avoid the process of rejection.
6. Structure cooperative (as opposed to a competitive or individualistic) efforts to create a context in which positive relationships among diverse individuals can be built.

7. Manage conflicts constructively with controversy and the Peacemaker Program.
   a. Controversy: Encouraging intellectual conflicts as part of learning and decision-making situations
   b. Peacemaker Program: Engaging in problem-solving negotiations and mediation to resolve conflicts of interests
8. Make your life an expression of pluralistic, democratic values, including the commitment to the equal worth of all persons and each individual's inalienable right to life, liberty, and the pursuit of happiness.

The first issue is covered in this chapter. The rest of these issues are discussed in subsequent chapters of this book.

SUMMARY

Diversity is inevitable, pervasive, and increasing. We cannot avoid interacting with diverse individuals in school, work, and community settings. Diversity potentially is a risk; it can result in either positive or negative outcomes. Diversity can increase productivity, creative problem solving, positive relationships, and general sophistication in interacting and working with individuals from a variety of cultural and ethnic backgrounds. Diversity can also lower productivity, increase closed-minded rejection of new information and egocentrism, and create negative relationships characterized by hostility, stereotyping, and prejudice. Whether the promise or dangers of diversity and pluralism are realized depends on (a) the structure of the situation and (b) the competencies of the individuals involved.

One of the consequences of the pervasiveness of diversity is that all individuals are becoming multicultural. Culture is a shared way of life for a group of socially interacting people and almost everyone belongs to more than one culture. Multicultural individuals are people who have internalized several cultures, which take turns in guiding their thoughts and feelings, depending on the situation. Multicultural education encourages the development of multicultural individuals (and provides an equal opportunity to learn to all students) by ensuring educational opportunities are fair and equal, reforming curricula to include a more global perspective, promoting intercultural competence, and promoting the social action skills needed to combat prejudice and discrimination.

Diversity is an inherent aspect of U.S. culture. Our democracy has always been based on managing diversity among citizens. We have passed at least three laws ensuring that segregation cannot take place within our society and that the value of diversity is realized. Diversity may result from demographic factors, personal characteristics, and abilities and skills. Changes in world interdependence, immigration patterns, and economic practices all highlight the importance of utilizing the positive potential of diversity. Training individuals to manage diversity in constructive ways is commonly known as human relations. Human relations training has its roots both in business and industry and in education.

Diversity among individuals poses opportunities and challenges. Positive outcomes result when individuals recognize the value of diversity, build a coherent personal identity that includes their own cultural heritage, strive to reduce their stereotypes and prejudices, build cooperative relationships, resolve conflicts constructively, and adopt a set of pluralistic and democratic values. All these factors are discussed in this book. The following list explains expectations for participants using this book:

1. **Attend and actively participate in all class sessions.** Attending each session is only half the battle. Each participant needs to be active and not only concerned

about his or her own work, but also concerned about the work of the other people in the class. Expect to be actively working during most of the session and to be able to improve your skill in working with others during the course.

2. **Do all the weekly implementation assignments.** The weekly implementation assignments are the heart of the course and are designed to be practical in getting multicultural education and human relations started in your classroom. Keep in mind that each class session begins with a chance to share what you have done with the implementation assignment and to hear what the others in your base group have done. They are counting on you to bring back your results.

3. **Read the material in the text with care.** Each chapter of this book contains material that should be read with care. It is sometimes helpful to underline or highlight important points, write questions in the margin, and add your own thoughts to what is written.

4. **Plan and teach at least one lesson each week.** Except perhaps for the first week, you should try as many multicultural and human relations procedures and lessons as you can. Planning and implementing at least one lesson each week is the way that this course will become powerful for you. Part of the sharing in the base groups will center on what is happening in the teaching of the lessons.

5. **Plan and teach at least five specific social skills over the course.** One of the most interesting and productive parts of the course is to teach students to be more effective in the way they cooperate with one another. The interpersonal and small group skills include basic behaviors like using quiet voices and staying with your group, to more complex leadership and communication skills like disagreeing while confirming other's competence. There are many reasons why teaching students social skills is important. One of them is that students' efforts to work together become even more effective and, therefore, achievement continues to grow.

6. **Monitor with special attention the behaviors of at least two key students while they are working cooperatively.** Although it is important to monitor with care all students who are working cooperatively, you should pick out two particular students in whom you have a high interest, perhaps a student with a disability, a very bright student, or a student who has difficulty in working with others. Whomever you pick, you should regularly monitor him or her several times while he or she works in cooperative learning groups and keep track of your observations for a case study.

7. **Keep a journal analyzing your implementation of the material in the text.** From this journal will be developed assumptions about multicultural education and human relations and your most frequently used procedures and strategies.

8. **Develop a colleagial relationship with at least one person in your school.** Choose someone who is interested in what you are doing and perhaps even willing to try some multicultural or human relations lessons. Evidence shows that people who innovate in their classrooms need the support of at least one colleague to persevere. Think about your staff and select at least one colleague who would be interested in multicultural education and human relations and in interacting with you about these issues. If you are participating in training to be part of a team from the same school, you may still want to think about keeping other colleagues informed and interested.

9. **Take an active and supportive interest in the work of the other members of your base group.** The base group is only one of several groups of which you will be a part during this course, but it is important. At the beginning of each session members of the base group will meet and share their experience from the week before. They are expected to provide encouragement for each other and assist each other in accomplishing the course requirements. The assignments will be reviewed by the base group and direct communication with the

instructor is provided by the base group file folder (a folder where implementation assignments are stored and instructor feedback is written).

10. **Enjoy yourself and help those around you enjoy themselves during the course sessions.**   Begin by participating in Activity 1.6 on the following pages. This group activity combines research, persuasive writing, debate, and adoption of the opposing position. It provides the format for interaction with peers and cooperative learning.

ACTIVITY **1.6** ■ DIVERSITY: BENEFICIAL OR HARMFUL?

A controversy about the value of diversity is raging. Imagine you are a committee of top officials who are trying to decide whether diversity should be encouraged or discouraged. To ensure that both sides get a complete and fair hearing, you have divided the committee into two groups to present the best case possible for each side of the issue.

Task: Your tasks are two-fold: to (a) write a group report on the issue of whether diversity is beneficial or harmful and (b) individually pass a test on the information from both sides of the issue.

Cooperative: Write one report for the group of four. All members have to agree. Each member has to be able to explain the choice made and the reasons why the choice is a good one. To help you write the best report possible, your group of four has been divided into two pairs. One pair has been assigned the position that diversity is beneficial and the other pair has been assigned the position that diversity is harmful. Your report should provide details of both the advantages and disadvantages of diversity.

PROCEDURE

1. **Research and prepare your position.** Your group of four has been divided into two pairs. Each pair is to (a) research your assigned position, (b) organize it into a persuasive argument (thesis, rationale, conclusion), and (c) plan how to present the best case for your position to the other pair.

2. **Present and advocate your position.** Make sure your assigned position receives a fair and complete hearing. Forcefully and persuasively present the best case for your position to the opposing pair. Be as convincing as possible. Take notes and clarify anything you do not understand when the opposing pair presents.

3. **Open discussion (advocate, refute, rebut).** Argue forcefully and persuasively for your position. Critically evaluate and challenge the opposing pair's information and reasoning. Defend your position from attack.

4. **Reverse perspectives.** Reverse perspectives and present the best case for the opposing position. The opposing pair will present your position. Strive to see the issue from both perspectives simultaneously.

5. **Synthesis.** Drop all advocacy. Synthesize and integrate the best information and reasoning from both sides into a joint position that all group members can agree to. Then (a) finalize the group report, (b) plan how to present your conclusions to the class, (c) ensure that all group members are prepared to take the test, and (d) process how well you worked together as a group and how you could be even more effective next time.

CONTROVERSY RULES

1. I am critical of ideas, not people. I challenge and refute the ideas of the opposing pair, but I do not indicate that I personally reject the people.

2. I remember that we are all in this together, sink or swim. I focus on coming to the best decision possible, not on winning.

3. I encourage everyone to participate and to master all the relevant information.

4. I listen to everyone's ideas, even if I don't agree.

5. I restate what someone has said if it is not clear.

6. I first bring out all ideas and facts supporting both sides, and then I try to put them together in a way that makes sense.

7. I try to understand both sides of the issue.

8. I change my mind when the evidence clearly indicates that I should do so.

DIVERSITY IS BENEFICIAL

You represent the prodiversity perspective. Your position is, diversity is beneficial in many ways and should be encouraged in our society. Given below are arguments that support your position. Summarize the evidence given below. Research your position and find as much additional information to support it as possible. Arrange your information into a compelling, convincing, and persuasive argument that presents your position as valid and correct. Plan how best to present your assigned position to ensure it receives a fair and complete hearing. Make at least one visual to help you present a persuasive case for your position.

1. **Diversity decreases stereotyping and prejudice.** Only through direct contact and interaction with diverse individuals can stereotypes be disconfirmed, personal relationships be built, and prejudice be reduced.

2. **Diversity increases the positiveness of relationships.** There is evidence that we like people we work with because we all achieve mutual goals. The positive relationships can lead to acceptance, respect, appreciation, and a commitment to equality.

3. **Diversity renews the vitality of society.** Diversity provides a source of energy and creativity. Music, dance, art, literature, and other aspects of culture are enriched and advance by the mixture of different cultural traditions and ways of perceiving the world.

4. **Diversity increases achievement and productivity.** Diverse groups have a wider range of resources available for completing tasks and, therefore, tend to be more productive and successful achievers than homogeneous groups.

5. **Diversity increases creative problem solving.** Diverse groups tend to be more creative problem solvers than homogeneous groups. Conflicts and disagreements that arise from different perspectives and conclusions generate more creativity than is generated by homogeneous groups.

6. **Diversity fosters growth in cognitive and moral reasoning.** Cognitive and moral growth depend on at least two different perspectives being applied to the same issue. Without such diversity, cognitive and moral growth cannot take place.

7. **Diversity fosters perspective taking.** Diversity can help develop a broader, more sophisticated view of the world and what happens within it. Without exposure to other perspectives, perspective-taking abilities cannot develop. The more able a person is to take a wide variety of perspectives, the more sophisticated the person is. Being sophisticated means that one can see the world, events, and issues from a variety of perspectives. It is through diversity that sophistication is created.

8. **Diversity builds a commitment to U.S. democracy.** It is not possible to value fully U.S. democracy in a homogeneous environment. The values advocated in the Constitution and the Declaration of Independence can best be understood through

(continued)

ACTIVITY 1.6 *Continued*

the protection of minority rights and the ability of minorities to influence the decisions of the majority.

DIVERSITY IS HARMFUL

You represent the antidiversity perspective. Your position is, diversity is harmful in many ways and should be discouraged in our society. Given below are arguments that support your position. Summarize the evidence given below. Research your position and find as much additional information to support it as possible. Arrange your information into a compelling, convincing, and persuasive argument that presents your position as valid and correct. Plan how best to present your assigned position to ensure it receives a fair and complete hearing. Make at least one visual to help you present a persuasive case for your position.

1. **Diversity increases stereotyping and prejudice.** Before actual contact takes place, only vague impressions of members of other groups may exist. Actual contact with diverse individuals confirms stereotypes and strengthens prejudice.

2. **Diversity creates interaction strain.** Interaction strain is feeling discomfort and uncertainty as to how to behave. Interaction strain inhibits interaction, creates ambivalence, and fosters atypical behavior such as overfriendliness followed by withdrawal and avoidance.

3. **Diversity increases the negativity of relationships.** There is evidence that we like people who seem similar to ourselves and we dislike people who seem different. The dislike can lead to rejection, scapegoating, bullying, hostility, and even racism.

4. **Diversity lowers productivity.** Diversity creates difficulties in communication, coordination, and decision making. These difficulties result in more time being spent in trying to communicate and less time being spent on completing the task. Productivity suffers.

5. **Diversity makes life more complex and difficult.** People who are similar are easy to relate to. You don't usually have to stop and think about what to say or how to act. The more diverse the group is, the more statements and behavior must be monitored to ensure you do not inadvertently insult or hurt someone's feelings.

6. **Diversity requires more effort to relate to others.** Just talking to a person from another culture takes more concentration and effort. Accents can be distracting. Phrases can be unusual. Communicating effectively with diverse individuals takes more effort than with individuals like yourself.

7. **Diversity can be threatening.** Feeling threatened causes defensiveness, egocentrism, and closed-minded rejection of new information. The more defensive a person is, the more closed-minded and the less receptive to new information the person becomes.

8. **Diversity creates internal dissonance and anxiety.** Diversity challenges standard ways of thinking and doing things. Strange, new ways of perceiving the world and completing tasks can create dissonance about one's traditional behavior. Anxiety results. People are calmer and happier when they are with homogeneous peers.

LEARNING CONTRACT

Name: _____   Date: _____

Class: _____   Group: _____

Write down your major learnings from reading this chapter. Then write down how you plan to implement each learning. Share what you learned and your implementation plans with your base group. Listen carefully to their major learnings and implementation plans. You may modify your own plans on the basis of what you have learned from your groupmates. Volunteer one action you can take to help each groupmate with his or her implementation plans. Use the help groupmates offer to you. Sign each member's plans to seal the contract.

Major Learnings	Implementation Plans

Participant's signature: _____   Date: _____

Signatures of group members: _____

_____

PROGRESS REPORT

Name: _____   School: _____

Subject Area: _____   Grade: _____

Date	Lesson	Successes	Problems

Describe critical or interesting incidents:

LOG SHEET

Name: _____   School: _____

Subject Area: _____   Grade: _____

Week	Lessons Planned, Taught	Social Skills Included	Planning Partner	Observer
1				
2				
3				
4				
5				
6				
7				
8				
9				
10				
11				
12				
13				
14				
15				
Total				

CHAPTER TWO

MY CULTURAL IDENTITY

INTRODUCTION

If I am not for myself, who will be for me?
If I am for myself alone, what am I?   —*Rabbi Hillel*

Hans Christian Anderson tells the story of an ugly duckling. This duckling did not look like the other ducklings, did not walk like the other ducklings, and did not speak like the other ducklings. Perceived by his peers as being ugly, this duckling was depressed and perceived himself to be an ugly, unwanted, and disliked duck. His depression was lifted and his self-image changed dramatically when he discovered that in fact he was not a duck, he was a swan. He not only was a swan, he was a beautiful swan. As he matured, his identity was clarified, and he took pride in his appearance and being. ■

To interact effectively with diverse individuals, you must understand that you are as different to them as they are to you. Unless you understand who you are from a historical, cultural, and ethnic perspective, you may have a difficult time being aware of who others are. The purpose of this chapter, therefore, is to provide a framework for understanding your cultural, historic, and ethnic identity in a way that highlights (a) your uniqueness as an individual, (b) the uniqueness of others, (c) the common identity that binds you together, and (d) the pluralistic values underlying diversity.

THE PERSON YOU THINK YOU ARE

What kind of person are you? How would you describe yourself to someone who does not know you? Would your description be disjointed and contradictory, or would it be organized and consistent? Would it change from day to day, or would it stay the same over a period of years? Do you like yourself, or do you feel a basic sense of shame and contempt when you think of yourself? We all need a strong and integrated sense of personal identity that serves as an anchor in life (Johnson, 2000).

Early philosophers advised us to "know thyself" and poets have told us, "To thine own self be true." We have taken their advice. Hundreds of books have been written dealing with how to get to know yourself and the *Oxford English Dictionary* lists more than 100 words that focus on the self, from *self-abasement* to *self-wisdom*.

When you form a conception of who you are as a person, you have an identity (Johnson, 2000). Your *identity* is a consistent set of attitudes that defines who you are. It is a subjective self-image called a self-schema, which is a type of cognitive structure.

A *self-schema* is a generalization about the self, derived from past experience, that organizes and guides your understanding of the information you learn about yourself from interacting with others. It influences the way information about the self is retrieved and encoded (e.g., Kihlstrom & Klein, 1994) and the way people behave (Froming, Nasby, & McManus, 1998). If you want children to behave in prosocial and constructive ways, for example, you promote their development of a prosocial self-schema and increase their self-awareness. The combination of a prosocial self-schema and self-awareness results in prosocial behavior. To enhance a child's ability to interact effectively with diverse peers, therefore, you would want each child to develop a self-schema of a person who values diversity and increase their self-awareness in a situation in which they are interacting with diverse schoolmates.

You have multiple schemas, each an aspect of your identity and self-view. Your self-schemas include (1) your view of your physical characteristics (height, weight, sex, hair and eye color, and general appearance), (2) your social roles (student or teacher, child or parent, employee or employer, and so forth), (3) the activities you engage in (playing the piano, dancing, reading, and so forth), (4) your abilities (skills, achievements), (5) your attitudes and interests (liking rock and roll, favoring equal rights for females), and (6) your general personality traits (extrovert or introvert, impulsive or reflective, sensible or scatterbrained).

Your identity consists of various aspects of your current identity and the potential selves you would like to be or that you imagine you might be. These potential selves include ideals that you would like to attain and standards that you feel you should meet. The aspects of your identity are arranged in a hierarchy. The more important an aspect of your identity is, or the higher it stands in the hierarchy, the more likely it is to influence your choices and your behavior. Your *gender identity* is your fundamental sense of your maleness or femaleness. Your *cultural identity* is your fundamental sense of your cultural and historical background. Your *ethnic identity* is your sense of belonging to one particular ethnic group.

Each aspect of your identity has positive or negative connotations. You generally look at yourself in an evaluative way, approving or disapproving of your behavior and characteristics. This is referred to as self-esteem. The word *esteem* comes from the Latin *aestimare*, which means "to estimate or appraise." Self-esteem thus refers to positive and negative evaluations of ourselves.

WHY HAVE AN IDENTITY?

The central importance accorded to the self is as old as psychology itself (James, 1890/1981). Your conceptualization of your *self* is the heart of your identity. Having a clear identity is important for a number of reasons (Johnson, 1997). First, your identity provides stability to your life. The world can change, other people can change, your career and family life can change, but something about yourself remains the same. During infancy, childhood, adolescence, and early adulthood, your identity expands, grows, and develops. The physical changes involved in growth, the increasing number of experiences with other people, increasing responsibilities, and general cognitive and social development, all cause changes and adaptations in self-definition. The final result has to be a coherent and unified personal identity.

Second, your identity directs your attention to the information, out of a pool of all the available information, to which you select to attend. To make sense out of all the available information, you selectively process that which past experience indicates is important for you. Having an identity speeds the processing of information relevant to your view of yourself. Information congruent with your self-view is processed easily, while information that contradicts your view of yourself is resisted and may be screened out entirely. If you see yourself as intelligent, for example, you tend to see your high grades as a result of your abilities and efforts. If you receive two A's and two C's, you tend to notice the A's and ignore the C's.

Third, your identity provides consistency to your self-view. Generally, you work to minimize any contradictions in your view of yourself. Your identity organizes and revises the incoming information so that it is consistent with your view of yourself. The incoming information is revised to fit your identity by having information relevant to it added or by altering inconsistent information. A low grade is perceived to be the result of bad luck and incompetent teachers. If you get low grades, creative expression (not grades) may be seen to be an indication of intelligence. People twist what they perceive so that it will fit into their existing schemas.

Fourth, you remember what is consistent with your identity and forget what is not. You remember your successes and forget your failures. Your identity facilitates the memory of information relevant to your view of yourself. It even reconstructs memory so the events you remember fit your view of yourself.

Fifth, your identity provides the means for dealing with stressful events. The more complex your identity is, the greater the buffer against stress and adversity. The complexity of your identity reduces the stress you experience and helps you cope with the stress you face. People with more complex identities are less prone to depression and illness; they also experience less severe mood swings following success or failure in one particular area of performance.

Finally, you seek out information and experiences that validate your identity. When you see yourself as intelligent, you seek out evidence proving that you are an intellectually superior person.

MULTICULTURAL PERSPECTIVES ON SELF-IDENTITY

Cultural differences exist in the way individuals define themselves. In the United States, for example, individuals are likely to say that the squeaky wheel gets the grease and recommend to their children to be a cut above the rest. In Japan, on the other hand, parents are likely to remind their children that the nail that stands up gets hammered down. These differences have been described by Triandis (1994) as individualism versus collectivism.

Evidence shows that the most fiercely independent people live in the United States, Australia, Great Britain, Canada, and the Netherlands, whereas the most interdependent people live in Venezuela, Colombia, Pakistan, Peru, and Taiwan (Hofstede, 1980). Most North Americans and Europeans have an independent view of the self as an entity that is distinct, autonomous, self-contained, and endowed with unique dispositions (Markus & Kitayama, 1991). They tend to say that the only person you can count on is yourself and that they enjoy being unique and different from others (Oyserman, 1993; Singelis, 1994; Triandis, 1989).

However, most Asians, Africans, and Latin Americans hold an interdependent view of the self as part of a larger social network that includes one's family, coworkers, and others to whom we are socially connected (Markus & Kitayama, 1991). These groups tend to believe that they are partly to blame if a family member or coworker fails and that their happiness depends on the happiness of those around them (Oyserman, 1993; Singelis, 1994; Triandis, 1989).

Are you more independent or interdependent in your view of yourself? When asked to described yourself, do you think of individual traits ("I am shy") or group affiliations ("I am a college student")? Participating in Activity 2.1 may help you define how you think about yourself.

ACTIVITY 2.1 ■ **WHO AM I?**

My Characteristics and Competencies			
	Personal Characteristics	**Demographic Characteristics**	**Abilities, Competencies**
1.			
2.			
3.			
4.			
5.			
6.			
7.			
8.			
9.			
10.			

My Heroes	
People with Whom I Identified as a Child	**People with Whom I Identify Now**

(continued)

ACTIVITY 2.1   *Continued*

My Commitments	
To What Should I commit My Time and Energy?	**For Whom and What Am I Responsible?**

My Values	
What Goals Do I Hope to Achieve?	**What Are My Major Values?**

THE WRONG TURNS IN BUILDING YOUR IDENTITY

Building an identity can go wrong when you separate your identity from the communities of which you are part, when you separate your identity from your moral character, and when your identity is superimposed on you by others or the society as a whole.

The Fallacy of Individual Identity

> I have my own unique thoughts, feelings, and dreams!
> I am an individual. There is no one in the world quite like me.

We often think we are self-created individuals who exist separate and apart from all other humans in the world. Such an individualistic orientation to the question, Who am I? is answered by a list of characteristics that has little or no relation to others and the larger community and society in which one lives. A person might describe him- or herself as a tall person, physically strong, who loves animals and the out-of-doors and who spends time canoeing and backpacking. Although accurate, this description is based on the fallacy of individual identity. In fact, the self develops through interactions with other people.

The fallacy of individual's identity ignores two important points. First, the self develops through interactions with other people. Second, the fallacy leaves out our social identities, that is, the groups to which we belong. We initially see ourselves reflected in the ways other people act toward us, respond to us, and perceive us. A baby boy may say, "I am smart," but that self-perception reflects what others have said to and about him. Cooley (1902) calls this "the looking-glass self." George Herbert Mead (1934) noted that developing such a "reflected" self depends on the ability to take in the perspective of others. Both emphasize that without other people interacting with us, we cannot form a concept or an identity of ourselves.

The Fallacy of the Value-Free Identity

How do you answer the question, Who am I? Is your answer separate and apart from considerations of your moral character and values? Many approaches to building identity and self-esteem seem to do so. They assume that who you are as a person is a collection of personal traits and characteristics that have nothing to do with your moral values. This assumption ignores two questions, What sort of person am I? and, What sort of person do I want to become? Advocates of a value-free identity often express a consumerist morality that assumes people are economic beings driven by the desire to accumulate. Individuals do not exist in a moral vacuum isolated from others. Instead, people exist ethically within the constraints of a communal world. Moral experience is essentially social, and it begins with social identity.

The Fallacy of Superimposed Identity

Do you construct your own identity, or is it imposed on you by your family, community, and society? Some of the discussions of identity portray individuals as passive receptacles into which an identity is poured. This assumption of passive acceptance ignores the evidence that children, adolescents, and adults actively decide for themselves whom they want to be and how they see themselves.

The Fallacy of Biases in Self-Definition

Whereas having a coherent and complex identity has many positive influences on your life, a number of biases also influence how you think about yourself. Often, an *illusion of control* of events that occur purely by chance influences your thinking. If you win the New York lottery, for example, you tend to ascribe your success to your intelligence in picking the right number rather than as resulting from dumb luck.

You also may be influenced by a *false consensus effect,* which is the belief that most other people act the way you do. If you take home pencils and paper from the office, you tend to believe everyone does so. In contrast, when asked to list your special skills and abilities, a *false uniqueness effect* may cause you to underestimate peers' abilities and overestimate the uniqueness and distinctiveness of your own skills and abilities. If you play tennis regularly, for example, you may believe that compared to others you are a uniquely talented tennis player.

An *above average effect* causes the vast majority of people to view themselves as being above average on any category or trait that is socially desirable. You tend to see yourself as more positive than you really are. On the other hand, a small minority of people tend constantly to evaluate themselves in an unrealistically negative way.

A *self-serving attributional bias* may be operating when you claim credit for success and deny responsibility for failure. When students do well on examinations, for example, they state that the tests are valid, but when they obtain poor grades, they question the validity of the tests. In addition, *self-centered bias* causes individuals consistently to exaggerate their own contributions to shared activities and jointly produced outcomes (compared to other group members), regardless of whether the outcome is successful or unsuccessful. College basketball players, for example, may overestimate their role in recent games.

Cognitive conservatism effect is the tendency, once your view of yourself has developed, to maintain and reinforce this view and to resist changing it. A *self-reference effect* takes place in the case when information that is relevant to the self is recalled better than information that is not relevant. When you perceive and recall yourself as a central actor in past events, *egocentric bias* is operating.

Finally, *hindsight bias* is a tendency, once an event has occurred, to overestimate one's ability to have foreseen the outcome. We tend to think after the fact that we knew beforehand what would happen. You can test your knowledge of these biases in Activity 2.2.

These biases exist for several reasons. First, some of these biases are cognitive shortcuts that enable you to cut through masses of available information efficiently to reach an explanation. This enables you to form a coherent, clear understanding of your experiences with as much efficiency as possible. Second, some of these biases are ways to determine plausible causes for particular events. People routinely overestimate the strength of any cause of an outcome, and, once a cause is determined, they tend to look for evidence that supports that cause. Third, some of these biases arise from the need to satisfy needs and motives through (a) enhancing self-esteem and (b) feeling in control. Finally, some of these biases arise from the need to impress others. Often you want to enhance your self-presentation to increase other's positive perception of you as a person.

SOCIAL IDENTITY

I have three chairs in my cabin. One for solitude, two for friendship, and three for society.
—*Henry David Thoreau*

Your identity is inherently social because you can understand who you are only in relation to your relationships with other people. Some relationships are positive and some are negative. You define yourself through your family, friends, and people who like you, but you also define yourself through your enemies and people who dislike you. If you are politically conservative, for example, part of your identity is differentiating yourself from those people who are politically liberal.

Identity is social in that it defines who you interact with and relate to and who you are similar to and different from. Historically, identity has existed only as being a member of communities and groups (MacIntyre, 1984). On the basis of these memberships, everyone knew exactly who he or she was. In the Middle Ages, for example, self-definition was based on 10 sources (see Activity 2.3):

1. The geographical location of your community (city, region, country)
2. The family of which you are part (son, daughter, cousin, or uncle)
3. To whom you are married (husband, wife)
4. What your occupation is (guildsman, doctor, knight).
5. Your social rank (nobleman, serf)
6. Your gender (male, female)

ACTIVITY **2.2** ■ BIASES INFLUENCING SELF-DEFINITION

Demonstrate your understanding of the biases influencing self-definition by matching the definitions with the appropriate characteristic. Check your answers with your partner and explain the reasoning for your answers.

BIAS

_____ 1. illusion of control

_____ 2. false consensus effect

_____ 3. false uniqueness effect

_____ 4. above average effect

_____ 5. self-serving attributional bias

_____ 6. self-centered bias

_____ 7. cognitive conservatism effect

_____ 8. self-reference effect

_____ 9. egocentric bias

_____ 10. hindsight bias

DEFINITION

a. Once your view of yourself has developed, there is a conservative tendency to maintain and reinforce it and to resist changing it.

b. The consistent exaggeration of your contributions (compared to other group members) to jointly produced outcomes.

c. The belief that you are above average in any category or trait that is socially desirable.

d. The belief most other people share your beliefs and act the way you do.

e. A tendency, once an event has occurred, to overestimate one's ability to have foreseen the outcome.

f. Information is recalled better when it is relevant to the self than when it is not.

g. Perceiving and recalling yourself as a central actor in past events.

h. The belief that you control events that occur purely by chance.

i. The belief that, in comparison with others, you have unique and distinctive skills and abilities.

j. The belief that you are responsible for your successes but are not responsible for your failures.

---

7. Your age (young, old)
8. Your bodily characteristics (height, strength)
9. Your moral goodness (honesty, deceny)
10. Your religion (Catholic, Jewish)

Your identity defines your membership in certain groups and places you in relation to other people. These relationships can be positive or negative. Eric Erikson (1950), for example, stated that a person's identity has to be grounded in a cultural identity if it is to facilitate psychological health. He believed that identity is located in the core of communal culture and that, as a member of a community, an important part of identity was exemplifying the moral code of the community, which he referred to as *character.*

ACTIVITY **2.3** ■ SELF-DEFINITION IN THE MIDDLE AGES

The following chart contains the 10 methods of self-definition during the Middle Ages. Define yourself according to each category. Then rank order the 10 characteristics from most important (1) to least important (10) to your identity.

Self-Definition Methods	My Definitions	Rank
Geography		
Family		
Marriage		
Occupation		
Social rank		
Gender		
Age		
Bodily characteristics		
Moral goodness		
Religion		

IDENTITY AND MORAL CHARACTER

> In a general sense, ethics is the name we give to our concern for good behavior. We feel an obligation to consider not only our own personal well-being but also that of others and of human society as a whole.
> —*Albert Schweitzer*

An aspect of identity that is commonly neglected is the view of oneself as a moral person, with character, who acts with integrity. A moral orientation adds an obligatory "ought to" quality to identity. The question, What sort of person am I to become? can be answered only by considering the kind of purposes and goals you consider worthy of commitment and pursuit. Your identity and character depend on sustained commitment to meaningful goals. Meaningful goals are goals shared by other people, the accomplishment of which benefits others and the community as a whole as well as oneself. Character is understanding, committing oneself to, and acting on core ethical values such as honesty, responsibility, respect, kindness, and caring for others. Individuals with character act with integrity as part of a community to fulfill their responsibilities and obligations to others and the community as a whole.

The moral dimension of identity is experiencing your actions not only from your personal perspective, but also from a social perspective that includes the perspectives and interests of other people in a relationship. Individuals involved in a relationship have a mutual obligation to respect and protect the framework of social norms that define what is fair and unfair, what is appropriate and inappropriate, and what is respectful and disrespectful.

The moral orientation in a relationship differs according to whether a relationship is cooperative or competitive (Deutsch, 1985; Johnson & Johnson, 1997; 1999). The moral orientation in a cooperative relationship focuses on mutual respect, self-respect, and equality (unless inequality brings greater benefits and advantages than those less fortunate would otherwise have if all were treated equally). This egalitarianism implies a definition of injustice as inequalities that do not benefit all concerned (Rawls, 1971). Identity in a cooperative context defines the person as part of a community in which members are working together to achieve shared goals. Their interactions while doing so are egalitarianism and characterized by mutual respect.

The moral orientation in competitive relationships is based on inequality and the win–lose struggle to determine who will have superior and who will have inferior outcomes. The struggle may be regulated so that the competition takes place under fair rules (as in a duel of honor) or so that one's moral orientation includes an obligation to obey the rules, or the struggle may be a no-holds-barred competition in which any means to defeat the other can be employed. In a competition, both the victor and the losers are morally obligated to acknowledge the end of the competition. The victor is not supposed to defeat the losers over and over again, and the losers are morally obligated to acknowledge that they have lost without reopening the competition over and over again. Identity in a competitive context defines a person as a separate individual striving to win. The interactions while doing so (and afterwards) are based on inequality and often characterized by contempt and disdain.

CONSTRUCTING YOUR IDENTITY

To loosely paraphrase Goethe, character is produced in the stream of life, not in solitude. You construct your identity in at least three ways: by acquiring social roles, by identifying with other people and groups, and by seeking out a broad range of experiences (Johnson & F. Johnson, 1997).

Role Acquisition

One way your identity is created is through the acquisition of social roles. A *social role* is a set of expectations aimed at structuring interactions within a relationship. Social roles are often defined specifically as part of a reciprocal relationship. The roles of student and teacher or husband and wife are reciprocal in the sense that one could not exist without the other. Social roles may be assigned or voluntary. Assigned social roles include gender and nationality. Social roles that are voluntarily acquired include friend and husband (or wife). Social roles may be permanent or temporary. Some roles people acquire are permanent—the role of parent for example. Others are temporary—the role of student, for example. The social roles you adopt may also be influenced, or even determined, by how well you are perceived to satisfy social values and attain social status (see Box 2.1). Your identity may be most influenced by assigned, permanent social roles.

Acquiring a role requires that you learn to act, feel, and perceive the world in a manner somewhat similar to that of other people who have similar roles. You must master the needed technical and interpersonal competencies and learn what to expect from people in related roles. In addition, you personalize each of your roles by actively modifying them to fit your personality.

Through acquiring social roles, you learn large, integrated patterns of consistent behavior. In acquiring a social role, you (a) anticipate being in the role, (b) perform the role while responding to the formal expectations of those in reciprocal roles and those enacting the same role, (c) perform the role while responding to informal expectations for how things really get done and exploring the range of variability allowed in performing the role, and (d) perform the role while modifying and molding the role around one's personality characteristics and the demands of other social roles.

The social roles you adopt help define who you are, such as student, tutor, friend, neighbor, boss, subordinate, engineer, carpenter, sailor, skier, minister, or cook. The social roles you acquire define who you are both to yourself and to other people.

Identification

In its simplest form, *identification* occurs when you try to be like someone you love or admire. Through identifying with other people, you incorporate their qualities and attributes into yourself. You can admire a teacher's scholarship and strive to become a scholar yourself. You can like a teacher and imitate that teacher's friendliness and warmth. By actively selecting adults, older students, and even mythical figures such as people in stories and television programs with whom to identify you construct your own personality and transform yourself into the kind of person you want to be.

Several major types of identification are identification based on love or liking, identification based on admiration for superior competence, and identification based on anxiety or anger. Those based on love or liking or on admiration result in a fairly straightforward growth of the person. You pattern yourself after more resourceful, powerful, and competent people whom you admire and like. As a young child, you probably wanted to be "bigger," to have the skills and power of older people. As you progressed through school, you probably experimented with imitating powerful and

---

BOX 2.1
RESOURCE ATTRACTORS

When establishing your identity, it may be helpful to consider your resource attractors. A *resource attractor* is an attribute that tends to attract other resources because it gives the possessor an advantage in a competition for these other resources. Examples of resource attractors are ability, training, previous experience, drive, and character. In addition, certain physical characteristics are resource attractors, such as being attractive or tall. Other resource attractors may be gender, ethnic and historical background, and wealth.

More opportunities present themselves for members of the Kennedy or the Rockefeller families. Physically attractive people are treated more favorably than physically unattractive people. Individuals with a high number of resource attractors often have more opportunities and higher rewards than members with few resource attractors and may attribute their success to their worthiness and effort (implying that those who have fewer resource attractors are less worthy and more lazy).

likeable others by emotionally relating to them, conforming to their expectations, idealizing them, and partly basing self-esteem on their approval. You may have identified with teachers because of your positive feelings toward them, their superior competence, and the control they exercise over valued resources such as knowledge, skills, and grades.

Identification based on anxiety or anger, however, can be destructive. When a child experiences the loss of a loved or admired person through death, desertion, or rejection, he or she may internalize aspects of the person in an attempt to maintain the relationship. When a child experiences being controlled, frustrated, or mistreated in situations in which there is no escape, he or she may identify with the tormentor out of helplessness and anger. These identifications can hinder development.

Identifications result in personal growth: the outer relationship becomes a model for an inner restructuring. Parental love, the love of a teacher, and the love of other adults become internalized in a more secure self-image, a sense of trust, and higher self-esteem. The child comes to love himself or herself in the same way he or she is loved by significant others. If the love of a parent or teacher is conditional, self-love may also be conditional. If a parent or teacher is ambivalent toward a child, both loving and hating him, then the child may tend to feel ambivalent toward himself— one part hating himself and another part loving himself. Healthy social development and constructive socialization depend on students identifying with others primarily on the basis of love and a desire to become more competent. The destructive aspects of identifications based on being rejected and frustrated are so pervasive in psychologically ill people that Perls (1973) viewed psychotherapy as the process by which negative identifications are replaced with positive ones.

You do not always accurately and realistically perceive the people with whom you identify. You may therefore build personal myths about parents, teachers, and friends. What matters for identification is not the actual characteristics of the person being identified with, but rather the characteristics you attribute to the person. This is especially true in times of crisis. There are also many periods in life when a developmental crisis forces change. The most marked is adolescence, when sexual maturity revolutionizes your life. Identification is one of the tools you use to manage such crises. You identify with others who seem to have the competence and characteristics necessary to handle the crisis.

Your identity builds from identifying with real, historical, and fictional people. You imitate and internalize aspects of individuals who have emotional significance for you. You identify with your parents, older siblings, teachers, and friends. You also identify with historical characters such as Benjamin Franklin or Jane Addams. The formation and increasing integration of your identity continue throughout life. It is a process that is constantly occurring. Adolescence, however, is a marked crisis in which individuals struggle with integrating and updating their identities. The danger of adolescence is the failure to resolve this crisis by "getting it all together." Luckily, you are never too old to define more clearly who you are.

In addition to identifying with people, you also identify with reference groups. *Reference groups* are groups to which a person belongs or aspires to belong, identifies with, and uses as a basis for comparison. Group membership can be involuntary (gender, ethnicity, nationality) or voluntary (which clubs you join and which company you work for). It is from identifying with these groups that your historical, cultural, ethnic identity is derived.

Seeking Out a Broad Range of Experiences

You expand your identity by seeking out a broad range of experiences. The more varied and extensive your experiences are, and the more you experience a wide variety of social roles, the more clearly defined your identity becomes.

BUILDING PRIDE IN YOUR CULTURAL IDENTITY

> Each generation teaches the next. We are here now, and we will be here always.
> Our footsteps touch those who have gone before, those who are here now, and
> those who will live in these mountains and hills for all eternity.
> —*Pueblo saying*

Each person must develop an awareness and appreciation of his or her own historical, cultural, ethnic, and religious background. Part of your identity is based on your identification with and appreciation of the culture and history of your ancestors. Usually, the more respect you have for your cultural heritage, the more respect you have for yourself. Descriptions of four steps to identifying with your historical background and creating an *unum* from *pluribus* follow. (See Box 2.2 for a brief summary of these steps.)

First, you develop an appreciation for your historic, cultural, ethnic, and religious background as well as your other important personal characteristics. You should value and recognize the culture and history of your ancestors (for some, your culture may be a small town in the United States). It is part of your identity. Your identity consists of multiple subidentities that are organized into a coherent, stable, and integrated whole. The subidentities include a *gender identity* (fundamental sense of maleness or femaleness), a *cultural identity* (sense of origins and membership in a culture), an *ethnic identity* (sense of belonging to one particular ethnic group), a *religious identity* (sense of belonging to one particular religious group), and so forth. Each of these subidentities should be recognized and valued, and they need to be organized into a coherent, stable, and integrated overall sense of self. Respect for one's subidentities may be the basis for self-respect. Activity 2.4 is an exercise in developing an appreciation for your clutural, historical, and ethnic heritage.

Second, you develop an appreciation for the historic, cultural, ethnic, and religious backgrounds (and other important personal characteristics) of others. A critical aspect of developing a historical, cultural, and ethnic identity is whether ethnocentricity is inherent in one's definition of oneself. An ingroup identity must be developed in a way that does not lead to rejection of outgroups. Many examples of being a member of one group require rejecting other groups. However, many examples of being a member of one group require valuing and respecting other groups. Other heritages may be seen as collaborative rather than competitive. The degree to which a person's identity leads to respect and value for others' diversity depends on developing a superordinate identity that subsumes both one's own heritage and the heritage of all other students, faculty, and members of society. Activity 2.5 may contribute to your appreciation for other cultural identities.

Third, you develop a strong superordinate identity as an "American." Your own historical identity and the historical identities of others are united under the umbrella identity of being American. Being an American is creedal rather than racial or ancestral. It is based on our belief that all humans are created equal and endowed

---

■ ■ ■ ■ ■

BOX 2.2
BEING AN AMERICAN

- I respect, appreciate, and value my religious, ethnic, and cultural background.
- I respect, appreciate, and value the religious, ethnic, and cultural backgrounds of others.
- I have a strong superordinate identity as an "American." Being an American is creedal. I believe in the American creed.
- I have pluralistic values. I value democracy, freedom, liberty, equality, justice, the rights of individuals, and the responsibilities of citizenship.

ACTIVITY **2.4** ■ CULTURAL, HISTORICAL, AND ETHNIC HERITAGE

1. Describe your cultural, historical, and ethnic heritage: _____

_____

2. Find the other members of this class who share your cultural heritage.

3. Plan a 15- to 20-minute class presentation on your cultural heritage that includes the following:

    a. Definition of your cultural identity
    b. History of your culture
    c. Traditions of your culture
    d. Aspects of your culture (food, songs, art)
    e. Personal experiences as a member of your culture
    f. Traditions of your culture that you practice

ACTIVITY **2.5** ■ COMPARING CULTURAL IDENTITIES

What do we have in common, how are we different? The diagram below, presenting two overlapping circles, is known as a Venn Diagram. This diagram is provided in conjunction with the following exercises.

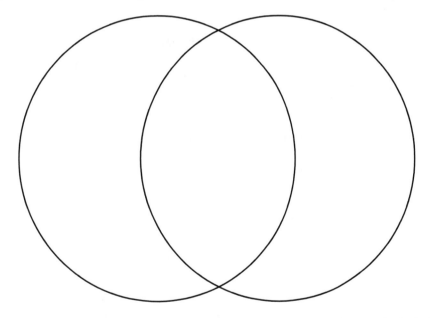

1. In the first circle write down the aspects of your cultural, historical, and ethnic identity that are unique to you and different from those of your partner.

2. In the second circle write down the aspects of the other person's cultural, historical, and ethnic identity that are unique to that person and different from yours.

3. In the overlapping part of the circles, write down the aspects of your cultural, historical, and ethnic identities that are similar.

4. Discuss how you are different and what you have in common.

5. Find a new partner and repeat the procedure.

by their creator with certain inalienable rights. That is, it is based on our commitment to the Constitution, Bill of Rights, and Declaration of Independence of the United States, which provide our superordinate identity as Americans. Our common commitment to equality, justice, and liberty for all unites us as one people, even though we are the descendants of many cultures, races, religions, and ethnic groups. Each cultural group is part of the whole and members of each new immigrant group, while modifying and enriching our national identity, learn they are first and foremost Americans. This country is one of the few successful examples of a pluralistic society in which different groups clashed but ultimately learned to live together through achieving a sense of common nationhood. In our diversity, there has always been a broad recognition that we are one people. Whatever our origins, we are all Americans. Complete Activity 2.6 to resolve cultural heritage and schooling.

Fourth, you adopt a pluralistic set of values concerning democracy, freedom, liberty, equality, justice, the rights of individuals, and the responsibilities of citizenship (Johnson & Johnson, 1994b). It is these values that form the American creed. All individuals are free to speak their minds and give their opinions. All individuals are considered to be of equal value. Every member has the right and responsibility to contribute their resources and efforts to achieving the group's goals. Each member has a right to expect other individuals to be considerate of his or her needs and wants. All individuals must at times put the good of the group above their own needs and desires. As Americans, we respect basic human rights, listen to dissenters instead of jailing them, and have a multiparty political system, a free press, free speech, freedom of religion, and freedom of assembly. These values were shaped by millions of people from many different backgrounds. Americans are a multicultural people knitted together by a common set of political and moral values that are primarily taught by the schools.

AM I ACCEPTABLE OR UNACCEPTABLE?

> Show me the sensible person who likes himself or herself. I know myself too well to like what I see. I know but too well that I'm not what I'd like to be.
> —*Golda Meir*

Most people use one or more of these processes for making judgments about their self-worth. It is important that you not only learn to accept yourself, but also learn a constructive method of judging your self-worth from the information that is available to you about yourself. Activity 2.7 provides an exercise for doing so. Usually, an unconditional, basic self-acceptance and an accurate understanding of how others perceive you are viewed as the most constructive ways to determine your self-esteem. Your psychological health may be related to believing you are intrinsically worthwhile and accurately understanding how others perceive you.

A common saying is "I can't be right for someone else if I'm not right for me!" *Self-acceptance* is a high regard for yourself or, conversely, a lack of cynicism about yourself (Johnson, 2000). Accepting yourself as you are has a number of benefits. Relationships exist through self-acceptance, self-disclosure, and being accepted by others. The more self-accepting you are, the greater your self-disclosure tends to be. The greater your self-disclosure is, the more others accept you. The more others accept you, the more you accept yourself.

A high level of self-acceptance, furthermore, is reflected in psychological health. Psychologically healthy people see themselves as being liked, capable, worthy, and acceptable to other people. All these perceptions are based on self-acceptance. Finally, considerable evidence abounds that self-acceptance and acceptance of others are related. If you think well of yourself, you tend to think well of others. You also tend to assume that others will like you, an expectation that often becomes a self-fulfilling prophecy.

ACTIVITY **2.6** ■ DO WE NEED A COMMON CULTURAL HERITAGE
IN SCHOOLS?

Complete the following tasks individually. Then find a partner and (a) share your answers and reasoning, (b) listen carefully to your partner's answers and reasoning, and (c) come to consensus about what the answers and reasoning should be.

1. *Culture* is a set of shared meanings that make social life possible. Do teachers and students need a common culture for instructional activities to be effective?

   _____ Yes _____ No

   Reasons: _____

   _____

2. The following list contains three aspects of shared identity and culture that may be required for effective teaching and learning to occur. Teachers may take it for granted that students are like themselves in these areas of functioning. Use the following scale to rate the importance of these aspects.

   1————————2————————3————————4————————5
   Unimportant   Very important

   _____ **Cultural functioning:** Teachers and students share a common cultural heritage that includes a common language, a large body of commonsense knowledge, and a knowledge of cultural heroes, popular tastes, and everyday customs and conversations.

   _____ **Psychological functioning:** Teachers and students are similar in the way their minds work, in the way they think and feel, in what makes them laugh and cry, and so forth.

   _____ **Physiological functioning:** Teachers and students react similarly to factors that create fatigue, how much stress can be tolerated, the conditions that bring on excitement or boredom, and so forth.

3. All children and adolescents in our society need to learn certain basic information and concepts to be able to read the newspaper, watch television programs, and communicate effectively. Examples are the Blarney Stone, *Alice in Wonderland,* the asteroid belt, and Saint Augustine.

   _____ Agree _____ Disagree

   Reasons: _____

   _____

INCREASING YOUR SELF-ACCEPTANCE THROUGH RELATIONSHIPS

Relationships begin when two people reach out to each other and identify common goals, interests, activities, and values. This is as true among diverse individuals as it is among homogeneous individuals. To build a relationship, both individuals must

ACTIVITY **2.7** ■ HOW I REASON ABOUT MYSELF

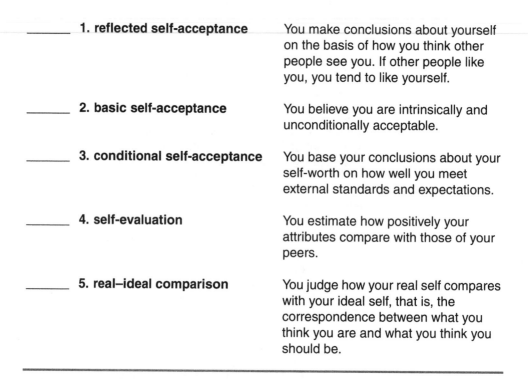

Working individually, rank the ways of deriving conclusions about your self-worth from what you most likely would do (1) to what you would least likely do (5). Write out the reasons for the order of your ranking.

Next find a partner. Share your ranking and reasons. Listen carefully to their ranking and reasons. Make any modifications you want to your ranking. Find a new partner and repeat the process.

_____ **1. reflected self-acceptance**	You make conclusions about yourself on the basis of how you think other people see you. If other people like you, you tend to like yourself.
_____ **2. basic self-acceptance**	You believe you are intrinsically and unconditionally acceptable.
_____ **3. conditional self-acceptance**	You base your conclusions about your self-worth on how well you meet external standards and expectations.
_____ **4. self-evaluation**	You estimate how positively your attributes compare with those of your peers.
_____ **5. real–ideal comparison**	You judge how your real self compares with your ideal self, that is, the correspondence between what you think you are and what you think you should be.

be open with and open to the other (Johnson, 2000). You are open with other persons when you disclose yourself to them, sharing your ideas and feelings and letting them know who you are as a person. You are open to other persons when you are interested in their ideas and feelings and want to know who they are as a person. It is only through disclosing yourself to diverse others that they can come to know you and accept you. Their acceptance and respect strengthens your own self-acceptance. It is only through disclosing themselves to you that you can come to know others and accept them. Your acceptance strengthens their self-acceptance. Your relationship grows and deepens as you and the other persons are more and more open with and to each other. Your awareness of the other person increases your self-awareness and vice versa. Your acceptance of yourself increases your acceptance of the other person and vice versa. Try sharing your past in Activity 2.8.

Feedback from people you trust can confirm your view of yourself or reveal to you aspects of yourself and reactions to your behavior you never knew. Feedback from other people can increase your self-awareness. You construct a *looking-glass self* by adopting, over time, other people's views of yourself. Receiving feedback from others enables you to understand that others have a different perspective and may see you differently from how you see yourself.

The relationship between disclosure, feedback, and self-awareness is represented in Figure 2.1 by the Johari Window, named after its two originators, Joe Luft and Harry Ingham (Luft, 1969). They believed that (a) certain things you know about

ACTIVITY **2.8** ■ SHARING YOUR PAST

The purpose of this exercise is to allow other people to get to know you by sharing your family history with them and to get to know them by learning more about their past. The procedure follows.

1. Fill in the following chart with the names (first and last) of your grandparents and parents. If you are not sure of all the names, ask your parents what they are. If you did not grow up with your parents, use whatever parent figures you have.

Maternal Grandfather	Maternal Grandmother	Paternal Grandfather	Paternal Grandmother

Mother	Father

You

2. For both your parents and each of your grandparents (both maternal and paternal), think about the answers to the following questions:

   a. Where was he or she born and raised?
   b. What was his or her early life like?
   c. What are (were) his or her outstanding characteristics?
   d. What is (was) his or her career?
   e. Can you trace any of your characteristics or attitudes to either of your parents or one or more of your grandparents?
   f. Do any family traditions (activities, foods, etc.) come from either one of your parents or one or more of your grandparents?

3. In small groups (from two to seven members), share your answers to the preceding questions and listen carefully to the answers of the other group members.

4. In the same small groups, discuss the following questions:

   a. How did you feel about doing this exercise?
   b. Did you learn anything new about yourself?
   c. Is it important for you to know about your family?
   d. How do you think an adopted person deals with this issue? (If you are adopted, how do you deal with it?)
   e. How did you react to what other members of your group said about their family roots?

FIGURE 2.1   Johari Window

	Known to Self	Unknown to Self
Known to Others	Free to self and others	Blind to self, free to others
Unknown to Others	Free to self, hidden to others	Unknown to self and others

AT THE BEGINNING OF A RELATIONSHIP

	Known to Self	Unknown to Self
Known to Others		
Unknown to Others		

AT THE END OF A RELATIONSHIP

	Known to Self	Unknown to Self
Known to Others		
Unknown to Others		

PRINCIPLES

1. Self-disclosure reduces the hidden area.
2. Feedback reduces the blind area.
3. Together they reduce the unknown area.

yourself and certain things you do not know about yourself and (b) certain things other people know about you and certain things they do not know. As a relationship grows and develops, your free area becomes larger and your blind and hidden areas become smaller. As you become more self-disclosing, you reduce the hidden area. As you encourage others to give you feedback, your blind area is reduced. Through reducing your hidden area, you give other people information to react to, thus enabling them to provide more informed and precise feedback, which better reduces your blind area. Through reducing your blind area, you increase your self-awareness; this helps you to be even more self-disclosing with others.

DIVERSITY WITHIN YOUR IDENTITY

You belong to many groups, and the demands of these memberships often conflict and sometimes contradict each other. You actually have a complex profile of group identities. A Caucasian person, for example, may be male or female, Roman Catholic or Jewish, lower class or upper class, southerner or Yankee. In addition, the person may be a mixture of Italian American, Swedish American, German American, and English American. In other words, you have multiple social identities that are internalized and integrated as you are growing up. The interaction of these multiple identities create internal complexity. You must be aware of and accept this complexity so that parts of yourself are not in conflict with other parts of yourself. The more you are aware of your own complexity, the more easily you can recognize the oversimplification of stereotypes and the less likely you are to see others in unidimensional, narrow ways.

SUMMARY

Who are you? You must know yourself to be able to know others. To understand, respect, and appreciate others' cultural and historical perspectives, you must be aware of your own. Your identity includes both personal and social facets. It provides stability to your life, influences what you attend to, provides consistency to your self-view, organizes your experiences, helps you manage stress and adversity, and influences the experiences and information we seek out. Although having a coherent and complex identity has many positive influences on your life, a number of biases also influence how you think about yourself. You build your identity by acquiring social roles, by identifying with other people and groups, and by seeking out a broad range of experiences.

Part of your identity is based on your identification with and appreciation of the culture and history of your ancestors. Usually, the more respect you have for your cultural heritage, the more respect you have for yourself. There are four steps to identifying with your historical background:

1. You develop an appreciation for your historic, cultural, ethnic, and religious background as well as your other important personal characteristics.
2. You develop an appreciation for the historic, cultural, ethnic, and religious backgrounds (and other important personal characteristics) of others.
3. You develop a strong superordinate identity as an "American."
4. You adopt a pluralistic set of values concerning democracy, freedom, liberty, equality, justice, the rights of individuals, and the responsibilities of citizenship.

Your identity may be positive or negative, depending on the process you use to make conclusions about your self-worth. Processes include making conclusions about yourself on the basis of how you think other people see you (reflected self-acceptance), believing you are intrinsically and unconditionally acceptable (basic self-acceptance), basing your conclusions about your self-worth on how well you meet external standards and expectations (conditional self-acceptance), estimating how positively your attributes compare with those of your peers (self-evaluation), and judging how your real self compares with your ideal self (real–ideal comparison). The more positive your conclusions about your self-worth (that is, the higher your self-acceptance), the more accepting you are of others and the more positively you view them.

If you think well of yourself, you tend to think well of others. This is especially important when others are from different cultural and ethnic backgrounds. You increase your self-acceptance by developing personal relationships in which you let others get to know you and you receive feedback on how they perceive you. This combination of self-disclosure and feedback increases your self-awareness and your self-acceptance.

This chapter details the first steps in building constructive relationships with diverse individuals. However, several barriers may prevent you doing so. They are discussed in the next chapter.

CHAPTER THREE

BARRIERS TO CONSTRUCTIVE DIVERSITY

INTRODUCTION

There are at least three approaches to theorizing and research on relationships among diverse individuals:

1. *Cognitive* approaches include the study of stereotyping, social categorization, and social identity.
2. *Attitudinal* approaches include the study of prejudice, racism, unconscious evaluation, and intergroup contact.
3. *Behavior* approaches include the study of discrimination, ingroup favoritism, aversive racism, institutional racism, and collective action.

These approaches have two foci: What takes place within the individual and what takes place between members of different, diverse groups (see Table 3.1). In the past 25 years, the majority of the research conducted on relationships among diverse individuals has dealt with intraindividual phenomena (beliefs, attitudes, and emotions). This chapter focuses on this body of theory, research, and practice. (The following chapter focuses on interpersonal and intergroup phenomena.)

DESEGREGATION OF SCHOOLS

Desegregation of schools in the United States was mandated in a historic Supreme Court decision in 1954 (*Brown v. Board of Education of Topeka*). (See Box 3.1 for a brief

TABLE 3.1   Approaches to Relationships among Diverse People

APPROACHES	FOCUS	
	Individual	*Interpersonal/Group*
Cognition	Stereotyping	Social categorization Social identity
Attitudes/Affect	Prejudice, racism Unconscious evaluation	Intergroup contact
Behavior	Ingroup favoritism Aversive racism	Discrimination Institutional racism Collective action

BOX 3.1

THE MAN WHO KILLED JIM CROW: CHARLES HAMILTON HOUSTON (1895–1950)

In the 1930s, not only did black and white children attend different schools in the South, the schools were grossly unequal. In 1930, for example, South Carolina spent 10 times as much on educating each white child as it did on educating each black child. Would knowledge of these statistics convince a nation that segregation was wrong? Charles Houston (the grandson of fugitive slaves who was then vice dean of Howard University's School of Law in Washington, D.C.) did not think so.

In 1935, he traveled through South Carolina with a 16-mm movie camera, filming schools—the buildings, teachers, buses, and students. He contrasted unheated cabins and tarpaper shacks (black schools) with tidy brick and stone structures (white schools). He titled his documentary, *Examples of Educational Discrimination among Rural Negroes in South Carolina.* He planned to use his film to take racial injustice in America's schools to court to overturn the 1895 Supreme Court decision, *Plessy v. Ferguson,* the case that legalized racial segregation and gave birth to the Jim Crow laws. He was little known at the time, but the results of his efforts were profound.

At age sixteen Charles Houston entered Amherst College in Massachusetts. Serving as an officer in World War I, he observed the mistreatment of black soldiers and concluded that if he survived, he would "fight for those who could not strike back" (Williams, 1987, p. 4). He entered Harvard University Law School in 1919 and was the first black elected to the editorial board of the Harvard Law Review. He received his law degree in 1922 and a doctorate in 1923. Houston began teaching at Howard Law School and in 1929 was appointed vice dean. He saw that litigation could do more than settle a case. It could shape society.

In 1935, the NAACP offered Houston an opportunity to direct a crusade against segregation. Houston accepted and decided on two long-range strategies. The first strategy was to train a cadre of top-notch black lawyers dedicated to making the legal system work for blacks. He advocated that every lawyer trained at Howard be knowledgeable about constitutional law, believing that the only worthy role for a lawyer was that of social engineer—someone who understood the Constitution and knew how to use it to better the living conditions of underprivileged citizens. A lawyer, he said, "is either a social engineer or he is a parasite on society" (Williams, 1987, p. 5). So tough that he was nicknamed Cement Pants, he trained black lawyers who could more than hold their own with white lawyers in the fight against racism.

The second strategy was to create a legal precedence for the courts to outlaw segregation. In 1935, working with his former student Thurgood Marshall, he convinced the Maryland courts to admit Donald Gaines Murray to the University of Maryland Law School, and in 1938 he convinced the Supreme Court to admit Lloyd Lionel Gaines into the University of Missouri Law School. This meant that every state in the Union had an obligation to provide an equal education for all citizens.

In 1944, President Franklin Roosevelt appointed Houston to the President's Committee on Fair Employment Practices. Houston constantly gave public speeches, believing, "Lawsuits mean little unless supported by public opinion…The truth is there are millions of white people who have no real knowledge of the Negro's problems." (Williams, 1987, p. 15)

Houston worked 15 to 18 hours a day, seven days a week, year after year. His dedication and hard work in ending Jim Crow made him one of the most important lawyers of the twentieth century. Worn out by his efforts, he died of heart failure at age 54 in 1950. In 1954, Houston's dream came true, and the Supreme Court ended segregation in schools with the historic *Brown v. Board of Education*

(continued)

BOX 3.1 CONTINUED

decision. Of his triumph in the Supreme Court in 1954, Thurgood Marshall remarked, "We were just carrying [Houston's] bags, that's all." The Supreme Court decision was very much Houston's triumph as a lawyer, educator, and NAACP advocate.

Williams, J. (1987). *Eyes on the prize: America's civil rights years: 1954–1965.* New York: Viking Penguin.

biography of the man whose life's work was to end segregation in schools.) Despite the Court's ruling, desegregation proceeds slowly, primarily because many people in the United States oppose it. Opponents argue that morality cannot be legislated; they engage in stalling tactics, lawsuits, and vocal opposition. The research conducted on desegregation, furthermore, does not support its effectiveness. Walter Stephan (1986) reviewed studies conducted during and after desegregation and found that 13 percent reported no change and 53 percent reported an increase in prejudice among whites. A brief history of desegregation is given in Box 3.2.

The effects of desegregation are difficult to determine for at least two reasons. First, the way schools are desegregated does not create the conditions under which interracial contact could be expected to have favorable consequences (Schofield, 1986; Taylor & Moghaddam, 1994). Second, the quality of the research is unsatisfactory, and the results are questionable. Despite these limitations, evidence indicates that desegregation has positive effects (Schofield & Sagar, 1983; Stephan, 1978, 1991).

Desegregation may improve black students' achievement, but only to a modest extent (Stephan, 1991). The average achievement of black students increased in proportion to the percentage of whites in their classroom (Coleman et al., 1966; McPartland, 1969) and in northern and western states, black students who attended desegregated schools achieved higher than those who attended segregated schools (Dawkins, 1994). A recent meta-analyses found greater achievement among minority students attending desegregated schools (Schneider, 1990). Perhaps the safest conclusion is that the achievement level of blacks sometimes increases and rarely decreases in desegregated schools.

Blacks who attend desegregated high schools are more likely to graduate from high school, attend and graduate from college, and attain higher GPAs than blacks who attended segregated schools (Crain & McPartland, 1984; Stephan, 1991). Blacks who attend desegregated schools or colleges are more likely to work in desegregated employment settings and to achieve higher incomes than blacks with segregated educational backgrounds (Braddock, 1985). Studies of white students attending black colleges have found positive effects on their self-concept as well as more favorable race relations (Comer, 1980; Pascarella et al., 1987).

The evidence from a nationwide survey indicates no long-term differences in self-esteem between blacks who attended segregated elementary and secondary schools and blacks who attended desegregated schools (Dawkins, 1994). Other evidence indicates that desegregation generally does not reduce the prejudices of whites toward blacks and leads to increases in black prejudice toward whites about as frequently as it leads to decreases (Schofield & Sagar, 1983; Stephan, 1978; 1991).

The research on the long-term benefits of desegregation indicates better and more integrated social relationships. A study involving 191 white adults found that early childhood contact with African American students had a significant positive effect on adults' current cross-ethnic attitudes (Wood & Sonleitner, 1996). Adults who attended desegregated schools have been found to live in integrated neighborhoods

■ ■ ■ ■ ■

BOX 3.2
SCHOOL DESEGREGATION

DATE	EVENT
Early 1800s	Public education was provided primarily in New England.
1860s	Almost all whites but only 7 percent of blacks received education in the North; no whites or blacks in the South received public education.
Post–Civil War	The Thirteenth Amendment freed the slaves, the Fourteenth Amendment guaranteed "equal protection of the laws" to all citizens of the United States, and the Fifteenth Amendment gave blacks the right to vote.
1896	The Supreme Court (*Plessy v. Ferguson*) interpreted the Fourteenth Amendment as allowing "separate but equal" facilities. Legalized segregation became common after this ruling.
1910	The NAACP was founded to fight against the widespread lynching of blacks by whites, unequal justice, and other forms of discrimination.
1930	The average per-pupil expenditure in U.S. public schools was $99; in the South it was $44 for white pupils but only $13 for black students (Stephan, 1999).
1954	The Supreme Court (*Brown v. Board of Education*) declared that in public schools separate was inherently unequal.
1955	The Supreme Court ordered the Brown decision implemented by the lower courts "with all deliberate speed." Yet in 1964, 99 percent of black children were still segregated (Edelman, 1973).
1964	The Civil Rights Act was passed by Congress.
	De jure segregation (segregation mandated by law) existed in the South; *de facto* segregation (segregation based on the fact of where people lived) existed in the North. By 1972, 44 percent of black children in the South were attending predominantly white schools whereas the figure was only 29 percent in the North (Pettigrew, 1975).
1970s	Many districts used bussing to integrate schools. Opponents to desegregation attacked the busing of students as the most vulnerable aspect of school desegregation.
	In large cities, white migration to the suburbs ended any possibility of integration. In Detroit, for example, over 80 percent of students were black.
1987	Thirty percent of black students attended segregated (all-black) schools and only 31 percent of white students attended schools that had 5 percent or more black students.
	Mandatory programs are more successful at reducing segregation than are voluntary programs, court-ordered programs, or school board–ordered programs (Rossell, 1990; Welch & Light, 1987).
2002	Desegregation is still far from complete. Should we give up or should we speed up the process?

more frequently (Crain, 1984; Pearce, Crain, & Farley, 1984). In an analysis of 21 studies of outcomes for ethnic minorities, Wells and Crain (1994) found that those who attended desegregated schools (compared to those who attended segregated schools) were more likely to experience success in college and to live in interracial neighborhoods. Interracial contact at young ages has been found to be related to African Americans' likelihood of interacting with white individuals as adults and being employed in more integrated work organizations (Braddock, Crain, & McPartland, 1984).

Diversity among peers is an important resource that can improve the group's productivity. Doing so may not be easy. A number of cognitive factors are barriers that prevent diverse peers from interacting effectively (see Johnson, 2000). They include stereotyping, prejudice, the tendency to blame the victim, and cultural clashes. They begin with the human need to classify.

THE HUMAN NEED TO CLASSIFY

> The Deity does not regard the human race collectively. He surveys all the beings of whom mankind is composed and discerns in each man the resemblances that assimilate him to his fellows, and the differences that distinguish them. God, therefore, stands in no need of general ideas.

> Such however is not the case with man.... Having superficially considered a number of objects and noticed their resemblance, he assigns to these a common name, sets them apart, and proceeds onward. These common names are ... proof of ... the insufficiency of the human intellect; for there are in nature no beings exactly alike.
> —*Alexis de Tocqueville (1945, p. 13)*

How do we understand other people? We cannot see another person's thoughts, motives, or intentions. We observe the other person, the situation, and the other person's behavior, we organize what we observe into categories, and then we make inferences and conclusions.

As Tocqueville so aptly noted, whereas God may be able to see each being in all its uniqueness, humans (in their limitations) must classify people and things in terms of their similarities and differences. Biologists, for example classify animals into families; archaeologists divide time into eras; and geographers split the Earth into regions. Likewise, people sort each other on the basis of gender, nationality, ethnicity, physical characteristics, and so forth.

You classify everything you attend to into categories and conceptual frameworks. This cannot be helped. It is how the human mind works. So many things need to be attended to that your cognitive capacity would be quickly overwhelmed if you did not classify what you perceive into categories. Without classification, you cannot reason, learn, grow and develop, accumulate knowledge, investigate interesting issues, or theorize. When you observe another person's appearance and behavior, for example, you immediately and spontaneously classify what you see into categories. You perceive the person to be male or female, tall or short, friendly or unfriendly, attractive or unattractive, a member of a certain cultural or ethnic group, and so forth.

This categorization process is immediate, rapid, spontaneous, and automatic. It occurs without any conscious thought. It speeds information processing time, changes the way in which you process information about the person (you add information connected with the category to the person), and makes impression formation simpler and more efficient.

Perception of another person begins with an act of categorization. You place the person somewhere within your prior knowledge of general social categories and person types. When you perceive another person, you move quickly from observable information (such as appearance and behavior) to inferences about the person's traits. From a number of verbal and nonverbal cues, you may decide the person is shy, intelligent, and sensitive. You then talk about the traits, not the verbal and non-verbal cues, if for no other reason than that it is a faster and easier way of describing a person. Moving from behavior to traits is especially economical because each trait may imply other traits. If a person is kind to animals, for example, you may infer that the person is warm, friendly, and caring. From one or two behaviors, you may construct a whole personality for the person. The implications that traits have for each other are known as *implicit personality theory.* The result is that you tend to form extensive impressions of others on the basis of very limited information.

Not all of the categorization process may be conscious. There is evidence that categorization on the basis of gender and ethnicity (and the activation of associated stereotypes) occurs prior to conscious awareness, involving information processing and interpretation that are not subject to conscious, controlled judgment and decision making. Given the research on the paradoxical effects of consciously attempting to suppress unwanted thoughts, trying to avoid stereotypes may boomerang. The more you try to avoid stereotyping, the more you may do so. Thus, deeply ingrained and culturally overlearned stereotypes may be unaffected by changing conscious attitudes and beliefs. You may need to change the underlying cognitive structures that determine the relative importance and accessibility of alternative social categories.

Whenever two people interact, they present each other with information about many different characteristics, such as age, gender, ethnicity, and socioeconomic status. Based on that information, the individuals classify each other in many different ways, some reflecting similarities and some representing differences. The categorization process both compels and allows you to decide quickly what other people are like based on minimal information, such as gender and appearance.

Categorizing behavior requires visual, verbal, and nonverbal cues. Even with minimal information, you form highly consistent impressions of others. What qualities you infer are influenced by (a) the person's physical features, (b) the salience of the person's behavior, (c) the social categories to which the individual belongs, and (d) your own motives and goals for forming the impression. Each quality you infer in the other person has an evaluative dimension. You either like or dislike it. In addition, you tend to weight each quality so that some qualities are perceived to be more important than others, and you then average the qualities to determine an overall impression of the other person.

The classification of persons into groups on the basis of common attributes is known as *social categorization.* By grouping people the way we group plants, animals, rocks, and so forth, we form impressions quickly and use past experience to guide new interactions. You categorize people on the basis of *inherited traits* (culture, sex, ethnic membership, physical features) and *acquired traits* (education, occupation, lifestyle, customs). Although this process has many advantages, it also has at least two serious drawbacks. First, it assumes that perceptions are accurate. Unfortunately, your perceptions about other people are not always accurate. Emotions are especially hard to identify, especially cross-culturally.

Second, perceptual biases can distort your judgments of others. They include the *halo effect* (we tend to think that a person we like is good in every dimension), the *positivity bias* (we tend to like most people), and the *negativity effect* (more emphasis is placed on negative than positive information). In forming impressions of other people, we tend to pay special attention to negative information (Fiske, 1980; Pratto & John, 1991), and we tend to weight negative information more heavily (Taylor, 1991).

Like lumping bananas and grapes together because they are fruit, categorizing people leads us to overestimate the differences between groups and to underestimate the differences within groups. Thus, social categorization can lead to discriminatory intergroup behavior and intragroup cohesion in the form of (a) more positive attitudes toward and more reported liking of ingroup than outgroup members, (b) ethnocentric biases in perception, evaluation, and memory, and (c) an altruistic orientation toward ingroup members (Howard & Rothbart, 1978; Turner, 1978). In fact, simply imposing a shared group membership on people can be sufficient to generate liking among them. The combination of inaccurate perceptions and overestimating the differences between groups can result in stereotyping and prejudice.

STEREOTYPES

> When we see a red-breasted bird, we say to ourselves "robin." When we see a crazily swaying automobile, we think, "drunken driver."... A person with dark brown skin will activate whatever concept of Negro is dominant in our mind.
> —*Allport (1954, p. 20)*

Stereotypes are everywhere and everyone has them. Stereotypes are a product of the way the mind stores, organizes, and recalls information. The use of stereotypes cannot be avoided. They are used to describe differences among groups and to predict how others will behave. They reduce complexity, help us make quick decisions, fill in the gaps in what we know, help us make sense out of who we are and what has happened to us, and help us create and recognize the patterns needed to draw conclusions. Unfortunately, stereotypes can also support unfairness and injustice.

The term *stereotype* was first used in the eighteenth century to describe a printing process designed to duplicate pages of type. In the nineteenth century the term *stereotypy* was used by psychiatrists to describe a behavior of persistent repetitiveness and unchanging mode of expression. Modern use of the term *stereotype* was originated by Lippmann (1922) in his book *Public Opinion.* He argues that "there is neither time nor opportunity for intimate acquaintance. Instead we notice a trait which marks a well-known type, and fill in the rest of the picture by means of the stereotypes we carry about in our heads" (p. 59). The world is simply too complicated to attend to every detail, and, therefore, the perceiver relies on stereotypes to simplify social perception. Katz and Braly (1933) conducted the first classic empirical study of stereotypes and linked them to attitudes and prejudice.

A *stereotype* is a belief that associates a whole group of people with certain traits. Stereotypes (a) are cognitive, (b) reflect a set of related beliefs rather than an isolated bit of information, (c) describe the attributes, personalities, and characters so groups can be compared and differentiated, and (d) are shared by individuals and groups holding them (Ashmore & Del Boca, 1979). Stereotypes function as simplifiers and organizers of social information. They reduce the complexity of the social environment and make it more manageable. Examples of stereotypes are the following: Women have been stereotyped as being more emotional than men. Men have been stereotyped as being more competitive than women. Tall, dark, and handsome men have been stereotyped as being mysterious. Stereotypes are often influenced by past events. Stereotypes of Japanese in the 1940s, for example, were heavily influenced by the surprise attack on Pearl Harbor in World War II.

You form stereotypes by categorizing (sorting single objects into groups rather than thinking of each as unique) and differentiating between the ingroup (the groups with which you identify) and outgroups. You commonly assume that the members of outgroups are quite similar while realizing that the members of the ingroup are quite diverse (*outgroup homogeneity effect*). The failure to notice differences among outgroup members may result from lack of personal contact with a representative sample of the outgroup. A white person, for example, may see all Hispanics as being alike, but someone with a wide variety of Hispanic friends may see little similarity among Puerto Ricans, Cubans, Mexicans, and Argentineans.

An efficient cognitive system does more than simply make things easy for people at all costs. Rather, it distributes limited resources in ways that maximize the informational value gained for the effort expended. Stereotyping is efficient for several reasons. First, the social categorization that precedes stereotyping reduces the amount of information that must be attended to. When you group social stimuli together and treat them as functionally equivalent, you reduce the need to form individualized impressions of each category member (Allport, 1954; Brewer, 1988; Fiske & Neuberg, 1990; Hamilton & Sherman, 1994; Lippmann, 1922).

Second, stereotypes expand your base of knowledge by allowing you to infer a person's attributes without having to attend carefully to the person's behavior (Brewer, 1988; Fiske & Neuberg, 1990; Hamilton & Sherman, 1994; Medin, 1988; Sherman, 1996). Through the relatively simple act of social categorization, stereotypes allow you to gain a large amount of "functionally accurate" information (Swann, 1984), thus resulting in a beneficial ratio of information gained to effort expended. Stereotypes are particularly useful when processing capacity is constrained, processing resources are scarce, and when accurate social perception is difficult to achieve. Stereotypes facilitate the encoding of both stereotype-consistent and stereotype-inconsistent information when processing capacity is low (Sherman, Lee, Bessenoff, & Frost, 1998). The energy saved by encoding stereotype-consistent information is then used to understand stereotype-inconsistent information. Stereotypes may be automatically activated when people experience a threat to their self-image (Spencer, Fein, Wolfe, Fong, & Dunn, 1998).

People who hold strong stereotypes are prone to *fundamental attribution error.* They attribute negative behavior on the part of a minority group member to dispositional characteristics, and positive behavior by a minority group member to situational factors; whereas one's own negative behavior is attributed to situational causes, and one's own positive behavior is viewed as dispositional. When a minority group member acts in an undesirable way, the attribution is "that's the way those people are" or "those people are born like that." If the minority group member is seen engaging in desirable behavior, the person holding the stereotype can view the minority person as an exception to the rule or view the minority person's behavior as due to luck, the situational context, or extraordinary motivation and effort.

Stereotypes are perpetuated and protected in four ways. The exercises in Activity 3.1 address why stereotypes persist. First, stereotypes influence what we perceive and remember about the actions of outgroup members. The social categories we use to process information about the world control what we tend to perceive and not to perceive. Our prejudice makes us notice the negative traits we ascribe to the groups we are prejudiced against. When individuals expect members of an outgroup to behave in a certain way, furthermore, they tend to recall more accurately instances that confirm rather than disconfirm their expectations. Hence, if an outgroup is perceived to be of low intelligence, (1) individuals would tend to remember instances in which an outgroup member was confused in class or failed a test, but (2) individuals would tend to forget instances in which an outgroup member achieved a 4.0 grade point average or became class valedictorian (Rothbart, Evans, & Fulero, 1979).

An association exists between power and stereotyping (Fiske, 1993; Fiske & Morling, 1996). The general premise of this work is that persons in positions of power are especially vulnerable to stereotyping subordinates because they pay less attention to them. High-power individuals may lack cognitive capacity to attend to subordinates because power requires attending to more people and more issues at the same time. High-power individuals may ignore subordinates because the high-power persons' outcomes do not depend on subordinates. High-power individuals may not attend to subordinates because they have a dominant personality. They may attempt to control their interactions with others to such an extent that they ignore the actions and motivations of others. Regardless of the cause, decreases in attention make powerful individuals more likely to depend on stereotypes in interacting with subordinates.

ACTIVITY **3.1**   ■   WHY DO STEREOTYPES ENDURE?

Given below are several reasons why stereotypes persist. Rank them from most important (1) to least important (7). Write down your rationale for your ranking. Find a partner and share your ranking and rationale, listen to his or her ranking and rationale, and cooperatively create a new, improved ranking and rationale. Then find another pair and repeat the procedure in a group of four.

_____ 1. People tend to overestimate the association between variables that are only slightly correlated or not correlated at all (i.e., *illusionary correlation*). Many people, for example, perceive that being poor and being lazy are associated. Any poor person who is not hard at work the moment you notice him or her may be perceived to be lazy. Low-power groups can acquire negative traits easily and once acquired, the stereotype is hard to lose.

_____ 2. Your prejudice makes you notice the negative traits you ascribe to the groups you are prejudiced against and you more readily believe information that confirms your stereotypes than evidence that challenges them. People tend to process information in ways that verify existing beliefs. This is known as the *confirmation bias* (the tendency to seek, interpret, and create information that verifies existing beliefs).

_____ 3. You tend to have a *false consensus bias* by believing that most other people share your stereotypes (poor people may be seen as being lazy). You tend to see your own behavior and judgments as quite common and appropriate, and to view alternative responses as uncommon and often inappropriate.

_____ 4. Stereotypes tend to be *self-fulfilling*. Stereotypes can subtly influence intergroup interactions in such a way that the stereotype is behaviorally confirmed. You can behave in ways that elicit the actions you expect from outgroup members, thus confirming your stereotype.

_____ 5. You dismiss individuals who do not match your stereotype as exceptions to the rule or representatives of a subcategory.

_____ 6. Your stereotypes often operate at an implicit level without your conscious awareness.

_____ 7. You often develop a rationale and explanation to justify your stereotypes and prejudices.

Second, stereotypes create an oversimplified picture of outgroup members. The act of categorization itself leads people to assume similarity among the members of a category. Even when the distinctions between groups are arbitrary, people tend to minimize the differences they see among members of the same group and to accentuate the differences between members of two different groups. When processing information about their ingroup and outgroups, people develop relatively simplistic and nonspecific pictures of outgroups. The larger the outgroup is, the more likely oversimplifications will occur. Individuals, furthermore, do more than simply note the differences between their ingroup and the outgroups. They attempt to emphasize the differences, and take actions that discriminate in favor of their own group. Activity 3.2 provides an opportunity to clarify stereotypes you hold about others, those others hold about you, and the opportunity to experience the process of stereotyping.

Third, individuals tend to overestimate the similarity of behavior among outgroup members. Because outgroups are perceived to be very homogeneous, the actions of one member can be generalized to all.

Fourth, stereotypes can lead to scapegoating. A *scapegoat* is a guiltless but defenseless group who is attacked to provide an outlet for pent-up anger and frustration caused by another group. The term comes from a biblical guilt-transference ritual:

> And Aaron shall lay both his hands upon the head of the live goat, and confess over him all the iniquities of the children of Israel, and all their transgressions in all their sins, putting them upon the head of the goat, and shall send him away by the hand of a fit man into the wilderness. (Leviticus 16:21)

In most instances, if Group 1 interfered with Group 2, the latter would respond by retaliating against Group 1. If, however, Group 1 is extremely powerful, too distant, or too difficult to locate, Group 2 may respond by turning its aggression onto Group 3. Group 3, although in no way responsible for the difficulties Group 2 experienced, would nonetheless be blamed and thereby become the target of Group 2's aggressive

ACTIVITY **3.2** ■ STEREOTYPING

The following exercise is aimed at clarifying (a) what stereotypes you have been taught about other groups, (b) what stereotypes they have been taught about you, and (c) how the process of stereotyping works.

1. Post the following list of words on sheets of paper around the room:

Male	Female
Teenager	Over age 70
Asian American	African American
Native American	Hispanic American
Blind	Deaf
Lower income	Middle Income
Roman Catholic	Protestant
Southern	Midwestern

2. Each participant is to circulate around the room, read the various categories, and write one stereotype he or she has heard under each heading. Participants are told not to repeat anything that is already written down. They are not to make up anything. They are to write down *all* the stereotypes they have heard about each of the groups listed.

3. After everyone is done writing, participants are to read all the stereotypes under each category.

4. Participants discuss the following:

   a. Their personal reactions
   b. How accurate the stereotypes of their identities are
   c. What they have learned about stereotyping others

actions. Stereotypes of certain outgroups can create a continual scapegoat that is blamed for all problems and difficulties no matter what their origins.

Stereotypes can be changed. The more personal information you have about someone, the less you stereotype. The more time and energy you have to consider the person's characteristics and behavior, the less you stereotype. The more motivated you are to form an accurate impression of someone, the less you stereotype. The more you perceive the person to be typical of the stereotyped group, the more your interaction changes your stereotypes. What these factors indicate is that for stereotypes to change, members of different groups need to interact for prolonged periods of time under conditions in which they get to know each other personally and see each other as being typical members of his or her group. Test your own reaction to stereotyping and how it affects your interactions with diverse others by participating in Activity 3.3

Stereotypes not only affect the ones who hold them, stereotypes also affect the ones targeted. When a widely known negative stereotype (e.g., poor intellectual ability) exists about a group, it creates for its members a burden of suspicion that acts as a threat. This threat arises whenever individuals' behavior could be interpreted in terms of a stereotype, that is, whenever group members run the risk of confirming the stereotype. Steele and Aronson (1995) in studying "stereotype threat" found that negative stereotypes about blacks' intellectual ability create a "situational pressure" that distracts black students and depresses their academic performance. They argue that the possibility of being judged by a stereotype can cause so much anxiety that intellectual performance is disrupted.

ACTIVITY **3.3** ■ INTERACTING ON BASIS OF STEREOTYPES

Stereotypes are rigid judgments made about other groups that ignore individual differences. The purpose of this exercise is to demonstrate how stereotypes are associated with primary and secondary dimensions of diversity.

1. Divide participants into groups of five. The group is to role play employees of a large corporation discussing the ways in which the percentage of people of color and women in higher-level executive positions may be increased from 10 percent to 50 percent.

2. Give each member of the group a headband to wear with a particular identity written on it for other group members to see. *Group members are not to look at their own headbands.* The five identities are

   Single mother of two young children
   Employee with physical disability
   Woman, age 72
   White male, company president
   Black female, union official

3. Stop the discussion after 10 minutes or so. The groups then do the following tasks:

   a. Guess what the label on their headband is
   b. Discuss their personal reactions
   c. Identify the participation pattern of each member—who dominated, who withdrew, who was interrupted, who was influential
   d. Relate what they have learned about stereotyping others

Steele and Aronson suggest that stereotype threat is the reason for the underachievement of black students. Seventy percent of black college students drop out of college (as opposed to about 35 percent of white students), and the drop-out rate is the highest among black students ranked in the top third by SAT scores. In addition, black students with the highest SAT scores fail more frequently than black students with lower scores and at a rate more than three times that of whites with similar scores. When placed in achievement situations, the negative stereotypes are activated and black students become more self-conscious and work less efficiently. Similar findings were reported on a study of lower-class individuals (Croizet & Claire, 1998). Stereotype threat is eliminated in programs such as the University of Michigan's 21st Century Program in which black and white students are randomly recruited, live together, study together cooperatively, and have personal discussions on social issues.

PREJUDICE

To know one's self is wisdom, but to know one's neighbor is genius. —*Minna Antrim*

To be prejudiced means to prejudge. *Prejudice* can be defined as an unjustified negative attitude toward a person based solely on that individual's membership in a group other than one's own. Prejudices are judgments made about others that establish a superiority/inferiority belief system. If one person dislikes another simply because that other person is a member of a different ethnic group, sex, or religion, we are dealing with prejudice.

One common form of prejudice is ethnocentrism. *Ethnocentrism* is the tendency to regard our own ethnic group, culture, or nation as better or more "correct" than others. The word is derived from *ethnic,* meaning a group united by similar customs, characteristics, race, or other common factors, and *center.* When ethnocentrism is present, the standards and values of our culture are used as a yardstick to measure the worth of other ethnic groups. Ethnocentrism is often perpetuated by *cultural conditioning.* As children we are raised to fit into a particular culture. We are conditioned to respond to various situations as we see others in our culture react. Stereotypes lead to prejudices. *Racism* is prejudice directed at people because of their ethnic membership. *Sexism* is prejudice directed at a person because of his or her gender. *Ageism* is prejudice against the elderly. There are many other types of "isms."

The concept *race* assumes biological differences that are most evident in physical appearances. The evidence indicates the existence of only one human race (with many variations). Although race has dubious value as a scientific classification system, it has had real consequences for the life experiences and life opportunities of African Americans. Race is a socially constructed concept that is the defining characteristic for African American group membership. Race has social meaning suggesting one's status within the social system. It introduces power differences as people of different "races" interact with one another. Racism and prejudice result from forming unfounded and often inaccurate opinions about a group, leading to biased behavior against members of that group. Racism justifies treating racial groups differently because it mistakenly assumes that (a) humans may be divided into clearly defined racial groups and (b) these groups vary in capabilities and aptitudes. The explanations for prejudice include evolutionary perspective, personality/individual differences approaches, theories of group identity, and various social cognitive viewpoints.

Evolutionary Theories. Evolutionary theories posit that the origin of prejudice against outgroup members is the need to protect and promote one's own group members' access to limited resources. This gives an evolutionary advantage to the ingroup and results in rational self-interest being the basis for conflict between groups (e.g., Buss, 1990; Fishbein, 1996; Sidanius, 1993).

Personality/Individual Differences Theories.   These theories view prejudice as resulting from traits or attributes that predispose individuals to be prejudiced (see Duckitt, 1992; Sidanius, 1993). Thus, emotional needs (rather than rational self-interest) underlie prejudice, and prejudice is seen as irrational. Research on the authoritarian personality, for example, found it related to conventionalism, submissiveness to authority, aggressiveness, and low tolerance for ambiguity (Taylor & Moghaddam, 1994). Prejudice may be reduced by increasing individuals' openness and flexibility.

Group Identity or Ethnocentrism Theories.   These theories posit that individuals are highly motivated to evaluate themselves positively and that these self-evaluations are highly related to their identities as members of special social groups (e.g., Abrams & Hogg, 1990; Tajfel & Turner, 1979). People typically judge their own group more favorably than other groups.

Social Cognitive Theories.   Social cognitive theories deal with the usefulness of stereotyping and the human tendency to categorize people into social groups, which contributes to prejudice, discrimination, and intergroup conflict (e.g., Brewer, 1991; Hewstone & Brown, 1986).

A number of other sociological theories emphasize social structure and power differentials in relationships as a source of intergroup conflict (Taylor & McKirnan, 1984). These theories have been used to analyze intergroup social movements and conflicts at the international level.

Modern Racism

Traditionally, in the United States racism and sexism were expressed through statements such as, Blacks are not as smart as whites and, Women are too emotional to be good managers. Traditional racism and sexism directly and explicitly contain negative evaluations of minorities and females and use the "natural world order" (nature intended it to be this way) as a justification.

Beginning with the civil rights movement in the 1960s, however, public pressure to see each person as an individual, not as a member of an ethnic group, has been increasing. This has influenced the way whites talk about minorities. Modern racism is a more subtle form of prejudice in which people appear, on the surface, not to be prejudiced, but actually do hold racist attitudes (Dovidio & Gaertner, 1991). Modern racism and sexism camouflage prejudices within more sophisticated principles of meritocracy and justice through statements such as, Blacks and women have gone too far—they are pushing for jobs they do not deserve (Swim, Aikin, Hall, & Hunter, 1995).

Modern racism and sexism use indirect and implicit negative evaluations of minorities and females to justify protecting cherished social values, such as meritocracy, from attack by minorities. The concept of modern racism posits that if we scratch the apparently nonracist surface of many people, we find bigotry lurking beneath. Modern racism arises because people can see themselves as being fair, humanitarian, and egalitarian while at the same time holding somewhat negative views of members of groups other than their own.

Having prejudiced thoughts, however, does not necessarily make you a racist (Devine et al., 1991). Even those who completely reject prejudice may sometimes experience unintentional, prejudiced thoughts and feelings due to prior learning. In this case, racism is like a lingering bad habit that surfaces despite people's best efforts to avoid it. As with all bad habits, with enough commitment and support, racism can be licked.

Discrimination

When prejudice is put into action, it is discrimination. *Discrimination* is an action taken to harm a group or any of its members. It is a negative, often aggressive action aimed at the target of prejudice. Discrimination is aimed at denying members of the targeted groups treatment and opportunities equal to those afforded to the dominant group. When discrimination is based on race or sex, it is referred to as *racism* or *sexism*. To reduce your prejudices and use of stereotypes, the following steps may be helpful (Johnson, 2000):

1. Admit that you have prejudices (everyone does, you are no exception), and commit yourself to reducing them.
2. Identify the stereotypes that reflect your prejudices and modify them.
3. Identify the actions that reflect your prejudices and modify them.
4. Seek feedback from diverse friends and colleagues about how well you are communicating respect for and valuing of diversity.

Blaming the Victim

It is commonly believed that the world is a just place where people generally get what they deserve. If you win the lottery, it must be because you are a nice person who deserves some good luck. If you are robbed, it must be because you were careless and wanted to be punished for past misdeeds. Any person who is mugged in a dark alley while carrying a great deal of cash may be seen as "asking to be robbed." Most people tend to believe that they deserve what happens to them. Most people also believe that others also get what they deserve in the world. It is all too easy to forget that victims do not have the benefit of hindsight to guide their actions.

Making a decision requires that information be gathered on each major alternative action and alternatives that will maximize gains and minimize costs be inferred from the information. But what happens when situations appear to be unjust? One method is to blame the victim by convincing ourselves that no injustice has occurred. When someone is a victim of prejudice, stereotyping, and discrimination, all too often they are seen as "doing something wrong." *Blaming the victim* occurs when we attribute the cause of discrimination or misfortune to the personal characteristics and actions of the victim. The situation is examined for potential causes that enable us to maintain our belief in a just world. If the victim can be blamed for causing the discrimination, then we can believe that the future is predictable and controllable because we will get what we deserve. See Table 3.2 for examples of the types of errors people make when evaluating diverse others.

ATTRIBUTION THEORY

Blaming the victim occurs as we try to attribute a cause to events. We constantly interpret the meaning of our behavior and the events that occur in our lives. Many times we want to figure out *why* we acted in a particular way or *why* a certain outcome occurred. If we get angry when someone infers we are stupid, but we could care less when someone says we are clumsy, we want to know why we are so sensitive about our intelligence. When we are standing on a street corner after a rainstorm and a car splashes us with water, we want to know whether it was caused by our carelessness, the driver's meanness, or just bad luck. This process of explaining or inferring the causes of events has been termed *causal attribution*.

An attribution is an inference drawn about the causes of a behavior or event. Any behavior or event can have a variety of possible causes. We observe the behavior

TABLE 3.2 Errors in Making Decisions about Diverse Others

ERRORS IN MAKING INFERENCES

Relying on Small Samples	Small samples are highly unreliable.
Relying on Biased Samples	People often ignore clear information about how typical and representative a sample is.
Underutilization of Base-Rate Information	People tend to pay more attention to a single concrete instance than to valid base-rate information, perhaps because the single concrete instance is vivid and salient and thus more compelling.

ERRORS FROM COGNITIVE HEURISTICS

Availability Heuristic	People tend to estimate the frequency of some event by the ease with which they can bring instances to mind. People tend to overestimate the frequency of events that are easy to remember.
Representativeness Heuristic	People evaluate how well the information matches some imagined average or typical person in the category; the closer the person is to the prototype, the more likely is the person judged to be in the category.

WEIGHING INFORMATION

Positive Frame	People avoid risks and opt for the "sure thing."
Negative Frame	People take risks to avoid "costs."
Postdecision Rationalization	The alternative chosen becomes more attractive, and the alternatives not chosen become less desirable.

or event and then infer the cause. When our boss criticizes our work, for example, we can attribute his or her behavior to a grouchy mood, being under too much pressure, disliking us, or the sloppiness of our work.

Early in childhood we begin observing our own behavior and draw conclusions about ourselves. We seem to have a fundamental need to understand both our own behavior and the behavior of others. In trying to understand why a behavior or event occurred, we generally choose either to attribute causes to (1) internal, personal factors (such as effort and ability) or (2) external, situational factors (such as luck, task difficulty, or the behavior and/or personality of other people). (See Table 3.3.) For example, if you do well on a test, you can attribute it to your hard work and great intelligence (an internal attribution) or to the fact that the test was incredibly easy (an external attribution). When a friend drops out of school, you can attribute it to a lack of motivation (an internal attribution) or lack of money (an external attribution).

People make causal attributions to explain their successes and failures. Frequently such attributions are *self-serving*, designed to permit us to take credit for pos-

TABLE 3.3 Dimensions of Attributions

	STABLE	UNSTABLE
Internal	Ability	Effort
External	Task difficulty	Luck

itive outcomes and to avoid blame for negative ones. We have a systematic tendency to claim our successes are due to our ability and efforts whereas our failures are due to bad luck, obstructive people, or task difficulty. We also have a systematic tendency to claim responsibility for the success of group efforts ("It was all my idea in the first place and I did most of the work") and avoid responsibility for group failures ("If the other members had tried harder, this would not have happened").

Attribution theory recommends that students be trained to make *self-serving attributions*. Students should attribute their academic success to ability and effort and avoid attributing successes to luck or other people. Students should attribute academic failures to bad luck or lack of effort and avoid attributing failures to personal factors such as lack of ability (see Table 3.4).

Attribution theorists assume that how people explain their successes and failures determines how hard they work on subsequent tasks. If minority students, for example, attribute academic failure to lack of ability, it can eventually lead to *learned helplessness* (the feeling that no amount of effort can lead to success) (Seligman, 1975). Learned helplessness is associated with shame and self-doubt. Students with a long history of attributing failure to lack of ability simply make no effort to learn. Teachers should ensure that students (especially minority students) think through why they succeeded or failed, and guide them toward the conclusion that their failure is caused by either (a) lack of effort or (b) using the wrong strategy. What emotions teachers express toward students seems to affect the attributions students make about the causes of their success or failure (Graham, 1991). Teacher sympathy for failure tends to be interpreted as indicating low ability whereas teacher anger towards failure seems to be interpreted as indicating low effort. Activity 3.4 is an exercise in considering what kinds of teacher statements are in accordance with attribution theory.

The attributions individuals make can determine how they feel. Depression and self-rejection can be induced by encouraging individuals to attribute their failures to personal factors ("It's all my fault!" "Everything I touch turns out rotten!") and their successes to luck or other people's altruism. The more a person attributes failures to causes that are stable and enduring (general personality), global (likely to affect many outcomes), and internal (something about him- or herself), the more likely the person is to become more depressed and self-rejecting. Life is full of personal failures. Minority and low-power students are especially likely to experience failures. You may receive bad grades, you may not get the job you want, your salary may be lower than you want, other people may not like you. The way you attribute causes for your failures can determine whether you are happy or depressed. Activity 3.5 will help you evaluate how negatively biases in attributing causes to events can affect your relationships to diverse individauls.

To maximize the achievement of students, and to encourage the development of achievement motivation, teachers should strive toward the following goals:

1. Praise students for effort as a personal characteristic rather than the effort itself ("You are a hard-working student" not, "You really worked hard").
2. Actively structure the classroom environment to emphasize the importance of student effort, to match task difficulty to student abilities, and to downplay the influence of luck on student achievement.

TABLE 3.4   Success Orientation

	STABLE	UNSTABLE
Success	Ability	Effort
Failure	Task difficulty	Luck

ACTIVITY **3.4** ■ WHAT SHOULD TEACHERS SAY?

Read the following teacher statements. Decide whether the teacher statement is helpful (H) or unhelpful (U) from the viewpoint of attribution theory. Write your answer in the appropriate space and write an explanation for your answer.

Find a partner. Share your answers and rationale. Listen carefully to his or her answers and rationale. Come to consensus as to whether each statement is helpful or unhelpful and why (according to attribution theory).

_____ 1. "Don't feel bad about your D David. Math is not your subject."

_____

_____

_____ 2. "You have a mental block against French, Calvin. Will you ever be able to get it straight?"

_____

_____

_____ 3. "Well done, Ralph! You worked hard and it paid off!"

_____

_____

_____ 4. "Congratulations on your A Jane. That was easy, wasn't it?"

_____

_____

_____ 5. "The test is going to be hard. Study a lot."

_____

_____

_____ 6. "You're good at science, Judy. Try harder on the next test."

_____

_____

_____ 7. "Kersten, you studied hard and you got an A. Study hard this week and the same thing will happen."

_____

_____

ACTIVITY **3.5** ■ BIASES IN ATTRIBUTING CAUSES TO EVENTS

Given below are biases in attributing causes to events. Rank order these causes in terms of most destructive (1) to least destructive (7) to relationships among diverse individuals. Write out your reasons for ranking the biases as you did.

Find a partner. Share your ranking and rationale. Listen carefully to his or her ranking and rationale. Create a new ranking and rationale that is better than either one.

_____ 1. **Cognitive heuristics.** Information processing shortcuts or rules-of-thumb can enable a person to make judgments quickly and result in error. Examples are *representativeness* (an individual is representative of his or her group) and *availability* (a cause that is most likely available for a member of that group).

_____

_____ 2. **Fundamental attribution error.** People tend to focus on the role of personal (dispositional) causes and underestimate the impact of situation factors on other people's behavior.

_____

_____ 3. **Actor–observer effect.** People tend to attribute their own behavior to situational causes and the behavior of others to personal factors.

_____

_____ 4. **Self-serving attributions.** People make favorable, self-serving, one-sided attributions for their own behavior by taking credit for positive outcomes and avoiding blame for negative ones.

_____

_____ 5. **Blaming the victim.** People believe in a just world: People get what they deserve and deserve what they get.

_____

_____ 6. **Learned helplessness.** People believe that no amount of effort will result in success.

_____

_____ 7. **Cooperative halo.** People tend to derogate and dislike competitors and see cooperators in positive ways.

_____

3. Minimize competition for underachieving students and instead emphasize individual improvement scores.

Attributing the causes of others' failure and misfortune to their actions rather than to prejudice and discrimination can be a barrier to building constructive relationships with diverse peers. Bad things do happen to good people. Racism does exist. Innocent bystanders do get shot. It is usually a good idea to suspend any tendency to blame the victim when interacting with diverse peers.

SOCIAL IDENTITY AND SOCIAL CATEGORIZATION THEORIES

In intergroup relations, three major barriers to constructive relationships are intergroup competition, bias favoring the ingroup over the outgroups, and depersonalization of members of the outgroups. The two theories that discuss the issues most directly are social identity and social categorization theories.

Social identity theory (formulated by Henri Tajfel, 1982, and John Turner, 1987) is based on the hypothesis that individuals seek a positively valued distinctiveness for their own groups compared to other groups to achieve a positive social identity. *Social identity* is the individual's knowledge that he or she belongs to certain social groups that have emotional value significant to the individual. According to social identity theory, people strive to enhance their self-esteem, which has two components: a personal identity and various social identities derived from the groups to which they belong. Thus, people may boost their self-esteem by viewing their ingroups more favorably than outgroups. In other words, our quest for a positive social identity leads us to inflate the positive aspects of the group to which we belong and to belittle groups to which we do not belong. When a group is successful, members' self-esteem can rise, conversely, when members' self-esteem is threatened, they feel a heightened need for ingroup favoritism (attraction to own group and disparagement of outgroups), which in turn enhances their self-esteem (Crocker & Luhtanen, 1990). (See Figure 3.1.)

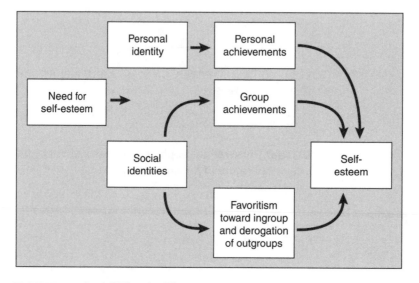

FIGURE 3.1   Social Identity Theory

The differentiation between ingroups and outgroups is based on *social categorization*. Social categories function as cognitive "labor-saving devices" by helping you place other people into meaningful categories. While you may use a wide range of categories for classifying people (for example, male, friend, stranger, Christian, neighbor, political, athlete), two very basic social categorizations are (1) member of my group and (2) member of another group (Hamilton, 1979). *Social categorization theory* is based on the hypothesis that personal and social identity are self-categorizations (Turner & Oakes, 1989) that in and of themselves are sufficient to create discriminatory intergroup behavior. Social identity is based on differentiating among groups (American, male, and protestant as opposed to Canadian, female, and Catholic) and is assumed to be a more inclusive, superordinate level of abstraction than personal identity in the categorization of the self.

A premise of social identity and social categorization theories is that the process of making categorical distinctions to understand the social world involves minimizing perceived differences within categories and accentuating intercategory differences (Tajfel, 1969). This results in three principles. First, the *intergroup accentuation principle* is assimilation within category boundaries and contrast between categories, such that all members of the ingroup are perceived to be more similar to the self than members of the outgroup. Second, the *ingroup favoritism principle* maintains that positive affect (trust, liking) is selectively generalized to fellow ingroup members but not to outgroup members. Third, the *social competition principle* maintains that intergroup social comparison is based on perceived negative interdependence (competition) between ingroup and outgroup. Some evidence exists that the desire to see oneself as fair-minded can mitigate discrimination against outgroup members (Singh, Choo, & Poh, 1998).

The second premise of social identity and social categorization theories is that because individual persons are themselves members of some social categories and not others, social categorization carries with it implicit ingroup–outgroup (we–they) distinctions resulting in (a) intergroup competition, (b) mutual distrust between ingroup and outgroups, and (c) ingroup members receiving preferred treatment (Turner, 1985). Even when social categorizations are imposed on people (given the acceptance and internalization of the categories), members of the ingroup are liked more and treated better than members of the outgroup. In addition, members of the ingroup tend to depersonalize members of the outgroup ("they" are all alike).

It should be remembered that people do not categorize themselves in the same way in every situation. When in Indiana, a person may say, "I'm from Muncie"; when in California, a person may say, "I'm from Indiana"; and in Singapore, a person may say, "I'm from the United States." As situations change, so do the ways people categorize themselves and others. Thus, categorization results in competition among groups, social identity, the depersonalization of members of the outgroups, and a bias toward the ingroup and against the outgroup. Social identity and social categorization theories explain how this happens. To overcome these effects, a process of decategorization and then recategorization must take place.

Decategorization: Personalizing Interaction

A primary consequence of categorization is the depersonalization of members of outgroups. Individual members of an outgroup tend to be treated as undifferentiated representatives, not as unique individuals. To reduce ingroup bias and the depersonalization of outgroup members, contact among members of the different groups is required. These intergroup interactions should be structured so as to reduce the salience of category distinctions and to promote opportunities to get to know outgroup members as individuals (Miller, Brewer, & Edwards, 1985). Contact is most effective when interactions are highly personalized rather than category based (Brewer

& Miller, 1984). Attending to personal characteristics of outgroup members tends to disconfirm category stereotypes and decrease the perception of outgroups as homogeneous units.

Recategorization: Building a Common Ingroup Identity

Johnson and Johnson (1992) and Gaertner and his associates (1993) posited that ingroup bias and the depersonalization of outgroup members can be reduced by structuring the contact among members of different groups so attention is focused on a superordinate category identification that encompasses both ingroup and outgroup in a single social group representation. Although there may be Caucasian Americans, African Americans, Asian Americans, and Hispanic Americans, for example, highlighting the superordinate identity of "American" can unite all citizens into a single social category and identification. Thus, attention to category differences is minimized by creating a new inclusive group identity. When individuals perceive the superordinate identity as a single entity, rather than as an aggregate of separate groups, evaluation of former outgroup members becomes more positive.

In addition to building a common identity as an American, within cooperative groups a common identity may be built by assigning majority and minority members the same role (Bettencourt & Dorr, 1998; Bettencourt et al., in press). Doing so results in all members perceiving that they share a common identity. It should be noted that decategorization and recategorization are not mutually exclusive. Cooperation and superordinate goals promote formation of common identity. Personalized interactions of equal status promote decategorization and individuation.

AWAKENING A SENSE OF INJUSTICE

Discrimination against outgroups may be decreased by reducing stereotyping and prejudice. Discrimination may be viewed as a form of injustice (Deutsch, 1985). Removing discrimination, therefore, requires awakening a sense of injustice in majority members about their treatment of minority and low-power group members. Deutsch posits that no change in discriminatory practices is possible until a sense of injustice is awakened. The following list of steps has been provided to awaken the majority's sense of injustice.

Step 1. Remove the majority's ignorance of the injustices experienced by minorities. Often the majority "insulates" itself from the victims by avoiding contact (living in all-white suburbs) or structuring the contact in ways that prevent the possibility of becoming aware of the discrimination (such as employee-of-the-month celebrations). This *insulated ignorance* protects majority group members from being aware of the consequences of their behavior (Hornstein & Johnson, 1966).

Step 2. Delegitimize the officially sanctioned ideologies and myths that "justify" the injustices (e.g., the cream rises to the top). Majority group members are largely content and tend to have a vested interest in preserving the status quo (which ensures their superior roles and privileges). Awaking a sense of injustice requires majority group members to become aware of their ideologies, questioning the ideologies, and deciding the ideologies are no longer legitimate.

Step 3. Expose the majority to new ideologies, models, and reference groups that support action to undo the disadvantages of the minorities. Majority group members must interact with minority group members, come to understand their perspectives and experiences, and form a new reference group that includes both majority and minority individuals. The new reference group must support change. The action steps must be clear.

Step 4. Stimulate the hope of the majority that they can effectively reduce injustice. Once victimization has become deeply embedded in social institutions, individual action to overcome it is frequently seen to be futile and costly. There must be hope of success for majority group members to take action.

Step 5. Increase the majority's belief that they will benefit from reducing injustice. This involves (a) reducing the fear of the majority that their new actions will have costly, harmful consequences for them and (b) enhancing the majority's prospect of material and psychic gains from a positive change in their relationships with the minority. Both the majority and the minorities must be seen as being better off as a result of decreasing discrimination.

Step 6. Increase the majority's belief that continuation of the old relationship will no longer produce the material benefits and gains that the majority has experienced in the past. Thus, continuing the status quo may have costly, harmful consequences for the majority.

Awakening a sense of injustice depends on prejudice being more than a uniform set of attitudes and values. Rather than having uniformly negative or positive attitudes toward outgroups, many individuals have conflicting tendencies (Gaertner & Davidio, 1986; Monteith, 1996b). A number of studies, for example, found that approximately 78 percent of the sampled populations indicated that they should respond with less prejudice than is apparent in their actual responses (Monteith, 1996a; 1996b). This finding held for both high- and low-prejudiced individuals.

Given that many people are highly prejudiced but feel conflicted about it, awakening their sense of injustice can tip the scales in favor of respect and appreciation. Monteith and Walters (1998) found that many high-prejudiced white individuals feel morally obligated to (a) be less prejudiced and (b) have relatively low-prejudiced personal standards for responding to blacks. These obligations appear to originate from an egalitarian self-image that defines egalitarianism in terms of equality of opportunity. Their belief in the right of every person to have an equal opportunity is more powerful than their prejudices.

THE PREJUDICED PERSONALITY

One view of prejudice emphasizes that certain personality characteristics predispose a person to be prejudiced. In their classic book, *The Authoritarian Personality*, Adorno, Frenkel-Brunswick, Sanford, and Levinson (1950) investigated the variables that related to anti-Semitism. Deeply concerned about the horrors of World War II and the threat posed by fascism, they wanted to defend the world from future Hilters. They believed that if technologically advanced nations such as Germany could be taken over by fascists, every country in the world was in danger. They reasoned that certain types of personalities had a potential for supporting fascism and thus posed a threat to democracies.

The researchers proposed that blind obedience and negative prejudices originated in families in which parents severely punish and shame their young children for even small misbehaviors. As a result, the children feel hostile toward their parents and other authority figures. But they do not want to express or acknowledge their hostility because doing so may (a) bring even more punishment and (b) create a powerful internal conflict between hating their punitive parents and believing that they ought to love and respect them. As a result, these children learn to repress their antagonisms toward their parents and other authorities and to displace their aggressive impulses onto weaker members of society.

To study the authoritarian personality, Adorno and his associates used a sample of 2,000 middle-class, white, non-Jewish, native-born residents of California to develop their *Potentiality for Fascism* or *F-Scale.* They found a strong relationship between anti-Semitism and ethnocentrism (rejection of all unlike groups—blacks, Asians, "Okies," and even "zootsuiters") and between anti-Semitism and political and economic conservatism (belief in traditional values and maintaining the status quo). Thus, anti-Semitism, rejecting all outgroups, and political conservatism all seem to be aspects of the same phenomenon. A list of 11 major characteristics of this personality syndrome follows:

1. Conventionalism (rigid adherence to middle-class values and conformity to social pressure)
2. Authoritarian submission (exaggerated emotional need to submit to ingroup authority)
3. Authoritarian aggression (belief in harsh punishment for people who deviate from conventional behavior)
4. Anti-intraception (rejection of emotions and fantasies)
5. Superstition and stereotypy (thinking in rigid, oversimplified, black-and-white categories with no tolerance of ambiguity or shades of gray)
6. Power and toughness (excessive concern with dominance and submission, identifying with and submitting to power figures)
7. Destructiveness and cynicism (generalized hostility that is rationalized as human nature)
8. Projectivity (projection of all negative affect onto others)
9. Sex (excessive concern about sex and harshly punitive about sexual behavior)
10. Rigidity
11. Intolerance of ambiguity

Overall, the authoritarian personality is characterized by exaggerated submission and obedience to authority, extreme levels of conformity to conventional standards of behavior, self-righteous hostility, and punitiveness toward minorities and those who violate conventional values (Stone, 1993). The F-Scale is one of the most reliable and valid scales ever constructed in psychology.

Rokeach (1960) reconceptualized the authoritarian personality as dogmatism, or closed-mindedness. He ignored the focus on right-wing conservative ideology and Freudian thought and viewed dogmatism as "(a) a relatively closed cognitive organization of beliefs and disbeliefs about reality, (b) organized around a central set of beliefs about absolute authority which, in turn, (c) provides a framework for patterns of intolerance toward others" (p. 57). It is a mode of thought characterized by rigidity, intolerance of ambiguity, belief in absolute authority, and intolerance toward others. Rokeach (1960, p. 57) states:

> . . . every person must be able to evaluate adequately both the relevant and irrelevant information he receives from every situation. This leads us to suggest a basic characteristic that defines the extent to which a person's system is open or closed, namely, the extent to which the person can receive, evaluate, and act on relevant information received from the outside on its own intrinsic merits, unencumbered by irrelevant factors in the situation, within the person, or from the outside.

Compared with open-minded individuals, closed-minded persons are

1. Less able to learn new beliefs and to change old beliefs
2. Less able to organize new beliefs and integrate them into their existing cognitive systems during problem solving, and thus take longer to solve problems involving new beliefs

3. Less accepting of belief-discrepant information
4. More resistant to changing their beliefs
5. More likely to reject information that is potentially threatening to their perceptual and attitudinal organization
6. Less able to recall information that is inconsistent with their beliefs
7. More likely to evaluate information consistent with their beliefs positively
8. Less able to discriminate between information received and its source; the status of an authority is confused with the validity of the authority's statements
9. Able to resolve fewer issues in conflict situations, more resistant to compromise, and more likely to view compromise as defeat

Dogmatism is a personality characteristic and mode of thinking independent of ideology. Rokeach believed anyone can be dogmatic whether they are conservative or liberal. To study dogmatism, Rokeach constructed the D-Scale, which updates the Fair-Mindedness Scale developed by Goodwin Watson (1925). The research on authoritarianism and dogmatism both point toward personality characteristics of highly prejudiced people.

EXPECTATIONS AND THE SELF-FULFILLING PROPHECY

The final cognitive issue in the cognitive influences on intergroup relations is the expectations of teachers and classmates on the performance of minority students. In essence, stereotypes are expectations of how members of other groups behave. Expectations, similar to biased perceptions, affect information processing, information seeking, and social interaction (see Hamilton, Sherman, & Ruvolo, 1990). The stronger the expectations are, the greater these effects.

Considerable evidence also exists that people's expectations of others can be influential in eliciting anticipated behavior (see Rosenthal, 1985; 1988). Robert Merton (1948) first referred to this phenomenon as the *self-fulfilling prophecy*. Gordon Allport (1954), in *The Nature of Prejudice*, extended this process to the realm of intergroup relations by stating, "In all human relations—familial, ethnic, international—the engendering power of expectancy is enormous. If we foresee evil in our fellow man, we tend to provoke it; if good, we elicit it" (p. 160). More specifically, the self-fulfilling prophecy is a set of expectations and actions that provokes the other into engaging in behavior that confirms one's original assumptions. An example is assuming that the other is belligerent and then proceeding to engage in hostile behavior thereby provoking the other into belligerent actions, which confirms the original assumption.

The self-fulfilling prophecy hardens and strengthens the original expectations. Members of groups engaged in violent and protracted conflict, for example, accumulate substantial evidence to support their negative views of outgroup members and consequently their hostile attitudes and expectancies are held with great certainty and are likely to be highly resistant to change. This creates barriers to the successful resolution of intergroup conflict and perpetuates and escalates intergroup hostilities.

Teacher Expectations: Pygmalion in Classrooms

Consider the following research study. In a high school, teachers were trained to communicate high expectations to incoming ninth-grade students who were assigned to the lowest track of English classes (Weinstein et al., 1991). After one year the students had higher English and history grades than comparable students whose teachers did not participate in the project, as well as higher overall grade point averages. The project students were less likely to drop out of high school and less likely to attend a continuation school than were the control students. A year after the project ended, however, there was no difference in achievement between project and control students.

Could the expectations of teachers make a significant difference in minority students' achievement and graduation? Many social psychologists would say yes. The *Pygmalion effect* is a self-fulfilling prophecy—teacher expectations for a student elicits behavior from the student that confirms the teacher's expectations. For a considerable time evidence has shown that low expectations of students can have harmful effects (Rosenthal & Jacobson, 1968). There are four key issues in this argument.

The first issue is whether teacher expectations influence student performance. A meta-analysis by Rosenthal and Rubin (1978) combined the results of 345 studies on interpersonal expectations and concluded that teacher expectancies do influence student performance. Harris and Rosenthal (1985) found the same results. Cooper (1993) called the effects of interpersonal expectations a "social fact," a strong conclusion from a scientific approach that bases findings on probabilities and statistical analyses. Teacher expectations can account for between 5 percent and 10 percent of the variance in student performance (Babad, 1993; Brophy, 1983).

The second issue is understanding how the expectations become reality. Rosenthal (1973), Harris (1993), and Harris and Rosenthal (1985; 1986) proposed four factors:

1. **Climate.** Teachers' affective behaviors (e.g., warmth, support, smiling, eye-contact) and the socioemotional climate they create for high- and low-expectancy students
2. **Feedback.** Teacher's praise and criticism of students, their acceptance or acknowledgment of a student's statement or request
3. **Input.** Amount or difficulty of material presented to the student
4. **Output.** Opportunities for the student to respond (e.g., frequency of contact between the student and teacher, questions asked by the teacher)

If teachers create a different learning climate for minority students, criticize their performance and refuse to recognize their good work, present material that is too easy or difficult for the students, and ignore the students and limit their opportunity to respond, then students may achieve lower than they would with another teacher who has high expectations. Climate and feedback behaviors are the most crucial actions in the expectancy confirmation process (Harris, 1993).

The third issue is whether teachers have different expectations for minority students than for white students. There is evidence that African American and Mexican American students receive lower teacher expectations for mental ability and academic performance than do white students (Baron, Tom, & Cooper, 1985). Teachers consistently had lower expectations for performance and ability for lower-class students than for middle-class students. Expectations for student performance and behavior are subject to a multitude of cognitive biases, including stereotypes of gender, ethnicity, social class, and age, to name a few.

The fourth issue is whether teachers can use what we know about expectations to increase student performance on a large scale. The answer to this issue may be more complex than it seems. Having high expectations of students is certainly advisable. The assumption that many teachers have low and inaccurate expectations for minority students, however, may not be valid. Some researchers argue that, in real life, (a) teachers generally form accurate expectations for their students and (b) inappropriately high or "pretend" expectations may do more harm than good (Brophy, 1985; Jussim, 1993).

Evidence indicates that performance on standardized aptitude tests can be significantly influenced by alternating the salience of negative expectancies. In one experiment, men and women with a history of successful performance in mathematics were given a portion of the advanced Graduate Record Exam in mathematics. In one condition, the participants were told that, in the past, men consistently performed higher on the test than did women. In the other condition, the participants were told that no sex differences had been previously found on this test. In the first condition, women performed significantly less well than did men with the same mathematics background. In the second condition, no significant differences occurred between men and women on the test.

Finally, evidence indicates that teacher perceptions regarding achievement and motivation differences between girls and boys, lower- and upper-class students, and African American and white students are mostly accurate, although the teachers occasionally relied on stereotypes to form their perceptions (Madon et al., 1998).

COMMITMENT TO LONG-TERM RELATIONSHIPS

The more committed majority and minority individuals are to their relationship, the less stereotyping and prejudice they will engage in. *Commitment level* represents long-term orientation toward another person and relationship, including psychological attachment and intent to persist through both good and bad times (Rusbult, 1980; 1983; Rusbult & Buunk, 1993; Rusbult et al., 1997). Strong commitment has been shown consistently to induce inclinations toward (a) responding in a constructive (rather than destructive) manner when the other person engages in potentially destructive behaviors, (b) tendencies to derogate tempting alternative relationships, (c) a merging of one's own and others' identities so that promoting the partners' interests is experienced as promoting one's own interests, (d) willingness to sacrifice one's own immediate well-being for the good of the other, and (e) tendencies toward positive illusion in which the other person's actions are perceived to be more constructive and positive than they actually are.

Commitment to the relationship tends to *inhibit* destructive patterns of thinking and processing information about the other person and his or her behavior rather than *activate* constructive patterns of thinking (Arriaga & Rusbult, 1998). Commitment results in scrupulously inhibiting destructive patterns of thinking (e.g., "I will not think bad things about us") (Rusbult, Yovetich, & Verette, 1996) and promotes thinking in collectivistic terms (e.g., *we, us, our* rather than *I, me, mine*) (Agnew et al., 1998). Thus, the greater the majority and minority individuals' commitment to their relationship is, the less likely they are to process information about each other and each other's behavior in negative and destructive ways. Stereotyping and prejudice are thereby reduced.

Success in Overcoming Prejudice

Success stories relate how people have overcome prejudice. In Brooklyn, New York, a Jewish high school teacher and an African American Baptist minister decided that the Hasidic Jewish and African American teens of the neighborhood needed to get to know each other. What resulted is the world's first African American Jewish rap group, Dr. Lax and the CURE.

In Galileo High School in San Francisco, a course in creating writing and poetry is offered in which the work of writers from different races and cultures is studied. Twice a week, white, Asian, Hispanic, and African American students talk about poetry, stories, and essays intended to reveal the humans behind the skin colors in the classroom.

In Memphis, Tennessee, both black and white high school students participate in the Bridge Builders program. It begins with a 1-week camp experience and lasts for 2 years (meeting monthly to talk or do role play or problem-solving exercises and other times to work together on community service projects). The founders thought it was a shame that the only way most black and white Memphis teens got to know each other was through competitive interactions on football fields and basketball courts. The purpose of Bridge Builders was to break down the racial barriers in

Memphis by giving teens who were natural leaders in their schools a chance to get to know each other, and to form bonds that could mean great things for Memphis as these teens grew up. In Memphis an insurance company paired a white student and a black student as summer interns and let them learn the business together.

These few of the many success stories of overcoming prejudice leave no doubt that it can be done. No matter what stereotypes and prejudices individuals develop, they can be unlearned, modified, and changed under the right conditions. In all these success stories, overcoming prejudice requires direct contact between majority and minority individuals and personal conversations about race relations. Not all contact, however, results in such positive outcomes. The next chapter focuses on what happens when contact occurs between members of different groups.

SUMMARY

Theorizing and research on relationships among diverse individuals include cognitive, attitudinal, and behavioral approaches. One area of diversity these approaches have been applied to is school desegregation. The research on desegregation indicates that in many cases it did not have the powerful, positive effects hoped for. This has lead to new research to understand why.

One set of explanations involves cognitive factors. Cognitive factors begin with the human need to classify people, objects, and events into categories to understand and respond to the events in their lives. Classifying people (social categorization) involves implicit personality theories in which a person's appearance and behavior are used to generate hypotheses about the person's traits, which then imply a cluster of traits that are assumed to go together. Unfortunately, the perceptions on which social categorization are based are not always accurate and the differences between groups tends to be overestimated.

A *stereotype* is a belief that associates a whole group of people with certain traits. Women have been stereotyped as being more emotional than men. You form stereotypes by (a) categorizing (you sort single objects into groups rather than thinking of each as unique) and (b) differentiating between the ingroup (the groups with which you identify) and outgroups. You commonly assume that the members of outgroups are quite similar while realizing that the members of the ingroup are quite diverse (*outgroup homogeneity effect*). Stereotypes are perpetuated and protected by (a) influencing what we perceive and remember about the actions of outgroup members, (b) creating an oversimplified picture of outgroup members, (c) overestimating the similarity of behavior among outgroup members, and (d) promoting scapegoating.

Stereotyping can lead to prejudice and discrimination as well as a tendency to blame the victim. *Prejudice* can be defined as an unjustified negative attitude toward a person based solely on that individual's membership in a group other than one's own. Overt racism may be replaced with *modern racism*, a more subtle form of prejudice in which people appear, on the surface, not to harbor prejudice but actually do hold racist attitudes. When prejudice is put into action, it is *discrimination* (actions taken to harm a group or any of its members). *Blaming the victim* occurs when the cause of discrimination or misfortune is attributed to the personal characteristics and actions of the victim (this maintains a belief in a just world). Blaming the victim and other dynamics of prejudice and discrimination involve making causal attributions that justify the mistreatment and disadvantage of minority groups. Activity 3.6 provides an aooportunity to review and test your knowledge of the important concepts presented in this chapter.

Just as categorization leads to stereotyping and prejudice, it also leads to self-categorizing that creates personal and social identity (social categorization theory). People may seek a positively valued distinctiveness for own groups compared to other groups to achieve a positive social identity (social identity theory). Thus, preju-

ACTIVITY **3.6** ■ IMPORTANT CONCEPTS

Demonstrate your understanding of the following concepts by matching the definitions with the appropriate concept. Find a partner. Compare answers.

CONCEPT

_____ 1. prejudice

_____ 2. ethnocentrism

_____ 3. stereotype

_____ 4. illusionary correlation

_____ 5. discrimination

_____ 6. blaming the victim

_____ 7. collusion

_____ 8. scapegoat

_____ 9. racism

_____ 10. modern racism

_____ 11. false consensus bias

_____ 12. stereotype threat

_____ 13. culture clash

DEFINITION

a. A belief that associates a whole group of people with certain traits

b. An action taken to harm a group or any of its members

c. An unjustified negative attitude toward a person based solely on that individual's membership in a group other than one's own

d. Attributing the cause of discrimination or misfortune to the personal characteristics and actions of the victim

e. The conflict over basic values that occurs among individuals from different cultures

f. The conscious or unconscious reinforcement of stereotypic attitudes, behaviors, and prevailing norms

g. The tendency for people to overestimate the association between variables that are only slightly correlated or not correlated at all

h. The prejudice directed at people because of their ethnic membership

i. Believing that most other people share their stereotypes

j. A guiltless but defenseless group who is attacked to provide an outlet for pent-up anger and frustration caused by another group

k. The subtle forms of prejudice in which people appear, on the surface, not to harbor prejudice, but actually do hold prejudiced attitudes

l. The tendency to regard own ethnic group, nation, religion, culture, or gender as being more correct than others

m. Whenever group members run the risk of confirming the stereotype

dice and discrimination may result from social categorizations that in turn result in intergroup competition, bias favoring the ingroup over the outgroups, and depersonalization of members of the outgroups. These effects can be mitigated through a combination of decategorization and recategorization.

Removing discrimination requires awakening a sense of injustice in majority group members about their treatment of minority and low-power group members. Finally, teacher expectations can affect the school performance and behavior of minority and low-power students. You are limited in how much you can change your cognitive processing without direct interaction with members of minority groups. The conditions under which that interaction should take place are discussed in the next chapter.

CHAPTER FOUR

INTERGROUP CONFLICT

INTRODUCTION

Among my experiments was this. In an hour I taught a cat and a dog to be friends. I put them in a cage. In another hour I taught them to be friends with a rabbit. In the course of two days I was able to add a fox, a goose, a squirrel and some doves. Finally a monkey. They lived together in peace; even affectionately. Next, in another cage I confined an Irish Catholic from Tipperary, and as soon as he seemed tame I added a Scottish Presbyterian from Aberdeen. Next a Turk from Constantinople, a Greek Christian from Crete, an Armenian, a Methodist from the wilds of Arkansas, a Buddhist from China, a Brahman from Benares. Finally, a Salvation Army Colonel from Wapping. Then I stayed away two whole days. When I came back to note results, the cage of Higher Animals was all right, but in the other there was such chaos of gory odds and ends of turbans and fezzes and plaids and bones and flesh—not a specimen left alive. These Reasoning Animals had disagreed on a theological detail and carried the matter to a Higher Court.

— Mark Twain (1974, pp. 180–181)

The goals of human relations are to respect, appreciate, and value the cultural, historical, and ethnic heritage of all individuals and to be able to interact with anyone effectively and constructively. Appreciating the cultural, historical, and ethnic heritages of your friends and associates begins with appreciating your own. Chapter 2 focused on building a positive cultural identity. Even for individuals who are quite accepting of themselves and others, barriers can prevent building positive relationships with diverse peers. The more aware you are of your own cultural heritage, for example, the more you may be aware of others. By categorizing yourself, you categorize all others. These and other cognitive influences on your appreciation of cultural diversity were covered in Chapter 3. This chapter focuses on the interpersonal and intergroup influences on respecting, appreciating, and valuing others' cultural heritages. The ways in which constructive relationships among diverse individuals can be created are discussed.

SEGREGATION STILL EXISTS

According to national surveys, about half the white population lives in neighborhoods that have no African Americans within half a mile, about two-thirds of whites are employed in a workplace that is all white, and only about one-fifth of whites have one or more African American acquaintances (Jackman & Crane, 1986; Kinder

& Mendelberg, 1995). This lack of contact reflects an avoidance of contact indicative of prejudice and intergroup anxiety (caused by expectations that contact with members of another group will make us feel awkward, self-conscious, irritated, or suspicious) (Islam & Hewstone, 1993). Today it is more important than ever to find ways to reduce prejudice. (See Box 4.1 for examples of organizations that work to do so.) Many theories of prejudice and discrimination have been developed to explain causes and effects of these phenomena. The following sections of this chapter describe a host of these theories.

PSYCHODYNAMIC THEORY

Psychodynamic theories posit that prejudice is the result of motivation tensions within the individual's personality. One such theory proposes that prejudice is displaced aggression. *Displaced aggression* occurs when a person is frustrated but cannot attack the source because of fear or simple unavailability and, therefore, the person attacks an innocent third party because the party is available and has less power. People who lose their jobs during an economic downturn, for example, may feel angry and aggressive, but have no obvious person to blame. They may then look for a scapegoat to blame and attack. There is evidence, for example, that lynching African Americans increased in bad economic times (Hovland & Sears, 1940).

Another psychodynamic theory posits that prejudice is a personality disorder. Prejudice, for example, can result from a person having an authoritarian personality (Adorno, Frenkel-Brunswik, Levinson, & Sanford, 1950). People with *authoritarian personalities* are characterized by exaggerated submission to authority, rigid conformity to conventional norms, self-righteous hostility, and harsh punitiveness toward deviants and members of minority groups. The authoritarian personality is associated with hostility toward homosexuals, AIDS victims, drug users, the homeless, and environmentalists (Peterson, Doty, & Winter, 1993). What is unclear is whether authoritarianism has its origin in personality conflicts or is taught to children by parents and peers. Believing it is inherent in the personality requires psychoanalysis to change it. Believing it is taught requires reteaching to change it.

INGROUP BIAS

Ingroup bias is acting to benefit members of one's own group over members of other groups (Brewer, 1979; Mullen, Brown, & Smith, 1992; Tajfel, 1982). The roots of ingroup bias probably lie in our evolutionary past (Eibl-Eibesfeldt, 1989; Fishbein, 1996; Fox, 1992; van der Dennen & Falger, 1990). Group living was (and is) necessary for survival. Within small communities, humans cooperated with each other and developed norms of reciprocity to further strengthen the group bonds (Axelrod & Hamilton, 1981; Trivers, 1971). The communities consisted primarily of biological relatives,

---

■ ■ ■ ■ ■

BOX 4.1
CIVIL RIGHTS ORGANIZATIONS

NAACP	National Association for the Advancement of Colored People
CORE	Congress for Racial Equality
SNCC	Student Nonviolent Coordinating Committee
SCLC	Southern Christian Leadership Conference

and concern for the group also meant that ingroup bias help ensure the likelihood that some members would survive and reproduce (Hamilton, 1964). For this and other reasons, it was advantageous for humans to think in terms of groups and to value the groups to which they belonged and to automatically favor one's own group over others (Perdue, Dovidio, Gurtman, & Tyler, 1990).

REALISTIC CONFLICT THEORY

Groups conflict. Both the aborigines and the Europeans wanted Australia, for example. The theory of *realistic group conflict* proposes that intergroup conflict emerges when groups find themselves competing for the same resources (e.g., Bonacich, 1972; Campbell, 1965; Sherif, Harvey, White, Hood, & Sherif, 1961/1988). It argues that the competition between groups creates hostility, antagonism, and prejudice toward each other. Therefore, prejudice is an inevitable consequence of conflict over resources that each group wants.

This theory is related to *frustration–aggression theory* because it assumes that prejudice arises when one group frustrates the other group's needs. Because conflicts will always occur among groups, intergroup prejudice is assumed to be inevitable. Gordon W. Allport (1954), in his classic treatise *The Nature of Prejudice,* stated, "realistic conflict is like a note on an organ. It sets all prejudices that are attuned to it into simultaneous vibration. The listener can scarcely distinguish the pure note from the surrounding jangle" (p. 226). He believed that even conflict rooted in objective characteristics of the situation eventually create subjective biases that divide the opposing groups.

Although realistic conflict theory posits that prejudice is a response to actual conflict and frustrations among groups, sometimes groups only perceive themselves to be deprived relative to others. Perceptions of *relative deprivation* can also create intergroup hostility. If a country's economy, for example, is growing, most citizens' economic situations may be improving, but some groups' situations may be improving more quickly than others. The group whose economic situation is improving more slowly may feel deprived as they see members of other groups increasingly able to afford things they cannot. They thus may feel antagonistic toward the better-off groups due to relative deprivation. White males, for example, may be upset when affirmative action leads to the economic advantage of females and minority individuals, even though the white males have secure jobs. Or females may feel relatively deprived when they receive raises because their white male counterparts are receiving even larger raises.

When prejudice exists before a realistic incident occurs, conflicts can light, flame, and burn quickly. The African American residents of Liberty City in Miami, for example, attacked white residents and their businesses when several police officers, accused of killing an African American robbery suspect, were not sent to prison. Rioting in Detroit in the late 1960s was precipitated by a police raid on a private drinking and gambling establishment (Goldberg, 1967). A crowd gathered during the arrests, and looting began after a window was broken by one spectator. Police withdrew for several hours in the hope that the residents would quiet down, but the looting continued. To quell the disorder, elite riot troops, complete with bayonets, swept through the streets. The African American residents responded with a series of fire bombings, and officials asked that the state police and national guard be brought in to control the mob. Rumors of sniping activity, the removal of restraints concerning the use of firearms, the lack of clear organization, and a desire for revenge prompted police violence, which in turn led to more widespread rioting. (See Box 4.2 for further illustrations of just such conflicts in a brief biography of Robert Moses.)

Given that groups have realistic conflicts, the way in which conflict is managed becomes a central issue to intergroup relations. This is especially true when groups are of unequal power.

■ ■ ■ ■ ■

BOX 4.2
ROBERT MOSES: THE GENTLE LEGEND

Robert Moses was known as the Black Ghandi of the civil rights movement in the 1960s. Born in Harlem and educated at Harvard, Robert Moses was pursuing his doctorate when he joined the Student Nonviolent Coordinating Committee (SNCC). At that time the state of Mississippi had no black voters. Together with NAACP organizer Amzie Moore, he began the Voter Registration Project.

In July 1961, he was at work in McComb, Mississippi, leading the first voter registration project in the Delta. He took 16 local blacks to register in Magnolia County. On August 29, he tried to do the same in Amite County, infuriating the state representative and fierce segregationist, E. W. Hurst. Hurst had his nephew, Billy Jack Caston, severely beat Moses at the courthouse.

Moses insisted on filing charges against Caston. Enraged whites, many with shotguns, poured into Liberty for the trial. Moses walked calmly through the mob, his courage making a deep impression on the black community. Caston went free.

Hurst struck again in late September. In McComb, on a busy Saturday morning, in the middle of a crowd, legislator Hurst chased and shot to death Herbert Lee, a father of nine who seemed to have done nothing more than occasionally lend his car to Moses. It was ruled self-defense and Hurst went free. In 1964 Louis Allen indicated he might testify against Hurst; he was murdered in his front lawn.

Moses registered voters in other Mississippi towns, notably Greenwood, in the face of more arrests, police dogs, beatings, and murders. He blamed himself for Allen's death. Believing that Mississippi would never change until the entire country had something at stake, he developed a plan to bring some 1,000 Northern white volunteers to Mississippi in the summer of 1964. He sought the help of the National Council of Churches to plan the training program for the volunteers. A committee was formed that included Goodwin Watson (a retired professor of social psychology at Columbia University), Robert Allen (a psychiatrist in New Jersey), and David W. Johnson (a social psychology graduate student at Columbia University). Moses led the training, inspiring everyone with his self-effacing style, humility, and deep convictions. By 1965, four years after Moses began, the registration books were opened and today Mississippi has more elected black officials than any other state in the Union.

Deeply distressed by the murders of three volunteers and SNCC members (Andy Goodman, Michael Schwerner, and James Chaney), Moses withdrew from the leadership of SNCC soon after the summer ended. Opposing the Vietnam War, Moses fled the country after being drafted by the military. By 1982 he was a mathematics professor at the University of Massachusetts. Helping his own children learn math, he developed a new system rooted in everyday life that won him a MacArthur genius award. By 1993 numerous schools across the country (and particularly in Mississippi) had adopted the Moses Algebra Project. To those involved in the civil rights movement of the 1960s, he remains a legend.

POWER MAJORITIES AND MINORITIES

The French social psychologist Serge Moscovici (1980; 1985a) proposed an intergroup conflict model of social influence, in which power defines whether a group is a majority or a minority. He assumed that both majorities and minorities are sources and targets of influence attempts. Majorities tend to use their power to force minorities to yield and to conform to the majorities' expectations. Minorities tend to convert the majorities to accept the minorities' position. What defines the majority and the minority groups is the amount of power they have.

A *power majority* is the group that has the most control over how important resources are distributed (they may be the numerical minority). A *power minority* is a group that has little control over the distribution of important resources (they may be a numerical majority). In the United States and Europe, for example, white males (a numerical minority) have traditionally controlled the distribution of the top posts in government and industry (they have been the power majority), whereas Asians and others are part of the power minorities (Shinagawa, 1997). In Japan, however, "pure Japanese" are the power majority and white Europeans are a power minority.

Unequal Power

One of the most common settings for realistic conflict exists between high- and lower-power groups. *Power* is the capacity to affect another person's goal accomplishment. *High power* is the capacity to have considerable influence on another person's goal accomplishment whereas *low power* is the capacity to have little influence on another person's goal accomplishment. When the distribution of power is obviously unequal, both the high- and the low-power members may have troubles, the overall group effectiveness may suffer, the gains members receive from being members decrease, and severe maintenance problems result. In discussions of theory and research pertaining to high and low power, the usual reference is to our society rather than to a small, problem-solving group. Yet the same dynamics between high-power and low-power persons can be found in a group of any size, even one as large as our society.

High-Power Members

Life generally seems good for high-power persons. Everything goes right, every problem is easily solved, everyone seems to like and appreciate them and everything they do. High-power persons are typically happy with their situation and tend not to see how much the use of power is involved in their relationships. They are convinced that low-power persons really do like them, that everyone communicates honestly with them, that no one hides information from them, and that they are really seen as "nice" persons.

When this enjoyable world is threatened by dissatisfaction expressed by low-power persons, however, high-power persons tend not to react benevolently. They are hard to move toward cooperation, conciliation, and compromise, and they largely ignore the efforts of their low-power groupmates to increase cooperative problem solving. To them, low-power persons somehow never learn to "know their place"; they insist on "rocking the boat" out of ignorance and spite.

High-power group members use at least two strategies that make it more difficult for low-power members to reduce the differences in power between them (Jones & Gerard, 1967). The first strategy is to institute norms or rules in the group that legitimize their power and make wrong any attempt by others to change the status quo. For example, in most communities the white power structure has established strong norms for where minority group members may live, what occupations they may have, and where they must go to school—as well as procedures for making both whites and nonwhites believe that the status quo is "legitimate" and "right." This strategy may be described as power defines injustice or might is right.

The second strategy high-power members employ to solidify their position is to make the risk of attempting to change the status quo so great that low-power members are deterred from trying to do so. They can invoke this strategy by establishing severe penalties against those who might attempt to change the status quo, and by offering the low-power members a variety of benefits or rewards on the condition that they refrain from rebelliousness. Of the two, the second seems to be more effective. The threat of punishment has never worked effectively to deter behavior, but the paternalistic leadership that tries to keep everyone happy has been applied successfully in combating labor and racial unrest in many parts of the country. This strategy may be characterized as "this hurts me more than it will hurt you" or "if only you would behave neither of us would go through this suffering."

Powerful group members have been found to (1) make more attempts to influence the behavior of the low-power members, (2) devalue the performance of the low-power members, (3) attribute the efforts of the low-power members to their own use of power rather than to the low-power members' motivations to do well, (4) view the low-power members as objects of manipulation, and (5) express a preference for the maintenance of psychological distance from the low-power members (Kipnis, 1972). Participants who were randomly assigned to central positions in a communication network (the more powerful positions) not only viewed themselves as powerful, but also rated themselves as more capable than the participants who were randomly assigned peripheral positions (Stotle, 1978).

Tjosvold (1978) notes that high-power group members (1) feel more secure than low-power members, (2) underestimate the low-power members' positive intentions, (3) devalue the low-power person, (4) are inattentive to the communications of the low-power person, (5) are unresponsive to cooperative gestures by the low-power members, and (6) attempt to protect their superior power by rejecting demands for change. High-power group members also seem uninterested in learning about the intentions and plans of low-power members (Tjosvold & Sagaria, 1978).

High-power individuals make fewer concessions in conflict situations (Lawler & Yoon, 1993), claim a larger share of available resources (Murnighan & Pillutla, 1995), and are less cooperative and more exploitative of the other's cooperation (Lindskold & Aronoff, 1980). High-power individuals tend to be more angered by a low-power person's harm than when positions are reversed (Baumeister, Smart, & Boden, 1996). As Aristotle noted, people think it "right that they should be revered by those inferior to them" (384–322 B.C./1991, p. 143), and they find it particularly vexing to be insulted or harmed by someone who should actually treat them with deference.

Using power may alter the high-power person (Kipnis, Castel, Gergen, & Manch, 1976). First, the desire for power becomes a need in and of itself, apart from the larger goals that power is intended to fulfill, such as accomplishing the task. Second, the ease in using power encourages power holders to use power to benefit themselves, at the expense of those under their power. Third, power holders received unwarranted positive feedback, even adulation, thereby producing an inflated sense of self-worth. Fourth, power may lead to the devaluation of others, reflected in a tendency to see the worst in others. Fifth, having an inflated view of one's power may also lead power holders to overstep the bounds of its appropriate use. Sixth, a recent meta-analysis indicates that as a person's power increases, the performance ratings of others become increasingly negative (effect size = 0.29) and self-evaluations become increasingly positive (effect size = 0.45) (Georgesen & Harris, 1998). High power seems to result in an egocentric or self-serving bias (Harris & Schaubroeck, 1988), resulting in inflating evaluations to maintain benefits such as employment, promotions, and perks.

The *power-devaluation theory* proposed by Kipnis and his colleagues (Kipnis, 1972; Kipnis, Castel, Gergen, & Manch, 1976; Kipnis, Schmidt, Prince, & Stitt, 1981; Wilkinson & Kipnis, 1978) posits that as a person's power increases, he or she makes more attempts to influence others. As more influence attempts are made, the person comes to believe that he or she controls the other people's behavior and is the causal agent in producing the outcomes. The performances of low-power others are devalued and the high-power person takes responsibility for any successes associated with the work of others.

High-status positions invoke a sense of privilege (Messe, Kerr, & Sattler, 1992). Holders of high-status positions come to believe they are entitled to special treatment simply because of the position they hold. Messe and his associates demonstrated that (a) privileged behaviors are a central component of people's role schema for supervisor, (b) due to this sense of privilege, supervisors expend less effort than subordinates on shared tasks, and (c) occupants of high-status positions act in a privileged manner by taking more than an equal share of the rewards offered to the group. In an earlier study, Johnson and Allen (1972) found that having high status and high power in an organization results in an enhanced self-perception that leads to altruistic behavior but disdain for the worker. But when individuals had high status but low power in an organization that rewarded high power, they engaged in selfish behavior (they deviated from the prescribed norms to increase their own rewards) but expressed respect for the worker. (See Activity 4.1 to participate in experiencing how minority members feel about various white majority behaviors.)

There is an association between power and stereotyping (Fiske, 1993; Fiske & Morling, 1996). The general premise of *power-stereotyping theory* is that persons in positions of power are especially vulnerable to stereotyping subordinates because they pay less attention to them. High-power individuals may lack the cognitive capacity to attend to subordinates because power requires attending to more people and more issues at the same time. High-power individuals may not attend to subordinates because they have a dominant personality trait and may attempt to control their interactions with others to such an extent that they ignore the actions and motivations of others. Regardless of its cause, decreases in attention make powerful individuals more likely to depend on stereotypes in interacting with subordinates. Complete Activity 4.2 to review aspects of having high power.

Low-Power Members

Low-power individuals generally find their relationship with high-power people threatening and debilitating. Low-power individuals are apt to feel frustrated and

ACTIVITY **4.1** ■ WHAT WHITE PEOPLE DO

1. Form a group of four members.

2. Each group is assigned a minority group membership (African American, Hispanic American, Asian American, Native American).

3. Each group writes down a list of behaviors that the white majority does that make them feel angry, frightened, or uneasy. Each member needs a copy of the list.

4. New groups of four are formed with one member from each group. Each member shares his or her list, listens to the other groups' lists, and adds something to his or her list to improve it.

5. The original groups of four meet. They finalize their list, place it on newsprint, and tape it to the wall for all other class members to read.

6. In your group of four, write down five conclusions about what you have learned from the experience.

7. Alternative: Have each member of the group role play being a white majority person. The other three members of the group tell the role player face to face what white people do that upsets them.

ACTIVITY **4.2** ■ WHAT TO REMEMBER WHEN YOU HAVE HIGH POWER

1. _____
_____

2. _____
_____

3. _____
_____

4. _____
_____

5. _____
_____

6. _____
_____

uncertain about their future goal facilitation because they depend heavily on the unpredictable behavior of the high-power members (Tjosvold, 1978). These feelings of uncertainty and anxiety provoke (1) increased vigilance and attempts to understand and predict high-power members' behavior, (2) distorted perceptions of the positive intent of high-power members toward them, (3) attraction to, mixed with fear of, high-power members, (4) stifling criticism of high-power members, (5) unwillingness to clarify one's position to high-power members, (6) ingratiation, conformity, flattery, and effacing self-presentation to induce high-power members to like and to reward them, and (7) expectation of exploitation (low-power members tend to believe that, because they have no retaliatory capability, they are vulnerable and helpless and will be exploited). Low-power members have been found to direct much of their communication and attention to high-power members to keep on good terms with them. (See Activity 4.3 to examine the interaction of unequal-power groups as they negotiate.)

On the other hand, low-power group members have been found to resist attempts by high-power members to control them. Tjosvold (1978) notes that low-power members have been found to defy threats, to counterthreaten, to refuse to comply with an influence attempt, even when resistance is costly, to dislike high-power members, and to perceive the relationship as competitive. Johnson and Allen (1972) found that low-power group members who believe they are equal to their high-power peers feel underrewarded and attempt to obtain increased rewards from the group while emphasizing the incompetence, uncooperativeness, lack of generosity, and unfairness of high-power members. In addition, they disliked their high-power peers.

Compared to high-power individuals, low-power individuals tend to be more cooperative (e.g., Lindskold & Aronoff, 1980), to make more concessions (e.g., Lawler & Yoon, 1993), and to be more compliant in response to threat while negotiating (e.g., Lawler & Yoon, 1993). Managers tend to yield to their superiors when interpersonal conflicts arise (e.g., Kramer, 1996). Low-power individuals tend to behave less aggressively than those having high power (e.g., Epstein & Taylor, 1967; Ohbuchi & Saito, 1986). It may be adaptive for the weaker person to be submissive (e.g.,

ACTIVITY **4.3** ■ POWER TO THE ANIMALS

INSTRUCTIONS

The objective of this exercise is to examine the interaction among groups of different power as they negotiate with one another. The exercise takes 2 hours. The coordinator should read the accompanying instructions regarding the distribution of marbles and then follow this procedure:

1. Introduce the exercise as one that highlights interaction among groups having unequal power. Divide the class into groups of 12. Explain that within each group are three mammals, four birds, and five fish; the status of the members in each group is determined by how well they negotiate for marbles. (Even when more than 12 participants are in a group, keep the number of mammals under five.) Hand out a copy of the general instructions to every participant.

2. Distribute 12 bags of marbles randomly within each group. Make sure that members understand their instructions. Give them time to examine what marbles they have, warning them not to let other group members see the marbles. Then begin negotiation session 1, which is to last 5 minutes.

3. During the negotiation session place on newsprint three headings: Mammals, Birds, and Fish. After 5 minutes stop the negotiating and have the participants compute their scores. Take the three highest scores and place them, along with the persons' initials, under the heading Mammals. (Even when more than 12 participants are in a group, keep the number of mammals under five.) Place the next four scores, together with the persons' initials, under the heading Birds. Place the remaining five scores, with the persons' initials, under the heading Fish. Have each person make a name tag indicating what he is and put it on.

4. Begin negotiation session 2. After 5 minutes end it and ask for scores. Read just the individual scores, placing the three highest in the mammals' column, the next four in the birds' column, and the next five in the fish column. Members who change columns on the basis of their score will have to exchange their name tags.

5. Conduct negotiation session 3 in the same way.

6. Conduct negotiation session 4 in the same way.

7. Announce that the mammals now have the authority to make the rules for the exercise, and that, although anyone else can suggest rules, the mammals will decide which ones will be implemented. Inform the mammals that they may make any rules they want, such as a rule that all marbles must be redistributed so that everyone has equal points, or a rule that all fish and birds must give mammals the marbles they ask for whether they want to or not. Have the mammals record their rules on newsprint.

8. After the new rules are established, conduct negotiation session 5. Then allow 5 minutes for the mammals to discuss and make any rule changes.

9. Repeat this cycle twice. Then give the birds and the fish copies of the list of strategies for influencing a high-power group. The birds and the fish have 10 minutes to discuss the strategies and decide which ones to adopt. Then continue with another negotiation session.

10. After a variety of strategies have been tried by the birds and the fish, or when they refuse to continue, conduct a discussion of the experience. The following questions may be used as guides:

    a. What were your feelings and your reactions to the experience?

    b. Do any parallels exist between the system set up by the game and the system in which we live?

    c. Would it have made much difference if the members who were fish had been mammals?

    d. Were the mammals acting with legitimate authority?

    e. Do any parallels exist between the exercise and the relations among racial groups, rich and poor, and adults and students?

    f. What negotiation strategies were used?

    g. What feelings arose from the unequal distribution of power? How did it feel to have high power? How did it feel to have low power?

    h. How did the strategies for changing the high-power group work? What contributed to their effectiveness or ineffectiveness?

    i. What conclusions about the use of power can be made from your experiences in the exercise?

DISTRIBUTION OF MARBLES

    1. The total number of marbles needed is 72 (six times the number of group members).

    2. The number of green marbles needed is 5 (the number of mammals plus 2).

    3. The number of yellow marbles needed is 10 (the number of birds plus the number of fish plus 1).

    4. The number of red, white, and blue marbles needed is 57, 19 of each.

Give each participant a bag of 6 marbles. Five bags contain 1 green marble, 1 yellow marble, and 4 marbles randomly selected from the colors red, white, and blue. Three bags contain 1 yellow marble and 5 marbles randomly selected from the colors red, white, and blue. The remaining 4 bags contain a random assortment of red, white, and blue marbles. These 12 bags are to be distributed at random within each group.

STRATEGIES FOR INFLUENCING A HIGH-POWER GROUP

    1. Build your own organizations and resources to make the low-power group less vulnerable.

    2. Form coalitions.

    3. Change the attitudes of high-power group members through education or moral persuasion.

    4. Use existing legal procedures to bring pressures for change.

    5. Search for ways in which to make high-power group members dependent on the low-power group.

    6. Use harassment techniques to increase the high-power group's costs of sticking with the status quo.

Gilbert, 1992), and the relationship can be seen as "the natural order of things according to which the big one's always peck the little ones" (Heider, 1958, p. 260).

Deutsch (1969) assumes that the goal of low-power members is to establish authentic, cooperative, equal-power relationships with the high-power members. He states that the ability of low-power members to offer and engage in authentic cooperation means that they are aware that they are neither helpless nor powerless, even though they are at a disadvantage. Cooperative action requires a recognition that a person has the capacity to "go it alone" if necessary; unless a person has the freedom to choose not to cooperate, there can be no free choice to cooperate. Thus, low-power members in a group need to build enough cohesiveness and strength to function independently of high-power members, if this is necessary. In addition, high-power members must be motivated to cooperate with low-power members. This means that the latter must find goals that are important to high-power members, especially goals they cannot accomplish without the cooperation of low-power members.

A variety of strategies for influencing high-power members are available to low-power members (Deutsch, 1969). By building their own organizations and developing their own resources, low-power members not only can make themselves less vulnerable to exploitation, but also can add to their power by providing themselves with alternatives that preclude being dependent solely on high-power members. Low-power members can add to their power by allying themselves with third parties. Another strategy is to try to use existing legal procedures to bring pressures for change (see Box 4.3 for legal actions pertaining to students with disabilities). Furthermore, low-power members can search for attachments with high-power members that, if made more obvious, can increase the latter's positive feelings toward or outcome dependence on low-power members. Low-power members can try to change the attitudes of those having high power through education or moral persuasion.

Finally, low-power members can use harassment techniques to increase high-power members' costs of maintaining the status quo. In planning how to increase their power in relation to high-power members, low-power members of a group should first clarify their goals, take stock of their resources, and finally study how to make high-power members more aware of their dependence on them and of their compatibility (if any) of goals. Complete Activity 4.4 to review how to manage low power.

INTERGROUP CONFLICT

A number of social scientists have worked to develop an intergroup theory explaining prejudice and discrimination. They include Muzafer Sherif, Robert Blake, and Jane Mouton. Conflicts also include clashes among cultures and clarifying resulting misunderstandings.

Sherif's Studies of Intergroup Conflict

The classic studies on intergroup conflict were conducted by Muzafer Sherif in the early 1950s (Sherif, 1962; 1966). The participants in the series of field experiments were 12-year-old boys who attended a summer camp run by the experimenters (the researchers were the camp staff). All boys were strangers to one another prior to attending the camp so no relationships were established among them. The campers were first divided into small cooperative groups who were assigned tasks requiring interdependent and coordinated action to achieve important goals, such as preparing meals to feed group members.

After creating cohesive, cooperative groups within which group members developed considerable interpersonal attraction, the groups were placed in competition with each other. As the intergroup competition became more and more intense,

■ ■ ■ ■ ■ ▬▬▬▬▬▬▬▬▬▬▬▬▬▬▬▬▬▬▬▬▬▬▬▬▬▬

BOX 4.3
STUDENTS WITH AND WITHOUT DISABILITIES

1. *Education for All Handicapped Children Act* (PL 94-142 of 1975) and its 1990 reauthorization as the *Individuals with Disabilities Education Act* (IDEA). The intent is to provide students with disabilities a free, appropriate public education in the least restrictive environment appropriate to their individual needs.

2. *Least restrictive environment* is defined by law:

   to the maximum extent appropriate, children with disabilities…are educated with children who are nondisabled, and that special classes, separate schooling or other removal of children with disabilities from the regular educational environment occurs only when the nature or severity of the disability is such that education in regular classes with the use of supplementary aids and services cannot be achieved satisfactorily (Public Law 94-142 of 1975).

3. The regulations require a "continuum of alternative placements" that includes "instruction in regular classes, special classes, special schools, home instruction, and instruction in hospitals and institutions," as well as the mandate that "supplementary services (such as resource room or itinerant instruction) be provided in conjunction with regular class placement."

4. Through the 1970s and much of the 1980s, the term *mainstreaming* was used to describe placing students with disabilities into academic or nonacademic settings for part of the day based on their educational and social needs.

5. In the late 1980s, the term *inclusion* was adopted. Inclusion is the placement of all students, regardless of the nature or severity of their disability or their behavior or academic level, in an age-appropriate general educational classroom. Some proponents believe the child may be removed from the general education classroom to receive related services.

6. The U.S. Supreme Court ruled that school districts are not required to maximize the potential of students with disabilities. Rather, they must offer only an education that confers some educational benefit upon the disabled child. Educational considerations are not the controlling factor in making placement decisions but are just one factor that must be taken into account.

7. Clarification of what is meant by "least restrictive environment" was made in 1989 (U.S. Court of Appeals for the 5th Circuit, *Daniel R. R. v. State Board of Education)*; in 1994 (U.S. Court of Appeals for the 9th Circuit, *Sacramento City School District v. Rachel H.);* and in 1997 (U.S. Court of Appeals for the 4th Circuit, *Harmann v. Loudoun County).* Four major themes are (a) individualization, (b) presumptive right to an integrated education, (c) appropriateness (what educational services are required takes precedence over questions of where they should be provided), and (d) options (alternative placements are possible to meet the needs of a particular child).

hostility mounted until food fights took place in the dining hall and constant name calling ensued whenever the groups were near each other. Plans for ambushes, raids, and other aggressive acts were designed.

A series of hypotheses on how to reduce intergroup hostility was tested. First, Sherif devised situations where members of the rival groups were given an opportunity to make social contact with each other in pleasant situations (such as watching a movie together). Group members used these contact situations as opportunities for further name calling and conflict. Second, Sherif brought in a new group from a

ACTIVITY **4.4** ■ WHAT TO REMEMBER WHEN YOU HAVE LOW POWER

1. _____

    _____

2. _____

    _____

3. _____

    _____

4. _____

    _____

5. _____

    _____

6. _____

    _____

nearby community to serve as an outside enemy. Having a common enemy united the groups of campers but did not end intergroup conflict. It only transferred it.

Finally, Sherif invented cooperative goals that were superordinate over the intergroup conflict among groups of campers. *Superordinate goals* are goals that cannot be easily ignored by members of two antagonistic groups, but whose attainment is beyond the resources and efforts of either group alone; the two groups, therefore, must join in a cooperative effort to attain the goals. Only after the successful arrangement of several contact situations that required the participation of both groups in joint action toward the achievement of superordinate cooperative goals did any reduction in intergroup conflict and stereotyping appear. Examples included repairing the water-supply system that had mysteriously broken down, pooling money to rent a movie that just happened to cost more than any one group could afford, and pushing a truck, which had suddenly broken down on its way to bringing food for a cook-out, that was too heavy for one group to move alone. After the campers had participated in a series of such activities, their attitudes toward members of the outgroup changed; several friendships among members of different groups were formed, members of the other groups were no longer disliked, and the conflict among the groups disappeared.

Although Sherif's studies provide clear documentation that cooperative groups can produce interpersonal attraction even when the individuals start out as enemies, the cooperative goals that were introduced were presented to the campers as "acts of God." Johnson and Lewicki (1969) conducted a study on intergroup conflict in which two types of superordinate cooperative goals were introduced, one appearing to be an "act of God" and the other introduced by one of the groups engaged in the conflict. The "act of God" cooperative goal did in fact resolve the intergroup conflict whereas the opposing group refused to accept the superordinate cooperative goal proposed by one of the parties involved. The opposing group tended to view the superordinate cooperative goal as part of a competitive strategy aimed at furthering the initiating group's vested interests. Thus, to be effective in promoting interpersonal attraction among "enemies," cooperative goals may have to be presented by a third party or appear to be natural tragedies or opportunities independent of the parties involved in the conflict. (Complete Activity 4.5 to participate in negotiating to advance your level of power.)

ACTIVITY **4.5** ■ NEGOTIATING WITH MARBLES

INSTRUCTIONS

In this game there are three levels of power, based on marbles in each group. Group members have the chance to progress from one level of power to another by obtaining marbles through negotiation. The three members who get the most power are declared the winners when the exercise ends. You are given six marbles each.

   The scoring system for the marbles is given in the charts below. Note that additional points are awarded if a member is able to get several marbles of the same color. For example, a person's total score if she had six green marbles would be 300 (6 × 50) plus 50 (for six of a kind), or 350 points.

Color	Points
Green	50
Yellow	25
Red	15
White	10
Blue	5

Number of One Kind	Points
4 or more	50
3	30
2	20
1	10

RULES FOR NEGOTIATION

1. You have 5 minutes to improve your score.

2. You improve your score by negotiating with other group members.

3. Members must be holding hands to have an agreement.

4. Only one-for-one trades are legal. Two-for-one trades or any other combinations are illegal.

5. Once a member touches the hand of another member, a marble of unequal value (or color) must be traded. If two members cannot make an agreement, they will have to hold hands for the entire negotiating round.

6. There is no talking unless hands are touching. This rule must be strictly followed.

7. Members with folded arms do not have to negotiate.

8. All marbles must be hidden. This rule must be strictly followed.

Blake and Mouton Studies of Intergroup Conflict

The more the intergroup conflict is defined as a win–lose situation, the more predictable are the effects of the conflict on the relationships of members within the group, on relationships between the groups, on negotiations between the groups, on the group that wins, and on the group that loses (Blake & Mouton, 1962; 1983). A group in the throes of an intergroup conflict experiences a strong upward shift in cohesion as members join together to defend their group against defeat. The group becomes more closely knit and gleans greater loyalty from its members; members close ranks and "table," or put aside, some of their conflicts with one another. There is a sharpening and banding together of the ingroup power structure as militant leaders take control and group members become more willing to accept autocratic leadership. Maintenance needs become secondary to task needs, and the group becomes more tightly structured and organized. Satisfaction among the members runs high, along with their sense of identification with the group and with its position on the issues in the conflict. At the same time the opposing group and its positions are belittled and devalued. Conformity is demanded; "a solid front" must be presented.

Between the groups, an attitude of hostility develops. Each sees the other as the enemy. Inaccurate and uncomplimentary stereotypes form. Distortions in perception (see Johnson, 2000) increase. Each group sees only the best parts of itself and the worst parts of the other group. Interaction and communication decrease between members of the conflicting groups. Doubt is cast on the validity of the position of the other group; its position is seen as distinctly inferior to that of one's own group. Group members tend to listen only to what supports their own position and stereotypes. They misperceive and fail to listen carefully to the other group's position. All these dynamics only intensify the conflict and deepen distrust.

In win–lose negotiations, judgments about the merits of the conflicting positions are distorted, with one's own position recognized as good and the other group's position assessed as bad. Negotiators are relatively blind to points of agreement between their own and the other side's proposals, and they tend to emphasize the differences. The orientation of the negotiators for the two sides is to win for their group, not to reach an agreement that satisfies everyone. This stance inevitably results in the *hero–traitor dynamic*—the negotiator who wins is seen as a *hero* and the one who loses as a *traitor.*

When a neutral third party decides who is right and who is wrong, the winner considers the third party to be impartial and objective; the loser views the third party as biased and thoughtless. Each side sees itself as objective and rational and the other side as unjust and irrational—thereby excluding from the negotiations any elements of genuine objectivity. With the only loyalty being to one's own group's position, the common result of win–lose negotiations is a deadlock. The win–lose strategy can result, of course, in the representative being caught in a conflict between his own beliefs and perceptions and the mandate of his group.

The group that wins becomes even more cohesive. It also tends to release tension, lose its fighting spirit, and become self-satisfied, casual, even playful. The leadership that was responsible for the victory is consolidated. Though concern for maintenance is high, the tendency to work is low. Winning confirms members' belief in their positive stereotype of their group and their negative stereotype of the other group. As a result there is little need to reevaluate perceptions or to reexamine group operations to learn how to improve them.

The group that loses frequently splinters, seeks the reasons for its defeat, and then reorganizes. Members bring to the surface unresolved conflicts among themselves in an effort to find the reasons for the defeat. Tension increases and the group begins to work even harder. Maintenance concerns abate as task concerns rise in a group effort to recover from defeat. The group often seeks someone to blame for the defeat—the leader, the judges, those who made the rules of the conflict situation, the least-conforming members, and so on—and replaces the leadership responsible for the loss.

If future victories seem impossible, members may become completely demoralized and assume a defeatist, apathetic attitude toward the group. The losing group tends to learn a great deal about itself because its positive stereotype of itself and its negative stereotype of the other group have been upset by the loss; therefore, it has to reevaluate its perceptions. Consequently, the losing group is likely to reorganize and become more cohesive and effective once it has realistically accepted the loss.

Blake and Mouton (1983) emphasize that those who use this procedure must avoid three basic traps that lead to increased, rather than decreased, conflict. The first to avoid is the *win–lose dynamic*—seeing every action of the other group as a move to dominate, create an advantage, or win. The participants must learn to recognize win–lose attitudes and behaviors and be able to set norms that stress their avoidance. The second trap to avoid is the *psychodynamic fallacy*—seeing the motivation for the behavior of members of another group in terms of personality factors rather than the dynamics of intergroup conflict. It is much easier to blame the conflict on sick, vicious, power-hungry persons than to view the other group's behavior as a predictable result of intense intergroup conflict. The final trap to avoid is the *self-fulfilling prophecy*. For example, one group assumes that the other is belligerent and proceeds to engage in hostile behavior in an attempt to defend itself by mounting a good offense—thereby provoking belligerence on the part of the other group, which confirms the original assumption. See Activity 4.6 to participate in Blake and Mouton's procedure for transforming the win–lose orientation to a problem-solving orientation during intergroup confrontation.

More recent evidence indicates that when third parties decide how to resolve intergroup and cross-cultural conflict (i.e., arbitration), the decision is evaluated more strongly through judgments about the treatment of disputants (relational concerns) in conflicts within groups and more strongly in terms of decision favorability (instrumental concerns) in disputes across groups (Tyler, Lind, Ohbuchi, Sugawara, & Huo, 1998).

Culture Clash

Another common barrier to building relationships with diverse peers is cultural clashes. *Culture clash* is conflict over basic values held among individuals from different cultures (see Activity 4.7). The most common form is when members of minority groups question the values of the majority. Common reactions by majority group members when their values are being questioned are:

1. **Threatened.** Their responses include avoidance, denial, and defensiveness.
2. **Confused.** Their responses include seeking more information in an attempt to redefine the problem.
3. **Enhanced.** Their responses include heightened anticipation, awareness, and positive actions that lead to solving the problem.

Many cultural clashes develop from threatening, to confusing, to enhancing. Once they are enhancing, they are no longer a barrier (see Activity 4.8).

Clarifying Miscommunications

Imagine that you and several friends went to hear a speaker. Although the content was good, and the delivery entertaining, two of your friends walked out in protest. When you asked them why, they called your attention to the fact that the speaker continually used the expression *you guys* even though half the audience were

ACTIVITY **4.6** ■ INTERGROUP CONFRONTATION

This procedure was developed by Blake and Mouton (1962). It has been used successfully in intergroup conflicts in a variety of organizations for every type of intergroup conflict you can imagine. Its purpose is to change the win–lose orientation to a problem-solving orientation. This exercise takes at least 2 hours to conduct (Blake and Mouton usually took about 20 hours to use the procedure in actual union–management conflicts).

1. Introduce the exercise as an experience in resolving conflicts between two or more groups. The objective is to change a win–lose orientation to a problem-solving orientation. Discuss the previous success Blake and Mouton have had with the procedure in difficult union–management conflicts. Use the accompanying description of a union–management conflict to set up a role play that participants can use in the exercise.

2. Each group meets separately and develops on newsprint (a) how it sees itself as a group and (b) how it sees the other group. Allow the groups at least 30 minutes to complete this task.

3. The two groups come together and share their descriptions. They compare how each side sees itself with how the other group sees it. Often each group sees the other as unreasonable, unethical, and unwilling to cooperate whereas it sees itself as extraordinarily reasonable, ethical, and cooperative. The differences in the perception of how each group sees the other group are then clarified.

4. The two groups meet separately for 20 minutes to diagnose their present relationship. They should answer questions such as, What problems exist? Why aren't the problems being constructively solved? What does the other group contribute to the conflict? What does one's own group contribute to the conflict? The groups should place this material on newsprint to share with the other group.

5. The groups meet together to share their diagnoses. They summarize the key issues causing the conflicts and the main sources of friction. The two groups should keep the integrative, problem-solving negotiation procedure in mind as they plan the next steps in resolving their conflict.

6. The two groups assess their reactions to the exercise and summarize what they have learned about resolving intergroup conflict. Conclusions about preventing intergroup conflict should also be presented and discussed.

UNION–MANAGEMENT CONFLICT

The union in a mid-size manufacturing company has asked the management for across-the-board increases in pay and fringe benefits. The management has refused to meet these "excessive demands" and has made an offer that the union leadership considers unacceptable. Still without a contract agreement at midnight of the day before the old contract expires, the union has voted to go on strike and remain on strike until a satisfactory agreement is reached. Divide into union and management groups and carry out the above procedure.

ACTIVITY **4.7** ■ TIME

Individuals living in industrialized societies are often seen as being "slaves of time." Individuals living in nonindustrialized societies are sometimes seen as being inconsiderate and unreliable. What happens when the two cultures meet?

The purpose of this exercise is to focus attention on the differences in time and timing in various cultures. The procedure follows.

1. Divide the class into groups of four. Divide each group into two pairs, Americans and Pinians (from a fictitious country named Pine). If possible give each pair something such as colored ribbons or armbands that visually distinguishes them from one another.

2. Ask all American pairs to go to one end of the room and the Pinian pairs to go to the other. They receive separate briefings.

3. The participants are to role play that they have an appointment with a photographer at 12:00 noon to have their picture taken.

   a. The *American pairs* are instructed that the appointment is at 12:00 sharp because the photographer has another appointment at 12:30 P.M. in another part of town. The photographer asked them not to be late.

   b. The Pinian pairs are instructed that to them time is not important. Today or tomorrow, it does not matter. Twelve o'clock or one o'clock, what difference does it make? Take it easy, have a cup of coffee, why rush?

4. The group of four meets. It is 11:55 in the morning and it takes 5 minutes to get to the photographer's studio. They role play the situation.

5. The group of four discusses the experience:

   a. What were the cultural differences?
   b. What communication barriers did the cultural differences create?
   c. How did the participants feel during the interchange between the Americans and Pinians?
   d. What are three conclusions about cross-cultural communication that can be made from the experience?

women, used only sports and military examples, only quoted males, and joked about senility and old age. Your friends were insulted.

Communication is actually one of the most complex aspects of managing relationships with diverse peers. To communicate effectively with people from a different cultural, ethnic, social class, and historical background, you must increase your use of the following:

1. **Language sensitivity.** Knowledge of words and expressions are appropriate or inappropriate in communicating with diverse groups. The use of language can play a powerful role in reinforcing stereotypes and garbling communication. To avoid this, individuals need to heighten their sensitivity and avoid using terms and expressions that ignore or devalue others.

2. **Awareness of stylistic elements of communication.** Knowledge of the key elements of communication style and how diverse cultures use these elements affect communication. Without awareness of nuances in language and differences in

ACTIVITY **4.8**   ■   MERGING DIFFERENT CULTURES

The purpose of this exercise is to merge individuals from two different cultures into one group. The procedure for the exercise follows:

MATERIALS

One envelope per participant

One die for each group in Atlantis

Poster board to construct 10 sets of Figure 4.1 for each participant in Atlantis and one set of Figure 4.2 for every participant taking part in this activity.

DIRECTIONS

1. Divide the class into citizens of Atlantis and Mu. Assign as many participants to the society of Mu as you assign to Atlantis. The citizens of Atlantis meet at one end of the room, and the citizens of Mu meet at the other end of the room.

2. At the Atlantis end of the room, assign participants to groups of four and seat each group around a table. Place enough pieces for 10 complete Ts per member in the center of each group (pieces for 40 Ts).

RULES FOR CITIZENS OF ATLANTIS

You are a worker in Atlantis who earns his or her living by constructing Ts. Life is hard in Atlantis so everyone looks out for Number One. A T is formed using four triangles and three squares (see Figure 4.1). You build your Ts by taking pieces from the center of the table.

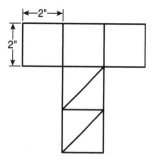

FIGURE 4.1

You take turns in acquiring the shapes. When it is your turn, you acquire shapes either by (a) taking two pieces from the pile or (b) rolling the die. If you roll an even number (2, 4, 6), you select that number of pieces; if you roll an odd number (1, 3, 5), you lose that number of pieces from those you have accumulated thus far, including those composing complete Ts.

The member with the greatest number of Ts is declared the wealthiest and survives. The poorest perish (lose). You can begin.

3. At the Mu end of the room, a second instructor divides the citizens of Mu into groups of four members and seats each group around a table. The instructor takes the 20 pieces that make up the four Ts for each group and randomly divides the pieces into four envelopes (5 pieces in each), making sure that no one envelope

contains the correct five pieces for completing a T. One envelope is given to each group member.

RULES FOR CITIZENS OF MU

You are a worker in Mu who earns his or her living by constructing Ts. Life is hard in Mu, so everyone looks out for everyone else. A T is formed using the five pieces shown in Figure 4.2. There are enough pieces among the members of your group to form one complete T for each member, but no one member has the right combination of pieces to complete his or her T. Mu, however, is a heterogeneous society that does not have a common language. The members of your group, therefore, do not speak to each other. *No verbal communication is allowed.*

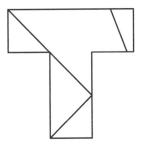

FIGURE 4.2

Group members must share pieces to be successful. You may offer pieces to another group member and accept pieces offered to you by another group member. You cannot offer pieces to more than one person at the same time. You may not ask for a particular piece by pointing, talking, nudging, grimacing, or any other method. When you give a piece to another member, simply hand it to the person without demonstrating how the piece fits into his or her T. You have 5 minutes to complete this task. You may open your envelopes and begin.

4. After 5 minutes the instructor collects each group's pieces and again places the pieces randomly into the envelopes. The Mu groups repeat the task, except this time they may use any form of communication they prefer. All other rules remain in effect. They have 5 minutes to complete the task.

5. When step 4 is completed, the Atlantis citizens join the Mu society. Evenly distribute the citizens of Atlantis among the Mu groups. Add to each group's Ts one additional T for each new member. Take the combined pieces and randomly distribute them into envelopes, one for each member of the integrated groups. Tell the participants:

RULES FOR ATLANTIS IMMIGRANTS AND CITIZENS OF MU

The citizens of Atlantis are immigrants to Mu. They are to have a part in the work of Mu, building Ts. The Ts are formed differently from those made in Atlantis. The sooner they learn to earn a livelihood, the better off Mu will be.

Members of Atlantis, however, do not speak Mu's language, and the meaning of nonverbal gestures in the two societies is quite different. Therefore, no verbal communication or nonverbal signaling, such as pointing or gesturing, is allowed. You have 10 minutes to complete your task. You can begin work.

6. Stop the groups when all groups have built their Ts or after 10 minutes, whichever comes first and have the groups discuss four questions:

a. How did the members of each society feel about working in integrated units?

(continued)

ACTIVITY 4.8   *Continued*

> **b.** How did the two societies differ?
> **c.** Why was your group successful or unsuccessful in integrating the two societies?
> **d.** What conclusions can be drawn about work groups consisting of members from more than one society?

style, the potential for garbled communication is enormous when interacting with diverse peers.

The English and their North American counterparts are sometimes seen as being impoverished when it comes to kinesthetic communication, using words to denote what gesture or tone would express in other cultures. In the United States and Canada, for example, people are often quite reserved when greeting others. Body contact is avoided. Yet in some Arab countries men kiss each other on the street when they meet. Nigerian men often walk hand in hand. Italian men embrace warmly and remain touching when engaged in conversation. In some African countries handshakes may be extended for long periods of time, and a hand on the knee among males is not an offense. All these differences create potential communication problems when members of the different cultures meet. (Participate in Activity 4.9 to experience these differences.)

Your ability to communicate with credibility to diverse peers is closely linked to your use of language. You must be sophisticated enough to anticipate how your messages will be interpreted by the listener. If you are unaware of nuances and innuendoes contained in your message, then you are more likely to miscommunicate. The words you choose often tell other people more about your values, attitudes, and socialization than you intend to reveal. Receivers react to the subtleties conveyed and interpret the implied messages behind words. The first step in establishing relationships with diverse peers, therefore, is to understand how language reinforces stereotypes. The second step is to adjust our usage accordingly. (Participate in Activity 4.10 to increase your awareness of cross-cultural communication barriers.)

You can never predict with certainty how every person will react to what you say. You can, however, minimize the possibility of miscommunicating by following some basic guidelines:

1. Use communication skills.
2. Negotiate for meaning whenever you think the other persons with whom you are talking misinterpreted what you said.
3. Use words that are inclusive rather than exclusive, such as *women, men, participants.*
4. Avoid adjectives that spotlight specific groups and imply the individual is an exception, such as *black doctor, woman pilot, older teacher, blind lawyer.*
5. Use quotes, references, metaphors, and analogies that reflect diversity and are from diverse sources, for example, from Asian and African sources as well as European and American.
6. Avoid terms that define, demean, or devalue others, such as *cripple, girl, boy, agitator.*
7. Be aware of the genealogy of words viewed as inappropriate by others. It is the connotations the receiver places on the words that is important, not your connotations. These connotations change over time so continual clarification is needed. There are "loaded" words that seem neutral to you but highly judg-

ACTIVITY 4.9 ■ GREETINGS AND GOODBYES

The purpose of this exercise is to increase awareness of how different cultural patterns of greetings and goodbyes can create communication problems. The procedure follows.

1. Divide the class into groups of four. Divide each group into two pairs, Americans and Lakians (from a fictitious country named Lake). If possible, give each pair something, such as colored ribbons or armbands, that visually distinguishes them from one another.

2. Ask all American pairs to go to one end of the room and the Lakian pairs to go to the other. They receive separate briefings.

3. The participants are to role play business associates who engage in an informal discussion of general economic conditions in their countries.

   a. The *American pairs* are instructed to greet their Lakian business associates in the traditional North American fashion. They are to shake hands, say "good to see you again," talk about the economic condition of North America for a while, and then say goodbye by shaking hands and waving.
   b. The *Lakian pairs* are instructed to greet their American business associates in the traditional Lakian fashion. They are to give the Americans a warm embrace and then to take and hold their hands for at least 30 seconds. They are to talk about the economic condition of Lake for a while. Then they are to say goodbye by giving the Americans a warm embrace, holding both their hands for at least 30 seconds, and telling them how great it was to talk to them.

4. The group of four meets. If they finish the conversation before other groups in the room do, each pair should find another pair from the other country and repeat the experience.

5. The group of four discusses the experience:

   a. What were the cultural differences?
   b. What communication barriers did the cultural differences create?
   c. How did the participants feel during the interchange between the Americans and Lakians?
   d. What are three conclusions about cross-cultural communication that can be made from the experience?

---

mental to people of diverse backgrounds. The word *lady,* for example, was a complement even a few years ago, but today it fails to take into account women's independence and equal status in society and, therefore, is offensive to many women. Words such as *girls, ladies,* or *gals* are just as offensive.

INSULATED IGNORANCE

An interesting aspect of the interaction between majority and minority group members is the belief by majority group members that ethnicity and historical background has little influence on a person's life. The dominance of the majority over minorities operates outside of the conscious awareness of the minority group members. Hornstein and Johnson (1966) and Johnson (1970) labeled this phenomenon

ACTIVITY **4.10** ■ CROSS-CULTURAL COMMUNICATION

The purpose of this exercise is to increase awareness of how cultural differences can create barriers to communication among group members. The procedure follows.

1. Form groups of six and divide each group into three pairs.

2. Each pair is assigned a particular cultural identity based on being a citizen of the country of Winkin, Blinkin, or Nod. Their task is to plan how they will act during the exercise based on the information about their country given on their briefing sheet. The pair is to work together cooperatively to ensure that both members understand how to act appropriately as a citizen of their country. They have 10 minutes to prepare.

3. Two triads are formed (one member from each country). Each triad is assigned the task of identifying the 10 most important principles of cross-cultural communication. They have 15 minutes to do so.

4. The group of six discusses the following questions:

   a. Compare the two lists. How are they different? How are they the same?
   b. How did members react to their assigned roles. Did they have any difficulties in enacting them?
   c. What were the communication barriers among the citizens of the three countries? Why did they occur?
   d. How could the communication barriers be avoided or overcome?
   e. What conclusions can be made from the exercise?
   f. What applications does the exercise have for everyday life?

CONFIDENTIAL BRIEFING: TO BE SEEN BY WINKIN CITIZENS ONLY

The following list contains the behavioral characteristics of the country of Winkin. Study this list carefully. Apply the characteristics to your role play.

1. **Orientation towards touch.** Touch as much as possible, stand and sit close to people, and give a long handshake (about 15–30 seconds) when you greet a person.

2. **Orientation toward eye contact.** Look other people in the eyes when you talk to them.

3. **Orientation toward disclosure.** You are interested only in yourself and you love to share yourself with other people. Talk only about yourself and what interests you. Do not listen to other people—they are boring. You do not want to understand the other person better, you want them to understand you. Whenever they start talking, you interrupt them and refocus the conversation on you.

4. **Orientation toward conflict.** You like to argue for the sake of arguing so that people pay attention to you.

5. **Orientation toward helping others.** You avoid helping people under any circumstances.

CONFIDENTIAL BRIEFING SHEET: TO BE SEEN BY BLINKIN CITIZENS ONLY

The following list contains the behavioral characteristics of the country of Blinkin. Study this list carefully. Apply the characteristics to your role play.

1. **Orientation toward touch.** Do not touch other people. Stand and sit far away from other people. Greet other people by nodding your head—do not shake hands.

2. **Orientation toward eye contact.** Do not look other people in the eyes when you talk to them. If you happen to look a person in the eyes, look for only a split second.

3. **Orientation toward disclosure.** You are genuinely interested in other people. You are inquisitive. You get to know other people by asking them questions about what they are interested in. You listen carefully and let other people finish what they are saying before you speak. You never interrupt. You never talk about yourself.

4. **Orientation toward conflict.** You are very uncomfortable with conflict and want to avoid it at all costs. You never argue about a point with which you disagree. Instead you change the subject and try to find something else to talk about.

5. **Orientation toward helping others.** You try to help other people (especially in solving a problem) as much as possible.

CONFIDENTIAL BRIEFING SHEET: TO BE SEEN BY NOD CITIZENS ONLY

The following list contains the behavioral characteristics of the country of Nod. Study this list carefully. Apply the characteristics to your role play.

1. **Orientation toward touch.** Touch people only occasionally when you are talking. Stand and sit about an arm's length from a person. Give a short handshake when you are greeting a person.

2. **Orientation toward eye contact.** Look other people in the eyes for only about 3 seconds at a time when you talk to them.

3. **Orientation toward disclosure.** You want to exchange ideas and thoughts. You share your interests and opinions, and you want other people to share their interests and opinions with you. You want to talk *with* other people instead of *to* them.

4. **Orientation toward conflict.** You seek reasoned judgments. You ignore who is right and who is wrong. You focus on the quality of ideas, seeking a synthesis or integration of different points of view. You listen carefully, add what you want to say, and make an informed judgment based on all positions and perspectives.

5. **Orientation toward helping others.** You help other people only when it benefits you, that is, when it is rational to do so.

"insulated ignorance." *Insulated ignorance* is the structuring of the relationship between majority and minority groups so majority group members are unaware of the inequities in the relationship and have minimal contact with minority group members. Insulated ignorance may result from the following process.

Step 1. The majority group creates a normative structure that structures their relationship with minorities.

Step 2. The normative structure becomes an indirect and invisible means to ensure majority group members receive the desired privileges and benefits without directly and personally having to discriminate against minority group members. Power is exercised indirectly in impersonal ways without the direct participation of majority group members. The normative structure can then operate without the conscious awareness of majority group members.

Step 3. Majority group members insulate themselves from understanding the impact of their actions on minority group members. Through largely segregated residential areas, world places, and recreational sites, members of the majority group can protect their ignorance of the dynamics of the intergroup interaction.

Insulated ignorance has several consequences. The first is that it protects majority group members from being aware of the consequences of their behavior (Hornstein & Johnson, 1966; Johnson, 1970). Members of the majority group can then believe that they personally are not prejudiced while at the same time participating in broad patterns of discrimination.

The second is that insulated ignorance protects the privileged status of the majority group members. In the United States, for example, few white individuals grasp the notion that being white entitles them to certain advantages and privileges not easily available to persons of color. As long as the members of the majority group are unaware of their participation in discriminatory practices, they tend to have no motivation to modify their privileged status and tend to perceive the efforts of minority group members to do so as being biased.

The third consequence of insulated ignorance is that it prevents majority group members from having an ethnic identity. Whites often have difficulty perceiving themselves as ethnic beings, whereas ethnic minorities tend to be constantly aware of their historical and cultural heritage. Members of the majority group assume that the pattern of benefits are the natural order of life. This tends to prevent them from feeling privileged and having an ethnic identity. Whereas members of minority groups always are aware of their ethnic and historical membership, members of the majority group live in an insulated ignorance, unaware of the impact of their ethnicity or historical group membership on their lives and their interactions with others.

The fourth consequence is that insulated ignorance prevents majority group members from understanding the perspective of minority group members. The lack of majority group members' awareness of the impact of their ethnicity on their privileges and benefits becomes a barrier to their understanding how the ethnicity of minority group members establishes limits on minority group members' benefits and how they perceive members of the majority group.

Finally, insulated ignorance helps create the illusion that the benefits received are due to majority group members' hard work rather than their position in society. Take a moment to review the important concepts introduced in this chapter by participating in Activity 4.11.

CONTACT THEORY

Intense, protracted, and often deadly conflicts occur between groups interacting with each other. Both Greek and Turkish Cypriots, for example, have, in the past, lived throughout the island, many in mixed towns and villages, yet intense conflict existed. Since the Turkish invasion in 1974, the two groups have lived separately with the conflict unresolved. In northern Ireland Protestants and Catholics live in close proximity, yet their conflict continues. The Hutus and Tutsis in Rwanda, and the Serbs, Croats, and Bosnians in Bosnia, shared a common language and culture and even a history of peaceful coexistence and intermarriage for extended periods of time. Yet deadly conflict broke out in both places, genocidal massacres were reported in which people systematically and brutally killed acquaintances and neighbors with whom they had harmonious relations in the past.

What these conflicts make clear is that contact per se does not preclude violent conflict between groups. Potential positive effects of contact between groups depend on the situational conditions in which the contact takes place. In the absence of essential conditions, contact between antagonistic groups is more likely to increase rather than reduce distrust, hostility, and stereotypes. As these examples indicate, even a

ACTIVITY **4.11** ■ **IMPORTANT CONCEPTS**

Demonstrate your understanding of the following concepts by matching the definitions with the appropriate concept. Find a partner. Compare answers.

CONCEPT

_____ 1. **psychodynamic fallacy**

_____ 2. **win–lose dynamic**

_____ 3. **hero–traitor dynamic**

_____ 4. **superordinate goals**

_____ 5. **power**

_____ 6. **relative deprivation**

_____ 7. **displaced aggression**

_____ 8. **authoritarian personality**

_____ 9. **realistic group conflict**

_____ 10. **self-fulfilling prophecy**

_____ 11. **culture clash**

_____ 12. **frustration–aggression theory**

DEFINITION

a. Seeing every action of members of other groups as a move to dominate, create an advantage, or win

b. The capacity to affect another person's goal accomplishment

c. Feelings of discontent aroused by the belief that one fares poorly compared to others

d. Seeing the motivation for the behavior of members of other groups in terms of personality factors rather than the dynamics of intergroup conflict

e. When a person is frustrated but cannot attack the source because of fear or simple unavailability, the person attacks an innocent third party because the party is available and has less power

f. Goals that cannot be easily ignored by members of two antagonistic groups, but whose attainment is beyond the resources and efforts of either group alone

g. Antagonism between groups arises from real conflicts of interests and the frustrations these conflicts produce

h. Your expectations cause you to behave in a way that provokes behavior from others that confirms your expectations

i. Prejudice arises when one group frustrates the other group's goal achievement and the frustrated group reacts with aggression

j. Conflict over basic values occurring among individuals from different cultures

k. The negotiator who wins is seen as a hero and the one who loses as a traitor

l. Person characterized by exaggerated submission to authority, rigid conformity to conventional norms, self-righteous hostility, and harsh punitiveness toward anyone considered different

history of positive contact may not prevent intergroup violence when situational conditions change.

In the United States, desegregation is based on the assumption that contact between majority and minority individuals results in positive relationships and a reduction of stereotyping, prejudice, and racism. Historically, social scientists believed that sheer ignorance about African Americans and their lives contributed to erroneous and oversimplified racial stereotypes (Myrdal, 1944). Contact was seen as the solution. A wide variety of studies conducted in the 1930s, 1940s, and 1950s indicated that such contact was not a straightforward matter. It seemed to be the nature of the contact between members of different ethnic groups, not the frequency, that promoted favorable intergroup attitudes.

Researchers studied the effects of actual contact between blacks and whites, utilizing visiting black lecturers in classrooms (Young, 1932), meetings with black professionals (Smith, 1943), school integration (Horowitz, 1936), joint recreational activities in integrated summer camps (Williams, 1948; Yarrow, Campbell, & Yarrow, 1958), voyages of white merchant seamen serving with black seamen (Brophy, 1945), and contact within combat infantry platoons (Mannheimer & Williams, 1949; Star, Williams, & Stouffer, 1965). Many of the earliest research studies used questionnaires in which respondents were asked to note their attitudes toward members of an ethnic group and then to describe the nature and frequency of their contact with members of that group (Allport & Kramer, 1946; Harlan, 1942; MacKenzie, 1948; Rosenblith, 1949). Somewhat later studies were based on postwar occupational and educational desegregation (Gray & Thompson, 1953; Gundlach, 1950; Harding & Hogerge, 1952; Minard, 1952; Reed, 1947; Rose, 1948; Williams & Ryan, 1954) and desegregated residential settings (Deutsch & Collins, 1951; Irish, 1952; Jahoda & West, 1951; Kramer, 1951; Wilner, Walkey, & Cook, 1952; 1955; Winder, 1952). These latter studies indicated that when the degree of cooperation growing out of involuntary residential proximity between white and black residents was greater, the development of friendly ethnic relationships was more likely.

Years later, we realize that the issue is not so simple. Sometimes intergroup contact is associated with less prejudice. According to national surveys, having more black friends or more contact with gay men and lesbians is associated with less prejudice (Herek & Capitanio, 1995; Jackman & Crane, 1986). Contact, however, is also correlated with more prejudice. Whites who have had the most contact with illegal immigrants (Espenshade & Calhoun, 1993) and whites living in areas of the South with the largest concentration of African Americans have the most prejudiced political attitudes (Giles & Buckner, 1993; Key, 1949). Thus, contact can either increase or decrease prejudice and discrimination (see Activity 4.12).

Based on these early studies, in 1947 Goodwin Watson published a review of the previous research and writings on intergroup relations. He concluded that contact between members of different ethnic groups was likely to be more effective in changing behavior and attitudes than were alternative experiences such as exposure to correct information or persuasive communication, given that the contact met a number of conditions. The conditions included the following:

1. Cooperative action to achieve mutual goals (diverse individuals had to engage in cooperative activities together)
2. Personal interactions among individuals that disconfirm stereotypes and encourage the transmission of individuating information about group members
3. Social norms and authorities favoring egalitarian contact
4. Equal status of all group members within the contact situation

In the same year, Williams (1947) published a similar list of conditions for constructive cross-ethnic contact, as did Kenneth Clark in 1953, and in 1954 Gordon Allport published his famous book, *The Nature of Prejudice*, in which he identified a similar list of conditions. Allport stated that prejudice is likely to be reduced only "by equal status contact . . . in the pursuit of common goals. The effect is greatly enhanced if this contact is sanctioned by institutional support . . . and . . . leads to the perception of common interests and common humanity between members of the two groups" (p. 281). Stuart Cook followed with a review in 1957.

Between the years of 1950 and 1970, there were approximately 40 studies on cross-ethnic interaction (Miller & Brewer, 1984; Schofield, 1997; Stephan, 1978; 1986).

ACTIVITY **4.12** ■ WHAT WOULD YOU DO?

A true account of how a Midwestern city attempted to deal with prejudice and discrimination follows. Read this case carefully and complete the tasks.

In 1991, the City of Dubuque, Iowa, conducted a controversial experiment in intergroup relations (Brewer, 1997). Although they had only a tiny racial minority of 331 black residents scattered among 58,000 citizens, a cross-burning had taken place in 1989 that had ignited a black family's garage. A city task force, formed to make recommendations for preventing future incidents of racial conflict, concluded that Dubuque needed more minority citizens.

In May 1991, the city council adopted a plan of incentives for local businesses to hire minorities with the goal of recruiting to Dubuque 20 new black families per year for 5 years. The community reacted negatively to the idea, and racial fights occurred in the local high school and additional cross-burnings took place. Rumors about the recruitment plan and its effect on local jobs, housing, and safety in the streets spread rapidly. Graffiti containing racial epithets appeared, and a group of young males organized a local chapter of the National Association for the Advancement of White People.

1. Write out your assessment of the pros and cons of the strategy the city adopted.

Pros	Cons

2. Write out what you would have done if you were the city council and why.

3. Find a partner. Share your assessment and plan. Listen carefully to the other person's assessment and plan. Create a new assessment and plan that is better than either of your originals. Write it down and both partners sign it.

4. Find another pair and combine into a group of four. Repeat the share–listen–create procedure in step 3.

The reviewers of this research aimed at answering the question, Has desegregation been successful, and if so under what conditions? Three of the measures assessing the success of desegregation were academic achievement, self-esteem, and intergroup relations. Some positive effects on black students' achievement were found whereas white students' achievement neither increased nor decreased in desegregated situations. No effects on the self-esteem of either black or white students have been found. In the short-term, desegregation has been found to both improve intergroup relations and create more negative attitudes and relationships.

Under favorable conditions contact seemed to reduce prejudice, and under unfavorable conditions contact seemed to increase prejudice. The major determinant of whether cross-ethnic contact produced positive attitudes and relationships was cooperative interaction among the individuals involved. The research on the long-term benefits of desegregation indicates better and more integrated social relationships. A study involving 191 white adults found that early childhood contact with African American students had a significant positive effect on adults' current cross-ethnic attitudes (Wood & Sonleitner, 1996).

Adults who attended desegregated schools have been found to live in integrated neighborhoods more frequently (Crain, 1984; Pearce, Crain, & Farley, 1984). In an analysis of 21 studies of outcomes for ethnic minorities, Wells and Crain (19954) found that those who attended desegregated schools (compared to those who attended segregated schools) were more likely to experience success in college and to live in interracial neighborhoods. Interracial contact at young ages has been found to be related to African Americans' likelihood of interacting with white individuals as adults and being employed in more integrated work organizations (Braddock, Crain, & McPartland, 1984).

The most recent formulations of contact theory specify that the following conditions must exist for contact to result in a reduction of prejudice, stereotyping, and racism:

Cooperative Action to Achieve Mutual Goals.   What largely determines whether interaction results in positive or negative relationships is the context within which the interaction takes place. Rather than requiring members of different groups to compete to see who is best or work individually on their own, they must work together to achieve mutual goals. This is the best supported of the conditions. Two meta-analyses indicated that cooperative experiences promote more positive relationships among heterogeneous individuals (Johnson & Johnson, 1989; Johnson, Johnson, & Maruyama, 1983). When people cooperate, they tend to like each other more, trust each other more, be more candid with each other, and be more willing to listen to and be influenced by each other than are people competing or working individually (Johnson & Johnson, 1989). In addition, considerable evidence shows that cooperative experiences, compared with competitive and individualistic ones, promote more positive, committed, and caring relationships regardless of differences in ethnic, cultural, language, social class, gender, ability, or other differences (Johnson & Johnson, 1989).

Personal Interactions to Disconfirm Stereotypes and Encourage Transmission of Individuating Information.   Ingroup members tend to assume that outgroup members are all alike. Through intimate, one-on-one interaction, those categories should break down and outgroup members should be perceived in more individualized terms (Brewer & Miller, 1984; Marcus-Newhall et al., 1993; Urban & Miller, in press; Wilder, 1984). In schools, individual contact among individuals from different groups is unusual and uncommon. Students associated with members of their own group. Tracking (ability grouping) ensures that white and minority students are separated. Desegregation does not ensure integration. Teachers must create the conditions and opportunities for personal interactions among diverse students for positive relationships to develop and stereotyping and prejudice to decrease. Such interactions also increase students' sophistication.

Support from Social Norms and Authorities.   The social norms, defined in part by relevant authorities, should favor intergroup contact. Norms have a powerful impact on individuals' behavior. Greenberg and Pyszczynski (1985) demonstrated that subjects expressed more prejudice after they overheard a confederate utter a racial slur. Blanchard and his associates (1991) demonstrated that college students being interviewed about a racial incident on campus conveyed more racist sentiment after they heard a fellow student do the same. Wilder and Shapiro (1991) demonstrated subjects were more likely to rate an outgroup member as "typical" when they were with fellow ingroup members than when they were alone.

The Two Groups Should Be of Equal Status in the Contact Situation. Desegregation situations that provided equal status contact, as in the army and public housing projects, have been successful (Pettigrew, 1969). When public schools were desegregated, however, white children were coming from more affluent families, were better prepared, and were academically more advanced than their black peers (Cohen, 1984).

In addition to these four conditions, recent research has focused on additional conditions that may be required for contact between diverse individuals and groups to have constructive rather than destructive effects. The first is the salience of social categories. When category distinctions are highly salient in an intergroup contact situation, group members are more apt to respond in ways that are category based (Brewer & Miller, 1984; Wilder & Shapiro, 1989a; 1989b) and are more biased in their intergroup attitudes (Haunschild, Moreland, & Murrell, 1994; Hong & Harrod, 1988). Three ways to reduce the salience of social categories follow:

1. Making shared categories salient. Ingroup bias is higher when people differ on two real social categories (such as ethnicity and gender) than when they differ on one category but share another (Brewer, Ho, Lee, & Miller, 1987; Urban & Miller, in press). Similar results have been found in laboratory studies on nominal group categories (Deschamps, 1977; Deschamps & Doise, 1978; Vanbeselaere, 1987; 1991).

2. Have equal representation of majority and minority members in cooperative groups (Rogers, Hennigan, Bowman, & Miller, 1984; Worchel, Andreoli, & Folger, 1977). Members of numerical minorities are more aware of their social category than are members of numerical majorities, express more ingroup bias than do numerical majorities, and are less accepting of members of other groups. Groups for whom category salience is high are more biased in their intergroup attitudes.

3. Create a common identity among majority and minority members (Johnson & Johnson, 1999). When majority and minority members are assigned the same role, for example, they perceive themselves as sharing a common identity (Bettencourt et al., in press; Bettencourt & Dorr, 1998).

The second potential addition to contact theory is the role of intergroup friendship. In a survey of 3,806 respondents in seven 1988 national probability samples of France, Great Britain, the Netherlands, and West Germany, Pettigrew (1997) found that intergroup friendship is a strong and consistent predictor of reduced prejudice and proimmigrant policy preferences. The reduction of prejudice among those with diverse friends generalized to more positive feelings about a wide variety of outgroups. There seems to be a benevolent spiral in which intergroup friendship reduces prejudice and, in turn, reduced prejudice increases the likelihood of further intergroup friendships. Similar effects were not found when the individual had an outgroup coworker or neighbor (but not a friend). Herek and Capitanio (1996) found that multiple outgroup friends have a strong negative relationship with prejudice. Wright, Aron, McLaughlin-Volpe, and Ropp (1997) found that knowledge that an ingroup member had a close relationship with an outgroup member results in more positive intergroup attitudes.

Since its original formulation 50 years ago, extensive research has been inspired by contact theory. The research has generally confirmed the theory across a variety of societies, situations, and groups. These include German children in school with Turkish children (Wagner, Hewstone, & Machleit, 1989), the elderly (Caspi, 1984), and the mentally ill (Desforges et al., 1991). The theory has been confirmed by laboratory (e.g., Cook, 1978; Johnson & Johnson, 1989), survey (e.g., Sigelman & Welch, 1993), field (e.g., Johnson & Johnson, 1989; Meer & Freedman, 1966), and archival (e.g., Fine, 1979) research.

There are problems with contact theory. The first is that the proliferation of required conditions renders the theory meaningless. As a result of all the diverse research, many social scientists have suggested revisions to contact theory. Some of the revisions have been situational, such as intimacy (Amir, 1976) or salience of social categories (Brewer & Miller, 1988) and some individual, such as low authoritarianism (Weigel & Howes, 1985). The danger to contact theory is that too many factors render it meaningless. Contact theory may become a "grocery list" of necessary conditions rather than a coherent model of attitude and behavior change.

The proliferation of conditions may result from social scientists confusing facilitating with essential conditions. Some of the conditions suggested for optimal contact may be catalytic (not essential for harmonious relationships but related to underlying mediating processes). Pettigrew (1997) suggests four broad, encompassing processes: (a) learning about the outgroup, (b) empathizing with the outgroup, (c) identifying with the outgroup, and (d) reappraising the ingroup. Some of the conditions proposed as requirements for constructive contact may actually be facilitators of one or more of these processes.

The second problem is the need to specify more precisely the mediation of contact effects. Social judgment theory, which is discussed at length in the next chapter, is an attempt to be more specific about the mediators of contact and positive relationships.

The third problem is that although contact theory concerns interaction among members of diverse groups, it focuses on interpersonal interaction. It needs to refocus on the contact between groups (Hewstone & Brown, 1986), rather than focusing on the contact of individuals from two groups. There is evidence that the perceived collective other is a qualitatively different kind of actor than a perceived individual other. Groups evoke stronger reactions than an individual engaging in the same behavior, and actions by groups and individuals elicit differing preferences for redress (Abelson, Dasgupta, Park, & Banaji, 1998).

When observers perceive individuals as part of a cohesive group (as opposed to an aggregate of unrelated individuals), the observers express stereotypic judgments about the individuals and infer that their behavior was shaped by the presence of others (Oakes & Turner, 1986; Oakes, Turner, & Haslam, 1991; Wilder, 1977; 1978). A racial slur by an individual, for example, provokes a different reaction than a racial slur delivered by a group. More research is considered needed on intergroup (as opposed to interpersonal) contact. See Box 4.4 for the reaction of a former slave to the theological attacks on women's rights during the 1851 Women's Rights Convention.

Gaining Sophistication
through Intergroup Relationships

Some people are *sophisticated* about how to act appropriately within many different cultures and perspectives. They are courteous, well-mannered, and refined within many different settings and cultures. Other people are quite *provincial*, knowing only how to act appropriately within their narrow perspective. To become sophisticated a person must be able to see the situation from the cultural perspective of the other people involved. Much of the information about different cultural and ethnic heritages and perspectives cannot be attained through reading books and listening to lectures. Only through knowing, working with, and personally interacting with members of diverse groups can individuals really learn to value diversity, utilize diversity for cre-

■ ■ ■ ■ ■

BOX 4.4
SOJOURNER TRUTH: "AIN'T I A WOMAN?"

Sojourner Truth (1797–1883) was a former slave and legendary figure in the abolition and suffrage movements. At the 1851 Women's Rights Convention in Akron, Ohio, she delivered her famous "Ain't I a Woman?" speech. After a group of ministers made a theological attack on women's rights, she ascended to the stage, stood at her 6-foot height, and defended women with her rich, soulful voice. Her words moved the audience to tears and thunderous applause, and her speech became a pivotal moment in the women's rights movement.

Truth could not read or write and, therefore, no formal record of the speech exists. The speech was published, however, in the *Anti-Slavery Bugle* newspaper on June 21, 1851, and in 1878, a second version of the speech (as convention president Frances Gage recollected it) was published in the "Narrative of Sojourner Truth." What follows is a composite of the two that historians believe accurately conveys her message.

Well, children, whar dar is so much racket there must be something out o'kilter. I think that 'twixt the negroes of the Souf, and the women of the Norf, all a talkin' 'bout rights, the white men will be in a fix pretty soon.

But what's all this here talking 'bout?

That man ober there says that women needs to be helped into carriages, and lifted ober ditches, and have the best place everywhar. Nobody ever helps me into carriages, or ober mud-puddles, or gives me any best place! And ain't I a woman? Look at me! Look at my arm! I have plowed and planted, and gathered into barns, and no man could head me! And ain't I a woman? I could work as much and eat as much as a man—when I could get it—and bear the lash as well! And ain't I a woman? I borne 13 children, and seen most all sold off to slavery, and when I cried out with my mother's grief none but Jesus heard me! And ain't I a woman?

Then they talk 'bout this thing in the head; what's this they call it? [A member of the audience whispers, "Intellect."] That's it, honey. What's that got to do with women's rights or negroes' rights? If my cup won't hold but a pint, and your'n holds a quart, wouldn't you be mean not to let me have my little half-measure full?

Then that little man in black there [one of the ministers], he says women can't have as much rights as men, 'cause Christ wasn't a woman! Whar did your Christ come from? Whar did your Christ come from? From God and a woman! Man had nothing to do with him.

If the first woman God ever made was strong enough to turn the world upside down all 'lone, these women together ought to be able to turn it back, and get it right side up again! And now they is asking to do it—the men better let 'em.

Obliged to you for hearing me. And now old Sojourner ain't got nothing more to say.

Williams, J. (1987). Eyes on the prize: America's civil rights years: 1954–1965. New York: Viking Penguin.

ative problem solving, and work effectively with diverse peers. Although information alone helps, it is only through direct and personal interaction among diverse individuals and developing personal as well as professional relationships with them that such outcomes are realized. Understanding the perspective of others from different ethnic and cultural backgrounds requires more than information. It requires the personal sharing of viewpoints and mutual discussion of situations.

To gain the sophistication and skills required to build relationships with diverse peers you need to develop friends from a wide variety of cultural, ethnic, economic, and historical backgrounds. Many aspects of relating to individuals different from yourself can be learned only from friends being candid about misunderstandings you are inadvertently creating. To gain the sophistication and skills you need to relate to, work with, and become friends with diverse peers, you need to develop the following attributes:

1. **Actual interaction.** Seek opportunities to interact with a wide variety of peers. You do so because you value diversity, recognize the importance of relating effectively to diverse peers, and recognize the importance of increasing your knowledge of multicultural issues.
2. **Trust.** Build trust by being open about yourself and your commitment to cross-cultural relationships and being trustworthy when others share their opinions and reactions with you. Being trustworthy includes expressing respect for diverse backgrounds and valuing them as a resource that increases the quality of your life and adds to the viability of your society.
3. **Candor.** Be candid by openly discussing your personal opinions, feelings, and reactions and encourage others to do likewise. Many events seem neutral to you that are offensive and hurtful to individuals from backgrounds different from yours. To understand what is and is not disrespectful and hurtful, your peers must be candid about their reactions and explain them to you.

If you are not sophisticated and skilled in building relationships with diverse peers, you are in danger of unconsciously colluding with current patterns of discrimination. *Collusion* is conscious and unconscious reinforcement of stereotypic attitudes, behaviors, and prevailing norms. People collude with discriminatory practices and prejudiced actions through ignorance, silence, denial, and active support. Perhaps the only way not to collude with existing discriminatory practices is to build friendships with diverse peers that allow you to understand when discrimination and prejudice occurs. The following list contains guidelines for action in learning how to build relationships with diverse others.

1. Recognize that diversity among members is everpresent and unavoidable.
2. Recognize that the more interdependent the world becomes, the more important it is to be able to work effectively with diverse groupmates.
3. Maximize heterogeneity among members in both personal characteristics and abilities to maximize the group's productivity and success.
4. With heterogeneous membership comes increased conflict. Structure constructive procedures for managing conflicts among group members.
5. Face and resolve the barriers to the utilization of diversity (stereotyping, prejudice, blaming the victim, cultural clashes).
6. Ensure that diversity is utilized as a resource by strengthening the positive interdependence within the group to create the context in which diversity is a resource, not a hindrance.
7. Ensure diversity is used as a strength by uniting the personal identities of members of diverse groups. Create a superordinate identity based on a pluralistic set of values. Encourage individuals to develop the following:
   a. An appreciation for their gender, religious, ethnic, and cultural backgrounds
   b. An appreciation for the gender, religious, ethnic, and cultural backgrounds of other group members
   c. A strong superordinate identity of "group member" that transcends the differences among members
   d. A pluralistic set of values concerning equality, freedom, the rights of individual members, and the responsibilities of group membership
8. Ensure that diversity is used as a strength by fostering personal relationships among members to allow candid discussions that increase members' sophistication about their differences.
9. Ensure that diversity is used as a strength by clarifying miscommunications among diverse group members.

OTHER INFLUENCES ON PREJUDICE
AND DISCRIMINATION

Education

The first strategy for reducing prejudice is to ensure that all members of our society stay in school longer. The more education an individual has, the less prejudiced that person tends to be; in fact, educational levels are perhaps the strongest predictor of how prejudiced people are (Campbell, 1971; Sniderman & Piazza, 1993). On current issues, however, such as affirmative action, young white people are no more sympathetic to minorities than are older generations (Steeh & Schuman, 1991). In other countries it seems that young white people are actually more prejudiced; British youths' antagonism toward black West Indians seems to have increased (Pettigrew & Meertens, 1995). Education, therefore, although a contributing factor to reducing prejudice, does not seem to be enough in and of itself to do the job.

Mass Media

Whereas laboratory studies indicate that some attitudes are quite susceptible to change with appropriate persuasive techniques, attempts to change attitudes in the world outside the laboratory have been much less successful. Survey studies, for example, show that racial and ethnic attitudes rarely change even over several years' time (Sears, 1983). Thus, it is likely that media messages in and of themselves are not enough to change stereotypes and prejudices.

Simulations: Eye of the Storm

Upset about the assassination of Martin Luther King, an Iowa schoolteacher developed a simulation to give children some experience of what it would be like to be discriminated against. For 1 day she assigned all blue-eyed students to a minority group. They had to eat and play alone, were ridiculed, or were ignored. The next day, the brown-eyed students were discriminated against. The experience was filmed and titled, "Eye of the Storm." Twenty years later, in follow-up television interviews, participants still reported that the day had tremendous impact on their awareness of what discrimination felt like. Participants in other simulations report heightened awareness and empathy for oppressed groups.

Role Playing

Role playing requires people to imagine what it would be like to be in a certain situation and act as if they are experiencing it. The forms of role playing vary from psychodrama to debates. Psychotherapists use role playing to have patients act as if they were another person and experience a situation from the other person's point of view. A teenager might role play his or her parents, a husband might role play his wife, or a person might role play a punitive boss, all to gain some insight into the motivations and consequences of others' behavior (Kelly, 1955; Moreno, 1953).

Janis and Mann (1965) used role playing to have smokers understand what it was like to die of lung cancer. The research on role playing indicates it is an excellent way to get individuals actively involved in identifying their attitudes toward different groups and to gain insight into what life is like for a minority person, which in turn results in empathy for minority groups and decreases in prejudice (Johnson & F. Johnson, 2000). Role playing also provides an opportunity for rehearsing plausible antiracism arguments, and providing a release from guilt or embarrassment about previous behavior. (See Activities 4.13 and 4.14.)

ACTIVITY **4.13** ■ IMAGINE THIS IS TRUE

1. Form a group of four members. Divide into two pairs.

2. Identify a series of statements concerning stereotypes and prejudice to which you disagree. Study the following examples:

   a. Anyone who wants to work can find a job unless he or she is just lazy.
   b. The welfare system undermines worker motivation because of coddling and fraud.
   c. Interracial marriages are okay but the children suffer.
   d. [Identify your own statement.]

3. Choose one statement to which you both strongly disagree. Then prepare the best case possible for arguing the validity of that statement to the other pair. You have 4 minutes to present your case to the other pair. Plan your presentation as a formal, persuasive argument:

   a. Thesis statement (statement that presents what you are attempting to persuade the other pair to agree with)
   b. Rationale (major points arranged in a logical order to point toward the conclusion)
   c. Conclusion (same as the thesis statement)

4. Each pair presents its "best case" to the other pair.

5. In your group of four, write down five conclusions about what you have learned from the experience.

ACTIVITY **4.14** ■ WHAT MY LIFE WOULD BE LIKE

1. Form a group of four members. Divide into two pairs.

2. If you are white, choose a minority toward which a great deal of prejudice exists in U.S. society (African Americans, Native Americans). If you are a minority group member, you are to role play being white. Working cooperatively with your partner, complete the following tasks:

   a. Imagine you are born a member of the group you have chosen. Write a one-page essay on what your infancy, childhood, adolescence, and young adult life would be like.
   b. Present the contents of your essay to the other pair.
   c. Listen carefully to their presentation.
   d. Working as a group of four, rewrite each essay to improve its insights into the life of a member of the group on which it focuses.

3. In your group of four, write down five conclusions about what you have learned from the experience.

CONCLUSIONS AND WHAT HAPPENS NEXT

The theories and research on intergroup relations identify three key steps in reducing stereotyping, prejudice, and discrimination. The first step is to establish a cooperative community in which individuals are united under a superordinate identity and a joint effort to achieve compelling mutual goals. Creating positive and productive relationships among diverse individuals requires that diverse individuals actually interact with each other. Contact among members of diverse groups is a necessity. The evidence is clear. Contact results in constructive outcomes only with a cooperative context. The more destructive relationships among the diverse groups in the past, the stronger the cooperation has to be. Without establishing a cooperative relationship, no reduction of stereotyping and prejudice among diverse individuals is possible.

Whether a community flourishes or disintegrates depends on how conflicts are managed. If stereotyping and prejudice have to be reduced, then by definition conflict has occurred in the past, is occurring in the present, and is expected to occur in the future. To improve relationships among diverse groups, conflicts have to be managed constructively. The idea is to change a negative relationship to a positive one so that future conflicts are managed constructively rather than destructively. The second step, therefore, is to ensure that all community members share a common set of procedures for managing conflicts. Two types of conflicts are important: conflicts over diverse opinions and conclusions that arise during decision making and conflicts of interests that must be negotiated in a problem-solving way.

Both cooperation and constructive conflict management are based on a set of civic values that underlie the building and maintenance of a growing and thriving community in which diversity is respected, appreciated, and used to enhance productivity. The third step is to teach all students a set of civic values.

SUMMARY

There are a number of interpersonal and intergroup theories of prejudice and discrimination. Psychodynamic theories posit that prejudice is the result of motivation tensions within the individual, such as displaced aggression and authoritarian personality. The theory of realistic group conflict argues that intergroup hostility, antagonism, and prejudice result from competition between groups over resources that each group wants. Realistic conflict theory is related to frustration–aggression theory. Perceptions of relative deprivation can also create intergroup hostility. One of the most common settings for realistic conflict exists between high- and lower-power groups. Whereas the use of power is everpresent in a relationship, it is during conflicts that high- and low-power individuals become most conscious of its use. There is a perennial problem of how low-power groups persuade high-power groups to be motivated to resolve conflicts in good faith.

There are also a number of intergroup conflict theories. Sherif conducted a series of studies on creating and then reducing intergroup conflict. He found that creating intergroup conflict was easy. Resolving it was not. Contact during a pleasant activity did not resolve intergroup conflict; instead the situations were used to engage in hostile activities. Establishing a common enemy did resolve the conflict by transferring it onto another group. The only effective procedure for resolving intergroup conflict was the establishment of superordinate goals.

Blake and Mouton investigated the process of resolving intergroup conflict by examining what happens within the group, between the groups, and between negotiators representing the groups. The most well-known theory is contact theory, which specifies that contact between members of diverse groups can have positive impact if the groups are involved in cooperative efforts, personal interactions take place among members of the different groups, the building of positive relationships is supported by authorities and norms, and the groups have equal status in the situation. Such interactions enhance the sophistication of everyone involved and provide the setting in which culture clashes and misunderstandings can be managed constructively.

CHAPTER FIVE

SOCIAL JUDGMENT THEORY

INTERPERSONAL RELATIONSHIPS

The sixth step of maximizing the promise (and minimizing the dangers) of diversity and pluralism is to understand the social judgment process and how to create the process of acceptance while avoiding the process of rejection. Although it is clear that contact among diverse individuals is necessary if negative attitudes are to be reduced and an appreciation for diversity is to be developed, the nature of the contact and the specifics of the required interaction are somewhat unclear. Social interdependence theory is an attempt to specify the dynamics of the interaction needed to develop positive interaction and attitudes among diverse individuals.

Relationships are built on *interdependence* (Johnson, 2000). People reach out to others because they have goals (a) they want to pursue that other people share and/or (b) that require the participation of other people as well as themselves. A change in state of one person, therefore, causes a change in the state of all persons involved. To form a relationship, interaction is necessary. All interaction is based on a *cycle of social interaction* that involves perceiving what the other person is doing, deciding how to respond, taking action, and then perceiving the other person's response (see Figure 5.1).

In this cycle individuals have (1) a set of *goals* based on their needs, interests, personality, and relevant roles, (2) a set of *roles* (male or female, adult or child,

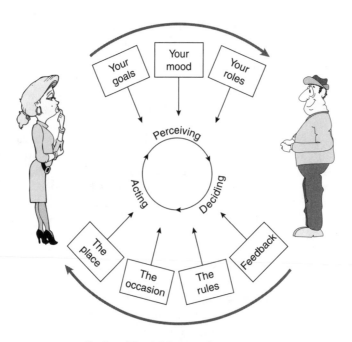

FIGURE 5.1   Cycle of Social Interaction

teacher or student, host or guest) that affect how they interact with each other, and (3) a *mood* based on personality, past events, others' behavior, physical setting, and significance of the interaction. The interaction takes place within a *physical setting* in which the purpose of the setting, color, noise, and lighting affect mood and the rules that prescribe appropriate behavior. The nature of the *occasion* (party, wedding, funeral, sports event) limits the goals participants can pursue. *Social rules,* both general and specific to the occasion and setting, influence behavior.

Finally, *feedback* is received as other people react to what participants say and do in the situation. On the basis of feedback, participants adjust their goals, reinterpret their roles, and refine their understanding of the rules. The social interaction cycle is fundamental to all interpersonal interaction and provides the context in which individuals build and sustain relationships.

Relationships are not always positive. Examples abound of human indifference to other's suffering and problems. Individuals have watched someone being killed without attempting to help; heard a woman in the next room fall off a stepladder and injure herself without asking whether she needed assistance; walked casually by, around, and over a woman with a broken leg lying on a sidewalk; administered, in blind obedience to an authority, painful electric shocks to another human being even after the person screamed in pain, pounded on the door, begged to be released, and then fell into ominous silence; physically and psychologically abused spouses and/or children; and through fear, hate, and prejudice deprived other people of their civil rights, robbed them of their freedom, and even killed them. Despite the suffering humans can cause each other, relationships are the key to human productivity and psychological health.

FORMING AND MAINTAINING POSITIVE RELATIONSHIPS

Thousand of years of speculating about the antecedents of interpersonal attraction have taken place. The most typical explanations are that people most like those (1) whose beliefs and interests are similar to their own; (2) who have some skills, abilities, and competencies they admire; (3) who have some pleasant or admirable qualities, such as loyalty, reasonableness, honesty, and kindness; (4) who like us; and (5) whom we expect to meet our needs (Johnson, 1970; Watson & Johnson, 1972).

A more adequate explanation of the antecedents and causes of caring and committed relationships may be found in the examination of three factors: preinteraction attitudes, physical proximity, and actual interaction. The following may be posited (Johnson & Johnson, 1980; 1989):

1. Preinteraction attitudes influence interpersonal attraction.
2. Physical proximity is a necessary but not sufficient condition for forming caring and committed relationships.
3. A cooperative context is a necessary and a sufficient condition for forming caring and committed relationships. A cooperative context promotes a process of acceptance whereas competitive and individualistic contexts promote a process of rejection.

Preinteraction Attitudes

In many cases, individuals do not meet each other without having some impressions of what the other individual is like. The most interesting case of preinteraction attitudes is when individuals are initially prejudiced toward each other. Individuals from different ethnic groups and people with and without disabilities have negative attitudes toward each other before they interact.

In the United States considerable prejudice and mistrust tends to come between members of majority and minority groups (Scott, 1979). When schools are desegregated, for example, both majority and minority students have initial prejudices and negative attitudes toward each other. Evidence indicates that white students have negative stereotypes of black students and vice versa (Johnson & Johnson, 1989). In one's own ethnic group, sociometric choices have been more common than other ethnic group nominations in the 1930s, the 1940s, consistently throughout the 1950s and 1960s, and into the 1970s. Even when students are asked to rate their associates as preferred playmates or work companions rather than as best friends, one's own ethnic group choices dominate other ethnic group choices. As individuals get older, furthermore, solidification of one's own ethnic group choices increases over other ethnic group choices.

Individuals with disabilities are viewed by their nondisabled peers in negative and prejudiced ways, whether the children and adolescents with disabilities are in the same or separate classrooms (Johnson & Johnson, 1989). Many teachers and students without disabilities have negative evaluations of students with disabilities and low expectations for their performance, regardless of (a) the amount of time spent in close physical proximity, (b) the fact that the behavior of students with disabilities has often been documented to be no different from the behavior of students without disabilities, and (c) the observation that the presence of students with a history of engaging in inappropriate behavior (i.e., emotionally disturbed) does not necessarily create a disrupting effect on the regular class. Some evidence, furthermore, suggests that the stigmas attached to disabilities transfer across settings. Even when children with learning disabilities attend new schools with new classmates, they continue to be rejected.

Thus, interpersonal attraction among individuals does not usually begin at a neutral point when they first meet. Stigmatization of each other by majority and minority individuals, as well as by individuals with and without disabilities, takes place even before direct contact begins. In fact, any categorization rule that provides a basis for classifying an individual as belonging to one social grouping as distinct from another can be sufficient to produce differentiation of attitudes toward the two groups in and of itself. In other words, preinteraction attitudes, both positive and negative, exist. Positive attitudes lead to an expectation of rewarding interaction, and negative attitudes lead to an expectation of nonrewarding interaction.

Physical Proximity

If physical proximity were sufficient to create positive relationships all theorizing could end at this point, especially if physical proximity could create positive relationships among heterogeneous individuals who were initially prejudiced toward each other. It does not. Physical proximity among heterogeneous individuals (in terms of ethnic membership and disability conditions) is the beginning of an opportunity, but like all opportunities, it carries a risk of making things worse as well as the possibility of making things better. When diverse individuals are brought into proximity, two results are possible:

1. Constructive, positive relationships characterized by a reduction of stereotyping and prejudice
2. Hostile, negative relationships characterized by increased prejudice, stereotyping, and even hatred

Physical proximity does not mean that minority and majority individuals will like and accept each other or that they will automatically stigmatize, stereotype, and reject each other. Whether positive or negative outcomes result from physical proximity among diverse individuals depends on how their interaction is structured (i.e., whether student–student interaction is structured competitively, individualistically, or cooperatively).

Ethnic Desegregation

The ethnic desegregation that has occurred in the United States' schools has produced a mixture of positive, negative, and neutral results (Johnson & Johnson, 1989). Negative outcomes seem more frequent than positive ones, with some reviewers finding mixed results with no predominant effect or with methodological problems so severe that no conclusion is possible. Stephan and Rosenfield (1978a) noted that desegregation reduced the prejudice of blacks toward whites in only 13 percent of the school systems studied; the prejudice of blacks toward whites increased in about as many cases as it decreased. Schofield (1978) and St. John (1975) noted that individuals in desegregated schools often become less accepting of members of other ethnic groups over time and that ethnic cleavage becomes more pronounced over time.

Relatively few cross-ethnic friendships seem to emerge in desegregated classrooms. Criswell (1939) found elementary children were significantly more likely to nominate as friends other children from their own ethnic group. Singleton (1974) found that third-graders rated a majority of same ethnic group peers as best liked. Rosenberg and Simmons (1971) report that even as many as 92 percent of third choices for friends by black individuals in a desegregated school are within their own ethnic group.

Studies of direct interaction between majority and ethnic minority individuals indicate that same ethnic group contact is more frequent than cross-ethnic interaction from preschool through early adolescence. Shaw (1973) found in a study (that lasted over a year) of fourth, fifth, and sixth grades in a recently desegregated school that association with members of the other ethnic group led to less acceptance of members of the other ethnic group. Schofield and Sagar (1977) conducted daily observation of seating arrangements in the cafeteria of a junior high school attended by adolescents who had chosen to attend (and whose families had chosen for them to attend) an integrated rather than a segregated school. A typical daily observation in this study involved 138 white and 190 black individuals. Random distribution of these individuals within the occupied seats in the cafeteria would have resulted in 67 side-by-side and 41 face-to-face interethnic adjacencies. They found that ethnic membership was a significant grouping criterion. Only 13 and 9 of the respected adjacencies were actually observed.

Perhaps the most extensive study of cross-ethnic proximity was conducted in Riverside, California (Gerard & Miller, 1975). They found increased ethnic encapsulation over time. Apparently as a consequence of being faced with social rejection, minority children showed little stability over time in the number of white children they picked as friends. Years after the schools were voluntarily desegregated, black, white, and Mexican American individuals tended not to associate with each other but rather to hang together in their own ethnic clusters. Relatively few cross-ethnic friendships emerged.

In cross-ethnic situations, therefore, physical proximity in and of itself is not sufficient to produce interpersonal attraction and positive interaction patterns. The conditions under which physical proximity does and does not lead to improved ethnic relationships are not clear from the general research on ethnic desegregation.

Inclusion

Consistent with the research on ethnic integration, several studies indicate that placing individuals with and without disabilities in close physical proximity (e.g., the same classroom) may increase prejudice toward, stereotyping of, and rejection of peers with disabilities in individuals without disabilities (Johnson & Johnson, 1989). On the other hand, evidence also shows that placing individuals with and without disabilities in the same classroom may result in more positive attitudes of individuals without disabilities toward their peers with disabilities.

Proximity Is Not Enough

The research on cross-ethnic and cross-disability interaction is consistent. Constructive interaction and positive relationships require something more than simple proximity. The same may be true for homogeneous populations as well. In an all-white college student sample, Marwell and Schmidt (1975) found that visibility of a partner did not reduce exploitation and antisocial behavior directed toward the partner. Some form of social contact had to be initiated. Thus, placing majority and minority individuals in the same classroom or situation may be a necessary condition for promoting positive relationships, but it does not seem to be a sufficient condition. Individuals must interact with each other.

The reasons why physical proximity is not sufficient to produce positive relationships among heterogeneous individuals may include (a) initial negative emotions and stereotypes, (b) the strain of interacting with a stigmatized person, (c) the paternalistic tendency to be overfriendly initially, and (d) ambivalent feelings.

NEGATIVE EMOTIONS AND STEREOTYPES

Interactions among members of diverse groups is commonly associated with negative emotions. Interactions with outgroup members, especially when group membership is highly salient, can be fraught with anxiety, discomfort, fears of appearing prejudiced or intolerant, and other negative emotions. These negative emotions increase the likelihood of self-censorship, misattribution, and stereotype confirmation (Bodenhausen, 1993; Stephan & Stephan, 1985; Wilder, 1993).

Anxiety about interacting with members of other groups may be especially destructive to building constructive relationships. Generally, groups that experience greater anxiety in an intergroup situation have more biased attitudes (Stephan & Stephan, 1985; Wilder & Shapiro, 1989a; 1989b). Being a numerical minority in a situation may especially raise anxiety levels. Islam and Hewstone (1993), for example, found that minority Hindus felt more anxious in intergroup contact situations than did majority Muslims. Balancing the membership of majority and minority individuals may reduce anxiety.

INTERACTION STRAIN

During the initial interaction between classmates with and without disabilities, the individuals without disabilities may feel discomfort and show *interaction strain*. A number of studies have found that persons without physical disabilities reported discomfort and uncertainty in interaction with peers who had physical disabilities (Johnson & Johnson, 1989). Individuals interacting with a person who has physical disabilities have been found to exhibit greater motor inhibition; greater physiological arousal; less variability in their behavior, quickly terminating interaction, expressing opinions not representative of their actual beliefs, fewer gestures, and more reported discomfort in the interaction; and in the case of a person said to have epilepsy, greater maintenance of physical distance. Jones (1970), furthermore, found that college students without disabilities who performed a learning task in the presence of a blind confederate (as opposed to a sighted confederate) reported stronger beliefs that they would have performed better on the task if the blind person had not been present, even when the actual performance data indicated that the presence of a blind or sighted person had no significant effects on the college students' achievement.

Individuals without disabilities may not be the only ones experiencing interaction strain in the mainstreaming situation (Johnson & Johnson, 1989). Individuals with disabilities may feel tension and discomfort when interacting with peers without disabilities, often feel less appreciated, find tasks more difficult, perform at a lower level, and expect to be viewed negatively and to be rejected by others.

Paternalism

Another aspect of interaction between individuals with and without disabilities is that the norm to be kind to the former may result in overfriendliness by the latter in initial encounters, which usually decreases with further interaction (Kleck, 1966). Individuals with disabilities tend not to receive accurate feedback concerning the appropriateness of their own behavior and tend not to experience the normal behavior of peers without disabilities (Hastorf, Northcraft, & Picciotto, 1979). As a result, they become socially "handicapped" and believe that other people like them less the better those others get to know them.

Ambivalence

There seems to be considerable ambivalence on the part of individuals without disabilities when interacting with individuals with disabilities (Johnson & Johnson, 1989). Public, verbalized attitudes toward people with disabilities are often favorable, whereas deeper, unverbalized feelings frequently involve rejection. Help tends to be more readily given to a person with disabilities when the helping does not entail sustained social contact. Reactions to a person with disabilities or minority person's actions tend to be amplified (positive or negative) depending on whether they have favorable or unfavorable consequences for the person without disabilities or majority person.

Due to negative preinteraction stereotypes and prejudices, interaction strain, paternalism, and ambivalence, physical proximity may be more likely to increase prejudice and rejection than to result in acceptance and liking. In addition to physical proximity, the interaction among heterogeneous individuals has to be carefully structured.

Cooperative Context

Preinteraction attitudes influence but do not guarantee positive or negative relationships. Physical proximity is a necessary but not sufficient condition for positive relationships. Whether positive or negative relationships develop depends on whether interaction actually takes place among individuals and whether the interaction occurs within a cooperative, competitive, or individualistic context. There is considerable evidence that cooperative experiences, compared with competitive and individualistic ones, promote more positive, committed, and caring relationships regardless of differences in ethnic, cultural, language, economic, gender, ability, or other differences (Johnson & Johnson, 1989).

When people cooperate, they tend to like each other more, trust each other more, be more candid with each other, and be more willing to listen to and to be influenced by each other (Johnson & Johnson, 1989). When people compete or work individualistically, liking, trust, influence, and candor tend to decrease. The impact of positive interdependence is enhanced when members have equal status and social norms and authorities promote positive relationships and friendship formation

(Allport, 1954; Watson, 1947; Williams, 1947). Social judgment theory was developed to explicate the powerful effects a cooperative context has on relationships among diverse individuals.

SOCIAL JUDGMENT THEORY

To establish that a relationship between cooperation and interpersonal attraction exists is not enough. The more important question is, Why does the relationship exist? To determine why a relationship between cooperative experiences and interpersonal attraction exists, the mediating variables must be specified. The answer may be that a process of acceptance or rejection takes place depending on whether interaction takes place within a context of positive, negative, or no interdependence (Johnson & Johnson, 1980; 1989).

Process of Acceptance

The *process of acceptance* may be defined as relationships becoming more and more caring and committed as proximity and interaction continue (see Figure 5.2). The process of acceptance begins with *positive interdependence,* which exists when group members perceive that they can reach their goals if and only if the other members also do so (Deutsch, 1962; Johnson & Johnson, 1989). Group members must believe that they "sink or swim together" in striving to achieve important mutual goals. Positive interdependence may be structured through mutual goals, joint rewards, shared resources, complementary roles, divisions of labor, and a mutual identity.

Striving for mutual benefit requires *promotive interaction*—assisting, helping, sharing, and encouraging each other's efforts to achieve. Promotive interaction may be contrasted with *oppositional interaction*—individuals attempting to obstruct and frustrate each other's goal achievement, and with *no interaction*—individuals ignoring, neither facilitating nor frustrating, each other's goal achievement (see Figure 5.3). The more promotive (as opposed to oppositional or no) interaction among

FIGURE 5.2   Process of Acceptance

FIGURE 5.3   Process of Rejection

individuals, the greater the resulting interpersonal attraction (Johnson & Johnson, 1989).

It may be posited that positive interdependence leads to promotive interaction, which, in turn, leads to interpersonal attraction via a number of mediating variables. More specifically, the following propositions may be made (Johnson & Johnson, 1980; 1989).

The relationship between cooperative experiences and interpersonal attraction may be partially caused by the frequent and accurate communication occurring among collaborators. Frequent, accurate, and open communication (a) is required to coordinate efforts to maximize mutual benefit and gain; (b) involves giving and receiving help, assistance, encouragement, and support; and (c) results in understanding each other's needs, interests, perspectives, abilities, and reasoning processes. To coordinate efforts to achieve, collaborators communicate as they encourage, support, help, and assist each other.

Effective coordination and communication requires understanding each other's conclusions, needs, interests, perspectives, abilities, and reasoning processes. Doing so results in realistically knowing each other on a personal level and in seeing each other as complexes of qualities (who persons are) rather than as complexes of performances (what persons do). The coordination, mutual helping, and personal relationships result in interpersonal attraction among group members. Thus, the more frequently, accurately, and openly the communication is aimed at facilitating each other's success, the greater the interpersonal attraction is.

The relationship between cooperative experiences and interpersonal attraction may be partially caused by the accuracy with which collaborators are able to understand each other's perspectives. *Social perspective-taking* is the ability to understand how a situation appears to another person and how that person is reacting cognitively and emotionally to the situation. The opposite of perspective taking is *egocentrism,* the embeddedness in one's own viewpoint to the extent that one is unaware of other points of view. Egocentrism is related to competitive and individualistic attitudes and efforts whereas perspective-taking ability and accuracy is related to cooperative attitudes and efforts.

Cooperative experiences tend to promote greater cognitive and emotional perspective-taking abilities than either competitive or individualistic experiences. The more accurate one's perspective taking is, the greater one's empathy with, understanding of, and altruism for others is. Mutual understanding resulting from efforts to enhance mutual benefit increase liking. Understanding the perspectives of others results in viewing the world from a broader and more sophisticated personal perspective. Accurate perspective taking results in an awareness that one is liked and accepted by others; one then reciprocates, which creates a cycle of increasing liking among cooperators. Thus, within a cooperative context, the more accurate the understanding of other's perspectives is, the greater the interpersonal attraction is.

The relationship between cooperative experiences and interpersonal attraction may be partially caused by the mutual influence that occurs among collaborators. *Inducibility* exists when individuals are receptive to others' attempts to influence them. Cooperation tends to increase one's openness to be influenced by others whereas competitive and individualistic experiences tend to create resistance to other's influence. Being influenced to engage in more effective and efficient actions (thereby being more successful) creates appreciation and liking. Generally, we like people we can influence and we like people who use friendly (persuasion and problem-solving) influence strategies when interacting with us. Within a cooperative context, therefore, the greater the inducibility among individuals is, the greater the interpersonal attraction is.

The relationship between cooperative experiences and interpersonal attraction may be partially caused by the differentiated and multidimensional views collaborators hold of each other. The more *differentiated* (taking into account many different characteristics), *dynamic* (being modified from situation to situation), and *realistic* (accurate) one's views of collaborators are, the more one likes and identifies with them and the greater the group cohesion is. A multidimensional, dynamic, and realistic view of another person incorporates many different categories—each category is assigned a weight as to its importance according to the demands of any specific situation, and the weight or salience of each category changes as the requirements of the situation change. New information concerning the person is admitted to one's impression as it becomes relevant. The conceptualization of the person stays in a dynamic state of change, open to modification with new information and takes into account situational factors.

The more *monopolistic* (single-dimensional) and *static* (unchanging from situation to situation) the views of others are, the less they will be liked. A *monopolistic, stereotyped, and static* view of another person focuses on only one or two dimensions and is permanently fixed regardless of new information received. Thus, unrealistic, stereotypic views of others generally result. Monopolistic impressions by their very nature are static and oversimplified because of their rigid weighting of a few characteristics of primary potency regardless of the demands of the current situation. In competitive and individualistic situations, individuals tend to organize information about others on the basis of the few characteristics most salient for individual high performance. The perceived distribution of ability becomes polarized and shared. A person is a winner or a loser, but nowhere in between.

Within cooperative situations, a multidimensional, dynamic, and realistic view of others is generated. Negative stereotypes tend to lose their primary potency and to be reduced when interactions reveal enough detail that group members are seen as individuals rather than as members of an ethnic group. All collaborators become "one of us." In other words, cooperation widens the sense of who's in the group, and "they" become "we."

The relationship between cooperative experiences and interpersonal attraction may be partially caused by the higher self-esteem of collaborators. The better one is known, liked, and supported, the higher one's self-esteem tends to be. High self-esteem tends to be related to self-acceptance, liking of others, and a lack of prejudices. Fein and Spencer (1997), for example, found that increases in self-esteem resulted in decreases in negative stereotyping, and decreases in self-esteem resulted in increases in negative stereotyping (aimed at increasing the person's self-esteem). Individuals who like themselves tend to like others. Cooperation tends to promote higher self-esteem and healthier processes for deriving conclusions about one's self-worth than does competition or individualistic experiences.

The relationship between cooperative experiences and interpersonal attraction may be partially caused by the greater productivity of collaborators. The greater one's psychological success is, the more one likes those who have contributed to and facilitated that success. Cooperation tends to produce higher achievement and greater productivity than does competitive or individualistic efforts. Liking for collaborators (including majority and minority members) has been found to become progressively more favorable as the groups' success increases.

Finally, the relationship between cooperative experiences and interpersonal attraction may be partially caused by the expectations for enjoyable and productive interactions in the future. The more one expects future interactions to be cooperative, positive and productive, the more one likes others. When one expects to interact with another person, the extent to which one expects the other to facilitate one's goal accomplishment largely determines one's attraction for the other (Johnson & S. Johnson, 1972; S. Johnson & Johnson, 1971).

Process of Rejection

The *process of rejection* may be defined as relationships becoming more and more negative as proximity and interaction continue (see Figure 5.3). It results from interaction within a context of negative or no goal interdependence. Negative goal interdependence promotes oppositional interaction and no goal interaction results in no interaction with peers. Both lead to an avoidance of and/or inaccurate communication; egocentrism; resistance to influence; monopolistic, static, and stereotyped views of others; feelings of rejection and low self-esteem; psychological failure; and expectations of distasteful and unpleasant interactions with others. All these factors promote dislike and rejection among individuals. The diversity among individuals may amplify these characteristics once the process begins.

Each Part of the Process Elicits All Other Parts

The factors involved in the processes of acceptance and rejection are interdependent and each influences the others (see Figure 5.4). Deutsch's (1985) crude law states that positive interdependence creates a variety of interrelated and interdependent outcomes, which, in turn, create greater positive interdependence. Any part of the process elicits all other parts of the process. Frequent and open communication results in better understanding of each other's perspectives, and increased understanding of each other's perspectives leads to more frequent and open communication. The more multidimensional and dynamic is the perception of each other, the higher the self-esteem of everyone involved. This in turn, makes it easier to have multidimensional

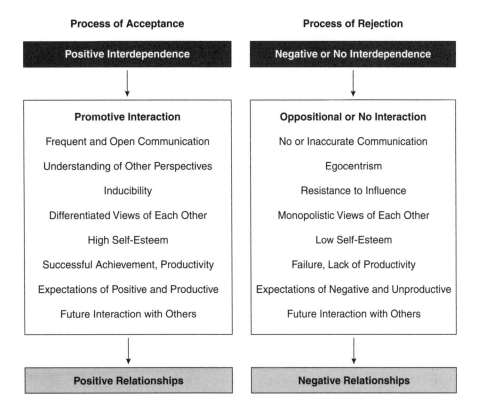

Process of Acceptance	Process of Rejection
Positive Interdependence	**Negative or No Interdependence**
Promotive Interaction	**Oppositional or No Interaction**
Frequent and Open Communication	No or Inaccurate Communication
Understanding of Other Perspectives	Egocentrism
Inducibility	Resistance to Influence
Differentiated Views of Each Other	Monopolistic Views of Each Other
High Self-Esteem	Low Self-Esteem
Successful Achievement, Productivity	Failure, Lack of Productivity
Expectations of Positive and Productive	Expectations of Negative and Unproductive
Future Interaction with Others	Future Interaction with Others
Positive Relationships	**Negative Relationships**

FIGURE 5.4   **Processes of Acceptance and Rejection**

and dynamic views of each other. The many variables related to positive interdependence are interconnected so that they can influence each other. The variables are a gestalt, with each variable being a door into the whole process. You can review the process of acceptance and rejection by completing Activity 5.1.

THE EVIDENCE ON COOPERATIVE EFFORTS

One-hundred eighty studies comparing the relative impact of cooperative, competitive, and individualistic experiences on interpersonal attraction have been conducted. From Table 5.1 it may be seen that cooperation generally promotes greater interpersonal attraction among participants than does competitive (251 to 7, with 151 no difference) or individualistic (184 to 18, with 133 no difference) efforts. These find-

---

ACTIVITY 5.1 ■ **PROCESSES OF ACCEPTANCE AND REJECTION**

Demonstrate your understanding of the processes of acceptance and rejection by matching the definitions with the appropriate characteristic. Check your answers with your partner and explain why your answers are correct.

CHARACTERISTIC

_____ 1. **effective coordination and communication**

_____ 2. **social perspective taking**

_____ 3. **inducibility**

_____ 4. **multidimensional view of others**

_____ 5. **healthy self-esteem**

_____ 6. **achievement**

_____ 7. **expectations for productive future interactions**

DEFINITION

a. Being influenced to engage in more effective and efficient actions (thereby being more successful) creates appreciation and liking.

b. High self-esteem tends to be related to self-acceptance, liking of others, and a lack of prejudices.

c. The more *differentiated* (taking into account many different characteristics), *dynamic* (being modified from situation to situation), and *realistic* (accurate) one's views of others are, the more one likes the other individual.

d. The more one expects future interactions to be positive and productive, the more one likes others.

e. Liking for collaborators (including majority and minority members) tends to become progressively more favorable as the groups' success increases.

f. Liking for others tends to increase the more frequently, openly, and accurately perceptions, ideas, opinions, and beliefs are exchanged.

g. The more one stands in others' shoes and sees the world from the others' viewpoint, the greater one's empathy with, understanding of, altruism for, and liking for others is.

TABLE 5.1 Impact of Social Interdependence on Interpersonal Attraction: Effect Sizes

	MEAN	SD	N
Overall			
Cooperative vs. competitive	0.66	0.49	93
Cooperative vs. individualistic	0.60	0.58	60
Competitive vs. individualistic	0.08	0.70	15
Ethnic Desegregation			
Cooperative vs. competitive	0.52	0.50	40
Cooperative vs. individualistic	0.44	0.51	12
Competitive vs. individualistic	–0.65	0.40	3
Inclusion of Disabled			
Cooperative vs. competitive	0.70	0.35	12
Cooperative vs. individualistic	0.64	0.47	25
Competitive vs. individualistic	–0.16	0.68	5
Homogeneous			
Cooperative vs. competitive	0.76	0.46	53
Cooperative vs. individualistic	0.64	0.60	48
Competitive vs. individualistic	0.26	0.64	12

Source: From *Cooperation and Competition: Theory and Research,* by D. W. Johnson and R. Johnson, 1989, Edina, MN: Interaction Book Company.

ings are strong (effect sizes = 0.66 and 0.60, respectively); the probability that they have occurred by chance is less than 1 in 100,000 or so (z-scores = 17.83 and 12.05, respectively), and it would take thousands of new studies finding exactly no difference to reduce the overall finding to statistical nonsignificance. There seems to be little difference between the relationships developed within competitive and individualistic situations (effect size = 0.08). Cooperation seems to promote better relationships when intergroup competition is absent (effect sizes = 0.77 and 0.63, respectively).

Many of the earliest studies on cross-ethnic relationships found that it is the nature of the contact between members of different ethnic groups, not the frequency, that promotes favorable intergroup attitudes (Johnson & Johnson, 1989). Actual contact between blacks and whites, visiting black lecturers speaking in classrooms, meetings with black professionals, school integration, joint recreational activities in integrated summer camps, voyages of white merchant seamen serving with black seamen, contact within combat infantry platoons, occupational and educational settings, and desegregated residential settings. The results indicate that the greater the degree of cooperation is between majority and minority individuals, the more likely it is that friendly ethnic relationships develop.

Sixty-one studies were found and reviewed comparing the relative effects of two or more goal structures on interpersonal attraction between majority and minority individuals. Cooperative experiences promoted significantly better relationships between white and minority individuals than did competition (effect size = 0.52) or individualistic efforts (effect size = 0.44). Individualistic efforts promoted more positive cross-ethnic relationships than did competition (effect size = –0.65), but the small number of studies makes this finding suggestive only.

Forty-one studies comparing the relative effects of two or more goal structures on interpersonal attraction between individuals with and without disabilities were found and reviewed. Cooperative experiences resulted in much greater interpersonal attraction between these individuals than did competitive (effect size = 0.70) or individualistic (effect size = 0.64) experiences. Individualistic experiences tended to promote greater cross-disability interpersonal attraction than did competition (effect size = 0.16).

One-hundred eleven studies comparing the relation of two or more goal structures on interpersonal attraction between homogeneous subject populations (in terms of ethnic membership and disability status) were found and reviewed. Cooperative experiences promoted greater interpersonal attraction among homogeneous individuals than did competitive (effect size = 0.76) or individualistic (effect size = 0.64) experiences. Competition promoted greater interpersonal attraction than did individualistic experiences (effect size = 0.26).

A central question concerning the impact of social interdependence on interpersonal attraction is whether the relationships formed within cooperative groups extend beyond the group situation. Even though individuals express liking for peers from other ethnic groups or with disability conditions, and in fact interact with them in constructive ways during achievement-oriented situations, whether these relationships and interaction patterns generalize to free-choice situations in which individuals can interact with whomever they wish needs to be determined.

A number of recent studies have demonstrated two results. First, when individuals were placed in postinstructional, free-choice situations, more cross-ethnic interaction occurred when individuals had been in a cooperative rather than a competitive or individualistic situation. Second, individuals who participated in cooperative learning groups had more noninstructional ethnic interactions within the school and more out-of-school interactions than did individuals who participated in individualistic learning situations (Johnson & Johnson, 1989). In other words, the relationships formed within cooperative groups among heterogeneous peers do in fact transfer and carry over into voluntary noninstructional situations both within and outside the school.

One of the most extreme tests of the relationship between cooperative experiences and interpersonal attraction is when "enemies" are placed in a situation within which they have to cooperate. The classic studies were conducted by Muzafer Sherif (1966). These were discussed in Chapter Four. In the early 1950s, Sherif conducted a series of field experiments with 12-year-old boys attending a summer camp. The camp staff consisted of Sherif and his colleagues and students. First, they worked to create cohesive, cooperative groups with a high level of interpersonal attraction among members. Second, they created such a high level of competition among groups that hostility became intense, resulting in food fights, name calling, and sabotage of each other's work whenever the groups were near each other. In testing various methods of reducing the intergroup animosity and creating positive relationships between the "warring" groups, Sherif found that (a) creating social contact in pleasant situations only resulted in the pleasant situation being transformed into an opportunity to express animosity towards each other, and (b) creating an outside enemy suppressed the intergroup conflict by transferring hostility onto a new group. The only method that transformed the animosity into friendships was the creation of superordinate goals that required the participation of all groups in joint action to achieve the goal or avert the disaster. Such goals seem to work only when they are perceived to result from "an act of God" or outside circumstances rather than from a project proposed by one of the groups (Johnson & Lewicki, 1969).

These results provide hope for the future. There are conflicts among diverse groups and individuals that appear to be *intractable* (i.e., conflicts that are deeply important to disputants, unresolved for long periods of time, that have resurfaced repeatedly, and are managed in destructive ways). Intractable conflicts include those over inequality between majority and minority groups, issues such as abortion rights or the death penalty, and among different historical groups in places such as the Middle East, the Balkans, and Northern Ireland. In many areas of the world, countries are faced with violent and deeply acrimonious conflicts among diverse cultural, religious, and ethnic groups that seem intractable. Yet, no matter how intractable a conflict may seem, no matter how much animosity exists among members of different groups, the research demonstrates that regardless of their initial diversity, when individuals are involved in cooperative efforts, positive, caring, and committed relationships result. More specifically, the experience of cooperating to achieve compelling goals that each group cannot achieve on its own can (a) build positive relationships among members of the diverse groups and (b) provide a context within which conflicts may be resolved constructively. (See Box 5.1 for the description of a movement that attempted to unite disparate groups to their advantage.)

OUR RESEARCH ON SOCIAL INTERDEPENDENCE AND CROSS-ETHNIC RELATIONSHIPS

To confirm or disconfirm our model of the processes of acceptance and rejection, we have conducted a 20-year program of research consisting of more than 80 studies (see Johnson & Johnson, 1989). Several of those studies were highly controlled field-experimental studies of cross-ethnic relationships. The measures of interpersonal attraction used included (a) an observation system that classified student–student interactions into task, maintenance, and social statements; (b) an observation system that classified student–student interactions during classroom free time; (c) a social-schema, figure-placement measure consisting of having students position all class members on a classroom diagram according to where they would be during classroom free time; and (d) a sociometric measure of interpersonal attraction consisting of having students write down the names of three students they would like to work with in a future learning group. Our studies addressed five questions.

The first question we addressed was whether cooperative, competitive, and individualistic experiences differentially affected cross-ethnic interaction and relationships. Cooper, Johnson, Johnson, and Wilderson (1980) compared the effects of

■ ■ ■ ■ ■

BOX 5.1
THE AMERICAN INDIAN MOVEMENT

The American Indian Movement (AIM) began formally in the late 1960s under the direction of Clyde Bellecourt, Russell Means, NeeGawNway WeeDun, and others. Prior to that time, the Native Americans belonged to separate and quite distinct tribes. Most of the widely diverse and numerous Native American cultures and languages have disappeared during the past 500 years due to disease, genocide, and ruinous government policies.

In an attempt to eliminate the divisive effects of tribalism, AIM was founded to unite all Native Americans into one organization. AIM's national headquarters are in Minneapolis, Minnesota. AIM's purposes are to promote a philosophy of self-determination deeply rooted in traditional spirituality, cultures, languages, and history. AIM's vision is to articulate clearly the claims of Native Nations, renew the spirituality of Native Americans, and reverse the policies of the United States and Canada and the colonialist governments in Central and South America.

The first mandate of AIM was to ensure the fulfillment of treaties made with the United States. In addition, AIM promotes unifying all Native Americans within a common culture, develops partnerships to address the common needs of the Native Americans, and creates programs and organizations that serve Native Americans. AIM is a powerful voice representing all that is best of surviving Native American cultures and peoples.

cooperative, competitive, and individualistic experiences on cross-ethnic relationships. Sixty students were randomly assigned to conditions stratifying for sex, ethnic membership, and ability. The students were from lower- and working-class families from an inner-city junior high school. The same curriculum was used in all conditions, and teachers were rotated across all conditions. Students participated in the study for 3 hours a day (English, geography, and science classes) for 15 instructional days. The results indicated that cooperation promoted more positive cross-ethnic relationships than did competitive or individualistic experiences.

In a similar study, Johnson and Johnson (1982) randomly assigned 76 students to cooperative, competitive, and individualistic conditions on a stratified random basis controlling for ethnic membership, ability, and sex. The same curriculum was used in all conditions, and teachers were rotated across all conditions. Both behavioral and sociometry measures of interpersonal attraction were used. Students participated in two instructional units for 45 minutes a day for 15 instructional days. Behavioral and attitudinal measures were taken for cross-ethnic interaction during the instructional sessions and during daily free-time periods. They found that cooperative learning promoted more cross-ethnic interaction and more positive cross-ethnic attitudes and relationships than did competitive or individualistic learning.

The second question was whether intergroup competition increased or decreased positive cross-ethnic relationships. Two studies were conducted comparing intergroup competition and intergroup cooperation. Johnson, Johnson, Tiffany, and Zaidman (1984) randomly assigned 51 fourth-grade students to intergroup competition and cooperation conditions, stratifying for minority status and sex. The same curriculum was used in all conditions and teachers were rotated across conditions. Students participated in the study for 55 minutes a day for 10 instructional days. Both behavioral and sociometric measures of interpersonal liking were used. Whereas no differences appeared for within-group cross-ethnic liking, inclusion of minority students and cross-ethnic liking for members of different cooperating groups within the intergroup cooperation condition increased. In other words, the positive cross-ethnic relationships established in the cooperative groups tended to generalize to other cross-ethnic relationships more within the intergroup cooperation than within the intergroup competition condition.

In a follow-up study, Johnson and Johnson (1985) randomly assigned 48 sixth-grade students to intergroup cooperation and competition conditions, stratifying for minority status, ability, and sex. The same curriculum was used in all conditions, and teachers were rotated across all conditions. The students participated in the study for 55 minutes a day for 10 days. Both behavioral and paper-and-pencil measures of interpersonal attraction were used. More positive cross-ethnic relationships within and between groups were promoted by intergroup cooperation than by intergroup competition.

The third question was whether minority students who achieved at a lower level than their majority classmates would be liked. When minority students achieve at a lower level than their majority classmates, they have, in essence, two strikes against them. They may be disliked because they are from a low-status minority, and, additionally, they may be disliked because their low achievement decreases the likelihood of the group winning. Johnson, Johnson, Tiffany, and Zaidman (1983) compared the effects of cooperative and individualistic learning experiences on the relationship between majority students and lower-achieving minority peers.

Forty-eight students (20 minority and 28 majority) were assigned to conditions on a stratified random basis controlling for ethnic membership, sex, social class, and ability level. They participated in the study for 55 minutes a day for 15 instructional days. The same curriculum was used in all conditions, and teachers were rotated across all conditions. Both behavioral and sociometric measures of interpersonal attraction were used. Minority students did in fact achieve at lower levels than did their majority peers. Yet more positive cross-ethnic interaction and relationships were found in the cooperative than in the individualistic condition.

Johnson, Johnson, Tiffany, and Zaidman (1984) found that intergroup competition accentuates the salience of ability and status within cooperative learning groups. Intergroup cooperation produced more participation and more inclusion of minority students than did intergroup cooperation. Although minority students achieved at a lower level than majority students, perceived themselves to be less able as students, and were perceived as needing more academic help, they were viewed as being equally valuable members of the learning groups in the intergroup cooperation condition. In the intergroup competition condition, they were viewed as being less valuable members.

The fourth question was whether the presence of conflict within cooperative groups would create divisive cross-ethnic relationships. Within cooperative groups disagreements and intellectual challenges occur frequently. Such conflicts are "moments of truth" that strengthen relationships or create divisiveness and hostility. Low-achieving students may be at a disadvantage in academic conflicts. When low achievers are minority students, academic conflicts could (a) increase cross-ethnic hostility and rejection and (b) decrease the academic self-esteem of minority students.

Johnson, Johnson, and Tiffany (1984) compared the effects of controversy, debate, and individualistic learning on cross-ethnic relationships. Seventy-two sixth-grade students were randomly assigned to conditions on a stratified random basis controlling for sex, reading ability, and ethnic membership. The same curriculum was used in all conditions, and teachers were rotated across all conditions. Both behavioral and sociometric measures of interpersonal attraction were used.

In all three conditions students studied a controversial issue with materials representing both pro and con views. In the controversy condition each learning group was divided into two pairs representing the pro and con sides. In the debate condition each member of a learning group was assigned a pro or con position to represent in a competition to see who could make the best presentation. In the individualistic condition subjects were given all the pro and con materials and told to learn the material without interacting with other students. Controversy promoted the most cross-ethnic interaction, the most supportive cross-ethnic relationships, and the greatest cross-ethnic liking. It seems that despite the existing prejudices and hostility between majority and minority students, structured academic conflicts characterized by high positive interdependence promote considerable cross-ethnic liking. Minority students, furthermore, felt more successful in the controversy condition than in the debate and individualistic conditions.

The fifth question was whether the cross-ethnic relationships formed within cooperative groups generalize to postinstructional situations. Even though individuals interacted constructively with peers from other ethnic groups and expressed liking for them during achievement-oriented situations, whether these relationships and interaction patterns generalize to free-choice situations in which individuals can interact with whomever they wish needs to be determined. A number of our studies demonstrated that when individuals were placed in postinstructional, free-choice situations there was more cross-ethnic interaction when individuals had been in a cooperative rather than a competitive or individualistic situation (Johnson & Johnson, 1981, 1982; Johnson, Johnson, Tiffany, & Zaidman, 1983). Warring, Johnson, Maruyama, and Johnson (1985) surveyed 74 sixth-grade and 51 fourth-grade students in an ethnically integrated, inner-city elementary school as to the cross-ethnic interactions they had engaged in during the academic year. An Activity Report Scale was given to students to determine with whom they interacted in structured class activities, unstructured class activities, school activities outside of class, and activities in their homes. They found that individuals who participated in cooperative learning groups had more noninstructional ethnic

ACTIVITY **5.2** ■ WHO ARE THESE PEOPLE?

Match the people with their achievements. Check your answers with your partner.

PERSON	ACHIEVEMENTS
_____ **1.** Jane Addams	**a.** Noted author and lecturer (born 1880)
_____ **2.** Helen Keller	**b.** Civil rights and labor activist, diplomat, author (born 1884)
_____ **3.** Florence Nightingale	**c.** Abolitionist feminist, orator (died 1883)
_____ **4.** Eleanor Roosevelt	**d.** Anthropologist born (1901)
_____ **5.** Sojourner Truth	**e.** Operated underground railroad and lead hundreds of slaves to freedom
_____ **6.** Deborah Sampson	**f.** Founded the American Birth Control League
_____ **7.** Margaret Mead	**g.** Nobel laureate, social reformer, pacifist, suffragist (born 1860)
_____ **8.** Margaret Sanger	**h.** First woman elected to Congress
_____ **9.** Nellie Bly	**i.** Revolutionary war soldier who fought as a man (born 1760)
_____ **10.** Jeanette Rankin	**j.** Activist nurse (born 1858)
_____ **11.** Harriet Tubman	**k.** Journalist

interactions within the classroom and school and more out-of-school interactions than did individuals who participated in individualistic learning situations.

The results of our research indicate that cooperative efforts promote more positive cross-ethnic relationships than do competitive or individualistic efforts, that intergroup cooperation increases the frequency of positive cross-ethnic relationships within a class whereas intergroup competition may reduce them, that positive cross-ethnic relationships form within cooperative efforts even when the minority students achieve at lower levels than do the majority students, that intellectual conflicts between majority and minority students can increase cross-ethnic liking within cooperative groups, and that the cross-ethnic relationships formed within cooperative groups generalize to free-time, school, and out-of-school situations.

LATERAL TRANSMISSION OF VALUES

An underlying assumption of school desegregation is that intergroup contact increases educational opportunity and improves the academic performance of minority children. This assumption in turn is based on the assumption that the relation between achievement and characteristics, such as social class, ethnic membership, and so forth, is not immutable but can in fact be altered by processes within the school environment. A specific set of values facilitates achievement. Many, if not

> ■ ■ ■ ■ ■
>
> **BOX 5.2**
> ## PARTIAL HISTORY OF WOMEN'S MOVEMENT
>
> 1848   Seneca Falls Conference is organized by Elizabeth Cady Stanton and Lucretia Mott.
>
> 1869   National Woman Suffrage Association is founded by Elizabeth Cady Stanton and Susan B. Anthony.
>
> 1869   American Equal Rights Association is founded; Susan B. Anthony is elected first president.
>
> 1869   Wyoming becomes the first territory to give women the vote on equal terms.
>
> 1870   Women vote for first time in Utah Territory.
>
> 1871   Victoria Woodhull presents petition to Judiciary Committee of House of Representatives, making case for universal female suffrage (rejected by congressmen).
>
> 1872   Susan B. Anthony is arrested for voting.
>
> 1879   Women lawyers gain right to practice law before Supreme Court by act of Congress.
>
> 1912   Girl Scouts is founded by Juliette Low.
>
> 1913   Harriet Tubman, who operated underground railroad and lead hundreds of slaves to freedom, dies.
>
> 1916   Jeanette Rankin of Montana is first woman elected to Congress.
>
> 1917   Margaret Sanger founds the American Birth Control League.
>
> 1920   Nineteenth Amendment to U.S. Constitution is ratified.
>
> 1925   Florence Sabin becomes first woman in National Academy of Sciences.
>
> 1932   Amelia Earhart is first woman pilot to fly the Atlantic Ocean solo.
>
> 1953   Clare Booth Luce is first U.S. woman appointed to major diplomatic post.
>
> 1966   National Organization for Women (NOW) is founded.
>
> 1972   Equal Rights Amendment is passed by Congress, but in 1982 fails three states short of ratification.
>
> 1972   Title IX legislation is passed by Congress.
>
> 1973   *Roe v. Wade* decision on abortion is made by Supreme Court.
>
> 1994   In *NOW v. Scheidler*, Supreme Court gives okay to treat antiabortion terrorists like racketeers.

most, white middle-class children possess these values. A lesser proportion of lower-class children do. The *lateral transmission of values* hypothesis states that mixing lower-class and middle-class children in the same classroom where there is a numerical majority of middle-class individuals results in lower-class children internalizing these achievement-related values and that internalization leads them to improve their academic performance.

Elements of support for the lateral transmission of values may be found. Mussen (1953) documented that achievement-related values are more prevalent among middle-class white than among lower-class minority children. Documentation exists that specific values facilitate achievement (e.g., McClelland, 1961), social influence processes result in the norms of the numerical majority being passed on to the minority (e.g., Asch, 1952; Duval, 1976; Jones & Gerard, 1967), and, within limits, performance levels are responsive to standards (e.g., Atkinson, 1964). Thus, it seems logical that lower-class children who are in the same classroom as middle-class children internalize the achievement-related values held by the middle-class children.

Direct testing of the hypothesis, however, has not met with success (Maruyama, Miller, & Holtz 1986). Several reasons may explain why. First, as has been well documented in this chapter, proximity does not mean acceptance. For values to be transmitted from one person to another, a positive relationship must exist (Johnson, 1979). Simply placing individuals in the same classroom does not mean they will interact, get to know each other, clarify their values, and modify their values on the basis of the success and effectiveness of the values.

Second, the vast majority of classrooms follow a competitive or individualistic model of instruction that creates a process of rejection rather than a process of acceptance. For the lateral transmission of values hypothesis to be tested, individuals must be placed in heterogeneous cooperative learning groups for most of the school day (not just an hour a week).

Third, it may take some time for values to be clarified, learned, transmitted, and internalized from one person to another. Years of working together cooperatively may be necessary.

SUMMARY

Social judgment theory states that individuals become involved in a process of acceptance or rejection that determines whether they like or dislike each other and perceive each other in positive or negative ways. The processes of acceptance or rejection are a gestalt within which any part of the process tends to elicit all other parts of the process. When individuals cooperate with each other, the positive interdependence and promotive interaction result in frequent and accurate communication, accurate perspective taking, inducibility, multidimensional views of each other, feelings of psychological acceptance and self-esteem, psychological success, and expectations of rewarding and productive future interaction. When individuals compete or work individualistically, the negative and no interdependence and oppositional or no interaction result in absent or inaccurate communication, in egocentrism, in resistance to influence, in monopolistic and static views of each other, in feelings of psychological rejection and low self-esteem, in psychological failure, and in expectations for oppositional interaction in the future.

To promote positive relationships among diverse individuals, therefore, situations need to be structured cooperatively, and the use of competitive and individualistic structures should be avoided. In the next two chapters, therefore, how learning situations can be structured cooperatively is discussed.

CHAPTER SIX

COOPERATIVE LEARNING

INTRODUCTION

The Penan tribe in Borneo have one word for "he," "she," and "it";
they have six words for "we."   —*Wade Davis*

The seventh step of maximizing the promise (and minimizing the dangers) of diversity and pluralism is to structure cooperative interaction among diverse individuals. There is power to working in groups. A group of staff and trustees at the Bronx Educational Services shaped the first nationally recognized adult literacy school. A group of citizens in Harlem founded and operated the first Little League there in more than 40 years. Motorola used small manufacturing groups to produce the world's lightest, smallest, and highest-quality cellular phones (with only a few hundred parts versus more than a thousand for the competition). Ford became America's most profitable car company in 1990 on the strength of using small groups to build its Taurus model.

Groups have existed for as long as there have been humans (and even before). Groups have been the subject of countless books. Every human society has used groups to accomplish its goals and celebrated when the groups were successful. It was groups that built the pyramids, constructed the Temple of Artemis at Ephesus, created the Colossus of Rhodes, and the hanging gardens of Babylon. It is obvious that groups outperform individuals, especially when performance requires multiple skills, judgments, and experiences. Many educators, however, overlook opportunities to use groups to enhance student learning and increase their own success. Complete Activity 6.1 to acquaint yourself with causes for missed opportunities to capitalize on the power of groups.

The opportunity to capitalize on the power of groups in schools begins with understanding the answers to the following questions:

1. What is cooperative learning
2. What are the differences among cooperative, competitive, and individualistic efforts?
3. Why use cooperative learning? What are the expected outcomes resulting from cooperative efforts?
4. What are the basic elements of cooperative learning that make it work? How do you structure the basic elements into cooperative lessons?
5. What are the ways positive interdependence may be structured into cooperative lessons?
6. How do you teach students the social skills they need to work effectively in groups?

ACTIVITY **6.1** ■ CAUSES OF MISSED OPPORTUNITIES TO CAPITALIZE ON POWER OF GROUPS

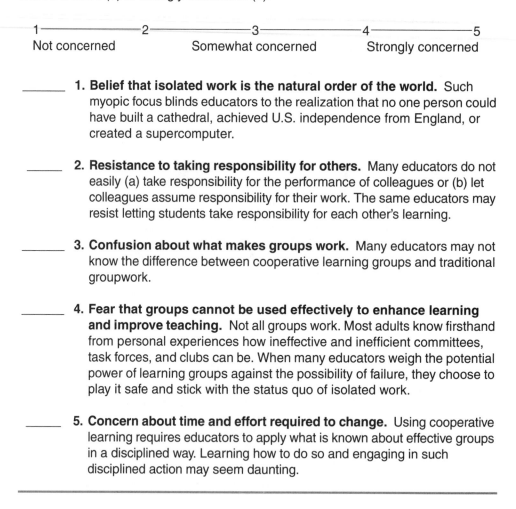

DIRECTIONS:

Consider the five sources of resistance to using cooperative learning described in the following list. Use the following rating scale to rate your attitude to each source from not concerned (1) to strongly concerned (5).

1————————2————————3————————4————————5
Not concerned   Somewhat concerned   Strongly concerned

_____ 1. **Belief that isolated work is the natural order of the world.** Such myopic focus blinds educators to the realization that no one person could have built a cathedral, achieved U.S. independence from England, or created a supercomputer.

_____ 2. **Resistance to taking responsibility for others.** Many educators do not easily (a) take responsibility for the performance of colleagues or (b) let colleagues assume responsibility for their work. The same educators may resist letting students take responsibility for each other's learning.

_____ 3. **Confusion about what makes groups work.** Many educators may not know the difference between cooperative learning groups and traditional groupwork.

_____ 4. **Fear that groups cannot be used effectively to enhance learning and improve teaching.** Not all groups work. Most adults know firsthand from personal experiences how ineffective and inefficient committees, task forces, and clubs can be. When many educators weigh the potential power of learning groups against the possibility of failure, they choose to play it safe and stick with the status quo of isolated work.

_____ 5. **Concern about time and effort required to change.** Using cooperative learning requires educators to apply what is known about effective groups in a disciplined way. Learning how to do so and engaging in such disciplined action may seem daunting.

7. How do you structure group processing to ensure cooperative groups continually improve their functioning?
8. How do you assess the quality and quantity of students' work in cooperative groups?
9. How do you structure cooperation among faculty and staff to ensure that cooperative efforts are institutionalized throughout school life?

LEARNING TOGETHER VERSUS LEARNING ALONE

This chapter explains how to use the power of groups to maximize each student's learning. Doing so requires educators to apply the basics of how groups work with discipline and diligence. Although the power of cooperative learning is obvious to many educators, the discipline needed to use cooperative learning effectively is not. The basic elements that make cooperation work cannot be taken for granted or treated lightly. They must be carefully and precisely structured into every learning group. Understanding how to use cooperation effectively begins with knowing the difference between cooperative, competitive, and individualistic efforts.

Students' learning goals may be structured to promote cooperative, competitive, or individualistic efforts. To accomplish this teachers may structure lessons in one of three ways, respectively:

1. Students can work together in small groups, ensuring that all members complete the assignment.
2. Students can engage in a win–lose struggle to see who is best in completing the assignment.
3. Students can work independently to complete the assignment.

In every classroom, instructional activities are aimed at accomplishing goals and are conducted under a goal structure. A *learning goal* is a desired future state of demonstrating competence or mastery in the subject area being studied. The *goal structure* specifies the ways in which students interact with each other and the teacher during the instructional session. Each goal structure has its place (Johnson & Johnson, 1989; 1994). In the ideal classroom, all students would learn how to work cooperatively with others, compete for fun and enjoyment, and work autonomously on their own. The teacher decides which goal structure to implement within each lesson. The most important goal structure, and the one that should be used the majority of the time in learning situations, is cooperation.

WHAT IS COOPERATIVE LEARNING?

To understand the nature of cooperative learning, it is necessary to place it within the broader context of social interdependence (see Figure 6.1, page 136). *Social interdependence* exists when each individual's outcomes are affected by the actions of others (Deutsch, 1949; Johnson & Johnson, 1989). Social interdependence may be positive or negative. *Positive interdependence* (cooperation) exists when individuals work together to achieve mutual goals, *negative interdependence* (competition) exists when individuals work against each other to achieve a goal that only one or a few may attain. *Social independence*, in which the outcomes of each person are unaffected by others' actions, is characterized by individualistic actions.

Cooperation is working together to accomplish shared goals. Within cooperative situations, individuals seek outcomes that are beneficial to themselves and beneficial to all other group members. *Cooperative learning* is the instructional use of small groups in which students work together to maximize their own and each other's learning. In contrast, *competitive learning* is when students work against each other to achieve an academic goal, such as a grade of A, which only one or a few students can attain; and *individualistic learning* is when students work by themselves to accomplish learning goals unrelated to those of other students. In cooperative and individualistic learning, you evaluate student efforts on a criteria-referenced basis whereas in competitive learning, you grade students on a norm-referenced basis. Whereas the appropriate use of competitive and individualistic learning is limited, you may structure any learning task in any subject area with any curriculum cooperatively. Activity 6.2 provides an exercise in reviewing the meanings of cooperative, competitive, and individualistic learning.

ACTIVITY **6.2** ■ CONCEPTS AND DEFINITIONS

Given below are three concepts and three definitions taken from Deutsch (1962) and Johnson and Johnson (1989). Match the correct definition with the correct concept. Find a partner and (a) compare answers and (b) explain your reasoning for each answer.

_____ **1. competitive efforts**

a. Exists when there is positive interdependence among students' goal attainments; students perceive that they can reach their goals if and only if the other students in the group also reach their goals

_____ **2. individualistic efforts**

b. Exists when there is negative interdependence among goal achievements; students perceive that they can obtain their goals if and only if the other students in the class fail to obtain their goals

_____ **3. cooperative efforts**

c. Exists when there is no interdependence among goal achievements; students perceive that the achievement of their goals is unrelated to what other students do

WHY USE COOPERATIVE LEARNING?

During the past 100 years, over 550 experimental and 100 correlational studies have been conducted by a wide variety of researchers in different decades with subjects of different ages, in different areas of study, and in different settings. (For a detailed review of the research on cooperative, competitive, and individualistic efforts, see Johnson and Johnson, 1989.) In our own research program at the Cooperative Learning Center (University of Minnesota), over the past 30 years we have conducted more than 90 research studies to refine our understanding of the nature of cooperation and how it works. Research participants varied as to economic class, age, sex, nationality, and cultural background. A wide variety of research tasks, ways of structuring cooperation, and measures of the dependent variables were used. Many different researchers conducted research with markedly different orientations working in different settings, countries, and decades. The research on cooperation has validity and generalizability rarely found in educational literature.

Working together to achieve mutual goals can have profound effects on the individuals involved. The type of interdependence structured among individuals determines how they interact with each other, which, in turn, largely determines outcomes. Structuring situations cooperatively results in individuals promoting each other's success by helping, assisting, supporting, and encouraging each other's efforts. Structuring situations competitively results in individuals opposing each other's success by obstructing and blocking each other's efforts. Structuring situations individualistically results in no interaction among individuals because individuals ignore each other and work alone. Assess how well you understand what attitudes comprise cooperative, competitive, and individualistic situations by completing Activity 6.3.

These interaction patterns affect numerous variables, which may be subsumed within three broad and interrelated outcomes (see Figure 6.1) (Johnson & Johnson, 1989):

ACTIVITY **6.3** ■ WHAT IS YOUR ATTITUDE?

Given below is a list of 12 attitudes. Form a pair and agree on whether each statement reflects a cooperative, competitive, or individualistic attitude. Identify each attitude as cooperative (1), competitive (2), or individualistic (3).

_____ **1.** Striving for everyone's success

_____ **2.** Striving to be better than others

_____ **3.** Striving for one's own success only

_____ **4.** Accruing benefits for oneself that do not affect others

_____ **5.** Celebrating joint success

_____ **6.** Accruing benefits for oneself that benefit others

_____ **7.** Celebrating only one's own success

_____ **8.** Being motivated to help and assist others

_____ **9.** Accruing benefits for oneself that deprive or hurt others

_____ **10.** Being motivated to maximize only one's own productivity

_____ **11.** Celebrating one's own success and others' failures

_____ **12.** Being motivated to ensure that no one else does better than oneself

1. **Greater efforts to achieve.** This includes higher achievement and greater productivity by all students (high-, medium-, and low-achievers), long-term retention, intrinsic motivation, achievement motivation, more time on task, higher-level reasoning, and critical thinking.
2. **More positive relationships among students.** This includes esprit-de-corps, caring and committed relationships, personal and academic social support, valuing of diversity, and cohesion.
3. **Greater psychological health.** This includes general psychological adjustment, ego strength, social development, social competencies, self-esteem, self-identity, and ability to cope with adversity and stress.

A focus on cooperative learning and persistence in implementing it in every classroom is instrumental in laying the foundation for a constructive learning environment (Johnson & Johnson, 1989). First, cooperative learning ensures that all students are meaningfully and actively involved in learning. Active, involved students do not tend to engage in disruptive, off-task behavior.

Second, cooperative learning ensures that students are achieving their potential and are experiencing psychological success so they are motivated to continue to invest energy and effort in learning. Those who experience academic failure are at risk for tuning out and acting up, which often leads to physical or verbal aggression.

FIGURE 6.1 Circles of Learning

Social Interdependence		
Cooperative	Competitive	Individualistic

Outcomes of Cooperative Learning		
Effort to achieve	Positive relationships	Psychological health

Five Basic Elements				
Positive interdependence	Individual accountability	Promotive interaction	Social skills	Group processing

COOPERATIVE LEARNING

Formal Co-op Learning	Informal Co-op Learning	Co-op Base Groups
Make preinstructional decisions	Conduct focused introductory discussion	Opening class meeting to check homework, ensure members understand academic material, complete routine tasks (such as attendance)
Explain task and cooperative structure	Conduct intermittent pair discussions every 10 or 15 minutes	Ending class meeting to ensure members understand academic material, homework assignment
Monitor learning groups and intervene to improve taskwork and teamwork Assess student learning and process group effectiveness	Conduct focused closure discussion	members help and assist each other learn between classes Conduct semester- or year-long school or class service projects

Cooperative School		
Teaching teams	Site-based decision making	Faculty meetings

Constructive Conflict			
Students		Faculty	
Academic controversy	Negotiating, mediating	Decision-making controversy	Negotiating, mediating

Civic Values				
Work for mutual benefit, common good	Equality of all members	Trusting, caring relationships	View situations from all perspectives	Unconditional worth of self, diverse others

Third, systematic use of cooperative learning promotes the development of caring and committed relationships for every student. Students who are isolated or alienated from their peers and who do not have friends are at risk for violent and destructive behavior compared to students who experience social support and a sense of belonging.

Fourth, cooperative groups provide an arena in which students develop the interpersonal and small-group skills needed to work effectively with diverse schoolmates. Students learn how to communicate effectively, provide leadership, engage in effective decision making, build trust, and understand others' perspectives.

Fifth, the cooperative base groups provide the arena for discussions in which personal problems are shared and solved. As a result, students' resilience, and ability to cope with adversity and stress tend to increase. Children who do not share their problems and who do not have caring, supportive help in solving them are at more risk for disruptive and destructive behavior.

Sixth, cooperative groups promote a sense of meaning, pride, and esteem by academically helping and assisting classmates and contributing to their well-being and quality of life.

Seventh, all the benefits of cooperation for students can also be found to result from cooperation among faculty, between faculty and administrators, and among administrators.

Finally, the systematic use of cooperative learning provides the context for resolving conflicts in constructive ways. To resolve conflicts constructively, students, faculty, and staff need a common set of procedures, which is why a schoolwide conflict resolution and peer mediation program is implemented. The powerful effects of cooperation on so many important outcomes separates it from other instructional methods and makes it one of your most important instructional tools.

TYPES OF COOPERATIVE LEARNING GROUPS

These problems are endemic to all institutions of education, regardless of level. Children sit for 12 years in classrooms where the implicit goal is to listen to the teacher and memorize the information in order to regurgitate it on a test. Little or no attention is paid to the learning process, even though much research exists documenting that real understanding is a case of active restructuring on the part of the learner. Restructuring occurs through engagement in problem posing as well as problem solving, inference making and investigation, resolving of contradictions, and reflecting. These processes all mandate far more active learners, as well as a different model of education than the one subscribed to at present by most institutions. Rather than being powerless and dependent on the institution, learners need to be empowered to think and learn for themselves. Thus, learning needs to be conceived of as something a learner does, not something that is done to a learner.
—*Catherine Fosnot (1989)*

There are three types of cooperative learning groups: formal cooperative learning groups, informal cooperative learning groups, and cooperative base groups (see Table 6.1).

Formal Cooperative Learning Groups

Formal cooperative learning consists of students working together, for one class period to several weeks, to achieve shared learning goals and jointly complete specific tasks and assignments, such as decision making or problem solving, completing a curriculum unit, writing a report, conducting a survey or experiment, or reading a chapter or reference book, learning vocabulary, or answering questions at the end of the chapter (Johnson, Johnson, & Holubec, 1998). Any course requirement or assignment may be structured cooperatively. In formal cooperative learning groups, teachers may participate in a number of tasks:

1. **Make preinstructional decisions.** Teachers specify the objectives for the lesson (both academic and social skills) and decide on the size of groups, the method

TABLE 6.1   **Understanding Cooperative Learning**

TYPES OF GROUPS	COOPERATIVE GROUPS	ESSENTIAL ELEMENTS	OUTCOMES
Pseudo groups	Formal cooperative learning	Positive interdependence	Effort to achieve
Traditional groups	Informal cooperative learning	Individual accountability	Positive relationships
Cooperative groups	Cooperative base groups	Promotive interaction	Psychological health
High-performing cooperative groups		Interpersonal and small-group skills	
		Group processing	

of assigning students to groups, the roles students are assigned, the materials needed to conduct the lesson, and the way the room is arranged.

2. **Explain tasks and positive interdependence.** A teacher clearly defines the assignment, teaches the required concepts and strategies, specifies the positive interdependence and individual accountability, gives the criteria for success, and explains the expected social skills to be used.

3. **Monitor students' learning and intervene within the groups to provide task assistance or to increase students' interpersonal and group skills.** A teacher systematically observes and collects data on each group as it works. When needed, the teacher intervenes to assist students in completing the task accurately and in working together effectively.

4. **Assess students' learning and help students process how well their groups functioned.** Students' learning is carefully assessed and their performances evaluated. Members of the learning groups then discuss how effectively they worked together and how they can improve in the future.

Informal Cooperative Learning Groups

Informal cooperative learning consists of having students work together to achieve a joint learning goal in temporary, ad-hoc groups that last from a few minutes to one class period (Johnson, Johnson, & Holubec, 1998; Johnson, Johnson, & Smith, 1998). During a lecture, demonstration, or film, informal cooperative learning can be used to:

1. Focus student attention on the material to be learned.
2. Set a mood conducive to learning.
3. Help set expectations as to what will be covered in a class session.
4. Ensure that students cognitively process and rehearse the material being taught.
5. Summarize what has been learned and precue the next session.
6. Provide closure to an instructional session.

During direct teaching, the instructional challenge for the teacher is to ensure that students do the intellectual work of organizing material, explaining it, summarizing it, and integrating it into existing conceptual structures. Informal cooperative learning groups are often organized so that students engage in 3- to 5-minute focused discussions before and after a lecture and 2- to 3-minute turn-to-your-partner discussions interspersed throughout a lecture.

Turn to Your Neighbor.   When a teacher asks a class who knows the answer and one student is chosen to respond, that student has an opportunity to clarify and extend what he or she knows through explaining. In this situation only one student is involved and active. The rest of the class is passive. A teacher may ensure that all students are active by using a procedure that requires all students to explain their answers simultaneously. When each student has to explain his or her answer and reasoning to a classmate, all students are active and involved. No one is allowed to be passive.

There are two basic ways of structuring simultaneous explaining: (a) the individual student formulates an answer and then explains to a classmate or (b) a small group formulates an answer and each member explains their group's answer and reasoning to a member of another group. The procedure follows.

Task: Students answer the question.

Cooperative: Students turn to the person next to them and create an answer they can agree on to the question. Students follow four steps:

Step 1. *Formulate* an individual answer to the question
Step 2. *Share* their answer with their partner
Step 3. *Listen* carefully to their partner's answer
Step 4. *Create* a new answer that is superior to their initial formulations through the processes of association, building on each other's thoughts, and synthesizing

Expected Criteria for Success: Each student must be able to explain the answer.

Individual Accountability: One member from the pair is randomly chosen to explain the answer. Teachers periodically use the simultaneous explaining procedure of having each group member explain the group's answers to a member of another group.

Expected Behaviors: All members are expected to be able to explain, listen, and synthesize.

Intergroup Cooperation: Whenever it is helpful, students should check procedures, answers, and strategies with another group.

Reading Comprehension Triads.   Alternatively, the same procedure can be used for reading assignments with cooperative groups. In addition, you may want to focus on developing a particular skill. Consider how the procedure can be adapted for this cooperative assignment.

Task: Read the assigned material (e.g., poem, chapter, story, handout) and answer the questions. Practice the skill of checking.

Cooperative: The group members develop one set of answers that they all agree on.

1. To facilitate the group's work, each member is assigned a role: reader, recorder, checker.
2. If all members score 90 percent or better on the test, each member receives 5 bonus points.

Expected Criteria for Success: Everyone must be able to answer each question correctly.

Individual Accountability: One member from the group is randomly chosen to explain the group's answers. Teachers give a test on the assigned reading that each member takes individually. Each group member is required to explain the group's answers to a member of another group.

Expected Behaviors: All members are expected to actively participate, check, encourage, and elaborate.

Intergroup Cooperation: Whenever it is helpful, students should check procedures, answers, and strategies with another group. When finished, students compare their answers with those of another group and discuss.

Cooperative Base Groups

Cooperative base groups are long-term, heterogeneous cooperative learning groups with stable membership (Johnson, Johnson, & Holubec, 1992; Johnson, Johnson, & Smith, 1998). Base groups give the support, help, encouragement, and assistance each member needs to make academic progress (i.e., attend class, complete all assignments, learn) and to develop cognitively and socially in healthy ways. Base groups are permanent (lasting from one to several years) and provide long-term, caring peer relationships necessary to influence members consistently to work hard in school. The use of base groups tends to improve attendance, to personalize the work required and the school experience, and to improve the quality and quantity of learning. Positive development is enhanced when base groups are given the responsibility for conducting a year-long service project to improve the school.

When you use formal, informal, and cooperative base groups repeatedly, you gain routine-level expertise in doing so. (See Activity 6.4 to review your knowledge of these learning groups.) *Expertise* is reflected in your proficiency, adroitness, competence, and skill in doing something. Expertise in structuring cooperative efforts is reflected in four ways:

1. Taking any lesson in any subject area with any age student and structuring it cooperatively
2. Being able to use cooperative learning (at a routine-use level) 60 to 80 percent of the time
3. Describing precisely what you are doing and why: (a) to communicate to others the nature and advantages of cooperative learning and (b) to teach colleagues how to implement cooperative learning
4. Applying the principles of cooperation to other settings, such as collegial relationships and faculty meetings

You usually gain expertise through a progressive refinement procedure: (a) teach a cooperative lesson, (b) assess how well it went, (c) reflect on how cooperation could have been better structured, and then (d) teach an improved cooperative lesson, repeating steps b, c, and d. You thus gain experience in an incremental, step-by-step manner. The routine-use level of teacher expertise is the ability to structure cooperative learning situations automatically without conscious thought or planning. You can then use cooperative learning with fidelity for the rest of your teaching career.

ACTIVITY **6.4** ■ TYPES OF COOPERATIVE LEARNING

Form a pair. In the spaces below, write out in your own words the definition of each type of cooperative learning situation.

1. Formal: _____

_____

2. Informal: _____

_____

3. Base groups: _____

_____

WHAT MAKES COOPERATION WORK?

> Together we stand, divided we fall.   —*Watchword of the American Revolution*

On July 15, 1982, Don Bennett, a Seattle businessman, was the first amputee ever to climb Mount Rainier (reported in Kouzes & Posner, 1987). He climbed 14,410 feet on one leg and two crutches. It took him 5 days. When asked to state the most important lesson he learned from doing so, without hesitation he said, "You can't do it alone."

What did he mean? During one very difficult trek across an ice field in Don Bennett's hop to the top of Mount Rainier, his daughter stayed by his side for 4 hours and with each new hop told him, "You can do it, Dad. You're the best dad in the world. You can do it, Dad." There was no way Bennett would quit hopping to the top with his daughter yelling words of love and encouragement in his ear. The encouragement of his daughter kept him going, strengthening his commitment to make it to the top. The classroom is similar. With members of their cooperative group cheering them on, students amaze themselves and their teachers with what they can achieve.

To structure lessons so students do in fact work cooperatively with each other, you must understand the basic elements that make cooperation work. Mastering the basic elements of cooperation allows you to do three things:

1. Take your existing lessons, curricula, and courses and structure them cooperatively.
2. Tailor cooperative learning lessons to your unique instructional needs, circumstances, curricula, subject areas, and students.
3. Diagnose the problems some students may have in working together and intervene to increase the effectiveness of the student learning groups.

Five Basic Elements of Cooperative Teams

For cooperation to work well, you explicitly have to structure five essential elements in each lesson (see Figure 6.1). The first and most important element is positive interdependence.

Positive Interdependence.   You must give a clear task and a group goal so students believe they sink or swim together. *Positive interdependence* exists when group members perceive that they are linked with each other in a way that one cannot succeed unless everyone succeeds. If one fails, all fail. Group members realize, therefore, that each person's efforts benefit not only him- or herself, but all other group members as well. Positive interdependence creates a commitment to other people's success as well as one's own and is the heart of cooperative learning. If there is no positive interdependence, there is no cooperation.

Instructors may structure positive interdependence by establishing *mutual goals* (maximizing one's own and each other's productivity), *joint rewards* (rewarding all group members when they achieve above the criteria, each member receiving bonus points), *shared resources* (members having different expertise), and *assigned roles* (summarizer, encourager of participation, elaborator).

Individual Accountability.   The second essential element of cooperative learning is *individual* and *group accountability*. The group must be accountable for achieving its goals. Each member must be accountable for contributing his or her share of the work (which ensures that no one "hitch-hikes" on the work of others). The group has to be clear about its goals and be able to measure (a) its progress in achieving them and (b) the individual efforts of each of its members. Individual accountability exists when the performance of each individual student is assessed and the results are evaluated by the group and the individual to ascertain who needs more assistance, support, and encouragement in completing the assignment. The purpose of cooperative learning groups is to make each member a stronger individual in his or her own right. Students learn together so that they can subsequently perform higher as individuals.

Promote Interaction.   The third essential component of cooperative learning is *promotive interaction,* preferably face to face. Students need to do real work together while promoting each other's success. Promotive interaction occurs when members share resources, and help, support, encourage, and praise each other's efforts to learn. Cooperative learning groups are both an academic support system (every student has someone who is committed to helping him or her learn) and a personal support system (every student has someone who is committed to himself or herself as a person). Important cognitive activities and interpersonal dynamics can only occur when students promote each other's learning. Instructors structure teams so that members sit knee to knee and talk through each aspect of the tasks they are working to complete. This includes orally explaining how to solve problems, discussing the nature of the concepts being learned, teaching one's knowledge to classmates, and connecting present with past learning. It is through promoting each other's learning face to face that members become personally committed to each other as well as to their mutual goals.

Social Skills.   The fourth essential element of cooperative learning is teaching students the required interpersonal and small-group skills. In cooperative learning groups, students are required to learn academic subject matter (taskwork) and also to learn the interpersonal and small-group skills required to function as part of a group (teamwork). Cooperative learning is inherently more complex than competitive or individualistic learning because students have to engage simultaneously in taskwork and teamwork.

Group members must know how to provide effective leadership, decision making, trust building, communication, and conflict management, and be motivated to use the prerequisite skills. Instructors have to teach teamwork skills just as purposefully and precisely as you do academic skills. Because cooperation and conflict are inherently related (see Johnson & Johnson, 1991; 1992), the procedures and skills for managing conflicts constructively are especially important for the long-term success of learning groups. Procedures and strategies for teaching students social skills may be found in Johnson (1991; 1993) and Johnson and F. Johnson (1997).

Group Processing.   The fifth essential component of cooperative learning is *group processing.* Group processing exists when group members have time allotted to discuss how well they are achieving their goals and maintaining effective working relationships. Groups need to describe what member actions are helpful and unhelpful and make decisions about what behaviors to continue or to change. Instructors structure group processing by assigning tasks such as (a) list at least three member actions that helped the group be successful and (b) list one action that could be added to make the group even more successful tomorrow. Instructors also monitor the groups and give feedback on how well the groups are working together. Continual improvement in the process of learning results from careful analysis of how members are working together and determining how group effectiveness can be enhanced.

Your use of cooperative learning becomes effective through disciplined action. The five basic elements are not just characteristics of good cooperative learning groups, they are a discipline that you have to apply rigorously (much like a diet has to be adhered to) to produce the conditions for effective cooperative action. See Box 6.1 for an analogy between teamwork in baseball and cooperative learning in the classroom that further illustrates the benefits and successes resulting from cooperation.

THE COOPERATIVE SCHOOL

W. Edwards Deming, Joseph Juran, and other founders of the quality movement have stated that more than 85 percent of the behavior of members of an organization

■ ■ ■ ■ ■

BOX 6.1
EXTRAORDINARY ACHIEVEMENT

Sandy Koufax was one of the greatest pitchers in the history of baseball. Although he was naturally talented, he was also unusually well trained and disciplined. He was perhaps the only major league pitcher whose fastball could be heard to hum. Opposing batters, instead of talking and joking around in the dugout, would sit quietly and listen for Koufax's fastball to hum. When it was their turn to bat, they were already intimidated.

Koufax's genius, however, could have been subverted in one simple way: by making the first author of this book his catcher. To be great, a pitcher needs an outstanding catcher (his great partner was Johnny Roseboro). David is such an unskilled catcher that Koufax would have had to throw the ball much slower for David to catch it. This would have deprived Koufax of his greatest weapon. Placing Roger and Edythe at key defensive positions in the infield or outfield, furthermore, would have seriously affected Koufax's success.

Sandy Koufax was not a great pitcher on his own. Only as part of a team could Koufax achieve greatness. In baseball, as in the classroom, it takes a cooperative effort. Extraordinary achievement comes from a cooperative group, not from the individualistic or competitive efforts of an isolated individual.

is directly attributable to the organization's structure, not the nature of the individuals involved. Your classroom is no exception. If competitive or individualistic learning dominates your classroom, your students will behave accordingly, regardless of whether you have temporarily put them in cooperative groups. If cooperative learning dominates your classroom, your students will behave accordingly and a true learning community will result.

The issue of cooperation among students is part of a larger issue of the organizational structure of schools (Johnson & Johnson, 1994). For decades schools have functioned as "mass production" organizations that divided work into component parts (first grade, second grade; English, social studies, science) to be performed by teachers who have been isolated from colleagues and work alone, in their own room, with their own set of students, and with their own set of curriculum materials. Students can be assigned to any teacher because students are considered interchangeable parts in the education machine. However, using cooperative learning the majority of the time changes the basic organizational structure of your classroom into a team-based, high-performance structure. In other words, cooperation is more than an instructional procedure. It is a basic shift in organizational structure that affects all aspects of classroom life.

In a *cooperative school,* students work primarily in cooperative learning groups, teachers and building staff work in cooperative teams, and district administrators work in cooperative teams (Johnson & Johnson, 1994). The organizational structure of the classroom, school, and district are then congruent. Each level of cooperative teams supports and enhances the other levels.

A cooperative school structure begins in the classroom with the use of cooperative learning the majority of the time (Johnson & Johnson, 1994). Work teams are the heart of the team-based organizational structure and cooperative learning groups are the primary work team. Cooperative learning is used to increase student achievement, create more positive relationships among students, and generally improve students' psychological well-being. Having teachers advocate cooperation to their students, furthermore, changes their own attitudes toward working collaboratively with colleagues.

Teaching Teams.   The first level in creating a cooperative school is to form collegial *teaching teams,* task forces, and ad hoc decision-making groups within the school (Johnson & Johnson, 1994). Teacher teams are just as effective as student teams. The use of cooperation to structure faculty and staff work involves (a) collegial teaching teams, (b) school-based decision making, and (c) faculty meetings. Just as the heart of the classroom is cooperative learning, the heart of the school is the collegial teaching team. Collegial teaching teams are small cooperative groups (two to five teachers) whose purpose is to increase teachers' instructional expertise and success (Johnson & Johnson, 1994).

Site-Based Decision Making.   A school-based decision-making procedure is implemented through the use of two types of cooperative teams (Johnson & Johnson, 1994). A *task force* considers a school problem and proposes a solution to the faculty as a whole. The faculty is then divided into *ad hoc decision-making groups* and considers whether to accept or modify the proposal. The decisions made by the ad hoc groups are summarized, and the entire faculty then decides on the action to be taken to solve the problem.

The third level in creating a cooperative school is to implement administrative cooperative teams within the district (Johnson & Johnson, 1994). Administrators are organized into collegial teams to increase their administrative expertise as well as task forces and ad hoc decision-making groups.

Willi Unsoeld, a mountain climber and philosopher, gave this advice "as the secret to survival" for all those who set off to climb a mountain: "Take care of each other, share your energies with the group, no one must feel alone, cut off, for that is when you do not make it." The same may be said for everyone entering a school.

CREATING A COOPERATIVE COMMUNITY

The Nature of Community and Social Interdependence

Positive development of children and youth begins with establishing a learning community based on cooperation (i.e., working together to achieve mutual goals). Scholarship and learning do not exist in isolation; they are products of a community and a culture characterized by mutual respect and trust. *Community* is a group of people who live in the same locality and share common goals and a common culture. The school community is made up of the faculty and staff, the students, their parents, and members of the neighborhood. Broadly, the school community of stakeholders further includes central administrators, college admission officers, and future employers.

To create a learning community, positive interdependence (i.e., cooperation) must be structured at all levels of the school: learning group, classroom, interclass, school, school–parent, and school–neighborhood. Members of the community must see themselves as partners, not adversaries. The school cannot be a learning community if students are pitted against each other in the classroom or if students are isolated with no friends in the classroom. Just as the family is the beginning of community in society, the learning group is the beginning of community in the school. The first step in creating a cooperative community is to use cooperative learning the majority of the time.

Classroom Interdependence

Ways to extend positive interdependence within learning groups to the classroom as a whole are numerous. Class goals may be established to create positive interdependence by setting a criterion each student must reach, a goal for each student to improve his or her performance level over previous scores, or a total class score as a specified criterion. Class rewards or celebrations may be created to establish positive interdependence by adding bonus points to all group members' academic scores when all class members achieve the criterion or by giving nonacademic rewards, such as extra free time, extra recess time, stickers, food, T-shirts, or a class party.

Positive interdependence may also be structured through class roles, such as establishing a classroom government (president, vice president, class council, and so forth), putting teams in charge of daily class cleanup, running a class bank or business, or engaging in other activities that benefit the class as a whole. Classroom interdependence may also be structured through dividing resources, such as having the class publish a newsletter in which each cooperative group contributes one article. Consider an example of divided resources.

One class was studying geography. The ceiling was turned into a large grid giving latitude and longitude. The class was divided into eight cooperative groups. Each group was assigned a geographical location on which to do a report. The groups summarized the essential information about their location on a placard, located on the ceiling where it should be placed, and placed it there. The class then planned an itinerary for a trip to visit all eight places. Yarn was used to mark their journey. As they arrived at each spot, the appropriate group presented its report on the location, including its latitude and longitude.

Class meetings can be held as a forum for discussing how well the class is functioning and how the quality of classroom life may be improved. The class also processes how well students are using social skills and civic values. Finally, a common identity, such as a class name, slogan, flag, or song, creates interdependence.

Interclass Interdependence

Cross-class cooperation can occur in many ways. An interdisciplinary team of three to six teachers may organize their classes into a "neighborhood" or a "school within a school" where classes work together and engage in joint projects for a number of years. Science and math, or English literature and social studies, may be integrated and the classes combined. Students of different ages can be involved in cross-class reading buddies that meet weekly throughout the year to share and explore literature. Several classes can do periodic projects on learning specific social skills and values so students from different classes can demonstrate these skills and values to each other and use them in the hallways, on the playground, and in the lunchroom. In these and many other ways, cross-class interdependence may be created.

School Interdependence

School-level positive interdependence is established in numerous ways (Johnson & Johnson, 1994). First, the school mission statement may articulate the mutual goals shared by all members of the school and may be displayed on the school walls and printed at the top of the agenda of every meeting involving faculty and staff. This "keeps the dream" visually prominent for faculty and staff and thus is a constant reminder of their commitment.

Second, just as students work in cooperative learning groups, ideally teachers can work in a variety of cooperative teams (Johnson & Johnson, 1994). All faculty and staff can meet weekly in teaching teams and/or study groups. Collegial teaching teams are formed to increase teachers' instructional expertise and success. They consist of two to five teachers who meet weekly and discuss how better to implement cooperative learning within their classrooms. The teaching teams plan lessons together, orchestrate their use of integrated curriculum units, schedule the times they can teach together and apart, and explore how best to promote each other's instructional success for the following week.

Regular teaming among faculty promotes collegial relationships, ongoing professional growth, and induction of new faculty. Collegial study groups are formed to meet regularly to discuss a book about an instructional method, such as cooperative learning, block scheduling, or creating an integrated curriculum. Teaching teams and study groups remind faculty and staff about important instructional procedures, involve faculty in a continual improvement process, and provide a procedure for socializing new teachers into the faculty. At one of the schools we work with, for example, a teacher stated:

> One challenge we face each year is bringing new faculty on board. We want them to become part of our school community as quickly as possible and that means training them in the components of our program. Study groups help accomplish this. We have one study group, for example, on the Nuts and Bolts of Cooperative Learning for new faculty who have not been trained in cooperative learning and another study group on Teaching Students to Be Peacemakers for new faculty who have not been trained in conflict resolution. A trained, experienced teacher leads each study group. Each meeting we take a chapter in the book and go over it in detail. Then we plan how to implement it in our classrooms. We make sure we have those programs in every classroom in the school. This is how we keep the climate the way it is.

Third, in addition to collegial teaching teams and study groups, teachers may be assigned to task forces to plan and implement solutions to schoolwide issues and problems such as curriculum adoptions and lunchroom behavior. Teachers may also be assigned to ad hoc decision-making groups during faculty meetings to involve all staff members in important school decisions. The use of cooperative teams at the school level ensures that a congruent, cooperative, team-based organizational structure is in place within both classrooms and the school (Johnson & Johnson, 1994).

Finally, school interdependence may be highlighted in a variety of schoolwide activities, such as the weekly student-produced school news broadcast, special activities organized by the student council, all-school projects, and regular school assemblies.

School–Parent Interdependence

Cooperation is built between the school and the parents by involving parents in establishing mutual goals and strategic plans to achieve the goals, in participating in a division of labor, in sharing resources to help the school achieve its goals, and in developing an identity as members of the school. Parents can produce a weekly school newsletter. Parents, with the help of students, can publish the school yearbook. Parents can volunteer in their children's classes and help conduct special projects. Parents may serve on all school committees and the site council. They can organize and conduct a variety of school activities, including a school carnival, a school gift-wrap sale, periodic parties in each classroom, and field trips. The PTA may raise money for additional supplies and technology. A faculty–parent task force may be formed to deal with serious discipline problems and ensure that parents are notified when a student misbehaves. The ideal goal is to have 100 percent of the parents participating in the school.

School–Neighborhood Interdependence

The school community may be extended into the neighborhood. The school mission can be supported by local merchants through such programs as giving a discount to students who have a card verifying that in the last grading period they achieved a B average or above. Members of the neighborhood could contribute resources to school activities, such as playing in the school band. Classes could do neighborhood service projects, cleaning up a park or mowing the yards of elderly residents. In many creative ways, the school and the neighborhood can join together to accomplish mutual goals. To review the important points covered in this chapter, complete Activity 6.5.

ACTIVITY **6.5** ■ COOPERATION IN THE CLASSROOM

1. Describe one example of a group being more powerful than separate individuals:

   _____

   _____

2. Give two reasons why many teachers fail to utilize the power of groups:

   a. _____

   _____

   b. _____

   _____

3. Define cooperative, competitive, and individualistic learning:

   Cooperative: _____

   Competitive: _____

   Individualistic: _____

4. Give three reasons based on the research why cooperative learning should be used:

   a. _____

   _____

   b. _____

   _____

   c. _____

   _____

5. Define the types of cooperative learning:

   Formal: _____

   Informal: _____

   Base groups: _____

6. Define the five different types of groups.

   a. _____

   b. _____

   c. _____

   d. _____

   e. _____

7. List and define the basic elements that make cooperation work:

   a. _____

   b. _____

   c. _____

(continued)

ACTIVITY 6.5   *Continued*

    d. _____

    e. _____

8. Explain why collaborators need to learn how to manage conflict constructively.

_____

_____

_____

9. What is the cooperative school?

_____

_____

_____

SUMMARY

This chapter has discussed three types of social interdependence: competitive, individualistic, and cooperative. Of the three, cooperation tends to promote the highest achievement, most positive relationships, and greatest psychological health. To harness the power of cooperation, however, it is necessary to know what makes it work and apply those elements with discipline and diligence. Like Sandy Koufax, natural talent is not enough to make a great teacher.

Being well trained in how to use cooperative learning and unusually well disciplined in structuring the five basic elements in every lesson are also necessary. The five essential components are positive interdependence, individual accountability, promotive interaction, social skills, and group processing. By structuring these five elements into lessons, teachers can create formal cooperative learning lessons, informal cooperative learning lessons, and cooperative base groups. Repetitive lessons and procedures may be turned into cooperative scripts.

The use of cooperative learning takes place within an organizational context. If the organizational context emphasizes mass production of educating students, it works against the use of cooperative learning. If the organizational context is a team-based, high-performance structure, it encourages and supports the use of cooperative learning. In a high-performance school, the five basic elements of cooperation are used to structure teaching teams, faculty meetings, and site-based decision making. Finally, the long-term success of cooperative efforts depends on members having frequent conflicts that are managed constructively.

COOPERATIVE LEARNING OBSERVATION FORM

Teacher: _____ Date: _____ Observer: _____

Teacher Actions	Implementation	Comments
Objectives	❑ Academic ❑ Social skills	
Positive Interdependence	❑ Group goal ❑ Group celebration/reward ❑ Resources shared/jigsawed ❑ Roles assigned ❑ Shared identity	
Group Composition	❑ Random ❑ Teacher selected	
Seating Arrangement	❑ Clear view/access to groupmates ❑ Clear view/access to materials	
Individual Accountability	❑ Each student tested individually ❑ Students check each other ❑ Random student evaluated ❑ Role: checker for understanding	
Definition of Social Skills	❑ Define (T-chart) ❑ Demonstrate/model ❑ Guided practice ❑ Assign as role	
Observation of Taskwork and Teamwork	❑ Teacher monitors and intervenes ❑ Students monitor ❑ Formal observation form ❑ Informal (anecdotal) observation	
Teacher Feedback: Teamwork Skills	❑ Class ❑ Group ❑ Individual ❑ Frequency and quality of use ❑ Charts and graphs used ❑ Positive feedback to each student	
Group Processing	❑ Reflection: teamwork and taskwork ❑ Goal setting for improvement ❑ Celebration	

Teacher Actions	Implementation	Comments
General Climate	❑ Group products displayed ❑ Group progress displayed ❑ Aids to group work displayed ❑ Comments	

CHAPTER SEVEN

USING COOPERATIVE LEARNING

TEACHER'S ROLE: BEING A "GUIDE ON THE SIDE"

At age 55, after his defeat by Woodrow Wilson for president of the United States, Teddy Roosevelt took a journey to South America. The Brazilian government suggested he lead an expedition to explore a vast, unmapped river deep in the jungle. Known as the River of Doubt, it was believed to be a tributary to the Amazon. Roosevelt accepted instantly. "We will go down the unknown river," he declared, and the Brazilian government organized an expedition for the trip. "I had to go," he said later, "it was my last chance to be a boy."

With his son Kermit and a party of 18, Roosevelt, headed into the jungle. "On February 27, 1914, shortly after midday, we started down the River of Doubt into the unknown," Roosevelt wrote. The journey was an ordeal. Hostile natives harassed them. Five canoes were shattered and had to be rebuilt. Their food ran short, and valuable equipment was lost. One man drowned when his canoe capsized. Another went berserk and killed a member of the expedition and then disappeared into the wilderness.

Roosevelt, ill with fever, badly injured his leg when he tried to keep two capsized canoes from being smashed against rocks. Unable to walk, he had to be carried. Lying in a tent with an infected leg and a temperature of 105°, he requested to be left behind. Ignoring such pleas, Kermit brought his father to safety with the help of the other members of the expedition.

Teddy Roosevelt barely survived, but he and his companions accomplished their mission. The party mapped the 1,000-mile River of Doubt and collected priceless specimens for the Museum of Natural History. The river was renamed in his honor, Rio Theodore. ∎

An expedition such as Roosevelt's consists of four phases:

1. You make a series of prejourney decisions about the number of people needed, the materials and equipment required, and the route to be taken.
2. You brief all participants on the goals and objectives of the journey, emphasize that members' survival depends on the joint efforts of all, and the behaviors you expect of members of the expedition.

3. You make the journey, carefully mapping the area traveled and collecting the targeted specimens.
4. You report your findings to interested parties, reflect on what went right and wrong with fellow members, and write your memoirs.

Conducting a cooperative lesson is done in the same way. You, the teacher, make a number of preinstructional decisions, explain to students the instructional task and the cooperative nature of the lesson, conduct the lesson, and evaluate and process the results. The following list outlines your specific tasks:

1. **Make preinstructional decisions.** In every lesson you (a) formulate objectives, (b) decide on the size of groups, (c) choose a method for assigning students to groups, (d) decide which roles to assign group members, (e) arrange the room, and (f) arrange the materials students need to complete the assignment.
2. **Explain the task and cooperative structure.** In every lesson you (a) explain the academic assignment to students, (b) explain the criteria for success, (c) structure positive interdependence, (d) explain the individual accountability, and (e) explain the behaviors you expect to see during the lesson.
3. **Monitor and intervene.** While you (a) conduct the lesson, you (b) monitor each learning group, (c) intervene when needed to improve taskwork and teamwork, and (d) bring closure to the lesson.
4. **Evaluate and process.** You (a) assess and evaluate the quality and quantity of student achievement, (b) ensure students carefully process the effectiveness of their learning groups, (c) have students make a plan for improvement, and (d) have students celebrate the hard work of group members.

In each class session teachers must make the choice of being "a sage on the stage" or "a guide on the side." In doing so they might remember that the challenge in teaching is not covering the material for the students, it's uncovering the material with the students.

PREINSTRUCTIONAL DECISIONS

Specifying the Instructional Objectives

The Roman philosopher Seneca once said, "When you do not know to which port you are sailing, no wind is favorable." The same may be said for teaching. To plan for a lesson you must know what the lesson is aimed at accomplishing. Every lesson has both (a) academic and (b) interpersonal and small-group skills objectives. You need to specify *academic objectives,* based on a conceptual or task analysis, and *social skills objectives* that detail what interpersonal and small-group skills you want to emphasize during the lesson. You choose social skills by:

1. Monitoring the learning groups and diagnosing the specific skills needed to solve the problems students are having in working with each other
2. Asking students to identify social skills that would improve their teamwork
3. Keeping a list of social skills you teach to every class, emphasizing the next one on the list for the next class lesson
4. Analyzing what social skills are required to complete the assignment

The most sophisticated way to determine the social skills students need to complete a lesson is by creating a flow chart. A *flow chart* is a simple yet powerful visual tool to display all the steps in a process. Creating a flow chart involves six steps (see Figure 7.1).

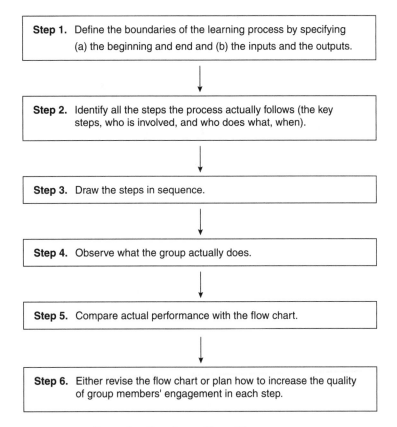

Step 1. Define the boundaries of the learning process by specifying (a) the beginning and end and (b) the inputs and the outputs.

Step 2. Identify all the steps the process actually follows (the key steps, who is involved, and who does what, when).

Step 3. Draw the steps in sequence.

Step 4. Observe what the group actually does.

Step 5. Compare actual performance with the flow chart.

Step 6. Either revise the flow chart or plan how to increase the quality of group members' engagement in each step.

FIGURE 7.1   **Steps for Creating a Flow Chart**

Deciding on the Size of the Group

There is a folk saying about snowflakes. Each snowflake is fragile and small. But when they stick together, it is amazing what they can do. The same is true for people. When we work together, there is no limit to human ingenuity and potential. For students to work together, they must be assigned to groups. To assign students to groups, you must decide (a) how large a group should be, (b) how students should be assigned to a group, (c) how long the groups will exist, and (d) what combination of groups will be used in the lesson (see Box 7.1).

Although cooperative learning groups typically range in size from two to four, the basic rule of thumb is, the smaller, the better. Although there is no ideal size for a cooperative learning group, groups of two or three members, or four at the most, are usually most effective. A common mistake is to have students work in groups of

■ ■ ■ ■ ■

BOX 7.1
GROUP SIZE DEPENDS ON TEAM

T = *Time Limits*
E = *Experience in working in groups*
A = *Age of students*
M = *Materials and equipment available*

four, five, and six members before the students have the skills to do so competently. In selecting the size of a cooperative learning group, remember the following advice:

1. **With the addition of each group member, the resources to help the group succeed increase.** As the size of the learning group increases, so does (a) the range of abilities, expertise, and skills; (b) the number of minds available for acquiring and processing information; and (c) the diversity of viewpoints.
2. **The shorter the period of time available, the smaller the learning group should be.** If only a brief period of time is available for the lesson, smaller groups, such as pairs, are more effective because they take less time to get organized, they operate faster, and each member has more "air time."
3. **The smaller the group is, the more difficult it is for students to hide and not contribute their share of the work.** Small groups increase the visibility of students' efforts and thereby make them more accountable.
4. **The larger the group is, the more skillful group members must be.** In a pair, students have to manage two interactions. In a group of three, student have to manage six interactions. In a group of four, students have to manage twelve interactions. As the size of the group increases, the interpersonal and small-group skills required to manage the interactions among group members become far more complex and sophisticated.
5. **The larger the group, the less frequent is the interaction among members is.** What results is less group cohesion, fewer friendships, and less personal support.
6. **The materials available or the specific nature of the task may dictate group size.** If you have 10 computers and 30 students, you may assign students to groups of three. When the task is tennis practice, a group size of two is natural.
7. **The smaller the group is, the easier it is to identify any difficulties students have in working together.** Problems in leadership, unresolved conflicts among group members, issues over power and control, tendencies to sit back and wait for others to do the work, and other problems students have in working together are more visible and apparent when groups are small. Groups need to be small enough to ensure all students are actively involved and participating equally.

Assigning Students to Groups

Sic parvis magna [Great things have small beginnings].   —*Sir Francis Drake*

There is no ideal group membership. What determines group productivity is not who its members are, but rather how well the members work together. You may use cooperative learning groups that are homogeneous in ability to teach specific skills or to achieve certain instructional objectives. Generally, however, assigning students to heterogeneous groups in which students come from diverse backgrounds and have different abilities, experiences, and interests has advantages:

1. Students are exposed to a variety of ideas, multiple perspectives, and different problem-solving methods.
2. Students generate more cognitive disequilibrium, which stimulates learning, creativity, and cognitive and social development.
3. Students engage in more elaborative thinking, give and receive more explanations, and engage in more frequent perspective taking in discussing material, all of which increase the depth of understanding, the quality of reasoning, and the accuracy of long-term retention.

To make groups heterogeneous, you assign students to groups using a random or stratified random procedure. The easiest and most effective way to group students is *random assignment*. You divide the number of students in your class by the size of the group desired. If you want groups of three and you have 30 students in your class, you divide 30 by 3. You have students number off by the result (e.g., 10). Students with the same number group together (all 1s get together, all 2s get together, and so forth).

A related procedure is *stratified random assignment*. This is the same as random assignment except that you choose one (or two) characteristics of students (such as reading level, learning style, task orientation, or personal interest) and make sure that one or more students in each group has that characteristic. A modified stratified random procedure is to assign students to groups by *preferences*. Have students write on a slip of paper what is their favorite sport to participate in. Then have them group with students who like to participate in the same sport. Variations include favorite food, celebrity, skill, car, president, animal, vegetable, fairy tale character, and so forth.

Teacher-selected groups can be either homogeneous or heterogeneous. When students select their own groups, they usually form homogeneous ones. Examples of four methods for assigning students to groups are provided. For additional methods for assigning students to groups as well as a variety of team-building and warm-up activities see R. Johnson and Johnson (1990).

Literature Characters. Give students cards with the names of characters from the literature they have recently read. Ask them to group with characters in the same story, play, or poem. Examples are Romeo and Juliet; Captain Hook, Peter Pan, and Wendy; Hansel, Gretel, the witch, and the stepmother.

Geographical Areas. List a number of countries or states and have students group themselves according to their most preferred choice to visit. Variations include grouping according to least preferred to visit, according to similarity of climate, according to similarity of geological features, according to similarity of exports, and so forth.

States and Capitols. To assign students to groups of two or four, divide the number of students in the class by 2 (30 divided by 2 = 15). Pick a geographic area of the United States and write out on cards the names of 15 states. Then on another set of cards write out the names of their capital cities. Shuffle the cards and pass them out to students. Then have the students find the classmate who has the matching state or capital. To form groups of four, have students with two adjacent states and their capitals combine.

Math Method. Variations to the math method of assigning students to groups are endless. The basic method is to assign each student a math problem and ask students to (a) solve their problem, (b) find the classmates whose problems have the same answer, and (c) form a group. This method may vary from simple addition in first grade to complex equations in high school classes. Thus, to form a group of three, you may distribute three equations throughout the class, for example, $3 + 3 = \square$, $4 + 2 = \square$, $5 + 1 = \square$. Students then follow steps a, b, and c.

Length of Group Life

A common concern is, How long should cooperative learning groups stay together? The type of cooperative learning group you use determines one answer to this question. Base groups last for at least one and ideally for several years. Informal cooperative learning groups last for only a few minutes or at most one class period. For formal cooperative learning groups, this question has no formula or simple answer. Groups usually stay together to complete a task, unit, or chapter. During a course every student should work with every other classmate.

Using Combinations of Cooperative Learning Groups

In many lessons you will want to use a combination of formal and informal cooperative learning groups as well as base groups. You may use more than one group size for any one lesson. You need ways to assign students to new groups quickly and procedures for making transitions among groups, for example, moving students from pairs to fours, to pairs, to threes, and so forth.

Assigning Roles to Ensure Interdependence

In planning the lesson, you think through what actions need to occur to maximize student learning. *Roles* prescribe what other group members expect from a student (and therefore what the student is obligated to do) and what that person has a right to expect from other group members who have complementary roles. Structure student–student interaction by assigning roles such as reader, recorder, encourager of participation, and checker for understanding. A progression exists for using roles to structure cooperative efforts:

1. Do not assign roles until students get used to working together.
2. Assign only simple roles to students, such as forming roles or the roles of reader, recorder, and encourager of participation. Rotate the roles so that each group member participates in each role several times.
3. Add to the rotation a new role that is slightly more sophisticated, such as checker for understanding. You assign functioning roles at this point.
4. Over time assign formulating and fermenting roles that do not naturally occur in the group, such as elaborator. Students typically do not relate what they are learning to what they already know until you specifically train them to do so.

At times students refuse to participate in a cooperative group or do not understand how to help the group succeed. You can solve and prevent such problems when you give each group member a specific role to play in the group. Assigning appropriate roles may be used to:

1. Reduce problems such as one or more members making no contribution to the group, or one member dominating the group.
2. Ensure that vital group skills are enacted in the group and that group members learn targeted skills.
3. Create interdependence among group members. You structure *role interdependence* by assigning each member complementary and interconnected roles.

The social skills represented by the roles should be taught like a spiral curriculum with a more complex version of the skill taught every year. You can familiarize yourself with group roles and corresponding skills by completing Activity 7.1.

Arranging the Room

The design and arrangement of classroom space and furniture communicates expectations for appropriate behavior and plans for learning activities. Desks arranged in a row communicate a different message and expectation than do desks grouped in small circles. Spatial design also defines the circulation patterns in the classroom. *Circulation* is the flow of movement into, out of, and within the classroom. It is movement through space. You determine what students see, when they see it, and with whom students interact with your classroom design.

ACTIVITY **7.1**   ■   IDENTIFYING THE VARIOUS TYPES OF ROLES

The list below contains four skills and eight examples of the roles that may be assigned to ensure students work together effectively. Form a pair and identify for each skill the two roles that teach that skill. Write the letters identifying those roles on the lines preceding the skill.

SKILLS	ROLES
_____ **1.** Forming skills	**a.** Encouraging everyone to participate
_____ **2.** Functioning skills	**b.** Using quiet voices
_____ **3.** Formulating skills	**c.** Relating new learning to previous learning
	d. Criticizing ideas, not people
_____ **4.** Fermenting skills	**e.** Staying with your group
	f. Changing your mind only if logically persuaded
	g. Explaining step by step one's reasoning
	h. Sharing one's ideas and conclusions

No single classroom arrangement meets the requirements of all lessons. Reference points and well-defined boundaries for work spaces are needed to move students from rows to triads, to pairs, to fours, to rows. Color, displays, and lighting (a) focus students' visual attention on points of emphasis in the classroom (e.g., the learning group, you, instructional materials) and (b) define the territorial boundaries of work spaces. You define boundaries in several ways:

1. **Labels and signs.** Use labels and signs to designate areas.
2. **Colors.** Use colors to attract visual attention and define group and individual spaces as well as different storage areas and resource centers.
3. **Taping lines.** Draw taping lines on the floor or wall to define the different work areas.
4. **Mobiles and displays.** Use mobiles and display (such as arrows) to direct attention. You can designate work areas by taping displays on the wall or hanging them from the ceiling or by hanging mobiles from the ceiling.
5. **Lighting.** Use lighting to define specific work areas. Directed light (illuminating part of the room while leaving other areas dim) intensifies and directs students' attention. Brightly lit areas can draw people toward the areas and suggest activity. More dimly lit areas surrounding the lighted ones become area boundaries. As the activity in the classroom changes, the lighting could also change.
6. **Furniture arrangement.** Move furniture to define work and resource areas. Even tall plants, when placed in pots with wheels, can be moved to provide spatial boundaries.
7. **Displays.** Display group work to designate work spaces. If a cooperative group is to remain together for a period of several days or weeks, members may construct a poster or collage to designate their work area.

Many of these same procedures can be used to control acoustically levels of noise in the classroom. Complete Activity 7.2 to discover which classroom design outcomes are most important to you.

ACTIVITY **7.2** ■ IMPORTANCE OF CLASSROOM DESIGN

Following is a list of outcomes resulting from various classroom designs. Form a pair and rank order the outcomes from most important (1) to least important (9).

_____ 1. **Academic achievement.** The way in which interior space is designed influences the amount of time students spend on task and other variables affecting achievement.

_____ 2. **Visual and auditory focus.** The way in which interior space is designed creates overall visual order, focuses visual attention, and controls acoustics.

_____ 3. **Patterns of participation.** Classroom design influences the patterns of student (and teacher) participation in instructional activities, the emergence of leadership in learning groups, and the patterns of communication among students and between students and teachers.

_____ 4. **Social contact.** Opportunities for social contact and friendships among students can be created through classroom design.

_____ 5. **Learning climate.** The design of interior space affects students' and teachers' feelings (such as comfort, enjoyment, well-being, anger, depression) and general morale. Good spatial definition helps students feel secure by delineating structured learning areas.

_____ 6. **Classroom management.** Spatial definition prevents discipline problems by defining how and where students work, how to interact with others, and how to move through the classroom.

_____ 7. **Ease of accessibility.** When students' accessibility to each other, teachers, and learning materials is unencumbered and convenient, learning is facilitated.

_____ 8. **Smooth transitions.** When classrooms are well designed, students are able to make quick transitions from one grouping to another.

_____ 9. **Teacher movement.** When teachers are able to move easily from group to group to monitor student interaction, they have more time and attention to spend doing so carefully during the lesson.

Planning the Instructional Materials

The types of tasks students are required to complete determine what materials are needed for the lesson. You, the teacher, decide how materials are to be arranged and distributed among group members to maximize their participation and achievement. Usually, you distribute materials to communicate whether the assignment is to be a joint or individual effort. For a joint effort, you can create interdependence through the use of materials, information, and outside enemies.

Materials Interdependence.   Create materials interdependence by giving each group only one copy of the materials. The students then have to work together to be successful. This is especially effective the first few times the group meets. After students are accustomed to working cooperatively, teachers can give a copy of the materials to each student.

Information Interdependence.   Create information interdependence by arranging materials as a jigsaw puzzle so that each student has part of the materials needed to complete the assignment. Each group member can receive different books or resource materials to synthesize. Such procedures require that every member participate for the group to be successful.

Interdependence from Outside Enemies.   Create interdependence from outside enemies by structuring materials into an intergroup tournament format and having groups compete to see who has learned the most. Such a procedure was introduced by DeVries and Edwards (1973). In the Teams–Games–Tournament format, students are divided into heterogeneous cooperative learning teams to prepare members for a tournament in which they compete with other teams. During the intergroup competition, students individually compete against members of about the same ability level from other teams. The team whose members do the best in the competition is pronounced the winner by the teacher.

STRUCTURING THE TASK AND COOPERATIVE LEARNING GROUP

Explaining the Academic Task

At this point you have planned the preinstructional decisions and preparations for your lesson. The next step is to explain the task, the objectives of the lesson, the concepts and principles students need to know to complete the assignment, and the procedures as they are to follow. Face your class and inform them (a) what to do to complete the assignment and (b) how to do it. The steps are explained on the flow chart in Figure 7.1.

Explaining Criteria for Success

When explaining to students the academic task they are to complete, you need to communicate the level of performance you expect of students. Cooperative learning requires criterion-based evaluation. *Criterion-referenced or categorical judgments* are made by adopting a fixed set of standards and judging the achievement of each student against these standards. A common version of criterion-referenced grading involves assigning letter grades on the basis of the percentage of test items answered correctly (see Box 7.2). Make clear your criteria for evaluating students' work. You might say, "The group is not finished until every member has demonstrated mastery." Sometimes improvement (doing better this week than last week) may be set as the criterion of excellence. To promote intergroup cooperation, you may also set criteria for the whole class to reach. "If we as a class can score more than 520 words correct on our vocabulary test, each student will receive two bonus points."

Structuring Positive Interdependence

Positive goal interdependence exists when a mutual joint goal is established so that individuals perceive they can attain that goal if and only if their groupmates attain that

■ ■ ■ ■ ■

BOX 7.2
EXAMPLE OF CRITERION-REFERENCED GRADING

GRADE	PERCENT CORRECT
A	95–100
B	85–94
C	75–84
D	65–74
F	64 or less

goal (see Johnson & Johnson, 1992b; 1992c). Members know that they cannot succeed unless all other members of their group succeed. Positive interdependence is the heart of cooperative learning. Without positive interdependence, cooperation does not exist. Students must believe that they are in a sink-or-swim-together learning situation.

Structure Positive Goal Interdependence.   First, you structure positive goal interdependence. Every cooperative lesson begins with positive goal interdependence. To ensure that students think *We, not me,* you tell students, "You have three responsibilities. You are responsible for learning the assigned material. You are responsible for making sure that all other members of your group learn the assigned material. And you are responsible for making sure that all other class members successfully learn the assigned material."

Supplement Positive Goal Interdependence.   Second, you supplement positive goal interdependence with other types of positive interdependence (such as reward, role, resource, or identity). *Positive reward interdependence,* for example, may be structured through providing group rewards, for example, tell students, "If all members of your group score above 90 percent on the test, each of you will receive 5 bonus points." Usually, the more ways positive interdependence is structured in a lesson, the better.

Structuring Individual Accountability

In cooperative groups, everyone has to do his or her fair share of the work. An underlying purpose of cooperative learning is to make each group member a stronger individual in his or her own right. You hold all group members accountable to learn the assigned material and help other group members learn in two ways. First you assess the performance of each individual member. Second, you give the results back to the individual and the group to compare to preset criteria. The feedback enables members to (a) recognize and celebrate efforts to learn and contributions to groupmates' learning, (b) provide immediate remediation and any needed assistance or encouragement, and (c) reassign responsibilities to avoid any redundant efforts by members.

Individual accountability results in group members knowing they cannot "hitch-hike" on the work of others, loaf, or get a free ride. Ways of ensuring individual accountability include keeping group size small, giving an individual test to each student, giving random individual oral examinations, observing and recording the frequency with which each member contributes to the group's work, having students teach what they know to someone else, and having students apply what they have learned to various problems.

Structuring Intergroup Cooperation

You can extend the positive outcomes resulting from cooperative learning to the whole class by structuring intergroup cooperation. You establish class goals as well as group and individual goals. When a group finishes its work, you encourage members to find other groups (a) who are not finished and help them understand how to complete the assignment successfully or (b) who are finished and compare answers and strategies. Extend the benefits of cooperation to the whole class.

Specifying Desired Behaviors

When you use cooperative learning you must teach students the small-group and interpersonal skills they need to work effectively with each other. In cooperative learning groups, students must learn both academic subject matter (taskwork) and the interpersonal and small-group skills required to work as part of a group (teamwork). Cooperative learning is inherently more complex than competitive or individualistic learning because students have to engage simultaneously in taskwork and teamwork. If students do not learn teamwork skills, they cannot complete the taskwork. The greater the members' teamwork skills are, the higher are the quality and quantity of their learning. You define the needed teamwork skills operationally by specifying the behaviors that are appropriate and desirable within learning groups.

The more specific you are about the behaviors you want to see in the groups, the more likely students will do them. Social skills may be classified as *forming* (staying with the group, using quiet voices), *functioning* (contributing, encouraging others to participate), *formulating* (summarizing, elaborating), and *fermenting* (criticizing ideas, asking for justification). Regularly teach the interpersonal and small-group skills you want to see used in the learning groups.

Three rules of thumb in specifying desired behaviors follow.

1. **Be specific.** Operationally define each social skill through the use of a T-chart.
2. **Start small.** Do not overload your students with more social skills than they can learn at one time. Emphasizing one or two behaviors for a few lessons is enough.
3. **Emphasize overlearning.** Having students practice skills once or twice is not enough. Keep emphasizing a skill until the students have integrated it into their behavioral repertoires and do it automatically and habitually.

MONITORING AND INTERVENING

> The only thing that endures over time is the law of the farm: I must prepare the ground, put in the seed, cultivate it, water it, then gradually nurture growth and development to full maturity... there is no quick fix.
> —*Stephen Covey*

Once students begin working in cooperative learning groups, the teacher's role is to monitor students' interaction and intervene to help students learn and interact more skillfully.

Monitoring Students' Behavior

Your job begins in earnest when the cooperative learning groups start working. Resist that urge to get a cup of coffee or to grade papers. You observe the interaction among group members to assess students' (a) academic progress and (b) appropriate use of interpersonal and small-group skills. You arrange face-to-face promotive interaction and conduct the lesson in ways that ensure that students promote each other's success face to face.

Observations can be formal, using an observation schedule on which frequencies are tallied, or anecdotal, using informal descriptions of students' statements and actions. Based on your observations, you can then intervene to improve students' academic learning and/or interpersonal and small-group skills. Remember, students respect what we inspect.

To *monitor* means to check continally. Monitoring has four stages:

Stage 1. Preparing. Prepare for observing the learning groups by deciding who will be the observers, what observation forms to use, and by training the observers.

Stage 2. Observing. Observe to assess the quality of cooperative efforts in the learning groups.

Stage 3. Intervening. Intervene when it is necessary to improve a group's taskwork or teamwork.

Stage 4. Assessing. Have students assess the quality of their own individual participation in the learning groups to encourage self-monitoring; have groups assess the level of their effectiveness; and have both individuals and groups set growth goals.

In monitoring cooperative learning groups, teachers can follow a number of guidelines:

1. Plan a route through the classroom and the length of time spent observing each group so that all groups are observed during a lesson.
2. Use a formal observation sheet to count the number of times appropriate behaviors are observed being used by students. The more concrete the data are, the more useful the data are to you and to students.
3. Initially, do not try to count too many different behaviors. At first you may want simply to keep track of who talks. Your observations should focus on positive behaviors.
4. Supplement and extend the frequency data with notes on specific student actions. Especially useful are descriptions of skillful interchanges that later can be shared with students or with parents in conferences or during telephone conversations.
5. Train and use student observers. Student observers can obtain more complete data on each group's functioning and may learn important lessons about appropriate and inappropriate behavior.
6. Allocate sufficient time at the end of each group session for discussion of the data gathered by the observers.

Providing Task Assistance

Cooperative learning groups provide teachers with a "window" into students' minds. Through working cooperatively students make hidden thinking processes overt and subject to observation and commentary. From carefully listening to students explain to each other what they are learning, teachers can determine what students do and do not understand. Consequently, you may intervene to clarify instructions, review important procedures and strategies for completing the assignment, answer questions, and teach task skills as necessary. In discussing the concepts and information to be learned, you should make specific statements, such as, "Yes that is one way to find the main idea of a paragraph," not, "Yes, that is right." The specific statement reinforces the desired learning and promotes positive transfer by helping students associate a term with their learning. Metacognitive thought may be encouraged by asking students, (a) "What are you doing?" (b) "Why are you doing it?" and (c) "How will it help you?"

Intervening to Teach Social Skills

Cooperative learning groups provide teachers with a picture of students' social skills. The social skills required for productive group work are discussed in detail, along with activities that may be used in teaching them, in Johnson and F. Johnson (2000), Johnson (1991; 2000), and Johnson and R. Johnson (2000). While monitoring the learning groups, you may intervene to suggest more effective procedures for working together or reinforce particularly effective and skillful behaviors. Choosing when to intervene is part of the art of teaching. When intervening, ask group members to

1. Set aside their task
2. Listen to your statement of the problem
3. Create three possible solutions
4. Decide which solution they are going to try first

EVALUATING LEARNING AND PROCESSING INTERACTION

Providing Closure to the Lesson

You provide closure to lessons by having students summarize the major points in the lesson, recall ideas, and identify final questions for the teacher. Students should be able to summarize what they have learned and to understand how they will use it in the future.

Assessing the Quality and Quantity of Learning

The quality and quantity of student learning should be regularly assessed and occasionally evaluated using a criterion-referenced system. This is covered in depth in Johnson and Johnson (1996c). Cooperative learning, furthermore, provides an arena in which performance-based assessment, authentic assessment, and total quality learning can take place. *Performance-based assessment* requires students to demonstrate what they can do with what they know by performing a procedure or skill. *Authentic assessment* requires students to demonstrate the desired procedure or skill in a "real-life" context and *Total quality learning* is continuous improvement in the process of students helping teammates learn. A wide variety of assessment formats may be used, and students may be directly involved in assessing each other's level of learning and then providing immediate remediation to ensure all group members' learning is maximized. Complete Activity 7.3 to assess which aspects of cooperative learning you think are most important.

Processing How Well the Group Functioned

When students have completed the assignment or come to the end of a class session, students describe what member actions were helpful (and unhelpful) in completing the group's work and make decisions about what behaviors to continue or to change. Group processing occurs at two levels—in each learning group and in the class as a whole. Processing involves four stages:

Stage 1. Feedback. You ensure that each student, each group, and the class receives (and gives) feedback on the effectiveness of taskwork and teamwork. Feedback given to students should be descriptive and specific, not evaluative and general (see Johnson, 2000).

ACTIVITY **7.3** ■ ASSESSING THE QUALITY AND QUANTITY OF LEARNING

Form a pair. Rank order each of the items in the following columns from most important to you (1) to least important to you.

WHAT IS ASSESSED	PROCEDURES	WAYS COOPERATIVE LEARNING HELPS
____ academic learning	____ goal setting	____ additional sources of labor
____ reasoning strategies	____ testing	____ more modalities in assessment
____ skills, competencies	____ compositions	____ more diverse outcomes
____ attitudes	____ presentations	____ more sources of information
____ work habits	____ projects	____ reduction of bias
	____ portfolios	____ development of rubrics
	____ logs, journals	____ implementation of improvement planning

Stage 2. Reflection. You ensure that students analyze and reflect on the feedback they receive. You avoid questions that can be answered yes or no. Instead of saying, "Did everyone help each other learn?" you should ask, "How frequently did each member (a) explain how to solve a problem and (b) correct or clarify other member's explanations?"

Stage 3. Improvement goals. You help individuals and groups set goals for improving the quality of their work.

Stage 4. Celebration. You encourage the celebration of members' hard work and the group's success.

Have groups routinely list three things they did well in working together and one suggestion to do something better tomorrow. To reinforce both individual and group learning, have students summarize their learning as a whole class.

Any assignment in any subject area may be structured cooperatively. In using formal cooperative learning, the teacher makes a number of preinstructional decisions, explains to students the task and the cooperative goal structure, monitors the groups as they work, intervenes when it is necessary, and then evaluates and helps groups process. In addition to formal cooperative learning, teachers use informal cooperative learning and cooperative base groups. These groups are discussed in the following sections.

INFORMAL COOPERATIVE LEARNING GROUPS

At times instructors may need to lecture, show a movie or videotape, give a demonstration, or have a guest speaker. In such instances, informal cooperative learning may be used to ensure that students are cognitively active (not passive). *Informal cooperative learning* consists of having students work together to achieve a joint learning goal in temporary, ad-hoc groups that last from a few minutes to one class period. Their purposes are to focus student attention on the material to be learned, set a mood conducive to learning, help organize in advance the material to be covered in a class session, ensure that students cognitively process the material being taught, and provide closure to an instructional session. Informal cooperative learning groups also ensure that misconceptions, misunderstandings, and gaps in understanding are identified and corrected, and learning experiences are personalized. They may be used at any time, but are especially useful during a lecture or direct teaching. See Activity 7.4 to evaluate the importance of the purpose of informal cooperative learning.

During lecturing and direct teaching the instructional challenge for the instructor is to ensure that students do the intellectual work of organizing material, explaining it, summarizing it, and integrating it into existing conceptual frameworks. This may be achieved by having students do the advance organizing, cognitively process what they are learning, and provide closure to the lesson. Breaking up lectures with short, cooperative processing times slightly decreases lecture time, but helps counter the main complaint about lectures: The information passes from the notes of the professor to the notes of the student without passing through the mind of either one.

USING INFORMAL COOPERATIVE LEARNING

The following procedure will help you plan a lecture that keeps students more actively engaged intellectually (see Figure 7.2). It entails having *focused discussions* before and after the lecture (i.e., bookends) and interspersing *pair discussions* throughout the lecture. Two important aspects of using informal cooperative learning groups are to (a) make the task and the instructions explicit and precise and (b) require the groups to produce a specific product (such as a written answer). The procedure follows.

ACTIVITY **7.4** ■ PURPOSES OF INFORMAL COOPERATIVE LEARNING

Form a pair. Rank order the following purposes of informal cooperative learning from most important (1) to least important (7).

_____ Focuses student attention on the material to be learned.

_____ Sets a mood conducive to learning.

_____ Helps cognitively organize in advance the material to be covered in a class session.

_____ Ensures that students cognitively process the material being taught.

_____ Provides closure to an instructional session.

_____ Allows for identifying and correcting misconceptions, misunderstandings, and gaps in comprehension.

_____ Personalizes learning experiences.

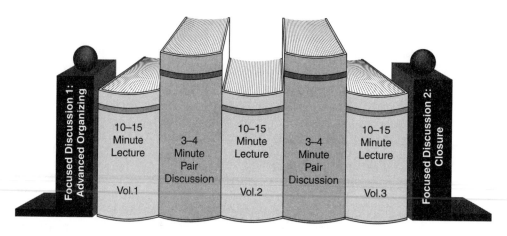

FIGURE 7.2   Informal Cooperative Learning

Introductory Focused Discussion.   Assign students to pairs. The person nearest them will do. You may prefer different seating arrangements each class period so that students meet and interact with a number of other students in the class. Give the pairs the cooperative assignment of completing the initial (advance organizer) task. Give them only 4 or 5 minutes to do so. The discussion task is aimed at promoting *advance organizing* of what the students know about the topic to be presented and *establishing expectations* about what the lecture will cover.

Intermittent Focused Discussions.   These discussions can be divided into two parts composed of a lecture segment and a pair discussion.

PART 1

Lecture Segment 1: Deliver the first segment of the lecture. This segment should last from 10 to 15 minutes. This is about the length of time a motivated adult can concentrate on a lecture. For unmotivated adolescents, the time may be shorter.

Pair Discussion 1: Give the students a discussion task focused on the material you have just presented that may be completed in 3 or 4 minutes. Its purpose is to ensure that students are actively thinking about the material being presented. The discussion task may be to (a) give an answer to a question posed by the instructor, (b) give a reaction to the theory, concepts, or information being presented, or (c) relate material to past learning so that it gets integrated into existing conceptual frameworks (i.e., students elaborate on the material being presented). Discussion pairs respond to the task in the following way:

1. Each student *formulates* his or her answer.
2. Students *share* their answer with their partner.
3. Students *listen* carefully to the partner's answer.
4. Pairs *create* a new answer that is superior to each member's initial formulation through the process of association, building on each other's thoughts, and synthesizing.

After students complete these four tasks, randomly choose two or three students to give 30-second summaries of their discussions. It is important that students are randomly called on to share their answers after each discussion task. This individual accountability ensures that the pairs take the tasks seriously and check each other to ensure that both are prepared to answer.

PART 2

Lecture Segment 2: Deliver the second segment of the lecture.

Pair Discussion 2: Give a discussion task focused on the second part of the lecture.

Repeat this sequence of lecture segment and pair discussion until the lecture is completed.

Closure Focused Discussion.   Give students an ending discussion task lasting 4 to 5 minutes to summarize what students have learned from the lecture. The discussion should result in students integrating what they have just learned into existing conceptual frameworks. The task may also point students toward what the homework will cover or what will be presented in the next class session. This provides closure to the lecture.

Informal cooperative learning ensures students are actively involved in understanding what they are learning. It also provides time for instructors to gather their wits, reorganize notes, take a deep breath, and move around the class listening to what students are saying. Listening to student discussions can give instructors direction and insight into how well students understand the concepts and material being taught (who, unfortunately, may not have any knowledge in the topic you are presenting). In the following sections more specific procedures for the initial focused discussion, the intermittent pair discussions, and the closure focused discussion is given.

NATURE OF BASE GROUPS

Committed relationships do not develop in a few hours or even a few days. They develop from spending long hours working together in which group members depend on and support each other. In schools, therefore, it is important that some of the relationships built through cooperative learning groups are long-term. School has to be more than a series of temporary encounters that last for only a few minutes, a class period, an instructional unit, or a semester. Students can be assigned to permanent cooperative base groups.

Cooperative base groups are long-term, heterogeneous cooperative learning groups with stable membership. Members' primary responsibilities are to (a) provide each other with support, encouragement, and assistance in completing assignments, (b) hold each other accountable for striving to learn, and (c) ensure all members are making good academic progress. Typically, cooperative base groups (a) are heterogeneous in membership (especially in terms of achievement motivation and task orientation), (b) meet regularly (for example, daily or biweekly), and (c) last for the duration of the class (a semester or year) or preferably until the students are graduated (see Table 7.1).

Types of Base Groups

Base groups may be used at the school level in two ways. The first is to have a base group in each course. Class base groups stay together only for the duration of the course. The second is to organize all students within the school into base groups and have the groups function as an essential component of school life. School base groups stay together for at least a year and preferably for four years or until all members are graduated. (See Table 7.2 for elements of forming base groups). The agendas of both types of base groups can include four tasks:

1. **Academic support tasks.** Base group members encourage each other to master course content and complete all assignments. Members check to see which

TABLE 7.1 Base Groups

TYPES	FUNCTIONS	NATURE
Class (meets at the beginning and ending of each session or week)	Provides academic support to members	Heterogeneous in membership
School (meets at the beginning and ending of each day or week)	Provides personal support to members	Meets regularly (daily, biweekly)
	Manages class routines and administrative requirements	Lasts for duration of class, year, or until graduation
	Personalizes class and school experience	Ensures all members are making good academic progress

TABLE 7.2 Forming Base Groups

GROUP SIZE	FOUR (OR THREE)
Assigning Students	Random assignment to ensure heterogeneity
Arranging Room	Permanent place for each group to meet
Preparing Materials	Standard forms students use each meeting; group file folders
Assigning Roles	Runner, explainer, accuracy, checker, encourager

assignments each member has and what help they need to complete them. The group discusses assignments, answers any questions about assignments, provides information about what a member missed, and plans, reviews, and edits papers. Members can prepare each other to take tests and go over the questions missed afterwards. Members can share their areas of expertise (such as art or computers) with each other. Above all, members monitor each other's academic progress and make sure all members are achieving.

2. **Personal support tasks.** Base group members listen sympathetically when a member has problems with parents or friends, have general discussions about life, give each other advice about relationships, and help each other solve nonacademic problems. Base groups provide interpersonal relationships that personalize the course.

3. **Routine tasks.** The base group provides a structure for managing course procedures such as attendance and homework.

4. **Assessment and evaluation tasks.** The base group provides a structure for assessing and evaluating student academic learning. Many of the more complex and important assessment procedures can best be used in the context of cooperative learning groups.

Class Base Groups

The larger the class and the more complex the subject matter, the more important it is to have class base groups. Base groups meet at the beginning and ending of each class session or (if the class session is 50 minutes or less) at the beginning of the first class session each week and at the end of the last class session each week. The members of base groups should exchange phone numbers and information about schedules as they may want to meet outside of class. Base groups have agendas that

TABLE 7.3   Base Group Agendas

OPENING TASKS	CLOSING TASKS
Greeting and welcome	Review and clarify assignments
Relationship and group-building task	Discuss what was learned
Check homework	Discuss applications of learnings
Review progress: ongoing assignments	Celebrate members' hard work

include specific and general tasks (see Table 7.3). All members are expected to contribute actively to the group's work, strive to maintain effective working relationships with other members, complete all assignments and assist groupmates in completing their assignments, and indicate agreement with base group's work by signing the weekly contract. At the beginning of each session students meet in base groups to carry out the following opening tasks (see Box 7.3):

1. Members greet each other and check to see that none of their group is under undue stress. Members ask,"How are you today?" and, "Are we all prepared for class?"

■ ■ ■ ■ ■ ■
BOX 7.3
BASE GROUP MEETINGS

- **When:** Base groups meet at the beginning and end of each class session.
- **Opening Tasks:** Ask and answer two or more of the following questions.
  1. How are you today? What is the best thing that has happened to you since the last class session?
  2. Are you prepared for this class session?
  3. Did you do your homework? Is there anything about it you do not understand?
  4. What have you read, thought about, or done relevant to this course since the last class session?
  5. May I read and edit your advanced preparation paper? Will you read and edit mine?
- **Closing Tasks:** Answer the following questions.
  1. Do you understand the assignment? What help do you need to complete it?
  2. What are three things you learned in today's class session?
  3. How will you use/apply what you have learned?
  4. How shall we celebrate the hard work and learning of group members?
- **Cooperative:** One set of answers from the group, everyone must agree, and everyone must be able to explain.
- **Individual Accountability:** One member of your group will be selected randomly to present your group's answers. At the beginning of the next class session, group members will ask you if you have followed through on your assignments and plans.
- **Expected Behaviors:** Active participating, encouraging, summarizing, and synthesizing.
- **Intergroup Cooperation:** Whenever it is helpful, check procedures, answers, and strategies with another group. When you are finished, compare your answers with those of another group and discuss.

2. Members complete the next task for the membership grid. This helps members get to know each other better. The task is to answer questions such as: What is the best thing that has happened to you this week? What is your favorite television show? Who is your favorite music group?

3. Members pick up their file folders with an attendance sheet, feedback form, and their assignments from the previous class session (with instructor's comments). The group members record their own attendance by writing the date and their initials in the Attendance section of the folder. They pass out the assignments from the previous class session and discuss any comments the instructor has made.

4. Members check to see whether members have completed their homework or need help in doing so. Members ask, "Did you do your homework?" "Is there anything you did not understand?" If extensive help is needed, an appointment is made.

5. In addition to the homework, members review what each member has read and done since the last class session. Each member may be prepared to (a) give a succinct summary of what he or she has read, thought about, and done; (b) share resources they have found; and (c) share copies of assignments they have completed.

6. Students collect each member's work, record it in their Base Group Progress Report Sheet, and place the assignments in their file folder. The file folder is returned to the instructor's desk. Periodically, the base groups may be given a checklist of academic skills to assess which ones each member needs to practice.

Generally, class base groups are available to support individual group members. If a group member arrives late, or must leave early on an occasion, the group can provide information about what that student missed. Group members may assist one another in writing required papers and completing other assignments. They can discuss assigned work, plan papers, review each other's progress, and edit each other's work. Questions regarding the course assignments and class sessions may be addressed in base groups.

The class session closes with students meeting in base groups. Some examples of closing tasks follow:

1. Ensure all members understand the assignments. Find out what help each member needs to complete the assigned work.

2. Summarize at least three things members learned in the day's class session.

3. Summarize how members will use and apply what they have learned.

4. Celebrate the hard work and learning of group members.

School Base Groups

At the beginning of their freshman year (or any academic year), students should be assigned to base groups. Base groups should stay together for at least a year and ideally, for four years (or until members are graduated). Class schedules should be arranged so members of base groups are assigned to as many of the same classes as possible. In essence, the computer is programmed to assign base groups to classes (whenever possible) rather than to individuals.

During the year, base groups meet either twice each day or week. When base groups meet twice a week, they meet first thing Monday morning and last thing Friday afternoon. Mirroring class base groups, school base groups meet at the beginning of each day to carry out the following opening tasks:

1. Members congratulate each other for showing up with all their books and materials and check to see that none of their group is under undue stress. Members ask, "How are you today?" and, "Are we all prepared for the day?"

2. Members check to see whether each student is keeping up with his or her class work or needs help and assistance in doing so. The questions to discuss are, Tell us how you are doing in each of your classes? Is there anything you did not understand? If there is not enough time to help each other during the base group meeting, an appointment is made to meet again during free time or lunch. Periodically, the base groups may be given a checklist of academic skills and assess which ones each member needs to practice.
3. Members review what they have read and done since the evening before. Members should be able to give a succinct summary of what they have read, thought about, and done. They may come to the group meeting with resources they have found and want to share, or copies of work they have completed and would like to distribute to group members.
4. Members get to know each other better and provide positive feedback by discussing questions such as, What do you like about each other? What do you like about yourself? and, What is the best thing that has happened to you this week?

At the end of the day students meet in their base groups to ensure everyone is doing their homework, understands the assignments to be completed, and has the help and assistance they need to do their work. In addition, base groups may discuss what members have learned during the day and check to see whether all members have plans to do something fun and interesting that evening.

When base groups meet twice each week (perhaps first thing on Monday and last thing on Friday), they meet to discuss the academic progress of each member, provide help and assistance to each other, and hold each member accountable for completing assignments and progressing satisfactorily through the academic program. The meeting on Monday morning refocuses the students on school, provides any emotional support required after the weekend, reestablishes personal contact among base group members, and helps students set their academic goals for the week (what is still to be done on assignments that are due, and so forth). Members should carefully review each other's assignments and ensure that they have the help and assistance needed. In addition, they should hold each other accountable for succeeding academically. The meeting on Friday afternoon helps students review the week, set academic goals for the weekend (what homework has to be done before Monday), and share weekend plans and hopes.

Quick Base Group Meetings

At times only a few minutes are available for base groups to meet. Even in as short a time as 5 to 10 minutes, base groups can address four tasks:

1. A quick *self-disclosure task,* such as asking members, "What is the most exciting thing you did during your vacation break? What is the best thing that happened to you last weekend? What is something you are proud of? What is your favorite ice cream?"
2. An *administrative task,* such as discussing which classes to register for next semester
3. An *academic task,* such as thinking about test-taking skills. Tell students, "You have midterms coming up. As a group, write out three pieces of advice for taking tests. I will type up the suggestions from each group and hand them out next week."
4. A *closing task,* such as wishing each other good luck for the day or week

Building a Group Identity

The effectiveness of base groups depends in part on the strength of the group identity. The first week the base groups meet, for example, base groups can pick a name, design a flag, or choose a motto. If an instructor with the proper expertise is available, the groups can benefit from participating in a challenge course involving ropes and obstacles. This type of physical challenge that the groups complete together builds cohesion quickly.

Base Group Grid

The more personal the relationships are among base group members, the greater is the social support that members can give each other. Although students get to know each other on a personal level while they work together, the process can be accelerated through the use of the base group grid (see Figure 7.3).

Each base group meeting begins with a self-disclosure task in which students complete a column in their base group grid. Consider the following examples: What is a positive childhood memory? What is your most memorable vacation? What is the best book you ever read? What is the most important thing you have ever done? What is the farthest place (from this room) you have traveled to? Members write down each student's response in enough detail so that they can remember it a year later.

Checking and Recording Homework

Homework is usually checked in base groups at the beginning of the class session. One member of each group, the *runner*, goes to the instructor's desk, picks up the group's folder, and hands out any materials in the folder to the appropriate members. The group reviews the assignment step by step to determine how much of the assignment each member completed and how well each member understands how to complete the material covered. Two roles are used: explainer and accuracy checker. The *explainer* explains step by step how the homework is correctly completed. The *accuracy checker* verifies that the explanation is accurate and provides coaching if needed. The role of explainer is rotated so that each member takes turns explaining step by step how a portion of the homework is correctly completed. The other members are accuracy checkers. The base groups concentrate on clarifying the parts of the assignment that one or more members do not understand. At the end of the review the runner records how much of the assignment each member completed, places members' homework in the group's folder, and returns the folder to the instructor's desk.

Base Group Folders

The base group folder provides direct communication between students and the instructor. Each base group creates a folder. The folders may be personalized with the

FIGURE 7.3 Examples of a Base Group Grid

Members	Topic 1	Topic 2	Topic 3	Topic 4
Frank				
Helen				
Roger				
David				

group's motto or symbol. The folder is a means for managing attendance, assignments, and feedback. In each folder is an attendance sheet that each member initials to indicate attendance at the session. The base group folder provides a structure for keeping track of student attendance.

During each class session students place their completed homework and other assignments in the folder and turn it in. At the beginning of the following session, the assignments are returned (in the folder) with the instructor's comments on them. Each member receives a score for the quality of the homework completed and the base group as a whole receives a score (the sum of the points each member received). If all base group members complete the assignments at a level of 100 percent, every member receives 5 bonus points. The base group folder provides a procedure for collecting and assessing assignments.

At the end of the session each member fills out a feedback form. The forms are collected and placed in the folder. The folder is then returned to the instructor as the session ends. The feedback form may ask for (a) the three most important things the student learned during the session, (b) students' favorite part of the session, and (c) the questions students have about the material presented. The base group folder thus provides a structure for obtaining immediate feedback as to students' reactions to each class session.

Learning Community

A number of years ago, a speeding car carrying five teenagers slammed into a tree, killing three of them. It was not long before small, spontaneous memorials appeared at the tree. A yellow ribbon encircled its trunk. Flowers were placed nearby on the ground. A few goodbye signs were posted. Such quiet testimonies send an important message: When it really matters, we are part of a community, not isolated individuals. We define ourselves in such moments as something larger than our individual selves—as friends, classmates, teammates, and neighbors.

Many students have the delusion that each person is separate and apart from all other individuals. It is easy to be concerned only with yourself. But when classmates commit suicide and when cars slam into trees killing classmates, the shock waves force individuals out of the shallowness of self into the comforting depth of community. In times of crisis, such community may mean the difference between isolated misery and deep personal talks with caring friends.

Being part of a community does not "just happen" when a student enters school. Being known, being liked and respected, and being involved in relationships that provide help and support do not magically happen when the freshman year begins. Although many students are able to develop relationships with classmates and fellow students that provide support systems, other students are unable to do so. Schools have to structure student experiences carefully to build a learning community.

INTEGRATED USE OF ALL THREE TYPES OF COOPERATIVE LEARNING

The third step in increasing your expertise in using cooperative learning is to integrate all three types of cooperative learning. When used in combination, formal, informal, and base cooperative learning groups provide an overall structure to classroom life (Johnson & Johnson, 1999a; Johnson, Johnson, & Holubec, 1998b). A class session may begin with a base group meeting, followed by a brief lecture in which informal cooperative learning is used. Students then work together in a formal cooperative lesson, which is followed by a a short lecture with informal cooperative learning that summarizes what has been learned. The class session ends with a base group meeting.

Tables 7.4, 7.5, and 7.6 illustrate ways in which the three types of cooperative learning may be integrated. Two integrated lessons are then explained in depth.

Examples of Lessons That Integrate All Three Goal Structures

Two examples have been provided to illustrate how a classroom lesson can integrate all three goal structures: cooperative, competitive, and individualistic (see Box 7.4).

Example 1: The Billion-Dollar Being. Students arrive at class and meet in their base groups to welcome each other, complete a self-disclosure task (such as identifying each member's favorite television show), check each student's homework to make sure all members understand the academic material and are prepared for the class session, and tell each other to have a great day.

The teacher then begins a lesson on the limitations of being human. To help students cognitively organize in advance what they know about the advantages and disadvantages of being human, the teacher uses informal cooperative learning. The teacher asks students to form a triad and ponder the question, What are five things you cannot do with your human limitations that a billion-dollar being might be designed to do? (See *Topic in Applied Science,* Jefferson County Schools, Golden, Colorado, for this Billion-Dollar Being lesson.) Students have 4 minutes to do so. In the next 10 minutes, the teacher explains that although the human body is a marvelous system, we (like other organisms) have specific limitations. We cannot see bacteria in a drop of water or the rings of Saturn unaided. We cannot hear as well as a deer or fly

TABLE 7.4 Integrating All Types of Cooperative Learning for a 50-Minute Session

ACTIVITY	MINUTES
Welcome and opening base group meeting	10
Choice 1: Direct teaching, informal cooperative learning	35
Choice 2: Work in formal cooperative learning groups	35
Choice 3: Direct teaching, formal cooperative learning groups	35
Choice 4: Academic controversy	35
Closing base group meeting	5

TABLE 7.5 Weekly Schedule for 50-Minute Class Sessions

SESSION 1		SESSION 2		SESSION 3	
Minutes	*Activity*	*Minutes*	*Activity*	*Minutes*	*Activity*
15	Base group meeting	5	Base group meeting	5	Base group meeting
30	Lecture with informal cooperative learning	35	Formal cooperative learning groups work on assignment or controversy	15	Formal cooperative learning groups work on assignment
5	Base group meeting	5	Base group meeting	10	Lecture with informal cooperative learning
				15	Base group meeting

TABLE 7.6   Integrating All Types of Cooperative Learning for a 90-Minute Session

ACTIVITY	MINUTES
Opening base group meeting	10
Direct teaching with informal cooperative learning	25
Work on assignment in formal cooperative learning	40
Direct teaching with informal cooperative learning	10
Closing base group meeting	5

■ ■ ■ ■ ■

BOX 7.4
INTEGRATED USE OF ALL TYPES OF LEARNING STRUCTURES

- **Task:** Plan a day (week) with cooperative learning being used 100 percent of the time. The objective is to provide an overall gestalt as to how the four different types of cooperative learning and a wide variety of the lesson structures may be used in an integrated way.
- **Cooperative:** Find a partner who teaches the same grade level and subject area as you do. Develop one plan for the two of you, both of you must agree that the plan will work, and both of you must be able to implement the plan.
- **Individual Accountability:** Each person will have to present the plan to a member of another group.
- **Expected Behaviors:** Explaining, listening, synthesizing by all members.
- **Intergroup Cooperation:** Whenever it is helpful, check procedures and plans with other groups.

Note: Now that it has been established that cooperative learning may be used 100 percent of the day, the issue of the supplemental use of competitive and individualistic learning becomes relevant. The next chapter focuses on this issue.

as an eagle does. Humans have never been satisfied with being limited, and, therefore, we have invented microscopes, telescopes, and wings. The teacher then instructs students to turn to the person next to them and answer the questions, What are three limitations of humans; what have we invented to overcome them, and what other human limitations might we be able to overcome?

Formal cooperative learning is now implemented in the lesson. The teacher has the 32 students count off from 1 to 8 to form random groups of four. Group members sit so they can face each other and face the teacher. Each member is assigned a role: researcher/runner, summarizer/time keeper, collector/recorder, and technical advisor (role interdependence). Every group gets one large 2-feet by 3-feet piece of paper, a marking pen, sheet of scratch paper for designing the rough draft of the being, an assignment sheet explaining the task and cooperative goal structure, and four student self-evaluation checklists (resource interdependence).

The *task* is to design a billion-dollar being who overcomes the human limitations thought of by the class and the group. The group members are to draw a diagram of the being on the scratch paper and when satisfied with the diagram, transfer it to the larger paper. The teacher establishes *positive goal interdependence* by asking for one group drawing that all group members contribute to and can explain. The *criterion for success* is to complete the diagram in the 30-minute time limit.

The teacher ensures *individual accountability* by observing each group to ensure that members are fulfilling their roles and that any one member can explain any part of the being at any time. The teacher informs students that the *expected social skills* to be used by all students are encouraging each other's participation, contributing ideas, and summarizing. The skill of encouraging participation is defined and each student practices it twice before the lesson begins.

While students work in their groups, the teacher *monitors* by systematically observing each group and intervening to provide academic assistance in using the interpersonal and small-group skills required to work together effectively. At the end of the lesson the groups hand in their diagrams of the billion-dollar being to be assessed and *evaluated.* Group members then *process* how well they worked together by identifying actions each member engaged in that helped the group succeed and one suggestion to improve their group next time.

The teacher uses *informal cooperative learning* to provide closure to the lesson by asking students to meet in new triads and write out six conclusions about the limitations of human beings and what can be done to overcome them. At the end of the class session the cooperative base groups meet to review what students believe is the most important thing they have learned during the day, what homework has been assigned, what help each member needs to complete the homework, and to tell each other to have a fun afternoon and evening.

Example 2: Global Economic Interdependence.   Students start the school day by meeting in their base groups to welcome each other, complete a self-disclosure task (such as identifying each member's favorite television show), check each student's homework to make sure all members understand the academic material and are prepared for the day, and tell each other to have a great day. The teacher then begins a lesson on world interdependence. The teacher has a series of objects and wants students to identify all the countries involved in creating the objects. To help students cognitively organize in advance what they know about the world economy, the teacher uses informal cooperative learning by asking students to turn to the person seated next to them and identify the seven continents and one product that is produced in each continent. They have 4 minutes to do so.

Formal cooperative learning is now implemented in the lesson. The objectives for the lesson are for students to learn about global economic interdependence and to improve their skill in encouraging each other's participation. The teacher has the 30 students count off from 1 to 10 to form random triads. They sit so they can either face each other or face the teacher.

The teacher hands out objects that include a silk shirt with plastic buttons, a cup of tea (a saucer and cup with a tea bag and a lump of sugar in it), and a portable tape player and earphones (with a cassette tape of a Nashville star) made by Phillips (a European company). She assigns members of each triad the roles of hypothesiser (who hypothesizes about the number of products in each item and where they came from), reference guide (who looks up each hypothesized country in the book to see what products it exports), and recorder. After each item the roles are rotated so that each student fulfills each role once. The teacher introduces the concept of world economic interdependence with several observations:

1. A hand-held calculator most often consists of electronic chips from the United States, is assembled in Singapore or Indonesia, placed in a steel housing from India, and stamped with the label Made in Japan on arrival in Yokohama. (The paper and ink in the label are all made from the trees and chemicals in Japan but are processed elsewhere; the plastic in the keys and body are also all processed elsewhere.)

2. Modern hotels in Saudi Arabia are built with room modules made in Brazil, with construction labor from South Korea, and with management from the United States.
3. Global economic interdependence is almost beyond imagining.

The teacher then assigns the *academic task* of identifying how many countries contributed to the production of each object. *Positive goal interdependence* is established by stating that it is a cooperative assignment, therefore, all members of the group must agree on an answer before it is recorded, and all members must be able to explain each of the group's answers. The criteria for success is to hand in a correctly completed report form and for each member to score 90 percent or better on a test to be given the next day on world economic interdependence. *Positive reward interdependence* is established by stating that if the record sheet is accurate, each member will receive 15 points, and if all members of the group achieve 90 percent or better on the test, each member will receive 5 bonus points.

Individual accountability is established by the roles assigned and the individual test. In addition, the teacher observes each group to make sure all students are participating and learning. The teacher informs students that the *expected social skill* to be used by all students is encouraging each other's participation. The teacher defines the skill and has each student practice it twice before the lesson begins.

While students work in their groups, the teacher *monitors* by systematically observing each group and intervening to provide academic assistance in using the interpersonal and small-group skills required to work together effectively. At the end of the lesson the groups hand in their report forms to be *evaluated* and *process* how well they worked together by identifying three things members did to help the group achieve and one suggestion to improve their group next time.

Next, the teacher uses a *generic cooperative lesson structure* to teach vocabulary. Studying vocabulary words is a weekly routine in this class. Teachers tell students to move into their vocabulary pairs, take the vocabulary words identified in the world interdependence lesson. For each word students (a) write down what they think the word means, (b) look it up in the text and write down its official definition, (c) write a sentence in which the word is used, and (d) learn how to spell the word. When they have completed these tasks for each word, the pair is to make up a story in which all the words are used. Pairs then exchange stories and carefully determine whether all the words are used appropriately and spelled correctly. If not, the two pairs discuss the word until everyone is clear about what it means and how it should be used.

The teacher uses informal cooperative learning to provide closure to the lesson by asking students to meet with a person from another group and write out four conclusions they derived from the lesson and circle the one they believe was the most important. At the end of the day the cooperative base groups meet to review what students believe is the most important thing they have learned during the day, what homework has been assigned, what help each member needs to complete the homework, and to tell each other to have a fun afternoon and evening.

SUMMARY

There is considerable research indicating that cooperative efforts, compared with competitive and individualistic ones, result in promotive interaction. This, in turn, results in greater efforts to achieve more positive interpersonal relationships and greater psychological health.These outcomes only result, however, if cooperation is implemented in ways that highlight positive interdependence, individual accountability, promotive interaction, appropriate use of interpersonal and small-group skills, and group processing. There are three types of cooperative learning: formal cooperative learning for entire lessons or unites, informal cooperative learning to make direct instruction active (not passive), and cooperative base groups to provide long-term support for academic progress. Formal cooperative learning consists of instructors making a set of preinstructional decisions (such as group size and assignment method), explaining the task and cooperative structure, monitoring the learning groups and intervening to improve taskwork and teamwork, assessing the quality of learning, and ensuring students process how effectively they are working together. Informal cooperative learning entails interspersing pair discussion throughout the lesson and having focused discussions before and after the direct teaching. Cooperative base groups are aimed at providing the support and encouragement needed to ensure that all members progress academically. There may be class base groups or school base groups.

When integrated correctly, these cooperative learning groups provide an overall structure to classroom life. A class session may begin with a base group meeting, followed by a brief lecture in which informal cooperative learning is used. Students then work together in a formal cooperative lesson, which is followed by a short lecture with informal cooperative learning that summarizes what has been learned. The class session ends with a base group meeting.

Creating a cooperative classroom provides the foundation for diversity becoming a valued resource. Whether the power of cooperation is fully utilized largely depends on how conflicts among diverse individuals are managed.

COOPERATIVE LESSON PLANNING FORM

Subject Area: _____   Date: _____

Lesson: _____

MAKING PREINSTRUCTIONAL DECISIONS

Academic objectives: _____

Social skills objectives: _____

_____

Group size: _____   Method of assigning students: _____

Roles: _____

Room arrangement: _____

Materials: _____

_____ One copy per group   _____ On copy per person

_____ Jigsaw   _____ Tournament

_____ Other: _____

EXPLAINING TASK AND COOPERATIVE GOAL STRUCTURE

1. Task: _____

_____

2. Criteria for success: _____

_____

3. Positive interdependence: _____

_____

4. Individual accountability: _____

_____

5. Intergroup cooperation: _____

_____

6. Expected behaviors: _____

_____

MONITORING AND INTERVENING

1. Observation procedure: _____ Formal _____ Informal

2. Observer: _____ Instructor _____ Students _____ Visitors

3. Intervening for task assistance: _____

   _____

4. Intervening for teamwork assistance: _____

   _____

5. Other: _____

   _____

ASSESSING AND PROCESSING

1. Assessment of members' individual learning: _____

   _____

2. Assessment of group productivity: _____

   _____

3. Small-group processing: _____

   _____

4. Whole-class processing: _____

   _____

5. Charts and graphs used: _____

   _____

6. Positive feedback to each student: _____

   _____

7. Goal setting for improvement: _____

   _____

8. Celebration: _____

   _____

9. Other: _____

   _____

COOPERATIVE LEARNING LESSON-PLANNING SHORT FORM

Subject Area: _____ Date: _____

Lesson: _____

Objectives: _____ Academic _____ Social Skills

Group size: _____ Method of assigning students: _____

Roles: _____ Materials: _____

Academic task: _____

_____

_____

Criteria for success: _____

_____

_____

Positive interdependence: _____

_____

_____

Individual accountability: _____

_____

_____

Expected behaviors: _____

_____

_____

Monitoring: _____ Instructor _____ Students _____ Visitors

Behaviors observed: _____

_____

_____

Assessment of learning: _____

_____

_____

Small-group processing: _____

_____

_____

Goal setting: _____

_____

_____

Whole-class processing: _____

_____

_____

Celebration: _____

Other: _____

INFORMAL COOPERATIVE LEARNING PLANNING FORM

Subject Area: _____ Date: _____

Lesson: _____

DESCRIPTION OF THE LECTURE

1. Lecture topic: _____

2. Objectives (major understandings students need to have at the end of the lecture):

    a. _____

    _____

    b. _____

    _____

3. Time needed: _____

4. Method for assigning students to pairs or triads: _____

5. Method of changing partners quickly: _____

6. Materials (such as transparencies listing the questions to be discussed and describing the formulate–share–listen–create procedure): _____

    _____

    _____

ADVANCED ORGANIZER QUESTION(S)

Questions should be aimed at promoting *advance organizing* of what the students know about the topic to be presented and *establishing expectations* as to what the lecture will cover.

    1. _____

    _____

    2. _____

    _____

    3. _____

    _____

COGNITIVE REHEARSAL QUESTIONS

List the specific questions to be asked every 10 or 15 minutes to ensure that participants understand and process the information being presented. Instruct students to use the formulate–share–listen–create procedure. Monitor by systematically observing each pair. Intervene when it is necessary. Collect data for whole-class processing.

1. _____

_____

2. _____

_____

3. _____

_____

4. _____

_____

SUMMARY QUESTION(S)

Give an ending discussion task and require students to come to consensus, write down the pair or triad's answer(s), sign the paper, and hand it in. Signatures indicate that students agree with the answer, can explain it, and guarantee that their partner(s) can explain it. The questions could (a) ask for a summary, elaboration, or extension of the material presented or (b) precue the next class session.

1. _____

_____

2. _____

_____

CELEBRATE STUDENTS' HARD WORK

1. _____

_____

2. _____

_____

CHAPTER EIGHT

THE CONFLICT-POSITIVE SCHOOL

THE SCHOOL AS A CONFLICT-POSITIVE ORGANIZATION

> If civilization is to survive, we must cultivate the science of human
> relationships—the ability of all peoples, of all kinds, to live together, in
> the same world at peace. —*Franklin Delano Roosevelt*

The eighth step in maximizing the promise (and minimizing the dangers) of diversity is to understand how to resolve conflicts constructively and gain skill in using the procedures for doing so. To ensure that diverse students build positive relationships and interact in constructive ways, conflicts must (a) occur frequently and (b) be managed constructively. In other words, schools must be conflict-positive organizations, not conflict-negative organizations (Tjosvold & Johnson, 1983; Tjosvold, 1991). (See Table 8.1.)

The Conflict-Negative School

In a *conflict-negative school* conflicts are suppressed and avoided and, when they occur, are managed in destructive ways. The assumption is that conflicts are destructive. Therefore, the goals of good management are twofold: (a) to try to eliminate all conflict from the school by suppressing, avoiding, and denying its existence and (b) to minimize the impact of any conflict that takes place. All conflicts are considered the same type and believed to be the source of problems in the school. The belief is that conflicts are inherently destructive, with no redeeming value.

People may react to conflicts with fear, anxiety, apprehension, insecurity, and defensiveness. Procedures are established to avoid conflict, such as isolating any person who seems likely to engage in a conflict and separating potential disputants from each other. Training students and faculty in conflict management procedures is avoided because it is perceived as ineffective or even as encouraging people to engage in conflicts.

The Conflict-Positive School

A *conflict-positive school* is one where conflicts are encouraged and managed constructively to maximize their potential in enhancing the quality of teaching, learning, and school life in general. Different types of conflicts are recognized. Conflicts are viewed as being inevitable and pervasive throughout school life. Even if we could avoid conflict, which we cannot, we would not want to. The occurrence of conflicts is not a

TABLE 8.1 Differences between Conflict-Positive and Conflict-Negative Organizations

CONFLICT-NEGATIVE VIEWS	CONFLICT-POSITIVE VIEWS
Conflict is unitary.	Conflicts are various and can assume many different forms.
Conflict is the problem.	Conflict is part of the solution.
Conflicts should be avoided.	Conflicts should be sought and encouraged.
Conflict is inherently destructive.	How conflict is managed determines whether outcomes are destructive or constructive.
Conflicts have no value.	Conflict has many values.
Conflicts cause fear, anxiety, apprehension, insecurity, and defensiveness.	Conflicts create excitement, interest, concentration, and a sense of promise.
Competent management should strive to suppress, avoid, and contain conflict.	Competent management should encourage and support conflict.
Individuals should be isolated and separated to avoid conflict.	Individuals should be organized into teams to promote conflict.
Procedures should be established to prevent conflict.	Procedures should be established to manage conflict.
Training encourages conflicts.	All members should be trained in procedures that ensure coorientation and normative support.
When cornered into a conflict, individuals should go for a "win."	In a conflict, individuals should try to "solve the problem."

cause for despair. Conflicts are not the problem, they are part of the solution. Many valuable outcomes are seen as resulting from conflicts. Conflicts are not only inevitable, they are healthy and valuable, revitalizing and rejuvenating the school.

These positive outcomes, however, are not automatic. The way in which conflict is managed determines whether it has positive or negative outcomes. Rather than suppressing conflicts, conflicts should be encouraged as long as they are managed constructively. Rather than fearing conflicts, the possibility of conflict creates feelings of excitement, interest, and promise.

Faculty and administration, therefore, create, encourage, and support the possibility of conflict. One way they do so is to organize students and themselves into teams. Students work in cooperative learning groups and faculty work in colleagial teaching teams. Within the teams, specific procedures for managing conflict are taught so that all members of the school use the same procedures. They are expected to face conflict and resolve it constructively. To create a conflict-positive school, educators must understand several issues:

1. What conflicts are
2. The difference between destructive and constructive management of conflicts
3. The positive outcomes of constructively managed conflicts
4. How to ensure that all students and faculty use the same procedures for managing conflicts
5. The steps for teaching students how to manage conflicts constructively

How conflict is managed in an organization is a key element in defining the organization's culture. *Culture* is a shared way of life of a group of socially interacting individuals. Culture is transmitted from generation to generation by the processes of enculturation and socialization. Although lasting over time, culture is recreated daily through interactions among individuals and between individuals and their surroundings. A positive, caring culture is created in a school through the combination of creating a cooperative community in which conflicts are managed constructively and all members internalize the same civic values.

WHAT IS CONFLICT?

Storms are a natural and unavoidable aspect of Earth's weather system. Storms range in intensity from mild rainstorms to hurricanes. Some storms are accompanied by gentle rain, others by thunder and lightning. Conflicts are the storms between individuals. They are a natural and unavoidable aspect of human relationships, and they vary in intensity from mild to severe. To manage your interpersonal storms, you need to know several things about conflicts.

According to the *World Book Dictionary,* a conflict is a fight, struggle, battle, disagreement, dispute, or quarrel. A conflict can be as small as a disagreement or as large as a war. Probably the most influential definition is that of Deutsch (1973), who states that a *conflict* exists whenever incompatible activities occur. An activity that is incompatible with another activity is one that prevents, blocks, or interferes with the occurrence or effectiveness of the second activity. Incompatible activities may originate in one person, between two or more people, or between two or more groups (see Activity 8.1).

Conflicts must be accepted as a natural part of life that must be faced and resolved in constructive ways. You might as well try to stop the earth from turning on its axis as try to eliminate conflicts from your life. Conflicts arise no matter what you do. Conflicts are especially frequent whenever you have goals you care about and are involved in relationships you value.

Whenever conflicts occur, destructive or constructive outcomes may result. Obtaining constructive outcomes requires (a) a set of procedures for managing conflicts constructively; (b) the opportunity to practice, practice, practice the procedures until real skill and expertise in their use is attained; and (c) the support and encouragement to use the procedures by the norms and values of the school (and home). If conflicts are to be managed constructively, everyone needs to use the same procedures to resolve them and be skilled in their use. All members of an organization (such as a school, business, or family) must use the same procedure. A constructive agreement results when (a) the agreement maximizes joint benefits and everyone goes away satisfied and pleased; (b) disputants are better able to work together cooperatively and have more respect, trust, and liking for each other; and (c) disputants are better able to resolve future conflicts constructively.

Conflicts occur continually, and because so many people are so unskilled in managing conflicts, learning how to resolve conflicts constructively is one of the best investments you can make. Once learned, conflict skills accompany you in every situation and in every relationship. Knowing how to resolve conflicts with skill and grace can increase your career success, quality of relationships with friends and colleagues, and happiness. Complete Activity 8.2 to examine what conflict means to you.

At least four important types of conflicts for schools (Johnson & Johnson, 1995a; 1995b) are controversy, conceptual conflict, conflict of interests, and developmental conflict. *Academic controversy* exists when one student's ideas, information, conclusions, theories, and opinions are incompatible with those of another, and the two seek to reach an agreement. Controversies are resolved by engaging in what Aristotle called *deliberate discourse* (i.e., the discussion of the advantages and disadvantages of proposed actions) aimed at synthesizing novel solutions (i.e., *creative problem solving*).

Closely related to controversies are *conceptual conflicts,* which occur when incompatible ideas exist simultaneously in a person's mind or when information being received does not seem to fit with what one already knows. An example is when the

ACTIVITY **8.1** ■ WHAT IS CONFLICT?

Working as a pair, write out your answers to the following questions. There should be one set of answers for the two of you, both of you have to agree on the answers, and both of you have to be able to explain your answers to the teacher or the entire class. When you have finished, find another pair and compare answers. Use some of their ideas to improve your answers.

1. Conflict begins when two people want the same thing. When one person says, "I want the ice cream bar" and another person says, "I want the ice cream bar," a conflict exists. What do you think a conflict is? Define the word *conflict* in your own words, using your own ideas.

2. Are conflicts good _____ or bad _____?

Give three examples of good conflicts. Give three examples of bad conflicts. Then list three small and three large conflicts. Finally, list three conflicts at home and three conflicts at school.

Good	Bad

Small	Large

Home	School

3. What is more important?

_____ Getting what you want

_____ Maintaining a good relationship with the other person

(What lasts longer, a cookie or a friend?)

---

same amount of water is poured into two glasses—one is tall and skinny and the other is short and fat. The student knows that each glass holds the same amount of water but at the same time believes that the tall glass has more water in it.

A *developmental conflict* exists when recurrent incompatible activities between adult and child, based on the opposing forces of stability and change within the child, cycle in and out of peak intensity as the child develops cognitively and socially. Examples of developmental conflicts include dependence versus independence and security in the status quo versus demand for growth and change. Each is a continuum. Conflicts appear at either end. The child, for example, may test the limits of dependence and then months later test the limits of independence.

To understand conflicts of interest, you must first understand what wants, needs, goals, and interests are (Johnson & Johnson, 1995a). Each of us want many things. A *want* is a desire for something. Each person basically has a unique set of

ACTIVITY **8.2** ■ WHAT CONFLICT MEANS TO ME

Think of what *conflict* means to you. Is it scary or exciting? Is it interesting or yucky? Write in the circles words that come into your mind when you think of conflict. (Make additional circles if needed.)

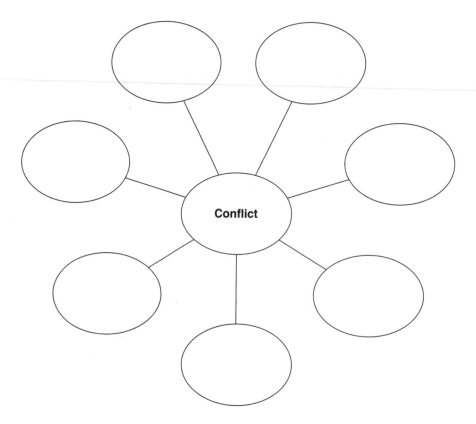

Compare your words with those of the other members of your group. Decide as a group what the word *conflict* means and write your answer below.

_____

_____

wants. A *need* is a necessity for survival. Needs are more universal. Every person has needs that must be satisfied for survival and reproduction (water, food, shelter, sex); for belonging (love, sharing, cooperation); and for power, freedom, and fun (Glasser, 1984). On the basis of our wants and needs we set goals. A *goal* is an ideal state of affairs that we value and are working to achieve. Our goals are related through social interdependence. When we have mutual goals, we are in a cooperative relationship; when our goals are in opposition, we are in a competitive relationship. Our *interests* are the potential benefits gained by achieving our goals.

Within schools and classrooms the interests of students, teachers, and administrators at times are congruent and at times are in conflict. A *conflict of interests* exists when the actions of one person attempting to reach his or her goals prevent, block, or interfere with the actions of another person attempting to reach his or her goals (Deutsch, 1973). Most conflicts of interests involve:

1. Use of something (computer, book, clothes, car)
2. Obtaining something (money, clothes, computer games, power)
3. Agreeing on something (what movie to see, where to eat, what to do)

In many classrooms teachers create a conflict of interests among students by having them compete for grades. Conflicts of interests are common among students, between students and faculty, among faculty members, and between faculty and administrators, both because they occur naturally and because they are deliberately created. (See Activity 8.3.)

CONFLICTS CAN BE DESTRUCTIVE OR CONSTRUCTIVE

It is not the presence of conflicts, but the way in which they are managed, that determines whether they are destructive or constructive. Conflicts are *constructive* to the following extent:

1. They result in an agreement that allows all participants to achieve their goals. The agreement maximizes joint outcomes, benefits everyone, and is in all participants' best interests.
2. They strengthen relationships among participants by increasing liking, respect, and trust for each other.
3. They increase participants' ability to resolve future conflicts constructively with each other.

Conflicts become more constructive when (a) individuals value their diversity and appreciate how it enriches learning, teaching, decision making, and problem solving;

ACTIVITY **8.3** ■ UNDERSTANDING CONFLICTS OF INTEREST

Given below are concepts and definitions. Match the correct definition with the correct concept. Find a partner and (a) compare answers and (b) explain your reasoning for each answer.

_____ **1. want**	**a.** When actions taken by person A to achieve goals prevent, block, or interfere with actions taken by person B to achieve goals
_____ **2. need**	**b.** Desired ideal state of future affairs
_____ **3. goal**	**c.** Potential benefits to be gained by achieving goals
_____ **4. interest**	**d.** Universal necessity for survival
_____ **5. conflict of interest**	**e.** Process by which persons who have shared and opposed interests come to an agreement to work out a settlement
_____ **6. negotiation**	**f.** Desire for something

(b) individuals seek mutual benefit, understand they have mutual interests, and seek common ground; (c) individuals are confident in their ability and that of their schoolmates or colleagues to use the same conflict resolution procedures skillfully; and (d) individuals regularly take stock and reflect on their effectiveness in managing conflicts. Practice resolving a difficult conflict in Activity 8.4. Then try a simpler conflict resolution with nonverbal interaction in Activity 8.5. Evaluate your methods of resolution and your reactions to the conflict in Activity 8.6.

Conflicts become more destructive when they (a) result in one participant winning at the other's expense; (b) create anger, resentment, hurt feelings, and distrust; and (c) decrease the possibility of resolving future conflicts constructively. Destructively managed conflicts are highly costly to an organization, destroying the organization's effectiveness, ripping apart relationships, sabotaging work, delaying and decreasing teaching and learning efforts, and devastating individual's commitment to the organization's goals, sense of security, and personal feelings (Janz & Tjosvold, 1985). Ill-managed conflicts result in faculty and students spending time brooding and fighting rather than teaching and learning.

THE VALUE OF CONFLICT

When conflicts are managed constructively, they have considerable value. The issue is not whether conflicts occur, but rather how they are managed. When managed constructively, they have many desirable outcomes (Deutsch, 1973; Johnson, 1970; Johnson & F. Johnson, 2000; Johnson & R. Johnson, 1979; 1991). First, conflicts can increase the quantity and quality of achievement, higher-level reasoning, and creative problem solving. Second, conflicts can increase the quality of decision making and problem solving. Higher-level moral reasoning results from conflicts.

Third, conflicts are essential for healthy cognitive, social, and psychological development. Conflicts help a person mature. It is through conflict that relationship issues are resolved at various stages of growth. Many times, developmental imperatives require conflicts between children or adolescents and adults. People take the perspectives of others and become less egocentric. They feel confident they can cope with difficulties by dealing directly with them. Competent adolescents, furthermore, tend to be more cooperative (as opposed to disruptive) and more proactive and involved (as opposed to withdrawn). The more students learn how to take a cooperative approach to managing conflicts through joint problem solving, the healthier psychologically they tend to be and the better able they are to deal with stress and adversity. Having procedures and skills to negotiate solutions to joint problems prepares children and adolescents to handle conflict and cope with life's challenges and unforeseen adversities.

Fourth, conflicts energize individuals to take action. Conflicts energize and increase our motivation to deal with relationship problems. Awareness of conflict can trigger a great deal of physical energy and an intensity of psychological focus, which in turn result in a strong motivation to resolve the conflict and put one's plans into action. The energy that students put into being angry and upset could be focused on learning when conflicts are resolved constructively.

Fifth, skills in managing conflicts constructively make students more employable, enhance their career success, and generally increase the quality of their life. The current opinion of many business leaders is that schools often provide a distorted view of work because students do not learn the importance of being part of a cooperative team and managing conflicts skillfully to "get the job done." Through experiencing numerous conflicts and perfecting the procedures and skills required to manage them effectively, students are able to maintain higher-quality friendships and family relationships; to maintain higher-quality relationships on the job with

ACTIVITY **8.4** ■ DIVIDING THE CANDY

Conflicts often begin because there is only so much of something several people want, and no one can have as much as he or she would like. When there is only so much candy, and not everyone can have some, there is a conflict. This exercise requires that three people divide an amount of candy between two people. If you participate actively in this exercise, you will become more aware of how you manage such conflicts.

1. Divide into groups of three. Six pieces of candy are placed in the center of the group.

2. The purpose of the exercise is to get as much candy for yourself as you can. Try to convince the other two members of your triad to give you all the candy. If the other two members agree to divide the candy between themselves (leaving you out), offer one of them a better deal.

3. The triad decides how to divide the candy between two people. Only two people can receive candy. It is all right for one person to end up with all the candy. A clear decision must be reached as to how the candy is to be divided between not more than two people.

   a. **No "chance" procedures are allowed.** The group cannot draw straws or flip a coin to decide who gets what amounts of candy.
   b. **No "side agreements" are allowed.** The two who get the candy cannot agree to give the person left out part of their lunch.

4. The majority rules. Whenever two members make a firm agreement to split the candy a certain way, the decision is made. Be sure, however, to give the third person a chance to offer one of the two a better deal.

5. When a decision is made, write your answers to these questions:

   a. What did I do to get the candy? What strategies did I try?

   b. How did I feel during and after the negotiations?

   c. What strategies did the other two group members use?

   d. What did I learn about how I manage conflicts?

ACTIVITY 8.5 ■ NONVERBAL CONFLICTS

Try your hand (or thumb) at playing out two different nonverbal conflicts. Do not do these exercises if there is a physical reason why you should not participate.

THUMB WRESTLING

Lock fingers with another person with your thumbs straight up. Tap your thumbs together three times and then try to pin the other's thumb so that the other person cannot move it.

SLAPPING HANDS

Person A puts his or her hands out, palms down. Person B extends his hands, palms up, under Person A's hands. The object of the exercise is for Person B to try to slap the hands of Person A by quickly moving his hands from the bottom to the top. As soon as Person B makes a move, Person A tries to pull his or her hands out of the way before Person B can slap them.

---

superiors, peers, and subordinates; and to advance to management and leadership positions more readily.

Sixth, conflicts are essential to promoting caring and committed relationships and increasing morale. Conflicts can deepen and enrich relationships, strengthening each person's conviction that the relationship can hold up under stress, communicating the commitments and values of each person that the other must take into account, and generally keeping the relationship clear of irritations and resentments so that positive feelings can be experienced fully. Resolving conflicts creates a sense of joint identity and cohesiveness within the relationship.

A good argument may do a lot to resolve the small tensions of interacting with others. Nothing divides humans more than poorly managed conflicts. Nothing brings humans together more than constructively managed conflicts. Like all communities, classrooms and schools are cooperative enterprises within which diverse and heterogeneous individuals work together to achieve mutual goals. Conflicts occur, and when they are constructively managed, the quality of community life within schools is enhanced (see Box 8.1).

Seventh, conflicts increase awareness that there is a problem that needs to be solved. Conflicts increase our awareness of what the problems are, who is involved, and how the problems can be solved. The irritations of relating to others is reduced when we become aware of the specific problems causing them.

Eighth, conflicts promote change. Conflicts create incentives to challenge and change outmoded procedures, assignments, structures, habitual patterns of interacting with others, and personal habits. Ninth, conflicts help students understand what they are like as a person and how they need to change. What makes them angry, what frightens them, what is important to them, and how they tend to manage conflicts are all highlighted when students are in conflict with others. Being aware of what they are willing to argue about and how they act in conflicts can help them learn a great deal about themselves. Such awareness encourages change. There are times when things need to change, when new skills need to be learned, when old habits need to be modified. Tenth, conflicts also help students understand what others are like as individuals. Knowing what people are willing to fight about increases students' awareness of what they are like as individuals—their values, attitudes, and perspectives.

ACTIVITY **8.6** ■ CONFLICT PERSONAL PROFILE 1

It is important that you are aware of your most frequently used strategies for managing conflicts. In the space provided below, write out what you did and how you felt during your participation in the conflicts in Activity 8.4 and 8.5.

DIVIDING THE CANDY

1. The strategy: _____

_____

2. My feelings: _____

_____

NONVERBAL COMPETITIONS

1. The strategy: _____

_____

2. My feelings: _____

_____

CONCLUSIONS

1. _____

_____

2. _____

_____

3. _____

_____

4. _____

_____

Eleventh, conflicts are essential for having an interesting and fun life. Being in a conflict often sparks curiosity and stimulates interest. Arguments about politics, sports, work, and societal problems make interpersonal interaction more intriguing and less boring. Skillful bargaining is a form of entertainment. When others disagree with your ideas, you may be inspired to find out more about the issue. Conflicts can be fun when they are not taken too seriously. Many persons seek out conflicts through such activities as competitive sports and games, movies, plays, books, and teasing. They do so because they enjoy being involved in conflict situations. Review your understanding of these issues by participating in Activity 8.7.

The benefits gained from learning how to manage conflicts constructively far outweigh the cost of learning time lost by students being upset and angry. From a cost-analysis perspective, one of the soundest investments educators and students can make in classroom and school productivity is teaching students how to manage

■ ■ ■ ■ ■ ■

BOX 8.1
CONFLICT AND DIVERSITY

1. Conflict occurs more frequently among diverse individuals.
2. Conflict is more intense and generates stronger emotions among diverse individuals.
3. Conflict results from misunderstandings more frequently among diverse individuals.
4. Conflicts are managed destructively more frequently among diverse individuals.
5. Relationships among diverse individuals are greatly strengthened every time a conflict is resolved constructively.
6. Relationships among diverse individuals cannot be maintained unless conflicts are resolved constructively.

conflicts constructively. When teachers want to maintain the focus on learning rather than on hurt feelings, the most useful thing they can do is ensure that conflicts currently being dealt with are managed constructively.

Conflicts only have value if they are constructively managed. When different members of the school use different strategies for managing conflicts, anarchy and other destructive outcomes can result. For the value of conflicts to be realized, all students and faculty must use the same constructive procedures for resolving their conflicts.

THE NEED FOR COORIENTATION

Different students have quite different ideas about how conflicts should be resolved. Some rely on physical dominance through threats and violence. Other students use procedures such as verbal attack, the cold shoulder, giving in, or getting back at the other person in some way in the future. The multiple procedures for managing conflicts within the classroom can create chaos. This is especially true when students are from different cultural, ethnic, social class, and language backgrounds.

For education to proceed and learning to occur, students need to be *cooriented* so that everyone understands and uses the same procedures for managing conflicts. All students need to operate under the same norms and adhere to the same conflict resolution procedures. *Norms* are shared expectations about what behavior is appropriate within the situation. Conflict resolution begins with a common set of norms concerning which behaviors are appropriate and which procedures to use. These norms must be clearly and publicly established. Physical violence against oneself or another person, public humiliation and shaming, and lying and deceit should be outlawed. Conflicts among students should be skillfully negotiated to solve the problem and improve the relationship. Students (and school personnel) should be expected to follow norms for appropriate social conduct without exception (see Activity 8.8).

Ensuring that all students use the same conflict resolution procedures is especially important when students are from different cultures, ethnic groups, and backgrounds. The United States has always been a nation of many cultures, races, languages, and religions. In the past 8 years alone, more than 7.8 million people journeying from more than 150 different countries and speaking dozens of different languages came to make the United States their new home. The school is the meeting ground for children from different cultural, ethnic, social class, and language back-

ACTIVITY 8.7 ■ **POINTS TO REMEMBER**

Given below are a series of points about conflict and conflict resolution. Using the rating scale below, rate each statement as to your degree of agreement from strongly disagree (1) to strongly agree (10). Then meet in a group of four. Come to agreement as to the degree of truth contained in each statement.

1———2———3———4———5———6———7———8———9———10
Statement is false   Statement is true

_____ **1.** Conflicts arise no matter what you do. They are inevitable.

_____ **2.** The more important your goals are, the more conflicts you will be involved in; the more important a relationship is, the more likely you are to be involved in conflicts.

_____ **3.** Any conflict has the potential for destructive or constructive outcomes.

_____ **4.** Whether a conflict is constructive or destructive depends on your skill in managing conflicts in positive ways.

_____ **5.** Ideally, you seek to resolve a conflict in a way that maximizes beneficial results for both yourself and the other persons involved.

_____ **6.** To manage conflicts with skill, finesse, grace, and class, you need to know a conflict resolution procedure and be skilled in its use.

_____ **7.** When two individuals involved in a conflict are using different procedures, destructive outcomes typically result. If conflicts are to be managed constructively, everyone needs to use the same procedures to resolve them.

_____ **8.** Because the procedures for resolving conflicts effectively are not learned in most families or from television, movies, or novels, you must learn how to resolve conflicts as part of your education at school.

_____ **9.** Knowing how to resolve conflicts with skill and grace increases your career success, quality of relationships with friends and colleagues, and happiness.

grounds. They come to know each other, appreciate the vitality of diversity, and internalize the common heritage of being American that binds them together.

Although this diversity represents a source of creativity and energy that few other countries have, it also provides a series of problems concerning how conflicts are managed in the classroom. Suspicions and fears of each other may need to be expelled. Differences may need to be recognized and adjusted to. All students need to use the same set of procedures to resolve conflicts so that their goals are achieved, relationships are strengthened, and their ability to manage future conflicts is improved. Students and faculty become cooriented to the procedures used in resolving conflicts through a training program. Such a program is primarily established and maintained day to day by classroom teachers.

ACTIVITY **8.8**   ■   HOW CONFLICTS SHOULD BE MANAGED

It may be helpful to devise a set of rules to help you manage current conflicts as well as future conflicts. A list of rules has been provided from another class as examples to help set you thinking about what kinds of rules would be effective in managing conflicts. Study these rules and complete the exercises below.

1. Deal with the present, not the past (ancient history does not count).

2. No name calling (it only makes things worse).

3. No pushing, shoving, or hitting (physical violence makes things worse).

4. Talk to each other face-to-face (not behind each other's back).

5. Do not spread the conflict (keep it between the two of you).

Working with a partner, write out five rules for resolving your conflicts. You should agree on one set of answers for the two of you and both of you need to be able to explain your answers.

1. _____

2. _____

3. _____

4. _____

5. _____

Combine with another pair. Share your rules. Listen carefully to theirs. Use their ideas to improve your list:

1. _____

2. _____

3. _____

4. _____

5. _____

MANAGING CONFLICTS CONSTRUCTIVELY

Classrooms need to become conflict-positive places where destructive conflicts are prevented and where constructive conflicts are structured, encouraged, and utilized to improve the quality of instruction and classroom life. Students need to learn constructive ways of managing conflict. Violence, fear, intimidation, threat, acquiescence, and abuse have no place within classrooms and schools. Yet without direct training in how to manage conflicts constructively, many students will never become able to do so. They will do so when students are directly taught the required conflict resolution procedures and skills and the classroom and school norms and values support the use of the procedures and skills. There are three steps in teaching students the procedures and skills they need to manage conflicts of interests constructively.

Step 1: Creating a Cooperative Context

The best way I know how to defeat an enemy is to make him a friend.   —*Abraham Lincoln*

The first step in managing conflicts constructively is to establish a cooperative environment. The context within which conflicts occur largely determines whether the conflict is managed constructively or destructively (Deutsch, 1973; Johnson & Johnson, 1989; Tjosvold & Johnson, 1983; Watson & Johnson, 1972). There are two possible contexts for conflict: cooperative and competitive. (In individualistic situations individuals do not interact and, therefore, no conflict occurs.)

Competitive Context.   For competition to exist, there must be scarcity: I must defeat you to get what I want. Rewards are restricted to the few who perform the best. In a competitive situation, individuals work against each other to achieve a goal that only one or a few can attain. You can attain your goal if and only if the other people involved cannot attain their goals. Thus, competitors seek outcomes that are personally beneficial but detrimental to all others in the situation.

Conflicts usually do not go well in a competitive context. Within competitive situations, individuals typically have a short-term time orientation in which all energies are focused on winning. Little or no attention is paid to maintaining a good relationship. The following circumstances are characteristic of competitive situations (Deutsch, 1973; Johnson & Johnson, 1989; Tjosvold & Johnson, 1983; Watson & Johnson, 1972):

- Communication tends to be avoided, and when it does take place, it tends to contain misleading information and threats. Threats, lies, and silence do not help students resolve conflicts with each other. Competition gives rise to espionage and other techniques to obtain information about the other that that person is unwilling to communicate, and to "diversionary tactics" to delude or mislead the opponent about oneself.
- There are frequent and common misperceptions and distortions about the other person's position and motivations that are difficult to correct. Students engage in self-fulfilling prophecies by perceiving another person as being immoral and hostile and reacting accordingly, thus evoking hostility and deceit from that other person. Students notice small misbehaviors of opponents whereas they ignore their own large misbehaviors (mote–beam mechanism). Double standards exist. Because preconceptions and expectations influence what is perceived, and because people interpret events in a biased way that justifies their own beliefs and actions, and because conflict and threat impair perceptual and cognitive processes; the misperceptions are difficult to correct.
- Individuals have a suspicious, hostile attitude toward each other that increases their readiness to exploit each other's wants and needs and refuse each other's requests.
- Individuals tend to deny the legitimacy of others' wants, needs, and feelings and consider only their own interests.

Cooperative Context.   For cooperation to exist, all parties must be committed to achieving mutual goals: I am not successful unless you are successful. The more successful you are, the more I benefit and the more successful I am. In a cooperative situation students work together to accomplish shared goals. Students seek outcomes that are beneficial to everyone involved. They are committed to each other's, as well as their own, well-being and success.

Conflicts usually go well in a cooperative context. Within cooperative situations, individuals typically have a long-term time orientation in which energies are focused both on achieving goals and on building good working relationships with others. The following circumstances are characteristic of cooperative situations (Deutsch, 1973; Johnson & Johnson, 1989; Tjosvold & Johnson, 1983; Watson & Johnson, 1972):

- Effective and continued communication is of vital importance in resolving a conflict. Within a cooperative situation, the communication of relevant information tends to be open and honest, with each person interested in informing the other as well as being informed. Communication tends to be more frequent, complete, and accurate.
- Perceptions of the other person and the other person's actions are far more accurate and constructive. Misperceptions and distortions such as self-fulfilling prophecies and double standards occur less frequently and are far easier to correct and clarify.
- Individuals trust and like each other and, therefore, are willing to respond helpfully to each other's wants, needs, and requests.
- Individuals recognize the legitimacy of each other's interests and search for a solution accommodating the needs of both sides. Conflicts tend to be defined as mutual problems to be solved in ways that benefit everyone involved.

Constructive Context.   Conflicts cannot be managed constructively within a competitive context. When competitive and individualistic learning dominates a classroom and school, conflicts are inevitably destructive. Instead of trying to solve interpersonal problems, students think short term and go for the "win." To resolve conflicts constructively, an instructor first has to establish a cooperative context, primarily through the use of cooperative learning procedures the majority of the day (Johnson, Johnson, & Holubec, 1998). The more cooperative the relationships are among students, the more constructively conflicts are managed. Because cooperative learning increases achievement and promotes a number of other important instructional outcomes (Johnson & Johnson, 1989), there can be little objection to using cooperative procedures.

In addition to its overall positive effects, cooperative learning promotes a long-term time perspective and enhances the learning of social skills. The constructive resolution of conflict in classes and schools requires students and staff to recognize that their long-term mutual interests and relationships are more important than is the result of any short-term conflict. Because cooperative efforts require individuals to interact and coordinate their actions, social skills become an essential part of making efforts work, especially skills involved in resolving conflicts constructively.

Finally, the overuse and inappropriate use of competitive and individualistic learning procedures should be avoided. The more competitive the relationships are among students, and the more students tend to focus on their own self-interests, the more destructive conflicts tend to be.

Step 2: Instructional Use of Academic Controversies

> It's best that we should not all think alike. It's difference of opinion that makes horse races.
> —*Mark Twain*

The second step is to promote intellectual controversies frequently to increase the quantity and quality of academic learning. Controversies promote conceptual conflicts. To maximize student achievement, student critical thinking, and student use of higher-level reasoning strategies, teachers need to engage students in intellectual conflicts in which they have to prepare intellectual positions, present them, advocate them, criticize opposing intellectual positions, view the issue from a variety of perspectives, and synthesize the various positions into one position. The frequent use of academic controversies allows students to practice their conflict skills daily. Academic controversies are discussed in depth in Chapter 9 and in Johnson and Johnson (1995c).

Step 3: Implementing a Conflict Resolution Program

> A soft answer turneth away wrath.   —*Bible*

Implementing a conflict resolution/peer mediation program consists of three steps: teaching students how to negotiate to solve problems, teaching students to mediate, and having an adult arbitrate when negotiation and mediation fail. Peacemaker training is discussed in depth in Chapter 10 and in Johnson and Johnson (1995a; 1995b).

Teaching Students to Negotiate to Solve Problems.   Students must be taught how to negotiate constructive resolutions to their conflicts. When two students both want to use the computer at the same time, a conflict arises. When such conflicts occur, settlements must be negotiated. *Negotiation* consists of persons who have shared and opposed interests and want to come to an agreement trying to work out a settlement. A person may negotiate to win or to solve the problem. Whenever a person is involved in a long-term relationship, the quality of the relationship is usually more important than any one immediate issue. A person, therefore, should never try to win when he or she has to interact or to work with the other disputant in the future. The only method of negotiating that is appropriate for ongoing relationships is problem-solving negotiations. Students need to be taught the procedures for negotiating to solve the problem.

Teaching Students to Mediate Schoolmates' Conflicts.   Students must be taught how to mediate schoolmates' conflicts when they are unable to negotiate a constructive resolution by themselves. *Mediation* exists when a neutral third person—a mediator—intervenes to help resolve a conflict between two or more people in a way that is acceptable to them. A mediator listens carefully to both sides and helps the disputants move effectively through each step of the negotiation sequence to reach an agreement that both believe is fair, just, and workable. Mediation is an extension of the negotiation process and is a collection of strategies aimed at promoting more efficient and effective negotiations. It is important that all students are given the opportunity to assume the role of mediator as doing so increases students' negotiation skills.

When students have received the initial negotiation and mediation training, the peer mediation program should be implemented in the school. Each day pairs of students are chosen to serve as class or school mediators. The responsibility is rotated so that all students serve as mediator an equal amount of time.

Each week further lessons on using negotiation and mediation procedures are taught to refine and upgrade students' skills. Whenever possible, the procedures are integrated into academic lessons. Overlearning the procedures is emphasized so that students go through the procedures hundreds of times. The training is a 12-year spiral curriculum so that the procedures are taught every year at an increasingly sophisticated and complex level.

Arbitrating Students' Conflicts.   When students are unable to negotiate an agreement and mediation fails, a faculty member or administrator may have to arbitrate the conflict. When mediation fails, the teacher or principal may have to decide. Arbitration is the submission of a dispute to a disinterested third party (such as a teacher or principal) who makes a final and binding judgment as to how the conflict will be resolved. The arbitrator carefully listens to both sides and makes a decision.

The process of having a teacher or principal decide who is right and who is wrong seldom satisfies anyone, leaving at least one student with resentment and anger toward the arbitrator. More importantly, it reinforces students' beliefs that they are not capable of working out future disputes themselves. For these reasons, arbitration is the last resort to resolving conflicts within the classroom and school. In a way, arbitration is a threat to encourage the success of negotiations and mediation.

CONFLICT RESOLUTION AS A MANAGEMENT PROGRAM

Management problems are by definition disruptions to the overall cooperative nature of the school. Management problems plague classrooms and schools. Students bicker, threaten, tease, and harass each other. Conflicts involving racial and cultural differences are increasing. Truancy is epidemic. Violence is escalating. Generally, conflicts among students and between students and staff occur with frequency and consume considerable teacher and administrator time.

To deal with these problems, schools institute management programs. Management programs in schools may be placed on a continuum:

External rewards/punishments 1—2—3—4—5—6—7 Competencies for self-regulation

At one end are management programs based on teacher-administrated external rewards and punishments that control and manage student behavior. At the other end are programs based on teaching students the competencies and skills required to regulate their own and their schoolmates' behavior. Peer mediation programs anchor the self-regulation end of the continuum.

External Rewards/Punishments. Most management programs are clustered at the end of the continuum labelled *external rewards/punishments.* This end of the continuum signifies adult administrations. Thus, it is up to the staff to monitor student behavior, to determine whether it is within the bounds of acceptability, and to force students to terminate inappropriate actions. When infractions are minor, staff often arbitrate ("The pencil belongs to Mary. Jane be quiet and sit down") or cajole students to end hostilities ("Let's forgive and forget. Shake hands and be friends"). If that does not work, students may be sent to the principal's office for a stern but cursory lecture about the value of getting along, a threat that more drastic action will ensue if the conflict continues, and a final admonition to go and fight no more. If that does not work, time-out rooms may be used. Eventually, some students are expelled from school.

Such programs teach students that adults or authority figures are needed to resolve conflicts. The programs cost a great deal in instructional and administrative time and work only as long as students are under surveillance. This approach does not empower students. Adults may become more skillful in how to control students, but students do not learn the procedures, skills, and attitudes required to resolve conflicts constructively in their personal lives at home, in school, at work, and in the community.

Competencies for Self-Regulation. At the other end of the continuum are programs aimed at teaching students self-responsibility and self-regulation. Self-regulation is the ability to act in socially approved ways in the absence of external monitors. It is the ability to initiate and cease activities according to situational demands. Self-regulation is a central and significant hallmark of cognitive and social development.

To regulate their behavior, students must monitor their own behavior; assess situations, taking other people's perspectives into account to make judgments as to which behaviors are appropriate; and master the procedures and skills required to engage in the desired behavior. In interaction with other people, students have to monitor, modify, refine, and change how they behave to act appropriately and competently.

If students are to learn how to regulate their behavior, they must have opportunities to (a) make decisions regarding how to behave and (b) follow through on the decisions made. Allowing students to be joint architects in matters affecting them promotes feelings of control and autonomy. Students who know how to manage their conflicts constructively and regulate their own behavior have a developmental advantage over those who do not. Ideally, students are given the responsibility of regulating their own and their classmates' behavior so that teachers can concentrate on instruction rather than on control.

To decide what type of management program to implement in a school, it helps to know what types of management problems are occurring. Typically, most management problems involve either conflicts among students or conflicts between students and (a) teachers or (b) standards concerning appropriate and acceptable conduct. By training students to manage conflicts constructively, a management program is created in which students are empowered to solve their own problems and regulate their own and their classmates' behavior. Although such programs have been suggested for years (Johnson, 1970), it is only recently that students have been trained to be peacemakers. Take a moment to review important concepts in this chapter by completing Activity 8.9.

A LIFE-LONG ADVANTAGE

Teaching students how to manage conflicts constructively may impact their later career success. A recent survey conducted for Accountempts (a large accounting, bookkeeping, and data-processing temporary personnel service that is a division of Robert Half International, Inc.) of vice presidents and personnel directors of 100 of the nation's 1,000 largest corporations found that people who manage U.S. leading corporations spend more than 4 working weeks a year dealing with the problems caused by employees who cannot resolve their conflicts with each other. In answer to the question, What percentage of management time is spent dealing with conflicts among employees, respondents revealed that executives spend an average of 9.2 percent of their time or, based on a 40-hour week, 4.6 weeks a year attempting to deal with employee conflicts and the difficulties and disruptions they cause.

In 1976, the American Management Association sponsored a survey on conflict management (Thomas & Schmidt, 1976). The respondents included 116 chief executive officers, 76 vice presidents, and 66 middle managers. They reported that about 24 percent of their time is spent dealing with conflict. The sources of conflicts they faced included misunderstandings, personality clashes, value and goal differences, substandard performance, disagreement over methods of work, lack of cooperation, competition, and noncompliance with rules and policies. School and hospital administrators, mayors, and city managers report that conflict resolution commands nearly 49 percent of their attention.

In addition to taking up valuable management time, employee conflicts can seriously reduce any company's productivity and its ability to compete effectively in the marketplace. Knowing how to negotiate constructive resolutions to conflicts of interest is an essential skill that may significantly affect students' career success.

These recent research studies found that executives in high-level positions spend much of their time dealing with conflicts, and the more skillful they are at

ACTIVITY **8.9** ■ CONCEPTS AND DEFINITIONS

Given below are eight concepts and definitions. Match the correct definition with the correct concept. Find a partner and (a) compare answers and (b) explain your reasoning for each answer.

_____ 1. conflict positive

a. Persons have shared and opposed interests and want to come to an agreement to work out a settlement

_____ 2. conflict

b. Shared expectations about the behavior that is appropriate within a situation

_____ 3. constructive conflict

c. Results in an agreement that allows all participants to achieve their goals

_____ 4. coorientation

d. Encouraging and managing conflicts constructively to maximize their potential in enhancing the quality of teaching, learning, and school life in general

_____ 5. norms

e. A neutral third party intervening to help resolve a conflict between two or more people in a way that is acceptable to them

_____ 6. negotiations

f. Disruptions to the overall cooperative nature of the school

_____ 7. mediation

g. Everyone using the same definition and procedures for managing conflicts

_____ 8. management problems

h. The occurrence of incompatible activities in which one activity prevents, blocks, or interferes with the occurrence or effectiveness of the second activity

---

doing so, the more successful their careers are. Because conflicts occur continually, and because so many people are so unskilled in managing conflicts, teaching students how to resolve conflicts constructively is one of the best investments schools can make. Once learned, conflict skills accompany students to every situation and every relationship. Students do not have to manage every conflict constructively, but the ability to do so should be in their repertoire. Knowing how to resolve conflicts with skill and grace gives students a developmental advantage; increases their future academic and career success; improves the quality of relationships with friends, colleagues, and family; and generally enhances their life-long happiness.

SUMMARY

To ensure that diversity results in constructive outcomes, students (and faculty) must be taught the procedures to manage conflicts constructively, and schools need to become conflict-positive organizations. Conflicts occur all the time. They are a natural, inevitable, potentially constructive, and normal part of school life. Students disagree concerning whom to sit by at lunch, which game to play during recess, when to work and when to play, when to talk and when to listen, and who is going to pick the paper up off the floor. Although schools and classrooms are filled with conflict, schools generally become conflict-negative organizations in which conflicts are denied, suppressed, and avoided. The potential constructive outcomes of conflicts are lost due to the educators' fear and anxiety over how conflicts may be managed.

The procedures most students use to manage their conflicts are frequently inadequate and destructive, making things worse rather than better. Different students often have different ideas about how conflicts should be resolved. Students may get angry, fight, hurl verbal abuse at each other, verbally harass each other, ignore the conflict, take their anger out on someone/something else, play head games, or fantasize how to get revenge. These methods generally provide little chance of resolving any problems and often result in alienating students from their peers and the school staff. Students, furthermore, generally receive little training in how to manage conflicts constructively. To create a conflict-positive school, in which conflicts are sought out, encouraged, and managed constructively, all students must be taught the same procedures for resolving conflicts constructively.

A conflict has been resolved constructively when it solves the problem, strengthens the relationships among participants, and increases their ability to resolve their conflicts constructively in the future. Such constructively managed conflicts promote learning, problem solving, healthy social development, change, life success, and make life more interesting and fun. Students learn how to achieve these outcomes when (a) the extensive use of cooperative learning creates a cooperative context for relationships, (b) academic controversies are structured by the teacher, and (c) peer mediation programs are implemented in which all students learn a basic negotiation procedure with which to mediate their schoolmates' conflicts and teachers arbitrate as a last resort. Finally, teaching students how to manage conflicts constructively is in essence a management program that empowers student to regulate and control their own and their schoolmates' behavior, inculcating self-control and self-autonomy.

CHAPTER NINE

ACADEMIC CONTROVERSY

INTRODUCTION

Diversity implies differences in experiences and perspectives. Differences in ways of perceiving the world and interpreting events further implies disagreement. When diverse individuals work together cooperatively, they often disagree. However, disagreements are potentially constructive, as they lead to increased sophistication of thought, insights into each other's experiences and viewpoints, more personal and positive relationships, ongoing dialogue about relationships between majorities and minorities, and continuing motivation to learn more about how values such as liberty and equality may be implemented in our society. In addition, when such debates involve academic work, the result is higher achievement, creative problem solving, and more complete and accurate retention of what is learned.

Given the potential opportunities for diverse individuals to discuss their differences, it is somewhat surprising how infrequently it happens. One of the few studies of the occurrence and nature of discussions among diverse individuals was conducted at Grinnell College (a small, exclusive college in a small Iowa town) (Trosset, 1998). Grinnell made a point of maximizing the diversity of students in expectation that they would talk about their differences with each other. What Trosset discovered is that such conversations rarely occurred.

Students reported that the primary reasons for engaging in such discussions was to advocate what one believed (not learning) and achieve consensus through conversion (not intellectual exchange). Personal experience was seen as the primary source of legitimate knowledge (if one has not had the experience, one cannot contribute anything worthwhile), and the statements of those who have had the experience cannot be challenged by those who have not. Knowledge that is available to everyone (such as scholarly writings) was considered irrelevant. Perhaps most important of all, students did not have a procedure that would allow a stimulating discussion that encouraged consideration of a variety of perspectives and experiences. This chapter deals with just such a procedure, namely, constructive controversy.

THE IMPORTANCE OF INTELLECTUAL CONFLICT

> Have you learn'd lessons only of those who admired you,
> and were tender with you, and stood aside for you?
>
> Have you not learn'd great lessons from those who reject you,
> and brace themselves against you? or who treat you with contempt,
> or dispute the passage with you?   —*Walt Whitman, 1860*

In 1859 Horace Greeley and Henry David Thoreau were having a discussion about John Brown's exploits at Harper's Ferry. "No matter how well intended John Brown was," Horace said, "his methods were completely unacceptable. The man broke the law! Terrorism for a good cause is still terrorism. It does not follow that because slavery is wrong, John Brown's actions were right. No matter how opposed to slavery one is, one cannot condone what John Brown did." "Now Horace," Henry replied, "you are missing the whole point. It does not matter whether John Brown broke the law or not. It only matters what he symbolizes. And he symbolizes eternal justice, glory, and devotion to principle. We should pay homage to the ideas John Brown represents, not get caught in a mundane discussion of legalities." ■

Thomas Jefferson would have applauded Greeley and Thoreau's discussion. Jefferson noted, "Difference of opinion leads to inquiry, and inquiry to truth." Jefferson had a deep faith in the value and productiveness of conflict. He is not alone. A number of twentieth-century theorists have pointed out the value of conflict.

Piaget (1950) proposed that disequilibrium within a student's cognitive structure motivates transitions from one stage of cognitive reasoning to another. He believed that conflict among peers is an essential cause of a shift from egocentrism to accommodation of other's perspectives. Piaget proposed that a person, with an existing way of organizing his or her cognitive structures, enters into cooperative interaction with peers. Conflicts inevitably result that create internal disequilibrium and the inability to assimilate current experiences into existing cognitive structures. The person then searches for a new equilibrium by decentering and accommodating the perspectives of others. This creates the need to organize the person's cognitive structures in a new way. Kohlberg (1969) adopted Piaget's formulation as an explanation for the development of moral reasoning.

Conflict theorists noted that conflict had many positive benefits (Coser, 1956; Johnson & Johnson, 1995c; Simmel, 1955). Berlyne (1966) emphasized that conceptual conflict creates epistemic curiosity, which motivates the search for new information and the reconceptualization of the knowledge one already has. Hoffman and Maier (1972) insisted that higher-quality problem solving depended on conflict among group members.

Bruner (1961) proposed that conceptual conflict was necessary for discovery learning and could be created by (a) presenting events that are discrepant with what the student already knows and understands, (b) presenting "mysterious" events that seem inexplicable on the basis of students' present knowledge, and (c) having students argue and disagree with the instructor or with each other. Johnson (1970) posited that because knowledge results from social processes (i.e., "truth" is derived by scholars seeking consensus through discussion), conflict among ideas, theories, and conclusions becomes an essential part of building a conceptual structure that everyone agrees is valid.

The power of conflict may be clearly seen in the arts. Creating a conflict is an accepted writer's tool for capturing an audience. All drama hinges on conflict. Playwrights and scriptwriters create a conflict whenever they want to gain and hold viewer's attention, create viewer interest and emotional involvement, and excite and surprise viewers. A general rule of modern novels is that if a conflict is not created within the first three pages of the book, the book will not be successful. Educators, on the other hand, often avoid and suppress any sort of intellectual conflict in the classroom.

Despite the daily demonstration of the power of conflict in dramatic productions and the recommendation by theorists that conflict be an essential aspect of learning and teaching, educators have by and large avoided and suppressed intellectual conflict. Far from being a standard instructional procedure, in most colleges creating intellectual conflict is the exception, not the rule. Why do faculty avoid creating intellectual conflict among and within students? The answer to that question is somewhat of a mystery.

A number of hypotheses have been developed to explain why conflict is so avoided and suppressed in academic situations (Johnson, 1970; Johnson & F. Johnson, 2000; Johnson, F. Johnson, & Johnson, 1976; Johnson & R. Johnson, 1979, 1989, 1995c). Complete Activity 9.1 to determine which hypothesis is the best explanation for the existence of obstacles to academic conflict. These obstacles must be overcome if faculty are to utilize the power of intellectual conflict in their teaching. To give faculty the courage to change their teaching practices and to include conflict as a centerpiece of instruction, faculty members must know what academic controversy is, the outcomes it promotes, and the procedures that operationalize its use in learning situations.

WHAT IS ACADEMIC CONTROVERSY?

> The best way ever devised for seeking the truth in any given situation
> is advocacy: presenting the pros and cons from different, informed
> points of view and digging down deep into the facts.
> —*Harold S. Geneen (Former CEO, ITT)*

In an English class students are considering the issue of civil disobedience. They learn that during the civil rights movement, individuals broke the law to gain equal rights for minorities. In numerous literary works, such as *The Adventures of Huckleberry Finn* by Mark Twain, individuals wrestle with the issue of breaking the law to redress social injustice. Huck wrestles with the issue of breaking the law to help Jim, his friend, a runaway slave. In the 1970s and 1980s prominent public figures from Wall Street to the White House have felt justified in breaking laws for personal or political gain.

To study the role of civil disobedience in a democracy, students are placed in a cooperative learning group of four members. The group is then divided into two pairs. One pair is given the assignment of making the best case possible for the constructiveness of civil disobedience in a democracy. The other pair is given the assignment of making the best case possible for the destructiveness of civil disobedience in a democracy. In the resulting conflict, students draw from such sources as the Declaration of Independence by Thomas Jefferson, *Civil Disobedience* by Henry David Thoreau, "Speech at Cooper Union, New York" by Abraham Lincoln, and "Letter from Birmingham Jail" by Martin Luther King, Jr. to challenge each other's reasoning and analyses concerning when civil disobedience is, or is not, constructive.

Academic controversy exists when one student's ideas, information, conclusions, theories, and opinions are incompatible with those of another, and the two seek to reach an agreement. Controversies are resolved by engaging in what Aristotle called *deliberate discourse* (i.e., the discussion of the advantages and disadvantages of proposed actions) aimed at synthesizing novel solutions (i.e., creative problem solving). The instructor guides students through five steps (Johnson, 1970; Johnson & F. Johnson, 2000; Johnson, F. Johnson, & Johnson, 1976; Johnson & R. Johnson, 1979; 1989; 1995c):

1. Research and prepare a position. Each pair develops the position assigned, learns the relevant information, and plans how to present the best case possible to the other pair. Near the end of the period pairs are encouraged to compare notes with pairs from other groups who represent the same position.

ACTIVITY **9.1** ■ THE AVOIDANCE OF INTELLECTUAL CONFLICTS

Form a pair. Rank order the following hypotheses from most likely reason (1) to least likely reason (6) for the existence of obstacles to intellectual conflict.

_____ **Fear blocks faculty and students from engaging in intellectual conflicts.** Because destructively managed conflicts create divisiveness and hostility, when conflicts among students occur, faculty and students may have some anxiety as to whether constructive or destructive outcomes will result. Palmer (1990; 1991), for example, believes that fear of conflict blocks good teaching and learning and recommends that faculty have the courage to promote intellectual conflict among students and between students and faculty despite apprehensions about doing so.

_____ **Ignorance of how to engage in intellectual conflict blocks faculty and students from engaging in intellectual conflicts.** Until the relatively recent development of the academic controversy procedure, no clear set of instructional procedures was used for creating and managing intellectual conflict.

_____ **Lack of training programs to teach faculty how to use intellectual conflict effectively blocks faculty and students from engaging in intellectual conflicts.** Most faculty members have not been trained in how to create intellectual conflicts among students and how to use the conflicts to increase students' learning. Such training programs exist only at a few institutions, such as the University of Minnesota.

_____ **Our culture is so anticonflict that faculty do not see the promotion of intellectual conflicts as a possibility.** The view that conflict is a potential positive and powerful force on learning may be culturally unacceptable. In our society conflicts may be perceived to be so destructive that most faculty believe a well-run classroom is one in which no conflicts arise among students.

_____ **Pedagogical norms may block faculty and students from engaging in intellectual conflicts.** Current pedagogy promotes the use of a performer–spectator approach to teaching. Faculty lecture, often in an interesting and entertaining way, and students sit and watch and take notes. In an attempt to cover a whole field in a semester or year, students are often exposed to a blizzard of information within a lecture. Departmental chairs and colleagues may equate telling with teaching.

_____ **Inertia (the power of the status quo) may be so great that faculty just do not try anything new.** Faculty may choose to play it safe by only lecturing because it is their personal tradition and the tradition of their college and colleagues.

2. Present and advocate their position. Each pair makes their presentation to the opposing pair. Each member of the pair has to participate in the presentation. Students are to be as persuasive and convincing as possible. Members of the opposing pair are encouraged to take notes, listen carefully to learn the information being presented, and clarify anything they do not understand.

3. Engage in an open discussion to refute the opposing position and rebut attacks. Students argue forcefully and persuasively for their position, presenting as many facts as they can to support their point of view. The group members analyze and critically evaluate the information, rationale, and inductive and deductive reasoning of the opposing pair, asking them for the facts that support their point of view. They refute the arguments of the opposing pair and rebut attacks on their position. They discuss the issue following a set of rules to help them criticize ideas without criticizing people, differentiate the two positions, and assess the degree of evidence and logic supporting each position. They keep in mind that the issue is complex and that they need to know both sides to write a good report.

4. Reverse perspectives. The pairs reverse perspectives and present each other's positions. In arguing for the opposing position, students are forceful and persuasive. They add any new information that the opposing pair did not think to present. They strive to see the issue from both perspectives simultaneously.

5. Synthesize and integrate the best evidence and reasoning into a joint position. The four members of the group drop all advocacy and synthesize and integrate what they know into factual and judgmental conclusions that are summarized into a joint position to which all sides can agree. They (a) finalize the report (the instructor evaluates reports on the quality of the writing, the logical presentation of evidence, and the oral presentation of the report to the class), (b) present their conclusions to the class (all four members of the group are required to participate orally in the presentation), (c) individually take the test covering both sides of the issue (if every member of the group achieves up to criterion, they all receive bonus points), and (d) process how well they worked together and how they could be even more effective next time.

Structured controversies are most commonly contrasted with concurrence seeking, debate, and individualistic learning (see Table 9.1). *Debate* exists when two or more individuals argue positions that are incompatible with one another and a judge declares a winner on the basis of who presented their position the best. An example of debate is when each member of a group is assigned a position as to whether more or less regulations are needed to control hazardous wastes and an authority declares the winner to be the person who makes the best presentation of his or her position to the group.

Concurrence seeking occurs when members of a group inhibit discussion to avoid any disagreement or arguments, emphasize agreement, and avoid realistic appraisal of alternative ideas and courses of action. Concurrence seeking is close to the *groupthink* concept of Janis (1982) in which members of a decision-making group set aside their doubts and misgivings about whatever policy is favored by the emerging consensus to be able to concur with the other members. The underlying motivation of groupthink is the strong desire to preserve the harmonious atmosphere of the group on which each member has become dependent for coping with the stresses of external crises and for maintaining self-esteem.

Individualistic efforts exist when individuals work alone at their own pace, with their own set of materials, without interacting with each other, in a situation in which their goals are unrelated and independent from each other (Johnson, Johnson, & Holubec, 1998). Complete Activity 9.2 to review the important concepts discussed thus far in this chapter.

A key to the effectiveness of conflict procedures for promoting learning is the mixture of cooperative and competitive elements within the procedure (see Table 9.2).

TABLE 9.1 Controversy, Debate, Concurrence Seeking, and Individualistic Processes

CONSTRUCTIVE CONTROVERSY	DEBATE	CONCURRENCE SEEKING	INDIVIDUALISTIC
Categorizing and organizing information to derive conclusions	Categorizing and organizing information to derive conclusions	Categorizing and organizing information to derive conclusions	Categorizing and organizing information to derive conclusions
Presenting, advocating, elaborating position and rationale	Presenting, advocating, elaborating position and rationale	Presenting, advocating, elaborating position and rationale	No oral statement of positions
Being challenged by opposing views results in conceptual conflict and uncertainty about correctness of own views	Being challenged by opposing views results in conceptual conflict and uncertainty about correctness of own views	Being challenged by opposing views results in conceptual conflict and uncertainty about correctness of own view	Presence of only one view results in high certainty about the correctness of own views
Epistemic curiosity motivates active search for new information and perspectives	Closed-minded rejection of opposing information and perspectives	Apprehension about differences and closed-minded adherence to own point of view	Continued high certainty about the correctness of own views
Reconceptualization, synthesis, integration	Closed-minded adherence to own point of view	Quick compromise to dominant view	Adherence to own point of view
High achievement, positive relationships, psychological health	Moderate achievement, relationships, psychological health	Low achievement, relationships, psychological health	Low achievement, relationships, psychological health

The greater are the cooperative elements and the less the competitive elements, the more constructive the conflict is (Deutsch, 1973). Cooperative elements alone, however, do not ensure maximal productivity. There has to be both cooperation and conflict. Thus, controversy is characterized by both positive goal and resource interdependence as well as by conflict. In a controversy, students are required to advocate opposing positions (conflict) with the intent of learning both sides so all group members can come to consensus about a synthesis of the two positions (positive goal interdependence) knowing that they need to learn the opposing perspective and information (resource interdependence).

Debate consists of positive resource interdependence, negative goal interdependence, and conflict. In a debate, students are required to advocate opposing positions (conflict), knowing that a judge determines who wins (negative goal interdependence) and that they have only one side of the information (resource interdependence).

Concurrence seeking comprises positive goal interdependence (students are required to reach consensus about the issue) and resource interdependence (students realize they have only half of the information), but no conflict. Individualistic learning situations contain neither interdependence nor intellectual conflict; students study both sides of the issue without having to advocate either.

Students benefit from the process of controversy in at least three ways:

1. Effort to achieve. Compared with concurrence seeking, debate, and individualistic efforts, controversy tends to result in greater motivation to achieve. The search for information about the topic being studied is greater. Mastery and retention of the subject matter being studied is more complete. The ability to generalize the principles learned to a wider variety of situations is greater. The use of higher-level reasoning

ACTIVITY **9.2** ■ TEST YOUR UNDERSTANDING

Given below are concepts and definitions. Match the correct definition with the correct concept. Find a partner and (a) compare answers and (b) explain your reasoning for each answer.

CONCEPT	DEFINITION
_____ 1. academic controversy	**a.** Two or more individuals argue positions that are incompatible and a judge declares a winner on the basis of who best presented their position.
_____ 2. deliberate discourse	**b.** Members of a decision-making group set aside their doubts and misgivings about whatever policy is favored by the emerging consensus so as to be able to agree with the other members.
_____ 3. creative problem solving	**c.** Group members inhibit discussion to avoid any arguments, emphasize agreement, and avoid realistic appraisal of alternative ideas and courses of action.
_____ 4. debate	**d.** This discussion generates novel solutions to a problem.
_____ 5. concurrence seeking	**e.** Individuals work alone at their own pace and with their own set of materials without interacting with each other.
_____ 6. individualistic effort	**f.** One student's ideas, information, conclusions, theories, and opinions are incompatible with those of another, and the two seek to reach an agreement.
_____ 7. groupthink	**g.** This discussion is composed of the advantages and disadvantages of proposed actions.

TABLE 9.2 Social Interdependence and Conflict

	CONTROVERSY	DEBATE	CONCURRENCE SEEKING	INDIVIDUALISTIC
Positive Goal Interdependence	Yes	No	Yes	No
Resource Interdependence	Yes	Yes	Yes	No
Negative Goal Interdependence	No	Yes	No	No
Conflict	Yes	Yes	No	No

strategies is more frequent. The quality of decisions and solutions to complex problems for which different viewpoints can plausibly be developed is higher. Creative insights into issues being discussed is more frequent. Syntheses combining more than one perspective are more frequent. Task involvement reflects greater emotional commitment to solving the problem. Feelings of stimulation and enjoyment of the process are heightened. Overall, controversy tends to be fun, enjoyable, and exciting.

2. Positive interpersonal relationships. Controversy promotes greater liking and social support among participants than does debate, concurrence seeking, no controversy, or individualistic efforts.

3. Psychological health and social competence. Compared with concurrence seeking, debate, and individualistic efforts, controversy tends to result in higher academic self-esteem and greater perspective-taking accuracy. Being able to manage disagreements and conflicts constructively enables individuals to cope with the stresses involved in interacting with a variety of other people.

PROCESS OF CONTROVERSY

> Since the general or prevailing opinion on any subject is rarely or never
> the whole truth, it is only by the collision of adverse opinion that the
> remainder of the truth has any chance of being supplied.
> —*John Stuart Mill*

Rique Campa, a professor in the Department of Fisheries and Wildlife at Michigan State University, asked his class, "Can a marina be developed in an environmentally sensitive area where piping plovers [a shorebird] have a breeding ground?" He assigned students to groups of four, divided each group into two pairs, and assigned one pair the developer position and the other pair the Department of Natural Resources position. He then followed the structured academic controversy procedure over several class periods and required students to do extensive research on the issue.

Students researched the issue, prepared a persuasive case for their position, presented their position in a compelling and interesting way, refuted the opposing position while rebutting criticisms of their position, took on the opposing perspectives, and derived a synthesis, or integration, of the positions. In conducting the controversy, Professor Campa operationalized the theoretical process by which controversy works (see Figure 9.1).

Campa followed the advice of a number of psychologists who theorized about the processes through which conflict leads to the outcomes just described. These psychologists consisted of the following types: developmental (Hunt, 1964; Kohlberg, 1969; Piaget, 1948; 1950), cognitive (Berlyne, 1966; Hammond, 1973), social (Janis, 1982; Johnson, 1970; 1979; 1980; Johnson & F. Johnson, 1975; 2000; Johnson, F. Johnson, & Johnson, 1976; Johnson & R. Johnson, 1979; 1989; 1995c), and organizational (Maier, 1970). On the basis of their work, we have proposed the following process (Johnson & Johnson, 1979; 1989; 1995c):

Step 1. Initial conclusion. When individuals are presented with a problem or decision, they have an initial conclusion based on categorizing and organizing incomplete information, their limited experiences, and their specific perspective. They often have a high degree of confidence in their conclusions and, consequently, freeze the epistemic process.

Step 2. Cognitive rehearsal. When individuals present their conclusion and its rationale to others who have different positions, students engage in cognitive rehearsal, use higher-level reasoning strategies, and deepen their understanding of their position.

Step 3. Uncertainty, disequilibrium, conceptual conflict. When individuals are confronted by other people's different conclusions based on other information, experiences, and perspectives, the individuals become uncertain as to the correctness of their views. A state of conceptual conflict or disequilibrium is aroused. They unfreeze their epistemic process.

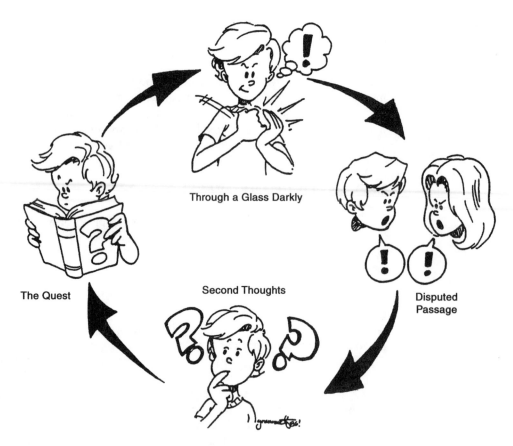

FIGURE 9.1 The Process of Controversy

Step 4. Epistemic curiosity. Individuals become curious and search for (a) more information and new experiences (increased specific content) and (b) a more adequate cognitive perspective and reasoning process (increased validity) in hopes of resolving the uncertainty. This motivation to learn more is called *epistemic curiosity*. Divergent attention and thought are stimulated.

Step 5. Refined conclusion. By adapting their cognitive perspective and reasoning through understanding and accommodating the perspective and reasoning of others, a new, reconceptualized, and reorganized conclusion is derived. Novel solutions and decisions are detected that, on balance, are qualitatively better.

The process of constructive controversy can be facilitated with five elements: a cooperative context, heterogeneous participants, relevant information, social skills, and rational argument.

1. **A cooperative context.** Communication of information is far more complete, accurate, encouraged, and utilized in a cooperative context than in a competitive context. Controversy in a cooperative context promotes open-minded listening to the opposing position whereas in a competitive context controversy promotes a closed-minded orientation in which individuals were unwilling to make concessions to the opponent's viewpoint and refuse to incorporate any of the opponent's viewpoint into their own position.
2. **Heterogeneous participants.** Heterogeneity among individuals leads to potential controversy and to more diverse interaction patterns and resources for achievement and problem solving.

3. **Relevant information distributed among participants.** The more information is available about an issue, the more successful is problem solving.
4. **Social skills.** For controversies to be managed constructively, individuals need a number of conflict management skills, such as disagreeing with each other's ideas while confirming each other's personal competence, and seeing the issue from a number of perspectives.
5. **Rational argument.** Rational argumentation includes generating ideas, collecting and organizing relevant information, using inductive and deductive logic, and making tentative conclusions based on current understanding.

STRUCTURING ACADEMIC CONTROVERSIES

> Conflict is the gadfly of thought. It stirs us to observation and memory. It instigates invention. It shocks us out of sheeplike passivity, and sets us at noting and contriving.... Conflict is a "sine qua non" of reflection and ingenuity.
> —John Dewey (*Human Nature and Conduct: Morals Are Human*)

Over the past 30 years, we have (a) developed and tested a theory of controversy (Johnson, 1970; 1979; Johnson & Johnson, 1979; 1985; 1987; 1989; Johnson, Johnson & Smith, 1986), (b) trained instructors and professors throughout North America and numerous other countries in the use of academic controversy to field test and implement the controversy procedure, and (c) developed a series of curriculum units on energy and environmental issues structured for academic controversies. A more detailed description of conducting academic controversies may be found in Johnson and Johnson (1995c). The basic format for structuring an academic controversy is as follows.

Make Preinstructional Decisions and Preparations

Topic.   The topic has to have at least two well-documented positions (pro and con). The choice of topic depends on the interests of the instructor and the purposes of the course. In math courses, controversies may focus on different ways to solve a problem. In science classes, controversies may focus on whether coal (or nuclear, wind, solar, or geothermal power) should be used as an energy source, whether hazardous wastes should be more regulated, or whether acid rain should be controlled. Because drama is based on conflict, almost any discussion of a piece of literature may be turned into a controversy, such as having students argue over who is the greatest romantic poet. Because most history is based on conflicts, controversies can be created over any historical event, such as the Federalist papers or the deportation of the Acadians. In any subject area, controversies can be created to promote academic learning and creative group problem solving.

Objectives.   Decide on academic and social skills objectives for the lesson.

Size and Makeup of Groups.   To ensure heterogeneity randomly assign students to groups and then randomly divide them into pairs. The size of groups is usually a function of the task, but too many students in one group can be counterproductive. The optimal number of students is usually four.

Instructional Materials.   Prepare instructional materials so that group members know what position they have been assigned and where they can find supporting information. (You can create resource interdependence by giving each pair half of the materials.) The following materials are needed for each position:

1. A clear description of the group's task
2. A description of the controversy procedure
3. A description of needed interpersonal and small-group skills
4. A definition of the position to be advocated with a summary of the key arguments supporting the position
5. Resource materials (including a bibliography) providing evidence for the elaboration of the arguments supporting the position to be advocated

Explain and Orchestrate the Academic Task, Cooperative Structure, and Controversy Procedure

Academic Task.   You explain the academic task so students are clear about the assignment and understand the objectives of the lesson. Direct teaching of concepts, principles, and strategies may take place at this point. The task must be structured around at least two well-documented positions (pro and con). The choice of topic depends on the interests of the instructor and the purposes of the course.

Cooperative Structure.   You structure positive interdependence by assigning two group goals. You tell students to

1. **Produce a group report detailing the nature of the group's decision and its rationale.** Members are to arrive at a consensus concerning the answer to the question posed. All group members must participate in writing a high-quality group report. Groups present their report to the entire class.
2. **Individually take a test on both positions.** Group members must master all the information on both sides of the issue and help each other score well on the test.

To supplement the effects of positive goal interdependence, the materials are divided among group members (resource interdependence) and bonus points may be given if all group members score above a preset criterion on the test (reward interdependence).

   The purpose of the controversy is to maximize each student's learning. You structure *individual accountability* by ensuring that each student participates in each step of the controversy procedure, by individually testing each student on both sides of the issue, and by randomly selecting students to present the group's report.

   You prepare students for academic controversy by providing instructions for engaging in the procedure (see Box 9.1) and by specifying social skills to be used during the controversy (see Box 9.2). In addition to explaining the procedure, you help students "get in role" by presenting the issue to be decided in an interesting and dramatic way. You specify social skills students are to master and demonstrate during the controversy. The social skills emphasized are those involved in systematically advocating an intellectual position and evaluating and criticizing the position advocated by others, as well as the skills involved in synthesis and consensual decision making. Students should be taught these controversy skills.

   You structure intergroup cooperation. The positive outcomes found in cooperative learning groups can be extended to the whole class by structuring intergroup cooperation. You explain that when preparing their positions, students can confer with classmates in other groups who are also preparing the same position. Ideas as to how best to present and advocate the position can be shared. If one pair of students finds information that supports its position, members can share that information with other pairs who have the same position. Bonus points may be given if all members of a class reach preset criteria of excellence (see Box 9.3). When a group finishes its

BOX 9.1
INSTRUCTIONS FOR CONTROVERSY PROCEDURE

Your overall goals are to learn all information relevant to the issue being studied and ensure that all other group members learn the information, so that (a) your group can write the best report possible on the issue and (b) all group members achieve high scores on the test. The controversy procedure helps you achieve these goals.

1. **Research, learn, and prepare your position.** Your group of four has been divided into two pairs. One pair has been assigned the pro position and the other pair has been assigned the con position. With your partner, prepare the best case possible for your assigned position:
   a. Research your assigned position and learn all relevant information. Read the materials supporting your position. Search for more information to support your position. Give the opposing pair any information you find that supports its position.
   b. Organizing the information into a persuasive argument that contains a thesis statement or claim (George Washington was the most effective U.S. president), the rationale supporting your thesis (He accomplished A, B, and C), and a logical conclusion that confirms your thesis (Therefore, George Washington was the most effective U.S. president).
   c. Plan how to advocate your assigned position effectively to ensure it receives a fair and complete hearing. Make sure both you and your partner are ready to present your assigned position so persuasively that the opposing pair comprehends and accepts your information and agrees that your position is valid and correct.
2. **Present and advocate your position.** Present the best case for your assigned position to the opposing pair to ensure it gets a fair and complete hearing. Be forceful, persuasive, and convincing in doing so. Use more than one media. Listen carefully to and learn the opposing position. Take notes and clarify anything you do not understand.
3. **Engage in an open discussion in which there is spirited disagreement.** Openly discuss the issue by freely exchanging information and ideas. Argue forcefully and persuasively for your position, presenting as many facts as you can to support your point of view. Listen critically to the opposing pair's evidence and reasoning, probe and push the opposing pair's thinking, ask for data to support assertions, and then present counterarguments. Take careful notes and thoroughly learn the opposing position. Compare the strengths and weaknesses of the two positions. Refute the claims being made by the opposing pair (give the other position a "trial by fire") and rebut the attacks on your position. Follow the rules for constructive controversy. A time-out period can be provided so you can caucus with your partner and prepare new arguments. Your instructor may encourage more spirited arguing, take sides when a pair is in trouble, play devil's advocate, ask one group to observe another group engaging in a spirited argument, and generally stir up the discussion. Remember, this is a complex issue and you need to know both sides to write a good report.
4. **Reverse perspectives.** Reverse perspectives and present the best case for the opposing position. Change chairs with the other pair. Present the opposing pair's position as if you were they. Use your notes to do so. Be as sincere and forceful as you can. Add any new facts you know of. Elaborate their position by relating it to other information you have previously learned. Strive to see the issue from both perspectives simultaneously. The opposing pair does the same.

(continued)

BOX 9.1 CONTINUED

5. **Synthesize.** Drop all advocacy. Find a synthesis on which all members can agree. Summarize the best evidence and reasoning from both sides and integrate it into a joint position that forms a new and unique solution. Change your mind only when the facts and rationale clearly indicate that you should do so.

   a. Write a group report on the group's synthesis and supporting evidence and rationale. All group members sign the report indicating that they agree with it, can explain its content, and consider it ready to be evaluated. Organize your report to present it to the entire class.

   b. Take a test on both positions. If all members score above the preset criteria of excellence, each receives 5 bonus points.

   c. Process how well the group functioned and how its performance may be improved during the next controversy. The specific conflict skills required for constructive controversy may be highlighted.

   d. Celebrate your group's success and the hard work of each member to make every step of the controversy procedure effective.

**BOX 9.2
CONTROVERSY RULES**

The following rules entail specific social skills required for effective controversy. These skills should be mastered and demonstrated during controversy.

1. I am critical of ideas, not people. I challenge and refute the ideas of the opposing pair, while confirming their competence and value as individuals. I do not indicate that I personally reject them.

2. I separate my personal worth from criticism of my ideas.

3. I remember that we are all in this together, sink or swim. I focus on coming to the best decision possible, not on *winning*.

4. I encourage everyone to participate and to master all the information.

5. I listen to everyone's ideas, even if I don't agree.

6. I restate what someone has said if it is not clear.

7. I differentiate before I try to integrate. I first distinguish *all* ideas and facts supporting both sides and clarify how the positions differ. Then I identify points of agreement and put them together in a way that makes sense.

8. I try to understand both sides of the issue. I try to see the issue from the opposing perspective to understand the opposing position.

9. I change my mind when the evidence clearly indicates that I should do so.

10. I emphasize rationality in seeking the best possible answer, given the available data.

11. I follow the Golden Rule of Conflict. The golden rule is, act toward your opponents as you would have them act toward you. I want the opposing pair to listen to me, so I listen to them. I want the opposing pair to include my ideas in their thinking, so I include their ideas in my thinking. I want the opposing pair to see the issue from my perspective, so I take their perspective.

■ ■ ■ ■ ■ ■

BOX 9.3
BONUS POINT SYSTEM

To encourage the interpersonal and small-group skills students need to demonstrate during controversies, a bonus point system can be used. Two points may be given for important skills, 1 point may be given for less difficult skills, and points may be taken away for negative behaviors.

DIFFICULT/IMPORTANT SKILLS (2 POINTS)	NEEDED SKILLS (1 POINT)	NEGATIVE ACTIONS (–1 POINT)
Reversing perspectives	Stating one's position	Insults
Criticizing ideas, not people	Explaining supporting information	Unparliamentary behavior
Synthesizing both sides	Paraphrasing other's remarks	Discounting
	Summarizing own or other's position	Quietness
	Stating we "sink or swim together"	
	Changing mind when logically persuaded	

work, the instructor should encourage the members to help other groups complete the assignment.

Monitor Controversy Groups and Intervene When Needed

While the groups engage in the controversy procedure, you monitor to see what problems they are having in completing the assignment: in skillfully presenting their positions, refuting the opposing position while rebutting attacks on their own position, reversing perspectives, and synthesizing. Use a formal observation sheet whenever possible and count the number of times you observe appropriate behaviors being used by students. Take notes on specific student actions to illustrate and extend the frequency data.

If a group does not understand the academic assignment, you may clarify instructions, review important concepts and strategies, answer questions, and teach academic skills as necessary. If a group is having problems engaging in the controversy procedure (researching their position, presenting it, refuting the opposing position while rebutting attacks on their position, reversing perspectives, or creatively synthesizing), you may provide clarification, coaching, and encouragement. You may also intervene to improve students' skills in working together and engaging in a controversy. Interpersonal and small-group skills (including conflict skills) may be directly taught (Johnson, 1993; Johnson & F. Johnson, 1997). You may also intervene to reinforce particularly effective and skillful behaviors that you notice.

Evaluating Students' Learning and Processing Group Effectiveness

At the end of each instructional unit, students should be able to summarize what they have learned. You may ask students to summarize the major points in the lesson, recall ideas, or give examples. You may provide your own summary and answer any final questions students have. You evaluate students' work and give feedback as to how their work compares with the criteria of excellence. Qualitative as well as quantitative aspects of performance may be addressed. Students receive a group grade on the quality of their final report and receive an individual grade on their performance on the test covering both sides of the issue.

You have groups process how well the group functioned. Students should have time to describe what member actions were helpful (and unhelpful) in completing each step of the controversy procedure and to make decisions about what behaviors to continue or change. Group processing occurs at two levels—in each learning group and in the class as a whole. In small-group processing, members discuss how effectively they worked together and what could be improved. In whole-class processing, the instructor gives the class feedback and has students share incidents that occurred in their groups.

CONDUCTING SUBJECT AREA–SPECIFIC CONTROVERSIES

Three academic controversies have been provided in Activities 9.3, 9.4, and 9.5. Participating in these controversies will help you experience the controversy procedure. The controversies involve social, political, and environmental issues, respectively. Suggestions for conducting controversies in math and science follow.

Controversy in Math.   In mathematics courses controversies may be conducted in a number of ways. One topic is reaching a decision under risk while comparing the relative advantages of using expected-value criterion and the minimax criterion. The instructional task is to determine the conditions under which each criterion is appropriate. Students may be given any problem to solve. The students are organized into cooperative learning groups with four students in each group. Two students are assigned the position that the solution should be derived by using the expected-value criterion. The other two students are assigned the position that the solution should be derived by the minimax criterion. The controversy procedure is then conducted. Another topic is to compare the Newton–Raphson and Bisection ways of solving for roots of a polynominal.

Structured Controversies in Science.   Within science classes any number of issues may be structured as academic controversies. A few topics we have used in our classes are acid rain (more research is needed vs. we know enough to act now), electrical power generation (coal vs. nuclear vs. renewable), hazardous waste (more regulations needed vs. fewer regulations needed), land use (preservation vs. economic/business planned utilization), and endangered species (endangered vs. protected). Faculty interested in these controversies may want to write the Cooperative Learning Center at the University of Minnesota for more complete descriptions and supporting materials.

WHAT ACADEMIC CONTROVERSY IS NOT

Often, misunderstandings about conducting an academic controversy and dealing with controversial issues and controversial subject matter in the classroom erupt. A *controversial issue* is an issue for which society has not found consensus, and is considered so significant that each proposed way of dealing with the issue has ardent supporters and adamant opponents. Controversial issues, by nature, arouse protest from some individual or group, because those who favor one position will be opposed by those who don't. The protest may result from a feeling that a cherished belief, an economic interest, or a basic principle is threatened. Academic controversy is aimed at learning, not at resolving political issues within a community.

ACTIVITY **9.3** ■ ARE AFFIRMATIVE ACTION PROGRAMS BENEFICIAL OR HARMFUL?

Definition: Affirmative action refers to a broad array of gender, race, national origin, and ethnicity outreach programs targeted at specific groups to notify them of education, employment, and contracting opportunities. It includes programs that favor (among similar candidates, all of whom are otherwise qualified) members of historically subordinated and still underrepresented groups. Affirmative action policies create opportunities in institutions in both the public and the private sectors. Programs may be voluntary or mandatory. For the past 35 years a controversy about the value of affirmative action has raged in our society.

Task: Your tasks are to (a) write a group report on the issue, Are affirmative action programs beneficial or harmful? and (b) individually pass a test on the research involved in the decision. Imagine you are a committee of the top officials in the U.S. government and are trying to decide whether affirmative action programs should be strengthened or abolished. Your report should provide details of the advantages and disadvantages of affirmative action. To ensure that both sides get a complete and fair hearing, you have divided your group into two groups to present the best case possible for each side of the issue. You will support one of two theses:

_____   Affirmative action is a positive program that is beneficial to our society and its future.

_____   Affirmative action is a negative program that is harmful to our society and its future.

Cooperative: Write one report for the group of four. All members have to agree. Everyone has to be able to explain the decision made and the reasons why the decision is a good one. To help you write the best report possible, your group of four has been divided into two pairs. One pair has been assigned the position that affirmative action is beneficial and the other has been assigned the position that affirmative action is harmful.

Procedure: Follow the steps outlined for controversy procedure in Box 9.1. Use the social skills specified in the controversy rules in Box 9.1.

AFFIRMATIVE ACTION IS BENEFICIAL

You represent the pro–affirmative action perspective. Your position is that affirmative action is beneficial in many ways and should be increased in the public and private sectors of our society. Given below are arguments that support your position. Summarize the evidence given below. Research your position and find as much additional information to support it as possible. Arrange your information into a compelling, convincing, and persuasive argument to support your position as valid and correct. Plan how best to present your assigned position to ensure it receives a fair and complete hearing. Make at least one visual to help you present a persuasive case for your position.

1. Affirmative action fights discrimination. Antidiscrimination laws are simply not enough as they tend to be underenforced and ignored.

2. Affirmative action compensates for past injuries. Past events can limit today's opportunities.

(continued)

ACTIVITY 9.3 *Continued*

3. Affirmative action ensures that society's opportunities and responsibilities of citizenship are fairly distributed. When resources are limited, they should be distributed in a just manner.

4. Affirmative action improves the general health of the national community. A great nation simply should not tolerate great inequalities.

5. Affirmative action promotes diversity. Commitment to diversity allows us to encounter people we have never known before who can introduce their own views into our discourse.

AFFIRMATIVE ACTION IS HARMFUL

You represent the anti–affirmative action perspective. Your position is that affirmative action is harmful in many ways and should be abolished in the public and private sectors of our society. Given below are arguments that support your position. Summarize the evidence given below. Research your position and find as much additional information to support it as possible. Arrange your information into a compelling, convincing, and persuasive argument to support your position as valid and correct. Plan how best to present your assigned position to ensure it receives a fair and complete hearing. Make at least one visual to help you present a persuasive case for your position.

1. Affirmative action increases discrimination. Antidiscrimination laws are sufficient to deal with discrimination. By definition, affirmative action discriminates against groups that are seen as privileged. A double standard is introduced.

2. Affirmative action does not compensate for past injuries. Past events cannot be erased by today's opportunities. Affirmative action creates new injuries that will have to be compensated for in the future.

3. Affirmative action ensures that society's opportunities and responsibilities of citizenship are unfairly distributed. Where resources are limited, they should be distributed in a just manner. Discriminating against privileged groups does not increase fairness. Preferential treatment is fundamentally unfair.

4. Affirmative action harms the general health of the national community. Affirmative action does not work and only causes new problems.

5. Affirmative action forces diversity onto people whether they want it or not. It violates individual freedom to force people to associate with diverse others who have different views and perspectives.

Second, many parents are concerned about certain curriculum materials and topics for study. Controversial subject matter varies from college to college and community to community. Any issue or topic has the potential to become controversial at some time or place. Academic controversy is a procedure for learning, not specific subject matter, curriculum materials, or topics.

Academic controversies create interest in subject matter and motivate students to investigate issues and points of view they would not ordinarily be interested in. Controversial issues and subject matter are just the opposite. They involve issues that students may be so emotionally involved in and feel so strongly about that a rational discussion is difficult. When unplanned and/or highly emotionally charged issues

ACTIVITY **9.4** ■ FEDERALISTS VERSUS ANTIFEDERALISTS

Task: Your task is to write a report giving your best reasoned judgment as to whether the Constitution of the United States should be ratified. The political struggle over ratification in the states was intense, sometimes bitter, and lasted 10 months. The arguments for and against the Constitution focused on three basic questions: (a) Will the new Constitution maintain a republican form of government? (b) Will the national government have too much power? (c) Is a bill of rights needed? In making your decision and planning your report you must make sure the views on both sides of the issue receive a fair and complete hearing. You will support one of two views:

_____   The Federalists wrote the Constitution and wished the country to ratify it (the Federalists included Alexander Hamilton, James Madison, and John Jay).

_____   The Antifederalists wished to defeat the Constitution (the Antifederalists included George Mason, John Hancock, Samuel Adams, and Patrick Henry).

Cooperative: Write one report for the group, everyone must agree, and everyone has to be able to explain the decision made and the rationale as to why the decision is a good one.

THE ANTIFEDERALISTS

You represent the Antifederalist perspective. Your position (thesis statement) is that the Constitution must not be ratified. In preparing your position write several slogans against the ratification of the Constitution. Also make at least one visual to help you present a persuasive case against ratification.

1. **A federal government will resort to tyranny to keep its power.** Free government requires the active participation of the people. The national government provided by the Constitution would be located too far from most people's communities to allow them to participate. As a result, the only way the government would be able to rule would be through the use of military force. The result would be a tyranny.

2. **The state governments will be destroyed.** The Constitution gives the national government too much power at the expense of the state governments. It gives the government the power to tax citizens and to raise and keep an army. The supremacy clause means all the national government's laws are superior to laws made by the states. As a result, it would be only a matter of time until the state governments were destroyed.

3. **The limits to the federal government's power is not clear.** The necessary and proper clause is too general and, as a result, gives too much power to the national government. It is dangerous not to list the powers of the government to put clear limits on them.

4. **The freedom of individuals is not protected.** The Constitution does not include a bill of rights which is essential for protecting individuals against the power of the national government.

THE FEDERALISTS

You represent the Federalist perspective. Your position is that the Constitution must be ratified. In preparing your position write several slogans for the ratification of the

(continued)

ACTIVITY 9.4   *Continued*

Constitution. Also make at least one visual to help you present a persuasive case for ratification.

1. **If factions control government for their personal gain, a republic will not work.** History proves that all the small republics in the past were destroyed by special interests. The citizens' civic virtue was not enough to prevent them from seeking their own selfish interests rather than the common welfare. Special interests can be more easily controlled in a large republic in which (a) the government is organized on the basis of checks and balances and (b) power is divided between the national and the state governments.

2. **The power of the central government is limited.** The Constitution will give the national government greater power than it has under the Articles of Confederation. But its powers are limited to dealing with tasks that face the entire nation such as trade, currency, and defense. A stronger national government is needed to deal with these problems. The Constitution provides adequate protections for the state governments.

3. **A national balance of power protects the states.** The powers of the national government are separated and balanced among the three branches so one cannot dominate the others. A strong executive branch is necessary for the national government to be able to fulfill its responsibilities. The Constitution gives Congress and the Supreme Court ways to check the use of power by the executive branch so it cannot become a monarchy.

4. **It is better to keep individual rights ambiguous.** A national bill of rights may give the impression that people would only be given protection for those rights that were actually listed.

---

arise in a classroom, however, faculty need a procedure and plan for dealing with them.

LEARNING HOW TO BE A CITIZEN IN A DEMOCRACY

The word *democracy* comes from the Greek word *demokratia,* which is a combination of *demos* (the Greek word for people) and *kratos* (the Greek word for rule). One admirer of Athenian democracy was Thomas Jefferson. Jefferson believed that free and open discussion should serve as the basis of influence within society, not the social rank within which a person was born. Jefferson was also influenced by one of his professors at William and Mary College, Dr. William Small of Scotland. Small advocated a new method of learning in which students questioned and discussed, examining all sides of a topic, with scant regard for the pronouncements of established authorities. A few years before his death, Thomas Jefferson (1818) described his experiences as a student at the College of William and Mary in a letter to Dr. Thomas Cooper: "I was bold in the pursuit of knowledge, never fearing to follow the truth and reason to whatever results they led, and bearding every authority which stood in the way" (p. 1).

Based on the beliefs of Thomas Jefferson and his fellow revolutionaries, U.S. democracy was founded on the premise that "truth" results from free and open

ACTIVITY **9.5** ■ ACID PRECIPITATION

Definition: Acid precipitation is popularly known as acid rain, but rain is not the only culprit. Acid precipitation includes acid rain, acid snow, acid sleet, acid hail, acid frost, acid rime, acid fog, acid mist, acid dew, and "dry" deposits of acid particles, aerosols, and gases. It is not only a problem in the United States, but also elsewhere in the world.

PRO-ENVIRONMENT POSITION

You are members of an environmental organization that believes a chemical leprosy is eating away at the face of the United States. The United States needs to recognize the extreme dangers of acid precipitation and take steps to remedy it before the damage becomes so pervasive that it is irreversible.

Your Position: Legislative action is immediately needed to rectify the problem of acid precipitation by controlling emissions of utility plants burning coal and petroleum. You believe that industry policy groups have not accepted responsibility for the damage utility plants are causing. They seem unconcerned about the human and environmental costs of their current practices. Certainly they will not change voluntarily.

Task: Whether you agree with this position, argue for it as strongly as you can. Use arguments that make sense and are rational. Be creative and invent new supporting arguments.

Procedure: Remember to learn the rationale for both your position and the industrial position. Challenge the industrial position, think of loopholes in their logic, and demand facts and information to back up their arguments. Study the following points to start preparing your position. Read the text materials, go to the library, and interview experts to gather additional material to support your position.

1. Acid precipitation occurs when sulfur dioxide and nitrogen oxides combine in the atmosphere and change chemically into acid, which falls to the earth mixed with some form of precipitation. The pollutants come primarily from burning coal and petroleum. About 90 percent of the sulfur in the atmosphere of the northeastern United States comes from human-made sources.

2. Acid precipitation can kill fish and other aquatic life outright. In Scandinavia, which is downwind of pollution pumped into the skies of Western Europe, acid precipitation has already destroyed fish life in 5,000 lakes in southwestern Sweden, in several Atlantic salmon rivers, and in 1,500 lakes in southern Norway.

3. Acid precipitation can have damaging effects on human health through inhalation and through leaching toxic materials into drinking water.

PRO-INDUSTRY POSITION

You are members of an industrial policy group that believes the listed causes of acid precipitation are only hypotheses advanced by scientists to explain certain facts that puzzle them. Scientists, however, have not conducted experiments tracing acid precipitation from the emission sources. Until cause and effect can conclusively be established, stringent controls on industry are presumptuous and costly.

Your Position: Legislative action is not needed to increase the controls on emissions of utility plants burning coal and petroleum. You believe that no hard scientific evidence

(continued)

ACTIVITY 9.5   *Continued*

has been presented to justify new controls. In addition, environmentalists are vague about the level of control required and do not mention other remedial measures to control emissions from sources other than utilities.

Task: Whether you agree with this position, argue for it as strongly as you can. Use arguments that make sense and are rational. Be creative and invent new supporting arguments.

Procedure: Remember to learn the rationale for both your position and the industrial position. Challenge the industrial position, think of loopholes in their logic, and demand facts and information to back up their arguments. Study the following points to start preparing your position. Read the text materials, go to the library, and interview experts to gather additional material to support your position.

1. Environmentalists are implying causality by association rather than by scientific proof of linkage. If the relationship between power plant emissions and acid precipitation is so overwhelming, then why have investigators been unable to trace acid precipitation back to the source emissions?

2. If both nitrate and sulfate in rain can be halved, the precipitation pH at most changes from 4.2 to 4.5. If sulfate alone is halved, the precipitation pH may change at most from 4.2 to 4.4. Emission controls, therefore, may be ineffective in changing precipitation pH values.

3. If interstate atmospheric deposition were regulated, at a minimum 2,980 mining jobs and $191 million in annual economic input could be affected. The effect on these mines depends on the control scheme adopted.

---

discussion in which opposing points of view are advocated and vigorously argued. Every citizen is given the opportunity to advocate for his or her ideas. Once a decision is made, the minority is expected to go along willingly with the majority because they know they have been given a fair and complete hearing. To be a citizen in our democracy, individuals need to master the process of organizing their conclusions, advocating their views, challenging opposing positions, making decisions, and committing themselves to implementing whatever decision is made (regardless of whether one initially favored the alternative adopted or not).

BUILDING A LEARNING COMMUNITY

Students have to learn how to be contributing members to a learning community to achieve the goals of the college and to prepare themselves for most careers in which group decision making is an everyday occurrence. For classes and colleges to be learning communities, these steps must be taken.

Positive Interdependence.   The first step in creating a learning community is creating positive interdependence among all members of the class or college. The easiest way to create such a cooperative context and a learning community is to use cooperative learning procedures the majority of the day (Johnson, Johnson, & Holubec, 1998). From making learning a cooperative effort, faculty may establish the mutual goal of searching for truth and knowledge and build commitment to achieving it. Increasing knowledge and understanding is achieved through cooperative interaction, not isolated thought. Truth and knowledge are consensual, based on intersubjectivity in which different individuals reach the same conclusions and make the same inferences after considering theory and facts.

Intellectual Conflict.   The second step is to make intellectual conflict a way of life. Faculty need to engage students in intellectual conflicts within which they have to prepare intellectual positions, present them, advocate them, criticize opposing intellectual positions, view the issue from a variety of perspectives, and synthesize the various positions into one position. Without intellectual conflict, a learning community in which faculty and students seek truth and knowledge cannot be achieved.

Joint Action.   The third step is to make the epistemology and pedagogy used congruent with the need for joint action toward mutual goals and the continued presence of intellectual conflict. The epistemology resulting from (a) a competitive context in which students are ranked from highest to lowest performer and (b) making students passive recipients of lectures and reading mitigates against the formation of a learning community. Developing a learning community requires an epistemology based on the predominant use of cooperative learning and academic controversies. Because cooperative learning increases achievement, committed and caring relationships, increased social competencies, and a number of other important instructional outcomes (Johnson & Johnson, 1989), there can be little objection to making it the dominant mode of learning.

In addition to cooperative learning, faculty use academic controversies to create the intellectual conflict and internal disequilibrium needed to increase student critical thinking and use of higher-level reasoning strategies. Finding consenual truth requires mutual commitment to do so and intellectual disagreement and challenge. The combination of cooperative learning and academic controversies makes the epistemology and pedagogy congruent with faculty and students working together to accomplish mutual goals and engaging in continual intellectual conflict. These two instructional procedures thereby promote the creation of a true learning community.

Peer Mediation.   The fourth step is to establish a peer mediation program (see Johnson & Johnson, 1995b). Maintaining a learning community requires members to manage their conflicts of interests constructively. Doing so involves training students how to (a) engage in problem-solving negotiations and (b) mediate the conflicts occurring among fellow students. Implementing such a peer mediation program provides the framework for ensuring that good relationships are maintained among community members.

SUMMARY

Thomas Jefferson based his faith in the future of democracy on the power of constructive conflict. To achieve Jefferson's vision, and promote student interest, curiosity, inquiry, and open-minded problem solving, teachers must use two interrelated instructional procedures: cooperative learning and academic controversy. Academic controversy results in many positive benefits for students, including higher achievement, more positive relationships with classmates, and increased self-esteem.

The academic controversy procedure involves dividing a cooperative group into two pairs and assigning them opposing positions. The pairs then develop their position, present it to the other pair, listen to the opposing position, engage in a discussion in which they attempt to refute the other side and rebut attacks on their position, reverse perspectives and present the other position, and then drop all advocacy and seek a synthesis that takes both perspectives and positions into account. Academic controversies may be used in any subject area.

To implement academic controversies successfully, students need to learn the interpersonal and small-group skills required to cooperate, engage in intellectual inquiry, intellectually challenge each other, see a situation from several perspectives simultaneously, and synthesize a variety of positions into a new and creative decision. Students also need to learn the academic skills of researching a position, conceptualizing and organizing an intellectual position, using inductive and deductive logic, presenting a scholarly and reasoned position, refuting others' positions, rebutting attacks on one's own position, and integrating information and reasoning from different perspectives and positions.

Walter Savage Landor once said, "There is no more certain sign of a narrow mind, of stupidity, and of arrogance, than to stand aloof from those who think differently from us." It is vital for citizens to seek reasoned judgment on the complex problems facing our society. Especially important is educating individuals to solve problems for which different points of view can plausibly be developed. To do so individuals must enter empathetically the arguments on both sides of the issue and ensure that the strongest possible case is made for each side, and arrive at a synthesis based on rational thought.

CONTROVERSY LESSON PLANNING FORM

Grade Level: _____   Subject Area: _____   Date: _____

Lesson: _____

OBJECTIVES

Academic skills: _____

Social skills: _____

PREINSTRUCTIONAL DECISIONS

Group size: _____   Method of assigning students: _____

Roles: _____

Room arrangement: _____

Materials: _____

Pro position: _____

Con position: _____

TASK AND COOPERATIVE GOAL STRUCTURE

1. Task: _____

_____

2. Criteria for success: _____

_____

3. Positive interdependence: _____

_____

4. Individual accountability: _____

_____

5. Intergroup cooperation: _____

_____

6. Expected behaviors: _____

_____

CONTROVERSY PROCEDURE

1. Preparing positions: _____

2. Presenting positions: _____

3. Discussing issue: _____

4. Reversing perspectives: _____

5. Reaching a decision: _____

MONITORING AND INTERVENING

1. Observation procedure: _____ Formal _____ Informal

2. Observer: _____ Teacher _____ Students _____ Visitors

3. Intervening for task assistance: _____

_____

4. Intervening for teamwork assistance: _____

_____

5. Other: _____

_____

EVALUATING AND PROCESSING

1. Assessment of members' individual learning:

2. Assessment of group productivity:

3. Small-group processing:

4. Whole-class processing:

5. Charts and graphs used:

6. Positive feedback to each student:

7. Goal setting for improvement:

8. Celebration:

CHAPTER TEN

TEACHING STUDENTS TO BE PEACEMAKERS

INTRODUCTION

"John pushed Perry down, so Perry kicked him." "Sally and Juanita were spitting in each other's faces and calling each other names." "Tyler threatened to beat up Richard. Richard said if Tyler tried to do anything he would get even." ∎

Considerable instructional, administrative, and learning efforts are lost because schools are filled with conflicts that students and faculty manage poorly. The frequency and severity of conflicts seem to be increasing, so that, for the first time, the category fighting, violence, and gangs has been found to be tied for the number one position with lack of discipline for the largest problem confronting local public schools (Elam, Rose, & Harris, 1994). When these conflicts exist among diverse individuals, the potential for destructive outcomes is considerable, and procedures to ensure that conflicts are managed constructively are greatly needed.

Teaching all students in all schools how to manage conflicts constructively helps ensure the following:

1. That positive outcomes of diversity are actualized
2. That positive outcomes of conflict are realized
3. That classrooms and schools are safe and orderly places
4. That students are prepared to manage conflicts constructively in career, family, community, national, and international settings

To manage conflicts constructively, students must be taught the steps of being a peacemaker (Johnson & Johnson, 1995a; 1995b):

1. Create a cooperative context.
2. Teach students to understand (a) what is and is not a conflict and (b) that conflicts have many potentially valuable outcomes.
3. Teach students the problem-solving negotiation procedure.
4. Teach students how to mediate their schoolmates' conflicts.
5. Implement the peer mediation program.
6. Teach follow-up lessons to refine and upgrade students' skills in using the negotiation and mediation procedures.
7. Each year, from the first through twelfth grades, repeat the above six steps.

TEACHING STUDENTS THE PEACEMAKER PROGRAM

The Teaching Students to Be Peacemakers program was developed in the mid-1960s at the University of Minnesota by researchers in the field of conflict resolution (Johnson, 1970; 1972; 1978; Johnson & F. Johnson, 1975; Johnson, F. Johnson, & R. Johnson, 1976). Its creators (the authors of this book) were interested in translating the theory on conflict resolution and the results of an ongoing research program in constructive conflict resolution into a set of practical procedures for students and faculty to use. Beginning in 1966, we trained teachers to teach students how to resolve conflicts constructively. Special attention was paid to helping (a) students resolve cross-ethnic conflicts arising from desegregation and (b) faculty resolve conflicts arising from site-based decision making and team teaching. Building positive relationships among disputants as well as reaching integrative agreements was and is, therefore, a major emphasis of the program.

Peacemaking training focuses on teaching students what are and are not conflicts, how to negotiate integrated solutions to their conflicts, and how to mediate schoolmates' conflicts. The negotiation and mediation procedures taught were based on the author's research in five areas:

1. Establishing a cooperative context for conflict, primarily through the use of cooperative learning (Johnson, 1970; Johnson & R. Johnson, 1975), establishing joint goals (Johnson & Lewicki, 1969), and expressing cooperative intentions (Johnson, 1971; 1971b; 1973)
2. Engaging in perspective taking in conflict situations (Johnson, 1967; 1970; 1971a; 1971b; 1971c; 1971d; 1975a; 1975b)
3. Expressing emotions such as warmth and avoiding expressing emotions such as coldness or anger in negotiations (Johnson, 1971b, 1971c)
4. Equalizing power between majority and minority students by teaching curriculum units aimed at strengthening the ethnic identity of minority students (Johnson, 1966a; 1966b)
5. Using problem-solving procedures in negotiations (Johnson, 1966; 1970; 1972)

The Peacemaker Program involves 20 hours of initial training in 30-minute lessons spread out over several weeks. Subsequently, teachers teach additional lessons to refine and upgrade students' negotiation and mediation skills. Important aspects of the Peacemaker Program include the following:

1. Training all students in the school to negotiate integrative agreements to their conflicts and mediate schoolmates' conflicts
2. Ensuring all students serve as peer mediators an equal amount of time so the benefits for doing so are experienced by everyone
3. Integrating the training into ongoing academic curriculum units
4. Repeating the training each year as a 12-year spiral curriculum
5. Ensuring the norms, values, and culture of the school promote and support the use of the negotiation and mediation procedures

The Peacemaker Program has been implemented in schools throughout North America, and in several countries in Europe, the Middle East, Africa, Asia, and Central and South America (Johnson & Johnson, 1987; 1991; 1998).

TWO APPROACHES TO ESTABLISHING
A PEER MEDIATION PROGRAM

A great diversity of conflict resolution/peer mediation programs exists in schools, but generally they can be described as either cadre or total student body programs.

The *cadre approach* emphasizes training a small number of students to serve as peer mediators. The community boards of San Francisco Conflict Managers Program and the School Mediators' Alternative Resolution Team (SMART) in New York City are examples. The training of a cadre of mediators usually consists of a 1- or 2-day workshop or a semester-long class. The cadre approach is based on the assumption that a few specially trained students can defuse and resolve constructively the interpersonal conflicts taking place among members of the student body. It is a relatively easy and inexpensive program for a school to adopt. It has not been clearly demonstrated, however, how the existence of a cadre of peer mediators decreases the severity and frequency of interpersonal conflicts among the general student population.

The *total student body approach* emphasizes training every student in the school to manage conflicts constructively (Johnson & Johnson, 1995a). The Teaching Students to Be Peacemakers program is the major example. It assumes all students are empowered to regulate their own behavior and resolve their interpersonal conflicts constructively when all students in the school are trained to negotiate integrative agreements to their conflicts and mediate schoolmates' conflicts. Training the whole student body and faculty in the same negotiation and mediation procedures requires considerable time and commitment by the faculty and administration and is, therefore, relatively costly.

STEP 1: CREATING A COOPERATIVE CONTEXT

The context within which conflicts occur largely determines whether the conflict is managed constructively or destructively (Deutsch, 1973; Johnson & Johnson, 1989; Tjosvold & Johnson, 1983; Watson & Johnson, 1972). Two possible contexts for conflict are cooperative and competitive (in individualistic situations individuals do not interact and, therefore, no conflict occurs). When competitive and individualistic learning dominate a classroom and school, conflicts are inevitably destructive. Instead of trying to solve interpersonal problems, students think in terms of short-term self-interest and go for the "win."

To resolve conflicts constructively, an instructor first has to establish a cooperative context, primarily through using cooperative learning procedures the majority of the day (Johnson, Johnson, & Holubec, 1998). The more cooperative the relationships among students are, the more constructively conflicts are managed. Because cooperative learning increases achievement and promotes a number of other important instructional outcomes (Johnson & Johnson, 1989), there can be little objection to doing so. The more competitive the relationships among students are, and the more students tend to focus on their own self-interest, the more destructive conflicts are. This step has been discussed in detail in the chapters on cooperative learning and in Chapter 8.

STEP 2: TEACHING STUDENTS THE NATURE AND DESIRABILITY OF CONFLICT

Many students have a negativity bias in which they tend to see conflicts as involving anger, hostility, and violence. They tend not to recognize that conflicts can result in insight, learning, problem solving, and laughter. Students, therefore, need to be taught (a) what is and is not a conflict, (b) the criteria for determining whether a conflict is resolved constructively, and (c) the value of conflict.

STEP 3: TEACHING ALL STUDENTS THE PROBLEM-SOLVING NEGOTIATION PROCEDURE

The heart of conflict resolution training is teaching students how to negotiate constructive resolutions to their conflicts. It is not enough to tell students to "be nice" or "talk it out," or "solve your problem." *All* students in all schools need to learn how to engage in problem-solving negotiations. *Negotiation* is a process by which persons try to work out a settlement when they (a) have both shared and opposing interests and (b) want to come to an agreement (Johnson & F. Johnson, 1997). There are two types of negotiations.

Win–Lose, or Distributive, Negotiations.   In win–lose or *distributive*, negotiations, the goal is to reach an agreement more favorable to oneself than to the other persons. It is appropriate primarily when disputants do not interact or work with each other in the future and, therefore, disputants focus more on maximizing their own gain than on the brief, ad hoc relationship with the other person.

At times you may negotiate to win (this means the other person loses). In win–lose negotiating, the goal is to maximize your outcomes while minimizing the other person's outcomes. Buying a used car is an example. In win–lose negotiations the goal is to make an agreement more favorable to you than to the other person. You go for the win when your wants, needs, and goals are important and you have a temporary, ad hoc relationship with the other person. The two of you plan to negotiate an agreement and then separate, never seeing each other again. Each wants, therefore, to gain an advantage over the other. You go for the win not caring whether the relationship is damaged or not. In some cultures, where bargaining is a way of life, this type of negotiating is an art form.

In going for the win you assume that the relationship is unimportant and has no future. This is often a mistake. There are very few times in your life when you negotiate with someone you will never interact with again. If you go for a win and then have to face the same person the next day, sooner or later the other person gets revenge! In most situations, therefore, you want to try to resolve the conflict by maximizing joint outcomes. Review some helpful hints for succeeding:

1. Make an extreme opening offer (if you are willing to pay $1,500, offer $500). Do not let the other person know how much you are willing to pay.
2. Compromise slowly (try to get the other person to compromise first).
3. Use threats, promises, and arguments to convince the other person what he or she wants is unreasonable and unattainable.
4. Be ready to walk away with no agreement.

Problem-Solving, or Integrative, Negotations.   In problem-solving, or *integrative*, negotiations, the goal is to reach an agreement that benefits everyone involved. The majority of the time, negotiations occur in ongoing relationships in which individuals are committed to the other's well-being as well as their own. In such circumstances, the disputants seek to solve the problem in a way that maximizes joint outcomes (see Box 10.1).

When you are dealing with someone with whom you have a long-term relationship (like family members, fellow students, neighbors, colleagues, or friends), you negotiate to solve the problem. In problem-solving negotiations, the goal is to discover a solution that will benefit everyone involved (to maximize joint outcomes). You do so to balance two concerns. First, you maximize joint outcomes by reaching an agreement that is advantageous to everyone involved (ensure that all participants benefit). Second, you improve the relationship and your ability to work together effectively.

In long-term relationships you are concerned about the other person's wants, needs, and goals. Protecting their interests and ensuring their well-being becomes one of your priorities. Maintaining a high-quality relationship, therefore, is usually more important than getting your way on any one issue. In problem-solving negotiations, therefore, the persons involved resolve the conflict as partners, not as adversaries. There is a hard-headed, side-by-side search for a fair agreement that is advantageous to both sides.

■ ■ ■ ■ ■

BOX 10.1
RULES FOR NEGOTIATING SOLUTIONS TO PROBLEMS

1. Realize that your interests (wants, needs, goals) differ.
2. Remember there is nothing wrong with conflict. It is how conflict is managed that is important.
3. Face conflicts. You want to deal with them frequently in positive ways. Do not let small conflicts build up to a big one. Nip them in the bud!
4. Remember that the shadow of the future interaction with the other person lies over any one conflict.
5. Use the procedure for problem-solving negotiations. Maximize joint outcomes.
6. Never walk away with a win. Make sure the other person is happy about the agreement and that the agreement is in both yours and the other person's best interests.
7. If problem-solving negotiations fail, seek help from a peer mediator.
8. Be ready to mediate other persons' conflicts when they ask you to.
9. Be ready to suspend negotiations if the other person is trying to win while you are trying to solve the problem.

When dealing with a person you have to associate with at work, in school, or in the neighborhood for some time, the rules are twofold. First, never walk away with a win! (Otherwise you must be careful whenever you pass dark doorways!) Do not end negotiations until the other person has what he or she wants (in a way that allows you to get what you want); otherwise the conflict may resurface later. One-sided settlements, imposed by whomever has the most power or is most persuasive, are rarely stable or long-lasting, and typically damage the relationship.

Second, make sure the long-term concern for each others' well-being is reciprocated. One-way relationships never last long. Ongoing relationships are guided by a *norm of mutual responsiveness,* that is, you help others reach their goals and they help you reach your goals. When the other person feels strongly about something, therefore, you are expected to take it seriously. When you feel strongly about something, they also should take you seriously.

In families and friendships, conflicts are often resolved by a procedure known as the *one-step negotiation.* Each person (a) assesses the strength of his/her interests, (b) assesses the strength of the other person's interests, and (c) agrees that whomever has the greatest need gets his or her way. The one-step negotiation procedure only works if it is reciprocal. Each should get his or her way half the time. If individuals are not equally responsive to each other's needs, the relationship breaks down. Knowing how to negotiate to solve the problem is a key to success and happiness. Problem-solving negotiating, however, is not easy to do well.

In ongoing relationships that have a future as well as a present, an integrative approach to negotiations is the only constructive alternative. All students, no matter how different their backgrounds and cultures, need to be (a) cooriented as to the integrative procedures used to resolve interpersonal and intergroup conflicts and (b) skilled in their use. The integrative negotiation procedure and skills need to be overlearned so that they are available for use when emotions such as fear and anger are intense.

Important Points about Negotiations

It takes two to negotiate. You cannot negotiate without the consent and participation of the other disputant. The two types of interdependence inherent in any negotiations are *participation interdependence* (negotiations cannot take place without the cooperation of the other disputant) and *outcome interdependence* (an agreement can only be achieved with the cooperation of the other disputant). No matter what happens disputants are dependent on each other to participate in the negotiating process and to reach an agreement.

Negotiations are a mixed-motive situation involving both cooperation and competitive elements. There is a desire to reach an agreement and a desire to make that agreement as favorable to oneself as possible. Thus, disputants face a *goal dilemma* between (a) maximizing their own outcomes and (b) reaching an agreement. The two goals can seriously interfere with each other.

Negotiators are dependent on each other for information about each other's wants, goals, and interests. Information dependence creates two dilemmas. First, should the negotiator trust the other disputant's statements about his or her wants, goals, and interests? Second, should the negotiator be honest and open in revealing his or her own wants, goals, and interests?

Negotiators strive for both primary and secondary gains. The *primary gain* is determined by the nature of the agreement. The *secondary gain* is determined by (a) the effectiveness of the working relationship with the other disputant and (b) the impact of the negotiations on interested third parties.

During negotiations contractual norms are developed. The norms become the ground rules for conducting the negotiations. Two common norms are the norm of reciprocity and the norm of equity. The *norm of reciprocity* requires disputants to return the same benefit or harm given him or her by the other disputant.) The *norm of equity* requires that the benefits received or the costs accrued by the negotiators are equal. In addition, not all issues are negotiable. (See Activity 10.1 for how to manage such conflicts.)

Negotiations have a beginning, a middle, and an end. The strategies and tactics used to initiate negotiations, exchange proposals and information, and precipitate an agreement can be quite different and sometimes contradictory. Negotiations are an ever-present factor in human life. Everyone has to negotiate every day. You cannot avoid negotiating, but it is not easy to do well. It takes years of practice to learn how to negotiate with skill, finesse, and grace.

Negotiations may rarely be used in most schools. DeCecco and Richards (1974) conducted a study of junior high and high schools students and found that students reported that negotiations were tried in only 17 percent of the conflicts; decisions were imposed by school authorities 55 percent of the time. Students, however, report that they prefer direct negotiations to resolve student–student and teacher–student conflicts and do want to learn how to negotiate.

Steps in Problem-Solving Negotiations

To negotiate integrative agreements, students need to define their conflict (e.g., Deutsch, Canavan, & Rubin, 1971; Deutsch & Lewicki, 1970), exchange positions and proposals (Johnson, 1977), view the situation from both perspectives (Johnson, 1971), invent options for mutual gain (Johnson, 1967; 1971; Deutsch, 1973; Pruitt, 1981), and reach a wise agreement (Deutsch, 1973). The steps in using problem-solving negotiations have been operationalized into the following procedure (Johnson & Johnson, 1995a; 1995b) (see Figure 10.1):

Step 1. Describe what you want. "I want to use the book now." You state what you want and listen carefully to what the other person wants. You use good communication skills and agree on a definition of the conflict that specifies it as a small and specific mutual problem to be solved.

Step 2. Describe how you feel. "I'm frustrated." You must understand how you feel and communicate it openly and clearly while listening carefully to how the other person is feeling.

ACTIVITY **10.1** ■ NEGOTIABLE VERSUS NONNEGOTIABLE ISSUES

Not every issue is negotiable, and you should know the difference between a negotiable and nonnegotiable issue. You must be able to say no when someone tries to negotiate a nonnegotiable issue. Your tasks are to make a list of negotiable and nonnegotiable issues and to practice saying no when someone brings up a nonnegotiable issue. To prepare, read the section on refusal skills in Chapter 5 of *Teaching Students to Be Peacemakers*.

1. Draw two columns on a sheet of paper. Label the first column Negotiable and the second column Nonnegotiable. In the first column write, "Eat a salad for lunch." In the second column write, "Shoplift." What you eat for lunch is negotiable. Breaking the law is not negotiable.

2. Working in a pair, list five issues that are negotiable and five issues that are not negotiable. Both of you need a copy.

3. Find a new partner. Share your list of negotiable and nonnegotiable issues. Listen to your partner's list. Create a new list from the best ideas of both of you.

4. Return to your original partner. Share your new list. Listen to his or her new list. Create a final list from the best ideas from both of you.

5. Role play a situation in which someone is trying to get you to do something you do not want to do. Pick one of the nonnegotiable issues. Try to negotiate it with your partner. Your partner should say, to your every attempt, "No, I won't do it. That issue is nonnegotiable." Then reverse roles. Your partner tries to negotiate one of the nonnegotiable issues with you. You reply to his or her every attempt, "No, I won't do it. That issue is nonnegotiable."

PERSON 1	PERSON 2
Help me cheat on this test.	No, I won't. That issue is nonnegotiable.
It's only one test. No one will ever know.	No, I won't. That issue is nonnegotiable.
If you're my friend, you'll help me cheat.	No, I won't. Cheating is nonnegotiable.

Step 3. Describe the reasons for your wants and feelings. "You have been using the book for the past hour. If I don't get to use the book soon my report will not be done on time. It's frustrating to have to wait so long." You state the reasons why you want what you do and feel how you do and listen carefully to the other person's reasons. In doing so, you express cooperative intentions, focus on interests not positions, differentiate before trying to integrate the two sets of interests, explore how disputants' interests are incompatible and compatible, and empower the other by giving choices.

Step 4. Take the other's perspective "My understanding of you is…" Summarize your understanding of what the other person wants, how the other person feels, and the reasons underlying both. You present the opposing perspective as completely and accurately as you can, summarizing the other's position and interests. This includes understanding the perspective of the opposing disputant and being able to see the problem from both perspectives simultaneously. Helpful procedures are paraphrasing (see Box 10.2) and checking their perceptions of the other person's interests and reasons.

FIGURE 10.1   Building a Bridge to Successful Resolution of a Conflict

BOX 10.2
RULES FOR PARAPHRASING

1. Put yourself in the other person's shoes.
2. Restate the other person's ideas and feelings in your own words. State as correctly as possible what the other person wants, feels, and why.
3. Start your remarks with, *You want . . . , You feel . . . ,* and *You think. . . .*
4. Show understanding and acceptance by nonverbal behaviors—tone of voice, facial expressions, gestures, eye contact, and posture.

Step 5. Invent three optional plans to resolve the conflict that maximize joint benefits. "Plan A is . . . , Plan B is . . . , Plan C is . . ." You invent options for mutual gain by inventing creative options and avoiding the obstacles to creative problem solving.

Step 6. Choose one plan and formalize the agreement with a handshake. "Let's agree on Plan B!" You strive to reach a wise agreement that (a) meets the legitimate needs of all participants and (b) is based on principles that can be justified on some objective criteria. Your plan maximizes joint benefits and strengthens disputants' ability to work together cooperatively and resolve conflicts constructively in the future. It specifies how each disputant should act in the future and how the agreement will be reviewed and renegotiated if it does not work.

Step 7. Try, try again until a wise agreement is reached. Students need to practice this procedure over and over again until it becomes an automatic habit (see Box 10.3 for a brief summary of these steps). Try the exercises in Activities 10.2 through 10.6 to practice the steps in problem-solving negotiations.

STEP 4: TEACHING ALL STUDENTS TO MEDIATE SCHOOLMATES' CONFLICTS

William Ury often tells a tale of an old gentleman who in his will requests that his estate be divided among his three sons in the following manner: One-half to his

BOX 10.3
STEPS TO PROBLEM-SOLVING NEGOTIATIONS

Six basic steps in negotiating a workable solution to a problem that maximizes joint outcomes follow:

1. Each person explains what he or she wants in a descriptive, nonevaluative way.
2. Each person explains how he or she feels in a descriptive, nonevaluative way.
3. Each person explains his or her reasons for wanting what he or she wants and feeling the way he or she does.
4. Each person reverses perspectives by summarizing what the other person wants and feels and the reasons underlying those wants and feelings.
5. The participants invent at least three good optional agreements that would maximize joint outcomes.
6. The participants choose the agreement that seems the wisest and agree to abide by its conditions.

ACTIVITY **10.2** ■ WHAT I WANT, WHAT YOU WANT

Conflicts begin when two people want the same thing. When one person says, "I want the ice cream bar" and another person says, "I want the ice cream bar," a conflict arises.

It is okay to want something. Every person has needs. Every person every minute of the day wants something. To stand up for yourself you have to let other people know what you want. You have a perfect right to stand up for yourself. So does the other person. You are both okay to stand up for what you want.

The first step of negotiationg is for each person to say what he or she wants. To practice the first and the last steps of negotiation, go through the steps of the procedure:

     1. I want . . . You want . . .
     2. Meet me in the middle.
     3. Okay. Shake.

Divide into groups of four. Form two rows of four students each. The two rows face each other. Each person says to the person he or she is facing:

I want the cookie. No, I want the cookie.
Let's meet in the middle. Each will get half. You cut and I'll choose.
Okay. Shake.

Then move to the next person and say the same thing. Do not stop until you have practiced the sequence four times.

Why is dividing the cookie in half a good idea?

Where else can you use this procedure? Divide into pairs. Write down three places where you can use this procedure.

     1. _____

     2. _____

     3. _____

ACTIVITY **10.3** ■ WHAT I WANT, WHAT YOU WANT. HOW I FEEL, HOW YOU FEEL.

It is not enough to say what you want. You also need to say how you feel. Sometimes you may feel angry. Sometimes you may feel frustrated. Sometimes you may feel afraid.

In conflicts, everyone has feelings. Both sides need to say how they feel. You need to say how you feel. The other person needs to say how he or she feels. To stand up for yourself you need to let other people know how you feel. To stand up for themselves, other people need to let you know how they feel. Both you and the other person have a perfect right to your feelings.

The second step of negotiation is for each person to say how he or she feels. To practice the first, second, and last steps of negotiation, go through the steps of the procedure:

1. I want... You want...
2. I feel... You feel...
3. Let's take turns. Flip a coin to see who goes first. Okay. Shake.

Divide into groups of four. Form two rows of four students each. The two rows face each other. Each person says to the person he or she is facing:

I want the book. No, I want the book.
I feel frustrated. I'm afraid you won't let me have the book.
Let's take turns. Flip a coin to see who goes first.
Okay. Shake.

Then move to the next person and say the same thing. Do not stop until you have practiced the sequence four times.

Where else can you use this procedure? Divide into pairs. Write down three places where you can use this procedure.

1. _____

2. _____

3. _____

Why is flipping a coin a good idea?

ACTIVITY **10.4** ■ WHY I WANT IT, WHY YOU WANT IT

It is not enough to say what you want. You must also say *why* you want it. You must have reasons for wanting something. You must share your reasons with the other person and the other person must share his or her reasons with you. The third step of problem-solving negotiations is to say why you want what you want and why you feel as you do. Practice these steps of negotiating.

PERSON 1	PERSON 2
I want . . .	I want . . .
I feel . . .	I feel . . .
My reasons are . . .	My reasons are . . .
We could do it together.	We could do it together.

WANTING TO PLAY THE SAME GAME

Divide into groups of four. Form two rows of four students each. The two rows face each other. Each person says to the person he or she is facing:

PERSON 1	PERSON 2
I want to play chess.	I want to play chess.
I feel frustrated!	I feel angry!
I'm frustrated because you are interfering with my daily practice to improve my chess game.	I'm angry because I've been waiting all day for my turn and now you are trying to crowd in line.
We could play chess together.	Okay. Shake.

Move to the next person and say the same thing. Do not stop until you have practiced the sequence four times.

Why is playing chess together a good idea?

---

eldest son, one-third to his middle son, and one-ninth to his youngest son. When the loving father died, his estate consisted of 17 camels. The three sons attempted to divide up the estate according to their father's wishes but quickly found that they could not do so without cutting some of the camels into pieces. They argued and argued without agreeing on how to divide the camels.

Eventually, a village elder rode up on her own dusty camel and inquired about their problem. The three brothers explained the situation. The elder then offered to make her own camel available if that might help. It did. With 18 camels, the brothers could solve the problem. The oldest soon took 9 camels (one-half of 18), the middle son choose 6 more (one-third of 18), and the youngest son extracted 2 camels (one-ninth of 18). The sum of 9 plus 6 plus 2 equals 17. Almost before the three brothers knew what had happened, the wise woman climbed back onto her own camel and rode off into the setting desert sun.

ACTIVITY **10.5** ■ MY UNDERSTANDING OF YOU, YOUR UNDERSTANDING OF ME

Resolving conflicts takes more than understanding what you want and feel and why. You must also understand the other person. And you must make sure the other person knows you understand him or her. The fourth step of problem-solving negotiations is to summarize what the other person wants and feels and why. Practice these steps of negotiating.

PERSON 1	PERSON 2
I want...	I want...
I feel...	I feel...
My reasons are...	My reasons are...
My understanding of you is...	My understanding of you is...
You need it more than I do. You can have it.	Thanks. Shake.

Face your partner. Go through the above steps to negotiate who gets to use the computer first. Emphasize your understanding of the other person. Repeat with a new partner.

PERSON 1	PERSON 2
I want to use the computer now!	I want to use the computer now!
I feel upset.	I feel frustrated.
I want to use the computer to try out a new computer game.	I want to use the computer to do my homework.
My understanding of you is that you will be frustrated if you do not get to do your homework on the computer now.	My understanding of you is that you will be upset if you do not get to play your new computer game now.
You need the computer more than I do. You can use it first.	Thanks. Shake.

Why is letting the other person use the computer first a good idea?

This story illustrates what a clever and creative mediator can do. A *mediator* is a neutral person who helps two or more people resolve their conflict, usually by negotiating an integrative agreement. A mediator is not a judge who decides what disputants should do, commands them to obey, or enforces rules. Nor does a mediator tell disputants what to do, decide who is right and who is wrong, or talk about what he or she would do in such a situation. The mediator is simply a facilitator with no formal power over either disputant.

ACTIVITY **10.6** ■ INVENTING OPTIONS FOR MUTUAL GAIN

Resolving conflicts takes more than understanding yourself and the other person. You must also identify several possible agreements that benefit both sides. The fifth step in problem-solving negotiations is to think of at least three plans to solve the problem.

PERSON 1	**PERSON 2**
I want...	I want...
I feel...	I feel...
My reasons are...	My reasons are...
My understanding of you is...	My understanding of you is...
Three plans to solve the problem are...	Three plans to solve the problem are...
We choose a plan and agree.	We choose a plan and agree.

WHERE IS MY BOOK?

Face your partner. Go through the steps of negotiating a solution to the problem. Be sure to create at least three plans before you choose one. Then repeat with a new partner.

PERSON 1	**PERSON 2**
I want you to return the book you borrowed.	I want you to stop bugging me about that book.
I'm angry.	I'm irritated.
I'm angry because you promised to return the book right away if I let you borrow it.	I'm irritated because you keep asking me to return the book when you know I can't find it.
My understanding of you is that you can't find my book and you are irritated because I keep asking you to return it to me.	My understanding of you is that you are angry because you didn't want to lend me your book but did only because I promised to return it right away.
One plan to solve the problem is...	Another plan to solve the problem is...
A third plan to solve the problem is...	A fourth plan to solve the problem is...
Let's pick plan ___.	Okay. Shake.

Plan A: _____

Plan B: _____

Plan C: _____

A good mediator is impartial, neutral, nonjudgmental, patient, understanding, imaginative, knowledgeable, analytical, respectful, and trustworthy. As a mediator you help disputants resolve the conflict themselves by negotiating a fair and wise agreement as to what (a) they will do for each other or (b) not do to each other. You do so by first participating in the mediation program. You accept the role, patrolling the playground and school, intervening in any conflicts where a mediator may be helpful, being available to schoolmates who request a mediator, and provide support and assistance to schoolmates who want to resolve their conflicts constructively. Second, you maintain fair procedures for negotiating by ensuring that disputants have an equal chance to present their perspective and wants without being interrupted or insulted by the other. Third, you act as a fact finder by determining (a) what happened to create the conflict and (b) what issues must be resolved. You may ask each disputant, "What has to happen for this conflict to be resolved to your satisfaction?" Fourth, you use impartial and nonjudgmental words and phrases that show you have not taken one side against the other. You say, "Do you know what happened to Ted's $10?" not, "Did you steal Ted's $10?" Fifth, you teach disputants how to negotiate to solve the problem by identifying the following conditions:

1. What each disputant wants; how each feels, the reasons for their wants and feelings, the degree to which each understands the other, three optional agreements that will satisfy all disputants, and the option chosen as the final agreement.
2. A logical order for discussing the issues and periodically summarizing in a neutral way to develop momentum for resolving the conflict
3. Disputants' agreement to principles as well as specific actions. You might say, "Can we agree that threats and put-downs will never solve the problem?"
4. The advantages and disadvantages gained or lost by reaching an agreement or not finding a mutually beneficial solution

Sixth, when disputants fail to reach an agreement, you thank disputants for their positive efforts and make an appointment to continue mediation some time in the future. Seventh, when disputants reach agreement, you complete the mediator report form and write out the agreement:

1. Write clearly and concisely, being as specific as possible, spelling disputants' names correctly, and making sure dates are correct.
2. Write out the promises and commitments each disputant has made to the other. Use separate paragraphs for each aspect of the agreement and number each paragraph. Do not use language that implies wrongdoing by one or both disputants.
3. Write out the issues that have been resolved. Then note the issues that were not resolved and specify when and how the disputants plan to resolve them.

You have all disputants sign the agreement, and you sign it as a witness. You give each disputant a copy of the agreement. You inform them that you are the "keeper of the contract" and, therefore, available to continue mediation if the agreement does not work.

Mediation is usually contrasted with arbitration. *Arbitration* is the submission of a dispute to a disinterested third party (such as a teacher or principal) who makes a final and binding judgment as to how the conflict is resolved. When mediation has been successful,

1. The conflict is resolved so that all disputants benefit.
2. The relationship between the students is as good as or even better than ever.
3. Students' negotiating skills and self-confidence in using them is increased. An important purpose of the mediator is to teach negotiation procedures and skills so that the individuals can manage their conflicts on their own in the future.

All students need to be taught the procedures and skills to mediate their classmates' conflicts of interests (Johnson & Johnson, 1995a). (See Activity 10.7 to practice being a mediator.) Mediation consists of four steps (Johnson & Johnson, 1995a):

Step 1. Ending hostilities. Break up hostile encounters and cool off students.

Step 2. Ensure disputants are committed to the mediation process. To ready students to negotiate in good faith, the mediator introduces the process of mediation and sets the ground rules. The mediator first introduces him- or herself. The mediator asks students whether they want to solve the problem and does not proceed until both answer yes. Then the mediator supplies the following explanations (see Activity 10.8):

   a. "Mediation is voluntary. My role is to help you find a solution to your conflict that is acceptable to both of you."
   b. "I am neutral. I will not take sides or attempt to decide who is right or wrong. I will help you decide how to solve the conflict."
   c. "Each person will have the chance to state his or her view of the conflict without interruption."
   d. "The rules you must accept are (1) agree to solve the problem, (2) no name calling (see Activity 10.9), (3) do not interrupt, (4) be as honest as you can, (5) abide by solutions you agree to (you must do what you have agreed to do) and (6) keep anything said in mediation confidential (you, the mediator, will not tell anyone what is said)."

Step 3. Help disputants successfully negotiate with each other. The disputants are carefully taken through the tasks in this negotiation sequence: (a) both persons jointly define the conflict, stating what they want and how they feel; (b) both disputants exchange reasons; (c) both reverse perspectives so that each person is able to present the other's position and feelings to the other's satisfaction; (d) both invent at least three options for mutual benefit; and (e) both reach a wise agreement and shake hands. (see Box 10.4 for an elaboration of this sequence of five tasks.)

Step 4. Formalize the agreement. The agreement is solidified into a contract. Disputants must agree to abide by their final decision and in many ways the mediator becomes "the keeper of the contract."

STEP 5: IMPLEMENTING THE PEACEMAKER PROGRAM

Once students understand how to negotiate and mediate, the teacher implements the Peacemaker Program. Two separate versions of the program exist, one for elementary and one for secondary students.

Peacemaker Program for Elementary Students

Each day the teacher selects two class members to serve as official mediators. The teacher may randomly choose students to be mediators, or the teacher may carefully match students into pairs so that introverted students may be paired with extroverts, students with low academic skills may be paired with high-achieving students, and so forth. Initially, mediators work in pairs. This ensures that shy or nonverbal students get the same amount of experience as more extroverted and verbally fluent students. When all students are experienced enough to be comfortable with being a mediator, then they may mediate individually.

   The mediators wear official T-shirts, hats, or armbands so that they are easily recognized. They patrol the playground and lunchroom. Generally, the mediators are

ACTIVITY **10.7** ■ MEDIATION MENU

As a *mediator* you help two classmates resolve their conflict. You are neutral. You keep everything fair. You stand in the middle and help them go through each step of negotiating.

You say:

My name is _____. I am a mediator. Would you like help in solving your problem [make sure both answer yes]? Mediation is voluntary. I cannot make you do anything. I will not take sides or attempt to decide who is right or wrong. You have to decide for yourselves how best to resolve your conflict. Our goal is to reach an agreement that is acceptable to each of you. I will not take sides.

Each of you will have a chance to state your side of the conflict. For us to resolve your conflict we must agree on a set of rules:

1. You must agree to solve the problem.
2. No name calling.
3. Do not interrupt.
4. Be as honest as you can.

If we are successful, we will reach an agreement. You must live up to your side of the agreement. You must do what you have agreed to do.

Anything you say in mediation is confidential. I will not tell anyone.

We will now proceed across the bridge.

The agreement is good if:

1. It tells when, where, who, and how.

2. Each student can do what he or she has agreed to.

3. Both students agree to do something.

Fill out the Mediator Report Form and have both students sign it.

You say:

"We now have a signed agreement. Shake!"

"I am the keeper of the contract."

"I will check back with you tomorrow to see if the agreement is working."

available to mediate any conflicts that occur in the classroom or school. Any conflicts students cannot resolve themselves are referred to the class mediators. The mediators end hostilities, ensure disputants are committed to the process of mediation, facilitate negotiations, and formalize the agreement. Any conflicts the students cannot resolve with the help of a peer mediator are referred to the teacher, who first mediates and then, if necessary, arbitrates by deciding who is right and who is wrong. If that fails, the principal mediates the conflict. If that fails, the principal arbitrates.

The role of class mediator is rotated throughout the class so that all students serve as class mediator an equal amount of time. Mediating classmates' conflicts is perhaps the most effective and dramatic way of teaching students the need for skill in using each step of the negotiation procedure. Refresher lessons are taught twice a week throughout the school year to refine students' negotiation and mediation skills.

Peacemaker Program for Secondary Students

The secondary program is similar, except that a certain number of school mediators are chosen from each grade level (two mediators for every 30 students or so), and the role of mediator is rotated throughout the school so that all students serve as school mediator an equal amount of time.

ACTIVITY **10.8** ■ PLANNING YOUR OPENING STATEMENT

1. Divide into pairs. Your task is to write out your opening statement in mediating a conflict among classmates. Work cooperatively to produce one statement from the two of you to which each of you contribute. Both of you need a written copy of the opening statement, including

   a. An introduction of yourself
   b. A description of the process of mediation
   c. A description of the role of the mediator
   d. A confirmation that both students want to solve their problem and will abide by the mediation rules
   e. A statement of the confidentiality inherent in mediations
   f. A statement of the goal of finding an agreement that meets both person's needs

2. Divide into new pairs. Give your opening statement to your partner. Listen to his or her opening statement. Discuss how the statement can be given better next time.

3. Find a new partner. Give your opening statement. Listen to your partner's. Discuss how the statements could be given better next time.

4. Form groups of four. Write out at least four pieces of advice on how to make an effective opening mediation statement.

5. Participate in a whole-class discussion on how to make an effective opening mediation statement.

STEP 6: CONTINUING LESSONS TO REFINE AND UPGRADE STUDENTS' SKILLS

Follow-up lessons are needed to upgrade and refine students' skills in using the negotiation and mediation procedures. These lessons may consist of further instruction on communication skills, controlling anger, appropriate assertiveness, problem solving, perspective taking, creative thinking, and a wide variety of other related interpersonal and small-group skills (Johnson, 1991, 2000; Johnson & F. Johnson, 2000). Take a moment to review the important concepts discussed so far in this chapter in Activity 10.10.

    Follow-up lessons may also consist of integrating the negotiation and mediation procedures into academic lessons. Any social studies or literature lesson and

---

BOX 10.4
FACILITATING NEGOTIATIONS

HELP DISPUTANTS DEFINE THE CONFLICT

1. Ask each disputant: *"What happened, what do you want, how do you feel?"*
2. Paraphrase what each disputant says when it is necessary to demonstrate you are listening and understand what they are saying, and when you believe one disputant does not clearly understand what the other disputant is saying. Paraphrasing is restating and summarizing what a person says and how they feel in an accurate, complete, and neutral way.
3. Enlarge the shadow of the future by highlighting the ways they have to work cooperatively with each other in the future.

HELP DISPUTANTS EXCHANGE REASONS FOR THEIR POSITIONS

1. Help disputants present their reasons and the rationale for their positions.
2. Help disputants understand the differences between their positions.
3. Keep disputants focused on the issue, not on tangents such as their anger toward each other.
4. Equalize power.
5. Recognize constructive behaviors during negotiations.
6. Reframe the issue by helping disputants change perspectives.

HELP DISPUTANTS REVERSE PERSPECTIVES

1. Have each disputant present the other's wants, feelings, and reasons to the other's satisfaction.
2. Role play the conflict and switch roles at critical points.

HELP DISPUTANTS INVENT OPTIONS FOR MUTUAL GAIN

1. Encourage creative thinking.
2. Complete a balance sheet on each alternative suggested.

FORMALIZE THE AGREEMENT

1. Complete the Mediation Report Form.
2. Have disputants sign it and commit themselves to implementing the agreement.

---

many science lessons may be used to teach students negotiation and mediation skills. Students are placed in cooperative groups and engaged in a series of instructional activities to teach them the conflict resolution procedures in the context of the academic lesson. Because all drama is based on conflict, any literary work contains many, many opportunities for students to use the negotiation and mediation procedures in role plays (see Activity 10.11).

For example, each major conflict among characters in a literary work can be the basis for students practicing conflict resolution procedures. Students can: role play in two ways: first to practice the negotiation procedure and second to practice the mediation procedure (see Activity 10.12). Students can analyze the characters' conflicts in terms of the negotiation and mediation frameworks. Discussions can center on what strategies the characters use to manage their conflict and the resulting consequences of their actions. Students can then speculate what would have happened had the characters used the problem-solving negotiation procedures.

ACTIVITY **10.9** ■ STOP CALLING ME NAMES

Find a partner and role play the following situation.

PERSON 1	PERSON 2
I want you to stop calling me names.	I want to keep calling you names
I feel hurt.	I feel fine when I call you names.
The reason I want you to stop calling me names is it upsets me so much I can't learn.	The reason I want to keep calling you names is that it makes me feel powerful to know I can hurt your feelings.
My understanding of you is that you want to call me names so you can feel powerful.	My understanding of you is that you want me to stop calling you names because it hurts your feelings and upsets you so much you can't do your schoolwork.
One way we could resolve our conflict is for one of us to give in. I could let you call me names. Or you could stop calling me names.	Another way we could resolve our conflict is for us to make a deal. I could stop calling you names. You could help me run for student council.
A third plan would be for us to decide on a time when you could call me names and a time you could not. We could have a half-hour a day name-calling time.	Perhaps we should plan to work together on several projects so we could get to know each other better. If we got to know each other, I would not call you names.
Let's try plan 4.	Agreed. Shake.

Where else can you use this procedure? Working with your partner, write down three situations in which you could use this procedure.

1. _____

2. _____

3. _____

With some training, it is not difficult for teachers to integrate the Peacemaker program into academic units. Such integration is necessary because gaining real expertise in resolving conflicts constructively takes years and years of training and practice. A few hours of training is clearly not sufficient.

STEP 7: REPEATING PEACEMAKING STEPS EACH YEAR

The Teaching Students to Be Peacemakers program is a 12-year spiral program that is retaught each year, from the first through twelfth grade, in a more sophisticated and complex way. It takes years and years to become competent in resolving conflicts. Not only is it necessary to remember the many skills involved in the negotiation pro-

ACTIVITY **10.10** ■ MATCHING EXERCISE

Match the correct definition with the correct concept. Find a partner and (a) compare answers and (b) explain your reasoning for each answer.

_____ 1. negotiation

_____ 2. win–lose negotiations

_____ 3. problem-solving negotiations

_____ 4. perspective

_____ 5. social perspective taking

_____ 6. egocentrism

_____ 7. mediator

_____ 8. arbitration

a. Process by which persons who have shared and opposing interests and want to come to an agreement try to work out a settlement

b. Each disputant has as his or her goal reaching an agreement more favorable to oneself than to the other negotiator

c. Each disputant has as his or her goal reaching an agreement that maximizes the benefits for everyone involved

d. Way of viewing the world and one's position in it

e. Ability to understand how a situation appears to another person and how that person is thinking and feeling

f. Being unaware that other perspectives exist and that one's own view of the conflict is incomplete and limited

g. Submission of a dispute to a disinterested third party (such as a teacher or principal) who makes a final and binding judgment as to how the conflict will be resolved

h. A neutral person who helps two or more people resolve their conflict, usually by negotiating an integrative agreement

cess but practicing these skills is necessary to achieve grace and automaticity. (See Box 10.5 for points to remember.) Any thought that a few hours of training is enough to train students in a high level of competence in managing their conflicts constructively is terribly misguided.

RESEARCH ON THE PEACEMAKER PROGRAM

We have conducted more than 15 studies on the effectiveness of the Teaching Students to Be Peacemakers program (Johnson & Johnson, 1995e; 1996; Johnson & Johnson, 2000). The studies focused on peer mediation programs in elementary, middle school, and high school settings. The programs were evaluated over a period of several months to a year. The schools were in urban and suburban school districts. Students varied from lower- to upper-middle class and were from diverse ethnic and cultural backgrounds. Mediators were drawn from a wide variety of ethnic backgrounds. The studies were carefully controlled field-experimental studies with high internal and external validity.

ACTIVITY 10.11 ■ HAMLET AND HIS FATHER'S GHOST

The scene is the battlements of the castle of the king of Denmark. It is midnight, the witching hour. The ghost of Hamlet's father appears and beckons Hamlet to follow the ghost for a private talk. They have a conflict that must be resolved. Find a partner. Flip a coin to see who will be Hamlet and who will be his father. Then resolve the conflict using the problem-solving negotiation procedure.

GHOST

I am your father's spirit. Listen to me. If you ever loved me, you must avenge my foul, strange, and most unnatural murder. I was not bitten by a poisonous snake. The serpent that bit me now wears my crown.

He is an incestuous beast. He seduced your mother, a seemingly virtuous queen. Then, when I was asleep in the garden, he poured poison into my ear. My own brother, your uncle, killed me to gain both my crown and my wife. This is horrible! Horrible! You must kill him!

You are my son and it is your duty to avenge my death. I cannot rest in my grave until my murder is avenged. You must fulfill your obligation and put me to rest. Denmark will not prosper with such a man on the throne. The king must be committed to the welfare of Denmark, not himself. And besides, if he has a son, you will lose your birthright.

HAMLET

I did not know you were murdered. I thought you died of a snakebite. This is a complete surprise to me. The fact that my uncle murdered you is even more a surprise. I have a relationship with this man. I certainly want justice, but let's not be hasty. Asking me to kill him is a serious request.

First, I may be too young and inexperienced to do it right. You would do better to ask one of your generals to do it. Second, killing my uncle could seriously damage my future career options and quality of life. Don't be so blood-thirsty. Think of my future! Third, this is not the time for me to kill someone. I am a carefree youth! I am in love. I'm still in school. I have years of learning and maturing left before I will be ready to kill someone. Fourth, I would never rest in my grave, and I might even go to hell, if I killed my uncle.

Finally, killing my uncle is a complex task. I have to catch him alone doing something wicked so his soul will go to hell. What use is it if I kill him when he is doing something virtuous and he goes to heaven? This killing is not your usual walk into the room and stab him. This one is very complex and difficult. I'm not sure I want to do that much work!

The findings of our research indicate that before training, students engage in conflicts daily and generally manage them through trying to win by (a) forcing the other to concede (either by overpowering the other disputant or by asking the teacher to force the other to give in) or (b) withdrawing from the conflict and the other person. One of the teachers, in her log, stated, "Before training, students viewed conflict as fights that always resulted in a winner and a loser. To avoid such an unpleasant situation, they usually placed the responsibility for resolving conflicts on me, the teacher." Students seem to lack all knowledge of how to engage in problem-solving, integrative negotiations. Try Activity 10.13 to test your expertise in problem-solving negotiations.

ACTIVITY **10.12** ■ ROLE PLAYS

1. The school has called an assembly. You took an aisle chair. Before the assembly begins you place your books on your chair and leave to get a drink of water. When you get back, you find your books sitting in the aisle and another student in your chair. What do you do? Role play the exchange.

2. You are standing in the hallway by your locker when another student smashes into you. You are thrown against your locker and drop your books. The other student laughs. What do you do? Role play the exchange.

3. You tell a friend in confidence about someone you would like to go out with. The next day several people comment on it. You get your friend alone to talk about it. What do you do? Role play the exchange.

4. You have been sick with mono for several weeks. Your science teacher refuses to extend the deadline for your final project. Because you cannot finish the project in time, you will receive a low grade in the class. You believe the teacher is being unfair. You decide to try talking to the teacher again. Role play the exchange.

5. Chris borrows your history book. The next day, when Chris returns your book, it is muddy and the cover is torn. You believe that when you borrow something, you are responsible for taking care of it. You have to spend 20 minutes cleaning the book and taping the cover back together. Chris laughs and calls you a "neatness freak." What do you do? Role play the exchange.

6. You are making a presentation to a class. Two classmates who are hostile toward you sit together in the back of the class and continually make sarcastic remarks in loud whispers that can be easily heard by the whole class. You decide to talk to the two classmates about it. Role play the exchange.

PREPARING FOR THE ROLE PLAY

Prepare to role play your assigned character by reading the description of the situation and your character's experiences. In doing so, write out the answers to the following questions:

1. What do you want? _____

_____

2. How do you feel? _____

_____

3. What are your reasons for wanting what you want and feeling like you do? _____

_____

_____

After the peacemaker training, students knew the negotiation and mediation procedures, retained their knowledge throughout the school year, were able to apply the procedures to conflicts, transferred the procedures to nonclassroom and non-school settings, used the procedures similarly in family and school settings, and

■ ■ ■ ■ ■

BOX 10.5

POINTS TO REMEMBER WHEN RESOLVING A CONFLICT

1. **You both have the conflict.** You must work together to solve it. Solve conflicts as friends, not enemies.
2. **You both have wants.** You have a perfect right to express them. For the conflict to be resolved constructively, both of you must honestly state what you want.
3. **You both have feelings.** They must be expressed for the conflict to be resolved constructively. Keeping frustration, anger, hurt, fear, or sadness inside only makes the conflict more difficult to resolve.
4. **You both have reasons for wanting what you want and feeling like you do.** Ask for each other's reasons and make sure you see the conflict from both perspectives.
5. **You both have your perspective or point of view.** To resolve the conflict constructively, you must see the conflict from both perspectives.
6. **You both need to generate several alternative wise agreements that maximize the benefits to both of you.** Wise agreements make both persons happy.
7. **You both need to select the agreement that seems most wise and seal it with a handshake.** Never agree on a solution that leaves one person happy and one person unhappy.

(when given the option) engaged in problem-solving rather than win–lose negotiations. The number of discipline problems the teacher had to deal with decreased by about 60 percent and referrals to the principal dropped about 95 percent.

The results further demonstrated that when the peacemaker training was integrated into academic units, not only did the students learn how to negotiate and mediate, they also achieved higher on tests of academic learning. Students developed more positive attitudes toward conflict and adults in the school and parents perceived the Peacemaker Program to be constructive and helpful. Many parents whose children were not part of the project requested that their children receive the training the next year, and a number of parents requested that they receive the training so they could use the procedures to improve conflict management within the family.

SUMMARY

The frequency of conflicts is not the problem facing schools. In many cases, schools are too conflict avoidant and need to increase the frequency with which conflicts occur among students and between students and faculty. Conflict has many positive outcomes that cannot occur unless conflict is encouraged. The problem facing schools is not how to reduce the occurrence of conflicts, but rather how to increase the occurrence of conflicts while ensuring that they are managed in constructive and healthy ways. The major barrier to doing so is students' lack of effective conflict resolution procedures.

Students do have procedures for managing conflicts, but often the procedures are not constructive and not shared among all classmates. The multiple procedures for managing conflicts within classrooms create some chaos in how conflicts are managed. This is especially true when students are from different cultural, ethnic, social class, and language backgrounds. Life in schools gets easier when *all* students

ACTIVITY **10.13** ■ WHICH BOOKS TO TAKE

Scientists have suddenly discovered that a large comet is going to strike the Earth. All life, if not the Earth itself, will be destroyed. You and your partner have been picked to move from Earth to a new planet. The conditions on the new planet will be harsh and difficult. You will be starting life over, trying to develop a farming and technological society at the same time. Because of the limited room in the spaceship, you can only bring one book for the two of you. "Think carefully," the captain says. "You will never return to Earth. You will never be able to get more books from Earth."

1. **Work by yourself.** Decide which book you personally want to bring. Choose the book you think is most important to save and most helpful for starting a new civilization.

2. **Work by yourself.** Plan how to convince the other person that the book you have chosen should be taken. Make sure you are clear about

   a. What book you want to take
   b. How you feel about the importance and value of the book and how you would feel if the book were not taken
   c. The reasons for wanting to take the book and for feeling as you do

3. **Meet with your partner.** Only one book can go. Follow the steps of problem-solving negotiations in deciding which book to take to the new planet and why. You cannot take half of one and half of another. You cannot choose by chance (such as flipping a coin). Each member should present the best case for the book he or she has chosen. Once an agreement is reached, each person must be able to explain the reasons why the book was chosen.

PERSON 1	PERSON 2
I want	I want
I feel	I feel
My reasons are	My reasons are
My understanding of your wants, feelings, and reasons is	My understanding of your wants, feelings, and reasons is
I have three plans to solve the problem:	I have three plans to solve the problem:
We choose a plan and agree	We choose a plan and agree

(and staff members) use the same set of negotiation and mediation procedures in managing conflicts.

When students are taught how to negotiate and are given opportunities to mediate their classmates' conflicts, they are given procedures and competencies to (a) regulate their behavior through self-monitoring, (b) judge what is appropriate given the situation and the perspective of the other person, and (c) modify how they behave accordingly. Students then have the opportunity to resolve their dispute themselves, in mutually satisfactory ways, without having to engage the attention of a teacher. This empowers the students and reduces the demands on teachers and administrators, who can devote less time to establishing and maintaining control over students and more time on instruction.

Teaching *all* students negotiation and mediation procedures and skills and implementing a peer mediation program results in a schoolwide discipline program focused on empowering students to regulate and control their own and their classmates' actions. When a conflict occurs, the students involved first try to negotiate a resolution. If that fails, a classmate mediates their conflict. If that fails, the teacher attempts to mediate the conflict. If that fails, the teacher arbitrates by deciding who is right and who is wrong. If that fails, the principal mediates the conflict. If that fails, the principal arbitrates.

Every student needs to learn how to manage conflicts constructively. Without training, many students may never learn how to do so. Teaching every student how to negotiate and mediate ensures that future generations are prepared to manage conflicts constructively in career, family, community, national, and international settings. There is no reason to expect, however, that the process is easy or quick. It took more than 30 years to reduce smoking in the United States. It took more than 20 years to reduce drunk driving. It may take even longer to ensure that children and adolescents can manage conflicts constructively. The more years students spend learning and practicing the negotiation and mediation procedures, the more likely they are to actually use the procedures skillfully, both in the classroom and beyond the school door.

PEACEMAKER LESSON PLANNING FORM

Class: _____ Subject: _____ Date: _____

Lesson: _____

What peacemaker skill are you going to teach? _____

_____

Step 1. How will students see the need for the skill?

_____ Ask students to brainstorm what skills are needed to engage in each peacemaker step.

_____ Tell students why the skills are needed.

_____ Have a bulletin board display.

_____ Jigsaw materials on the need for the skill.

I will   _____

_____

_____

Step 2. How will you help students understand what the skill is and when it should be used?

_____ Have students help make a classroom T-chart to analyze the skill.

_____ Have students discuss when it is appropriate to use the skill.

_____ Have students practice using the skill with a partner.

Fill in this T-chart with the skills you plan to teach your students.

Looks Like	Sounds Like
Nonverbal, Body Language	*Verbal Statements, Sentence Starters*

Step 3. How will you ensure students practice the skill?

_____ Announce that you will observe the skill.

_____ Have practice sessions.

_____ Give positive feedback to anyone who demonstrates the skill.

_____ Have role-playing exercises.

I will _____

_____

_____

_____

Step 4: How will you ensure students receive feedback and process their skill use?

❑ **Teacher monitoring.** How will you monitor students' use of the skill and give them feedback?

I will _____

_____

_____

_____

❑ **Peer monitoring:** How will you structure peer observation of the use the skill?

_____ Pair practice in which each gives the other feedback.

_____ Practice in small groups in which one member is appointed observer.

_____ Give a "secret note" to a group member asking them to use the skill; praise the whole group when the group member does it.

I will _____

_____

_____

_____

Step 5. How will you ensure that students persevere in practicing the skill until it becomes natural?

DAILY

_____ Remind them that you will be listening for their use of the skill.

_____ Give feedback on what you heard.

_____ Have them process their use of the skill.

PERIODICALLY

_____   Discuss with the class the stages of learning a skill (awkward, phony, mechanical, and automatic).

_____   Have students rate their level of use and chart progress.

_____   Give class reward if students use the skill a preset number of times.

_____   Have the principal, an aide, a parent, or another teacher observe and give feedback on how well students use the skill.

_____   Tutor or coach target students on the use of the skill.

_____   Have students think of places outside of class to use the skill, have them do so and report on how it went and what they noticed.

I will   _____

_____

_____

_____

When most students have reached the automatic stage, plan and teach them another skill!

SKILL-TEACHING PLANNING FORM

Class: _____ Subject: _____ Date: _____

Lesson: _____

Conflict skill: _____

Definition: _____

_____

Looks Like	Sounds Like

Help students see need for skill by: _____

_____

Encourage the use of the skill by: _____

_____

Process use by: _____

_____

Refine skill later by: _____

_____

Notes on levels of use, problems, things learned for next time:

CHAPTER ELEVEN

TEACHING CIVIC VALUES

INTRODUCTION

> We who now live are parts of a humanity that extends into the remote past, a humanity that has interacted with nature. The things in civilization we most prize are not of ourselves. They exist by grace of the doings and sufferings of the continuous human community in which we are a link. Ours is the responsibility of conserving, transmitting, rectifying and expanding the heritage of values we have received that those who come after us may receive it more solid and secure, more widely accessible and more generously shared than we have received it.
>
> —*John Dewey, ("A Common Faith," etched upon his memorial stone at the University of Vermont)*

Some historians claim that the decline and fall of Rome was set in motion by corruption from within rather than by conquest from without. Rome fell, it can be argued, because Romans lost their civic virtue. *Civic virtue* exists when individuals meet both the letter and spirit of their public obligations. For a community to exist and be sustained, members must share common goals and values aimed at increasing the quality of life within the community. No one should be surprised that in a community where competitive and individualistic values are taught, people behave in accordance with such values. When that happens in a society, for example, people may stop obeying the law. Running stoplights may become a common occurrence because the individualist thinks it rational to arrive at the destination sooner. If someone is killed, it will be a pedestrian, not the driver. But each of us is at some time a pedestrian.

Community cannot be maintained unless members value others and the community as a whole, as well as themselves.

> Students are sitting in a circle on the carpet. A class meeting is in progress. Today the issue is respect. One of the students risked telling her classmates that she felt hurt during recess the day before because she was trying to tell some kids the rules to a new game, but nobody would listen. So began a discussion on what it means to be respectful, why that is important, and the sharing of everyone's personal experiences of times they felt respected versus not respected.

To be an effective learning community, all students, faculty, and staff need to adopt a set of civic values (Johnson & Johnson, 1996b; 1999). To create the common culture that defines a community, common goals and shared values serve to define appropriate behavior (see Activity 11.1). A learning community cannot exist in schools dominated by (a) competition where students are taught to value striving for their

ACTIVITY 11.1 ■ WAS TOCQUEVILLE RIGHT OR WRONG?

Tocqueville believed that a common set of values and ideals held society together:

> Without common belief... there still may be men, but there is no social body. In order for society to exist... and prosper... it is necessary that the minds of all men should be held together by certain predominant ideas. (Tocqueville, 1945, p. 8)

Do you _____ agree or _____ disagree? Write down your reasoning for your answer. Find a partner, share your opinion and reasoning, listen carefully to his or her opinion and reasoning, and come to agreement as to what is necessary for our society to exist and prosper.

Answer:

---

personal success at the expense of others or (b) individualistic efforts where students value only their own self-interests.

Rather, students need to internalize values underlying cooperation and integrative negotiations, such as commitment to the common good and to the well-being of other members, a sense of responsibility to contribute one's fair share of the work, respect for the efforts of others and for them as people, behaving with integrity, caring for other members, compassion when other members are in need, and appreciation of diversity. Such civic values both underlie and are promoted by the cooperation and constructive conflict resolution that take place in the school. Complete Activity 11.2 to discover which values you think students should be taught in school.

WHY TEACH CIVIC VALUES?

> If civilization is to survive, we must cultivate the science of human relationships—the ability of all peoples, of all kinds, to live together, in the same world at peace.
> —*Franklin Delano Roosevelt*

Three different rationales for teaching civic values are (a) preparing students to live in a democratic society, (b) making students better people, and (c) creating a caring community in which students learn.

Preparing Students for Democratic Society

Our democracy was founded on the premise that an informed, educated populace makes better decisions than do kings or dictators. The founders of our democracy assumed that the primary role of education, therefore, would be to teach students how to

ACTIVITY **11.2** ■ WHAT WOULD YOU ADD AND WHY

Alexis de Tocqueville called civic values the "habits of the heart." Consider carefully his recommendations. Add five other habits of the heart that you think all children and adolescents should learn in school and write down the reasons why. Find a partner. Share your five additions and reasons. Listen carefully to his or her five additions and reasons. Create a list of five additional habits of the heart that you both can agree on.

Alexis de Tocqueville	My Additions
1. Taking responsibility for the common good	1.
2. Trusting others to take responsibility for the common good	2.
3. Being honest	3.
4. Having self-discipline	4.
5. Reciprocating good deeds	5.

engage in the democratic process in their communities and prepare students for their role as responsible citizens (Albert, 1996; Miller, 1988). Each student must develop civic competencies that include the ability to reflect on an issue of common concern and reach a reasoned conclusion, advocate one's conclusion persuasively, listen with an open mind to other people's conclusions, view the situation from all perspectives, judge the relative merits of the positions being advocated, vote to decide which position to officially adopt, and implement the decision made. Diversity of conclusions and perspectives is seen as vital to making good decisions (see Activity 11.3).

Making Students Better People

> Education and work are the levers to uplift a people. Work alone will not do it unless inspired by the right ideals and guided by intelligence. Education must not simply teach work—it must teach life.
> —*W. E. B. Dubois*

In 1748 Baron Charles de Montesquieu published *The Spirit of Laws,* in which he explored the relationship between people and different forms of government for the government to survive. He concluded that dictatorship survives on the fear of the people, monarchy survives on the loyalty of the people, and a free republic survives on the virtue (high ethical values) of the people. He added that the free republic is the most fragile of the three political systems.

Montesquieu believed that virtue requires balancing a person's own needs with those of society as a whole. Motivation to be virtuous comes from "a sense of belonging, a concern for the whole, a moral bond with the community whose life is at

ACTIVITY **11.3** ■ DEMOCRATIC VALUES

Given below are the preambles from the Declaration of Independence and the Constitution of the United States of America.

1. List the values contained in these statements. Find a partner. Explain your list. Listen to his or her list. Produce a combined list that is as accurate as possible.

2. Working as a pair, list the ways that schools can teach these values to every child and adolescence in our country.

DECLARATION OF INDEPENDENCE

When in the Course of human events, it becomes necessary for one people to dissolve the political bands which have connected them with another, and to assume among the powers of the earth, the separate and equal station to which the Laws of Nature and of Nature's God entitle them, a decent respect to the opinion of mankind requires that they should declare the causes which impel them to the separation. We hold these truths to be self-evident, that all men are created equal, that they are endowed by their Creator with certain unalienable Rights, that among these are Life, Liberty, and the pursuit of Happiness.—That to secure these rights, Governments are instituted among Men, deriving their just powers from the consent of the governed,—That whenever any Form of Government becomes destructive of these ends, it is the Right of the People to alter or to abolish it, and to institute new Government, laying its foundation on such principles and organizing its powers in such form, as to them shall seem most likely to effect their Safety and Happiness.

CONSTITUTION OF THE UNITED STATES

We, the People of the United States, in Order to form a more perfect Union, establish Justice, insure domestic Tranquility, provide for the common defense, promote the general Welfare, and secure the Blessings of Liberty to ourselves and our Posterity, do ordain and establish this Constitution for the United States of America.

Values	Ways to Teach Them
1.	
2.	
3.	
4.	
5.	
6.	

stake." This moral bond is cultivated by "deliberating with fellow citizens about common good and helping shape the destiny of the political community." A sense of belonging and the moral bond requires that we care about each other and treat each other with respect and civility. Caring, respect, and civility make up the fabric of our national community. If they are absent, national community is nonexistent.

It is not enough for the founders of our country to have been virtuous and committed to democracy. Each generation has to develop virtue and commitment to democracy. Our democratic culture and social well-being depends on the renewing energy of young people who have the sensitivities and vision to help create a better and better democracy.

The founders of U.S. democracy were firmly convinced that schools could and should bring democracy to life. Schools were to inculcate in students the conviction that democracy involves intelligent, collaborative participation in society. Through political discourse and decision making, creative individuality was to be balanced with concern for the common good and the welfare of others. Equality, justice, caring, and civic responsibility were to serve as both ends and means in relationships with other people. The nature and value of the democratic process was to be taught through the curriculum and the pedagogical methods used to foster student learning. Cooperative learning and constructive controversy are such pedagogical methods. Complete Activity 11.4 to evaluate your own sense of the purpose of education.

Developing a Caring Citizenry

A democracy cannot flourish if there are deep levels of hostility, animosity, and dislike among its citizens. If citizens are indifferent and uncaring about each other's plight and circumstances, a democracy will not last. Children and adolescents need to have the experiences necessary to build a caring commitment to all citizens within our society. Urie Bronfrenbrenner (1979) stated:

> No society can long sustain itself unless its members have learned the sensitivities, motivations, and skills involved in assisting and caring for other human beings. It is possible for a person of 18 years of age to graduate from high school without even having had to do a piece of work on which someone else truly depended ... without ever having cared for, or even held, a baby; without ever having looked after someone who was old, ill, or lonely; or without having comforted or assisted another human being who really needed help.

An important aspect of caring is civility (see Table 11.1). Civility is more than politeness and good manners. It is a reflection of conscious intention and awareness of the value and worth of the other person. Genuine civility is how human beings relate to and support one another for the common good. Activity 11.5 may enhance your personal understanding of your own civility toward others.

DO OUR VALUES CHANGE?

Inner Directed versus Outer Directed

Sociologist David Riesman (1950) in his classic, *The Lonely Crowd*, believed that the United States was in the midst of a great shift in social character. Americans were changing from "inner-directed" to "other-directed" individuals. Riesman believed that in the nineteenth century, Americans tended to be inner directed. They sought guidance for life from "first principles," and acted on an internalized code of behavior. Other-directed people seek guidance, not from an internalized moral code, but primarily from their peers and the mass media. Many children and youth do not

ACTIVITY **11.4** ■ MAKING STUDENTS BETTER PEOPLE

Given below are statements about the purpose of education. On the 5-point scale, indicate the level of your agreement or disagreement and write down your reasons for each rating. Find a partner. Compare your ratings and reasons. Come to consensus about your agreement with each statement.

1————————2————————3————————4————————5
Disagree   Agree

_____ **1.** "Education is helping people become both smart and good." (Socrates)

_____ **2.** "Schools must teach the ethical skills necessary to maintain a democratic community." (John Dewey)

_____ **3.** Schools should teach the skills and attitudes necessary to fulfill the dream of democracy; we must build good citizens so they, in turn, can build a good society. (The Founders of the United States)

_____ **4.** "To educate a man in mind and not in morals is to create a menace to society." (Theodore Roosevelt)

_____ **5.** "Intelligence plus character—that is the goal of true education." (Martin Luther King, Jr.)

_____ **6.** "Democracy cannot exist unless there is public education for all citizens." (Thomas Jefferson)

_____ **7.** "Common schools are needed for common American people pursuing a common American good." (James Madison)

_____ **8.** "Great learning and superior abilities, should you ever posses them, will be of little value and small estimation unless virtue, honor, truth, and integrity are added to them." (Abigail Adams, speaking to her son John Quincy Adams)

TABLE 11.1 Democratic Values

BENJAMIN FRANKLIN	SCOUTS	BENJAMIN FRANKLIN	SCOUTS
temperance	trustworthy	justice	cheerful
silence	loyal	moderation	thrifty
order	helpful	cleanliness	brave
resolution	friendly	tranquility	clean
frugality	courteous	chastity	reverent
industry	kind	humility	
sincerity	obedient		

ACTIVITY **11.5** ■ UNDERSTANDING OTHERS

The following list describes people by one of their roles. All these roles vary in how similar or different they are from yours.

1. Rank the roles from easiest for me to understand (1) to hardest for me to understand (10). Write down the reasons why you ranked them as you did.

2. Find a partner. Share your ranking and reasons. Listen to their ranking and reasons. Try to agree on how these roles should be ranked in terms of similarity or difference in comparison to both your self-conceptions.

3. Working as a pair, imagine yourself interacting with a person identified with role 2 and role 7 on your list. How would these experiences differ from each other?

RANK	PERSON
_____	French Canadian
_____	Grandmother
_____	Adolescent
_____	Murderer
_____	Teacher
_____	Salesperson
_____	Priest
_____	Professional athlete
_____	Chinese farmer
_____	Student

have experiences in the home or neighborhood that create an inner set of principles to provide the gyroscope they need to live productive and satisfying lives. We want to ensure that children and youth develop an inner set of principles that allow them to champion a course of action that may not be popular but is true. Those principles may be known as *civic values*.

Growing Dishonesty

Since the early 1900s, numerous companies in the United States have used children as salespersons. American Seed Company, for example, sent packs of garden seeds to grade-school children with the understanding that the children would go door to door to sell the packs of seeds and split the proceeds with the company or win prizes. In 1981 a company spokesperson said, "For more than 60 years, we are proud to say, selling our garden-tested seeds has become a part of the American way of growing up."

Beginning around 1975, however, the American way was to order seeds, sell them at 60 cents a pack and pocket all the money, refusing to send the company its 40 cents per pack share (or return all the money and get a prize). In 1981, unreturned money cost American Seed Company nearly half of what it collected in revenues. The Company went bankrupt. One New Jersey child responded to a dun letter with, "Just got back from Bermuda vacation. Will send you $20 but surely give me time! I have to unpack and everything." The second letter, sent to parents, often resulted in parents siding with their outlaw offspring. One parent wrote, "You're a big company; you don't need the money, and you're only trying to cheat my child."

Although the children came from all walks of life (even a Rockefeller once sold enough seeds to win a sleeping bag), the sales force was mostly suburban boys aged 8 to 12 years old. Although a number of economic factors in the late 1970s affected profits, basically child dishonesty killed American Seed and similar companies.

Values change continually. Whether they change in a positive or a negative direction depends on the socializing influences in the lives of children and adolescents. Schools need a constructive influence on the development of values. This is not easy. Like all aspects of socialization, values are learned through interpersonal interactions with peers and adults, and students are quite active in picking and choosing which values they wish to internalize. It is important to understand, therefore, how schools may teach civic values.

HOW TO TEACH CIVIC VALUES

Membership in a community requires the adoption of the community's values. Two approaches to teaching values are *content* and *process*. The first approach, content, is to teach values through direct instruction. Each day, for example, could be dedicated to one value. The teacher can define it, give examples of it, and reward students who demonstrate it.

Core values can be directly taught. They may be placed in the school's mission statement and posted in every classroom. Lessons may be taught in which they are defined. Examples may be given illustrating how they may be expressed in interactions with other people. Students may role play how to put the values into action. Teachers may point out instances where a student or a model demonstrated the values. The values may be integrated into the curriculum. Children's literature may be used to teach values. *The Great Gilly Hopkins* by Katherine Paterson may be used to focus attention on compassion and *The River* by Gary Paulson may be used to help students focus on responsibility. Class meetings provide a safe forum for talking about values and how they affect student and faculty lives. Being clear about what is valued enables aligned choice making throughout the curriculum—from instructional strategies, used to pursue topics of study, to instructional resources employed. Activity 11.6 provides an example of teaching values through direct instruction.

The second approach, process, is to teach values through the instructional and schooling processes students experience minute by minute during the school day. These processes include modeling and identification, the enactment of assigned and voluntary roles, group influences, and the hidden curriculum existing in the pattern and flow of daily school life (Johnson & F. Johnson, 1997). First, faculty and administrators can teach students values through identification by (a) building positive, caring, supportive relationships with the students and (b) consistently modeling the values in interactions with the students. In its simplest form, *identification* occurs when a student tries to be like someone (an adult, older student, or mythical figure) that the student likes or admires: a person usually perceived as resourceful, powerful, or competent. A student can admire a teacher's scholarship, for example, and strive to become a scholar, or a student can see a teacher behaving honestly and decide to do likewise.

Second, values may be taught by assigning students social roles. A *social role* is a set of expectations (containing rights and responsibilities) aimed at structuring interactions within a reciprocal relationship. In school, students not only learn the role of student, but also other roles, such as American, citizen, collaborator, and mediator.

Third, individuals adopt the values of their reference groups. *Reference groups* are the groups to which individuals believe they belong or to which they aspire to

ACTIVITY **11.6** ■ TEACHING VALUES

Task: Teach values.

Procedure: A *poster session* is when numerous people make a presentation simultaneously. It is called a poster session because participants create a poster to attract individuals to their presentation.

1. Find a partner who has a different perspective and background than you do.

2. Gather materials (a large sheet of newsprint, markers).

3. Working cooperatively as a pair, create a poster that outlines your insights, strategies, key points, surprises, and alternatives for teaching values.

4. Place your poster on the wall. While one of you stays with your poster to explain your procedures for teaching values (the explainer), the other partner visits other poster sessions (the visitor).

5. Reverse roles. The original explainer becomes the visitor and vice versa.

6. Working cooperatively as a pair, summarize what you have learned about teaching values. Select one you will try first.

7. Process by explaining how your partner has contributed to your learning.

belong (Johnson & F. Johnson, 1997). Individuals accept a system of values, attitudes, and behavioral patterns when they accept membership in a new group. The discussion and consensual validation that take place within a group result in personal commitments to adopt the values. Values are not inculcated by focusing on each individual separately, but rather by emphasizing membership in a group (or community) that holds the desired values. By adopting the school community as a reference group, students adopt its civic values.

Fourth, the value systems underlying competitive, individualistic, and cooperative situations and the ways that conflicts are managed are a hidden curriculum beneath the surface of school life. School life should be devoid of opportunities for students to behave in antisocial and destructive ways that express negative values. Instead school life should be full of opportunities, minute by minute, to express prosocial and caring values. If students tell lies, for example, the structure should change so that they can tell the truth.

The adoption of values is an internal activity. Children and adolescents must be given the opportunity to make sense of values such as fairness and courage. Students must be invited to reflect on complex issues; to recast them in the light of their own experiences and questions; and to figure out for themselves what kind of person they want to be, what traditions are worth keeping, and how to proceed when two values are in conflict. This is an interpersonal process in which students discuss with each other what they are thinking and how they are choosing their values.

INTERDEPENDENCE AND VALUES

The primary way to teach civic values is to have them pervade all aspects of classroom and school life. The value systems underlying competitive, individualistic, and cooperative situations exist as a hidden curriculum beneath the surface of school life.

This hidden values curriculum permeates the social and cognitive development of children, adolescents, and young adults. Each type of interdependence has a set of values inherently built into it and those values determine whether diversity is viewed as positive or negative.

Values Resulting from Competition

When a situation is structured *competitively,* individuals work against each other to achieve a goal that only one or a few can attain (Johnson & Johnson, 1989). Individuals' goal achievements are negatively correlated; each individual perceives that when one person achieves his or her goal, all others with whom he or she is competitively linked fail to achieve their goals. Thus, individuals seek an outcome that is personally beneficial but detrimental to all others in the situation. Inherent in competition is a set of values that is taught and retaught whenever a person engages in competition (see Box 11.1):

1. A commitment to get more than others. There is a built-in concern that one be smarter, faster, stronger, more competent, and more successful than others so that one wins and others lose.
2. The belief that success depends on beating, defeating, and getting more than others. What is valued is triumphing over others and being Number 1. Winning has little to do with excellence and may actually be opposed to excellence. Competition does not teach the value of excellence. Competition teaches the value of winning—doing better and getting more than other participants.
3. The opposition, obstruction, and sabotage of others' success as a natural way of life. Winning depends on a good offense (doing better than others) and a good

■ ■ ■ ■ ■ ▬▬▬▬▬▬▬▬▬▬▬▬▬▬▬▬▬▬▬▬▬▬▬▬▬▬

BOX 11.1
HOW AND HOW NOT TO TEACH VALUES

Alphie Kohn (1997) wrote a critique of character education. In doing so he addressed five questions.

1. At what level are problems addressed (individual or system)? Even more than focusing on the individual, values programs should focus on creating (a) situations in which the values can be expressed and emulated and (b) overall classroom and school structures that promote the desired values.
2. What is the view of human nature? Instead of seeing children and adolescents as broken and needing fixing, values programs should assume that humans are basically caring, loving, committed, altruistic, and community oriented.
3. What is the ultimate goal of teaching students values? Instead of trying to create compliant and obedient individuals, value programs should help students become active participants in a democratic society, principled and caring members of a community, advocates of social justice, and responsible for deciding which traditions are worth preserving and why.
4. Which values should be taught? Everything faculty and staff do teaches values. The values most desirable are those that encourage participation in our democracy and improvement of the quality of life for all citizens (not just oneself).
5. What is the theory of learning? The most significant and least discussed aspect of teaching values is the instructional procedures used. "Telling and compelling" should be avoided, and cooperative learning should be encouraged.

defense (not letting anyone do better than you). There are two ways to win—doing better and obstructing other's efforts. A smart competitor always finds ways to oppose, obstruct, and sabotage the work of others to win.

4. The association of the pleasure of winning with others' disappointment in losing. Winners feel great about winning and they automatically feel great about other people losing. When someone loses, it is a source of pleasure and happiness because it means that one has a better chance of winning.

5. The threat other people pose to one's success. Because smart competitors obstruct and sabotage the work of others, competitors are to be distrusted and watched closely; their efforts to win and their efforts to sabotage one's work are threats. Competition casts schoolmates as rivals and threats to one's success.

6. The belief that people's worth is contingent on their "wins." When a person wins, he or she has value. When a person loses, he or she has no value. The worth of a person is never fixed. It all depends on the latest victory. When a person stops winning, he or she no longer has value as an individual. Competition places value on a limited number of qualities that facilitate winning. Thus, most people have no value because only a few people can win. In school, for example, if a person did not score in the top 5 or 10 percent in math or reading on the last test, they would have no or limited value academically. The other 90 to 95 percent of students are losers and have no value.

7. The belief that self-worth is conditional and contingent on one's wins. Competition teaches that self-worth is contingent on victories. When a person stops winning, he or she stops having value as a person. Far from helping students to believe in themselves, competition creates perpetual insecurity.

8. The view that extrinsic motivation should be based on striving to win rather than striving to learn. Winning is the goal, not learning or practice or development. Inducing people to try to beat others, like other extrinsic motivators, has been shown to reduce students' interest in the task itself.

9. This attitude that people who are different from oneself are to be either feared or held in contempt. Other people are perceived to be potential obstacles to one's success. If they are different in a way that gives them an advantage, the difference is feared. If they are different in a way that gives one an advantage over them, they are to be discounted. High-performing students are often feared because they can win, and low-performing students are often held in contempt as losers who are no competition.

Values Resulting from Individualistic Efforts

When a situation is structured *individualistically,* there is no correlation among participants' goal attainments (Johnson & Johnson, 1989). Each individual perceives that he or she can reach his or her goal regardless of whether other individuals attain or do not attain their goals. Thus, individuals seek an outcome that is personally beneficial without concern for the outcomes of others. The values that individualistic experiences teach differ from those of competition:

1. Commitment to one's own self-interest. One's own success is viewed as important. Others' success is considered to be irrelevant. The calculation of personal self-interest is solitary. Self-centeredness is built in, but the plight of others is ignored.

2. The belief that success depends on one's own efforts. What is valued is reaching some standard for success. Individualistic work teaches the value of independent efforts to succeed.

3. The attitude that other people's success or failure is irrelevant and of no consequence.

4. The idea that the pleasure of succeeding is personal and isolated.

5. The view that other people are irrelevant to one's success. Because their success or failure has no impact on oneself, others are avoided and seen as unrelated to one's success.

6. The attitude that other people's worth is nonexistent because they have no relevance and no value to one's efforts to succeed. When others are evaluated, there is a unidimensional focus on the quality that most affects the success of a task (such as reading or math ability).

7. The unidemensional view that self-worth is based only on oneself. Only the characteristics that help the person succeed are valued. In school, that is primarily reading and math ability.

8. The condition that individualistic experiences result in valuing extrinsic motivation based on achieving criteria and receiving rewards rather than striving to learn. Achieving up to a criterion is the goal, not learning, practice, or development. The rewards received for success are the underlying motivator of learning.

9. The attitude that people who are perceived to be different are disliked whereas people who are perceived to be similar are liked. Other people are perceived to be unnecessary and irrelevant to one's success.

Values Resulting from Cooperation

Cooperation is working together to accomplish shared goals (Johnson & Johnson, 1989). Within cooperative activities individuals seek outcomes that are beneficial to themselves *and* beneficial to all other group members. Cooperative learning is the instructional use of small groups so that students work together to maximize their own and each other's learning (Johnson, Johnson, & Holubec, 1998a). Within cooperative learning groups students are given two responsibilities: to learn the assigned material and to make sure that all other members of their group do likewise. In cooperative learning situations, students perceive that they can reach their learning goals only if the other students in the learning group do so. The values inherent in cooperative efforts differ from both individualistic and competitive efforts:

1. Commitment to the common good. In cooperative situations, individuals' work contributes not only to their own well-being, but also to the well-being of all other collaborators. Concern for the common good and the success of others is built in because the efforts of others also contribute to one's own well-being.

2. The belief that success depends on the joint efforts of everyone to achieve mutual goals. Because cooperators sink or swim together, an all for one and one for all mentality is developed. What is valued is teamwork and civic responsibility. Succeeding depends on everyone doing his or her part. Cooperation teaches the value of working together to achieve mutual goals.

3. The facilitation, promotion, and encouragment of others' success is a natural way of life. Succeeding depends on everyone doing well. There are two ways to succeed—contributing all one can to the joint effort and promoting other cooperators' efforts to contribute. A smart cooperator always finds ways to promote, facilitate, and encourage the efforts of others.

4. The association of the pleasure of succeeding with others' happiness in their success. Cooperators feel great about succeeding and they automatically feel great about other people succeeding. When someone succeeds, it is a source of pleasure and happiness because it means that one's help and assistance has paid off.

5. The potential contribution other people can make to one's success. Because smart cooperators promote and facilitate the work of others, cooperators are trusted because their efforts to succeed promote one's own success. Cooperation casts schoolmates as allies, colleagues, and friends who contribute to one's success.

6. **The belief that other people's worth is unconditional.** A person may contribute to a joint effort in so many diverse ways that everyone has value all the time. This inherent value is reaffirmed by working for the success of all. Cooperation places value on a wide range of diverse qualities that facilitate joint success. Thus, everyone has value.

7. **The belief that self-worth is unconditional.** Cooperation teaches that self-worth results from contributing whatever resources one has to the joint effort and common good. A person never loses value. Cooperative experiences result in individuals believing in themselves and their worth.

8. **The condition that intrinsic motivation should be based on striving to learn, grow, develop, and succeed.** Learning is the goal, not winning. Inducing people to try to contribute to the common good, like other intrinsic motivators, increases students' interest in the task itself.

9. **The attitude that people who are different from oneself are to be valued.** Other people are perceived to be potential resources for and contributors to one's success. If they are different, that means more diverse resources are available for the joint effort and, therefore, the difference is valued. The diverse contributions of members results in the realization that, in the long run, everyone is of equal value and equally deserving, regardless of their gender, ethnic membership, culture, social class, or ability.

Cooperative learning is the pedagogy for democracy. It is a classroom practice that motivates students to pursue common goals and encourages them to become other centered rather than individualistic or egocentric. It invests power in people rather than in authority figures. It encourages the development of civic skills such as dialogue, multiple perspective taking, collective judgment, and collective action on issues of common concern.

Social interdependence can be framed in three ways: positive (cooperation), negative (competition), and none (individualistic efforts). Each type of interdependence teaches an inherent set of values. These values influence whether diversity results in positive or negative outcomes. This does not mean, however, that competitive and individualistic efforts should be banned in schools. Students should learn how to compete appropriately for fun and enjoyment, work individualistically to pursue personal goals, and work cooperatively as part of teams. Cooperative learning, however, should be used the majority of the school day because it promotes the most desirable values for the future well-being of students and the future well-being of society. Complete Activity 11.7 to ascertain which values you believe are most important to teach in school.

CONFLICT RESOLUTION AND VALUES

The value systems underlying the procedures for managing conflict are the second hidden curriculum beneath the surface of school life. Each time a conflict appears and is resolved, a set of values are inherently taught in the experience.

Intellectual Conflicts and Teacher Authority

Perhaps the most common way of resolving intellectual conflicts is on the basis of faculty authority. When a difference of opinion or interpretation arises in a lesson, or when students reach different conclusions, the teacher quickly steps in and pronounces the correct interpretation to the edification of students. The teacher's conclusions are by definition correct and valid. If students do not agree, it is because they misunderstand or are misinformed. The values taught by this procedure include blind acceptance of authority's statements, the importance of pleasing the teacher rather

ACTIVITY **11.7** ■ WHICH VALUES WILL YOU TEACH?

Given below are a list of values. Choose six you believe are the most important for children and adolescents to learn in school. Write down your reasons for your choices. Find a partner. Share your choices and reasons. Listen to his or her choices and reasons. Create a new list that you can agree on. Be ready to share your list and the reasons for your choices with the class as a whole.

_____ 1. **Assertiveness:** openly sharing your opinions in a positive manner

_____ 2. **Commitment:** willing to take responsibility and follow through

_____ 3. **Compassion:** sincerely caring about people in need

_____ 4. **Cooperation:** working and socializing together respectfully

_____ 5. **Courage:** holding to your beliefs and opinions even when it is difficult

_____ 6. **Discretion:** thinking before acting or talking

_____ 7. **Goal setting:** planning and working for something you want

_____ 8. **Honesty:** being trustful and sincere

_____ 9. **Initiative:** beginning a task without being told to do so

_____ 10. **Kindness:** being nice to everyone

_____ 11. **Patience:** waiting calmly

_____ 12. **Perseverance:** sticking to a task until it is completed

_____ 13. **Reliability:** doing what you say you will do

_____ 14. **Respect:** treating others as you would like to be treated

_____ 15. **Responsibility:** accepting consequences for your actions.

_____ 16. **Responsible decision making:** choosing what is best for yourself and others

_____ 17. **Self-control:** displaying emotions and behavior appropriately

_____ 18. **Self-esteem:** having a positive belief in yourself

_____ 19. **Service:** using your time and effort to help others

_____ 20. **Time management:** using time wisely

than engaging in an objective inquiry, and aspects of being other directed and authority oriented rather than inner directed and inquiring.

Controversy and Democratic Deliberation

Our experiences shape our perspectives on large and small issues. Academic controversies allow all students to participate in a deliberative process that includes the free exchange of ideas and opinions in which majority and minority views are heard. It provides a means to experience the ways ethnic, cultural, and gender differences promote creative problem solving and more sophisticated analysis of issues. Because conflicting ideas and positions are inherent in a multicultural, pluralistic democracy, the process by which people argue their views is critical.

Participating in the controversy process teaches a unique set of values. For example, you have both the right and the responsibility to derive a reasoned position and advocate it. "Truth" is derived from the clash of opposing ideas and positions. Insight and understanding come from a "disputed passage" whereby one's ideas and conclusions are advocated and subjected to intellectual challenge. Issues must be viewed from all perspectives, and a synthesis should be sought to subsume the seemingly opposed positions. These values are in direct contrast with those taught in lessons in which teacher authority is definitive (see Table 11.2). Complete Activity 11.8 to evaluate your own sense of the purpose of education.

Conflicts of Interests

Two methods of negotiating resolutions to conflicts of interest are win–lose, or distributive, negotiations and problem-solving, or integrative, negotiations.

Win–Lose Negotiations.   Win–lose negotiations are in essence a competition. It inherently teachers all the values associated with competition. In addition, win–lose negotiations teach values such as deceiving the other person to maximize one's outcomes at the other person's expense is admirable.

Problem-Solving Negotiations and Mediation.   Problem-solving negotiations and peer mediation are closely related to cooperation. They inherently teach all the

TABLE 11.2   Intellectual Conflict and Values

TEACHER AS AUTHORITY	CONTROVERSY AND DEMOCRACY
Accept "truth" as the teachers' conclusions.	Accept "truth" as derived from the clash of diverse opinions.
Derive insight and understanding from accepting the teacher's conclusions. Never argue with the teacher. Accept what he or she says as the truth.	Derive insight and understanding from a "disputed passage," whereby one's ideas and conclusions are advocated and subjected to intellectual challenge.
Rigidly adhere to the teacher's perspective, ignoring all others.	View issues from all perspectives.
Debunk and ignore all views that oppose or disagree with the teacher's conclusions.	Seek a synthesis that subsumes the seemingly opposed positions.
Seek the truth from outside authorities.	Seek the truth from concensus of one's own insights and conclusions with diverse others.

ACTIVITY **11.8** ■ CONTROVERSY AND VALUES

Given below are a series of statements about the purpose of education. Using the rating scale, indicate the level of your agreement or disagreement and write down your reasons for each rating. Find a partner. Compare your ratings and reasons. Come to consensus about your agreement with each statement.

```
1———————————2———————————3———————————4———————————5
Disagree                                              Agree
```

_____ 1. "Difference of opinion leads to inquiry, and inquiry to truth." (Thomas Jefferson)

_____ 2. "Where there is much desire to learn, there of necessity will be much arguing, much writing, many opinions; for opinion in good men is but knowledge in the making. (John Milton)

_____ 3. "One completely overcomes only what one assimilates." (Andre Gide)

_____ 4. "He that wrestles with us strengthens our nerves, and sharpens our skill. Our antagonist is our helper." (Edmund Burke)

_____ 5. "It's best that we should not all think alike. It's difference of opinion that makes horse races." (Mark Twain)

_____ 6. "By blending the breath of the sun and the shade, true harmony comes into the world." (Tao Te Ching)

_____ 7. "Since the general or prevailing opinion on any subject is rarely or never the whole truth, it is only by the collision of adverse opinion that the remainder of the truth has any chance of being supplied." (John Stuart Mill)

_____ 8. "Conflict is the gadfly of thought. It stirs us to observation and memory. It instigates invention. It shocks us out of sheeplike passivity, and sets us at noting and contriving. . . . Conflict is a 'sine qua non' of reflection and ingenuity." (John Dewey)

_____ 9. "Our . . . advantage was that we had evolved unstated but fruitful methods of collaboration. . . . If either of us suggested a new idea, the other, while taking it seriously, would attempt to demolish it in a candid but nonhostile manner." (Francis Crick, Nobel Prize winner and codiscoverer of double helix)

_____ 10. "The best way ever devised for seeking the truth in any given situation is advocacy: presenting the pros and cons from different, informed points of view and digging down deep into the facts." (Harold S. Geneen, former CEO, ITT)

_____ 11. "We must learn to explore all the options and possibilities that confront us in a complex and rapidly changing world. We must learn to welcome and not fear the voices of dissent." (J. W. Fulbright) values associated with cooperation. In addition, problem-solving negotiations and mediation teach values such as being open and honest about what one wants and how one feels, understanding the other person's wants and feelings, striving to see the situation from all perspectives, being concerned with the other person's outcomes as well as one's own, seeking to reach agreements that are satisfying to all disputants, and maintaining effective and caring long-term relationships. In other words, constructive conflict resolution inherently teaches a set of civic values aimed at ensuring the fruitful continuation of the community.

BENEFITS OF A CIVIC VALUES PROGRAM

So many developmental and personal benefits derive from learning civic values that they cannot all be detailed here. At the personal level, civic values provide the internal gyroscope each child and youth needs to guide his or her behavior. They ensure that all individuals becomes inner directed (as opposed to other directed) and have the inner principles needed to regulate their behavior. At the school management level, teaching civic values takes the guesswork out of knowing what the school stands for. The values guide decision making about the curriculum, instruction, and resources. They provide a standard for making selections of curriculum materials. The values provide a structure for faculty and staff to talk to parents, students, visitors, and each other about what is important and why.

CREATING COMMITMENT TO VALUES

In teaching students values, you must remember a set of rules that govern how committed students become to the values being taught (for a review of this literature, see Johnson & F. Johnson, 1997).

Rule 1: Focus on Changing Groups, Not Individuals.   It is easier to promote value and attitude acquisition as well as behavioral change by changing the norms and values of the groups to which individuals belong than by changing each individual separately. Individuals adopt and conform to the norms of reference groups to which they belong, aspire to belong, and identify with. Reference group norms are powerful influences on attitudes and behavior, provide social support for continuing to hold attitudes and behavior patterns, reinforce recommended attitudes and behaviors and punish deviation, and help teachers resist efforts to change their attitudes and behaviors. In addition, individuals are more willing to take risks within small groups than they are when they are working alone.

Rule 2: Have Students Publicly Commit Themselves to Values.   Have students adopt values and have their peers hold them accountable for doing so. The classic studies by Kurt Lewin and his associates indicate that if you want to change individuals' values, attitudes, and behavior, they should be involved in group discussions that lead to public commitment to the new values and behaviors, and they should perceive that they are held accountable by their peers to fulfill their commitments. Publicly saying, "I'm going to do it!" is a powerful influence on one's values and behavior in at least four ways.

First, values and behaviors that are made public are more likely to be adopted than are those that are private, especially when peers hold one accountable to fulfill one's commitments. Second, public commitment results in students more strongly defending the values and behaviors from attack and more strongly responding to other people's support of the values and behaviors. Third, public commitment increases the responsibility individuals assume for subsequent outcomes. Finally, when individuals publicly take a stand, they cannot easily deny or forget the attitudes and behaviors in subsequent situations.

Rule 3: Expose Students to Visible and Credible Social Models. People are most likely to accept new values when they come into contact with others who have successfully adopted them. Visible and credible models and discussion with others who have already adopted the values may be important influences.

Rule 4: Confront Students with Vivid and Personalized Appeals. Students need to discuss values face to face in ways that make clear how following them fits in with current demands on their behavior. People tend to weigh information in proportion to its vividness. Statistical data summaries and impersonal information sources are less vivid than face-to-face discussions, even when the more vivid information is less representative. Thus, to have maximal impact on values, information needs to be discussed, face to face, in ways that make clear the personal implications of the information.

Rule 5: Have Students Teach What They Have Learned to Others. Peers are frequently able to teach more effectively than specially trained experts. Higher-level conceptual understanding and reasoning are promoted when participants have to teach each other a common way to think about problem situations. The way people conceptualize material and organize it cognitively is markedly different when they are learning material for their own benefit than when they are learning material to teach to others.

Rule 6: Have Students Advocate New Values to Schoolmates. People are particularly prone to increase their commitment to values that they have attempted to persuade others to adopt. You can advocate values through demonstrations, working together on lessons and projects, and modeling.

SUMMARY

By the time citizens of our society reach 18 years of age (if not long before), they need to have civic virtue. For a community or a society to exist, members have to share common goals and values and be committed to increase the quality of life for all citizens. Civic values must be taught to prepare students to live in a democratic society, make students better people, and create a caring community in which students learn. A set of values are specifically spelled out in the Declaration of Independence and the Constitution that must be internalized by all U.S. citizens. Survival of a democracy depends on the virtue of its people, and without commitment to each other's well-being, democracy cannot thrive.

There can be little doubt that each individual's values do change. Schools can teach students values by direct instruction, modeling and identification, the enactment of assigned and voluntary social roles, group influences, and the hidden curriculum existing in the pattern and flow of daily school life. The hidden curriculum is most directly expressed in how instruction is structured (competitively, individualistically, or cooperatively) and the ways that intellectual conflicts and conflicts of interest are managed (controversy and peacemaker programs). The benefits of emphasizing civic values in the classroom and school are numerous. Values guide the choice of goals and the decision-making process. Values are an internal gyroscope that points toward one set of actions over another. Finally, values provide a structure for interaction among members of the school and the school's stakeholders.

CHAPTER TWELVE

REFLECTIONS
AND CONCLUSIONS

DIVERSITY: PROMISE OR PROBLEM?

Pluralism and diversity among individuals create opportunities, but, like all opportunities, their outcomes are potentially positive or negative, depending on the conditions under which diverse individuals interact. Positive outcomes are promoted by the following eight steps.

STEP 1: RECOGNIZE DIVERSITY EXISTS AND IS VALUABLE

U.S. culture has always been pluralistic and is becoming increasingly so. This diversity is a strength as long as diverse individuals are united in their commitment to democracy and U.S. values. U.S. commitment to diversity is reflected in our laws on ethnic desegregation, the rights of females, and the desegregation of individuals with disabilities. To help implement these laws, human relations training was initiated to achieve two goals: (a) to improve relationships between majority and minority citizens by eliminating prejudice and discrimination and (b) to increase participants' competencies in interacting effectively with diverse individuals.

The history of human relations in business and industry goes back at least to the middle of the nineteenth century. It includes the strengthening of unions, development of mass production and scientific management, technological advances in the workplace, the Hawthorne and Harwood studies, the development of the National Training Laboratories of Applied Behavioral Science, and the theorizing of McGregor, Maslow, and Rogers. In education, the emphasis on human relations began in the 1920s but is primarily the result of the civil rights movement in the early 1960s.

More recently, schools are emphasizing multiculturalism. By ensuring that educational opportunities are fair and equal, reforming curricula to reflect a global perspective, promoting intercultural competence, and teaching students social action skills, schools hope to enable students to internalize multiple cultural identities.

STEP 2: BUILD AN INCLUSIVE, UNIFYING IDENTITY

To build relationships with diverse individuals you must build an inclusive, unifying identity. First, you develop an appreciation of your historic, cultural, ethnic, and religious background as well as your other important personal characteristics. To understand, respect, and appreciate others' cultural and historical perspectives, you must be aware of your own. Your identity includes both personal and social facets. You build your identity by acquiring social roles, by identifying with other people and groups, and by seeking out a broad range of experiences. Your social identity is largely based on your identification with and appreciation of the culture and history of your ancestors. Usually, the more respect you have for your cultural heritage, the more respect you have for yourself.

Second, you develop an appreciation for the historic, cultural, ethnic, and religious backgrounds (and other important personal characteristics) of others. The more accepting you are of others, the more accepting your are of yourself (and vice versa). Third, you adopt a strong superordinate identity as an American. It is this broader identity that unifies and unites all citizens. Within the identity is a pluralistic set of values concerning democracy, freedom, liberty, equality, justice, the rights of individuals, and the responsibilities of citizenship.

STEP 3: UNDERSTAND COGNITIVE BARRIERS

Theorizing and research on relationships among diverse individuals include cognitive, attitudinal, and behavioral approaches. Cognitive factors begin with the human need to classify people, objects, and events into categories to understand and respond to the events in their lives. Classifying people (social categorization) involves *implicit personality theories* in which a person's appearance and behavior are used to generate hypotheses about the person's traits, which imply a cluster of traits that are assumed to go together. Unfortunately, the perceptions on which social categorization is based are not always accurate, and the differences between groups tends to be overestimated.

A *stereotype* is a belief that associates a whole group of people with certain traits. Women have been stereotyped as being more emotional than men. You form stereotypes by categorizing (sorting single objects into groups rather than thinking of each as unique) and by differentiating between the ingroup (the groups with which you identify) and outgroups. You commonly assume that the members of outgroups are quite similar while realizing that the members of the ingroup are quite diverse (*outgroup homogeneity effect*). Stereotypes are perpetuated and protected by (a) influencing what we perceive and remember about the actions of outgroup members, (b) creating an oversimplified picture of outgroup members, (c) overestimating the similarity of behavior among outgroup members, and (d) promoting scapegoating.

Stereotyping can lead to prejudice and discrimination as well as a tendency to blame the victim. *Prejudice* can be defined as an unjustified negative attitude toward a person based solely on that individual's membership in a group other than one's own. Overt racism may be replaced with *modern racism* with a more subtle form of prejudice in which people appear, on the surface, not to harbor prejudice, but actually do hold racist attitudes.

When prejudice is put into action, it is *discrimination* (actions taken to harm a group or any of its members). *Blaming the victim* occurs when the cause of discrimination or misfortune is attributed to the personal characteristics and actions of the victim (this maintains a belief in a just world). Blaming the victim and other dynamics of prejudice and discrimination involve making causal attributions that justify the mistreatment and disadvantage of minority groups.

Just as categorization leads to stereotyping and prejudice, it also leads to self-categorizing, which creates personal and social identity (*social categorization theory*). People may seek a positively valued distinctiveness for own groups compared to other groups to achieve a positive social identity (*social identity theory*). Thus, prejudice and discrimination may result from social categorizations, which in turn result from intergroup competition, bias favoring the ingroup over the outgroups, and the depersonalization of members of the outgroups. These effects can be mitigated through a combination of decategorization and recategorization.

Removing discrimination requires awakening a sense of injustice in majority group members about any unfair treatment of minority and low-power group members. Finally, teacher expectations can affect the school performance and behavior of minority and low-power students.

STEP 4: UNDERSTAND THE DYNAMICS OF INTERGROUP CONFLICT

Intergroup theories of prejudice and discrimination include psychodynamic theories, realistic group conflict theory, and relative deprivation theory. Psychodynamic theories posit that prejudice is the result of motivation tensions within the individual. Realistic group conflict theory explains that intergroup hostility, antagonism, and prejudice result from competition between groups over resources that each group wants. Relative deprivation theory is based on the idea that less privileged groups want to be equal to more privileged groups.

One of the most common settings for realistic conflict exists between high- and lower-power groups. There are also a number of intergroup conflict theories. Sherif found that creating intergroup conflict was very easy, but resolving it was not. Information about the other groups, contact during a pleasant activity, and establishing a common enemy did not resolve the conflict. The only effective procedure for resolving intergroup conflict was the establishment of superordinate goals. Blake and Mouton examined what happens in intergroup conflicts within the group, between groups, and between negotiators representing groups.

Contact theory specifies that contact between members of diverse groups can have positive impact if the groups are involved in cooperative efforts, personal interactions take place, building positive relationships is supported by authorities and norms, and the groups have equal status in the situation. Interaction under these conditions provides the setting in which culture clashes and misunderstandings can be managed constructively.

STEP 5: UNDERSTAND SOCIAL JUDGMENT PROCESS

Social judgment theory states that individuals become involved in a process of acceptance or rejection that determines whether they like or dislike each other and perceive each other in positive or negative ways. The process of acceptance may be summarized as follows. When individuals cooperate with each other, the positive interdependence and promotive interaction result in frequent and accurate communication, accurate perspective taking, inducibility, multidimensional views of each other, feelings of psychological acceptance and self-esteem, psychological success, and expectations of rewarding and productive future interaction.

The process of rejection may be summarized as follows. When individuals compete or work individualistically, negative and no interdependence and oppositional or no interaction result in an absence of or in inaccurate communication, egocentrism, resistance to influence, monopolistic and static views of each other, feelings of psychological rejection and low self-esteem, psychological failure, and expectations for oppositional interaction in the future.

STEP 6: CREATE A COOPERATIVE CONTEXT

Promoting the process of acceptance and creating the conditions for contact begins with creating a cooperative context. The three types of social interdependence are competitive, individualistic, and cooperative. Of the three, cooperation tends to promote the highest achievement, most positive relationships, and greatest psychological health. What makes cooperation work is five essential elements: positive interdependence, individual accountability, promotive interaction, social skills, and group processing. By structuring these five elements into lessons, teachers can create formal cooperative learning lessons, informal cooperative learning lessons, and cooperative base groups.

Cooperation can be extended to the class, several classes, the school, parents, the neighborhood, and the community. In a cooperative school, teachers work in teaching teams, faculty meetings are structured cooperative, and site-based decision making utilizes cooperative groups. When diverse individuals work together to achieve mutual goals, the context is created for the process of acceptance, that is, for developing positive relationships free of negative stereotypes and prejudice.

STEP 7: TEACH CONFLICT RESOLUTION PROCEDURES

The more diverse are the individuals cooperating, the more frequently conflicts occur. To manage conflicts, students (and faculty) must be taught the procedures to resolve conflicts constructively and the school needs to become a conflict-positive organization in which conflicts are sought out, encouraged, and managed constructively. Constructively managed conflicts promote learning, problem solving, healthy social development, change, success, and life experiences that are interesting and fun.

When diverse students work together cooperatively, intellectual conflicts arise concerning how to complete an assignment or how best to proceed to achieve their goal. Such intellectual conflicts are known as controversies. *Academic controversy* exists when one student's ideas, information, conclusions, theories, and opinions are incompatible with those of another, and the two seek to reach an agreement. Teachers guide students through (a) researching and preparing a position, (b) presenting and advocating their position, (c) engaging in an open discussion in which they refute the opposing position and rebut attacks on their own position, (d) reversing perspectives, and (e) synthesizing and integrating the best evidence and reasoning into a joint position. Engaging in an academic controversy results in higher achievement, continuing motivation to learn, creative problem solving, higher-level reasoning, more positive relationships, and increased self-esteem.

When diverse students interact, conflicts of interests often occur. Two students may both want to use the same computer or read the same book. Both may claim the same pencil. A rivalry may occur over the same boy- or girlfriend. When such conflicts occur, students (and faculty) have to know how to negotiate constructive agreements.

Negotiation is a process by which persons try to work out a settlement in which they (a) have both shared and opposing interests and (b) want to come to an agreement. Two types of negotiations are win–lose, or *distributive,* negotiations and problem-solving, or *integrative,* negotiations. In win–lose negotiations, the goal is to reach an agreement more favorable to oneself than to the other persons. In problem-solving negotiations, the goal is to reach an agreement that benefits everyone involved. In ongoing relationships that have a future as well as a present, an integrative approach to negotiations is the only constructive alternative.

After students are taught the procedure for problem-solving negotiations, they are taught how to mediate schoolmates' conflicts. A *mediator* is a neutral person who helps two or more people resolve their conflict, usually by halting hostilities, ensuring commitment to the mediation process, facilitating problem-solving negotiations, and formalizing the agreement. Once students are trained to be mediators, a peacemaker program can be implemented. All students serve as peer mediators an equal amount of time so everyone experiences the benefits from doing so.

The negotiation and mediation training may be integrated into ongoing academic curriculum units. The training is repeated every year (the Peacemaker Program is a 12-year spiral curriculum). Teaching *all* students negotiation and mediation procedures and skills and implementing a peer mediation program results in a schoolwide discipline program focused on empowering students to regulate and control their own and their classmates' actions.

STEP 8: TEACH CIVIC VALUES

For diversity to be a strength, individuals must learn and internalize pluralistic, democratic values. By the time citizens of our society reach 18 years of age (if not long before), they need to have civic virtue. For a community or a society to exist, members have to share common goals and values and be committed to increasing the quality of life for all citizens. Civic values must be taught to prepare students to live in a democratic society, to make students better people, and to create a caring community in which students learn. A set of values is specifically spelled out in the Declaration of Independence and the Constitution of the United States that must be internalized by all citizens.

Survival of a democracy depends on the virtue of its people, and without commitment to each other's well-being, democracy cannot thrive. Schools can teach students values by direct instruction, modeling and identification, the enactment of assigned and voluntary social roles, group influences, and the pattern of ebb and flow of daily school life. Values are most directly expressed in the way instruction is structured (competitively, individualistically, or cooperatively) and the way that intellectual conflicts and conflicts of interest are managed (controversy and peacemaker programs). Values guide the choice of goals and the decision-making process. Values are an internal gyroscope that points toward one set of actions over another. Finally, values provide a structure for interaction among members of the school and the school's stakeholders.

SUMMARY

If these eight steps are followed, relationships among diverse individuals can be positive, constructive, effective, and caring. The legitimacy of group differences is recognized and intergroup conflicts are managed in just and equitable ways. The importance of making diversity a strength and ensuring that positive outcomes result from interaction among diverse individuals cannot be overemphasized.

The dominant form of war today, for example, is not international conflict, but rather intrastate conflict defined by ethnicity, religion, and communal identity. Such conflicts have occurred in the past few years in Bosnia, Rwanda, Armenia, and Guatemala and many other places. Because ethnic conflicts are often fought in and around communities rather than on well-defined battlefields, more than 80 percent of the causalities are civilians, notably women and children.

Within the United States and many other countries, furthermore, ethnic hate crimes are increasing. Although these conflicts are complex and difficult to resolve, it can be done. In South Africa, apartheid has been dismantled, proving that violent ethnic conflict can be managed, reduced, and prevented. By following the eight steps outlined in this book, the goals of multicultural education and human relations can be achieved, and diverse children and adolescents can build positive relationships with each other.

REVIEW AND CELEBRATION

The greatest rewards come only from the greatest commitment.
— *Arlene Blum (mountain climber and leader,*
American Women's Himalayan Expedition)

ACTIVITY 1: REVIEW OF PROGRESS

Meet in your base groups. Every member should have the following:

1. Journal
2. Case studies
3. Log sheet
4. Lessons and units planned (and taught)
5. Completed implementation assignments
6. Papers written

Task: Group members have 10 minutes to summarize their implementation of human relations. The summary should include personal learnings as recorded in their journals, the impact of the human relations lessons on the students being followed for case studies, the number and type of lessons they have conducted, and their overall experiences in teaching human relations skills to students.

Procedure: Once all members have summarized their implementation of human relations, the group makes at least three conclusions about their experiences to share with the entire class. This is a *cooperative* activity; everyone should participate, listen carefully to groupmates, provide support and encouragement, and celebrate the group's effort in implementing human relations into their classrooms and schools.

ACTIVITY 2: SHARING SUCCESSES

Task: Share your successes in implementing human relations and help each groupmate do the same.

Procedure: Stay in your base groups and work cooperatively in answering the following questions:

1. How have your students benefited from human relations?
2. What human relations lesson was most successful?
3. Which student benefited most from working cooperatively?
4. What human relations lesson was most important to you personally?

ACTIVITY 3: HUMAN RELATIONS REVIEW QUIZ

Task: Answer each question in the Review Quiz correctly.

Procedure: Divide your base group into pairs and work cooperatively. Each pair takes the quiz together, producing one answer for the pair, with both members in agreement and able to explain each answer. When finished, reform as a base group and take the review quiz again. If there is any disagreement as to the answer to a question, find the page number in the book that contains the answer and clarify until all members are in agreement and can explain the answer.

ACTIVITY 4: BASIC CONCEPTS REVIEW

Task: Starting with Chapter 1, identify the basic concepts in each chapter.

Procedure: Divide your base group into pairs. Partners ensure both members can correctly define each concept. When finished, reform as a base group and compare the concepts identified for each chapter and their definitions. If members disagree as to the correct definitions, identify the page on which the definition appears and clarify the definition until all members of the group agree and are able to explain it. Make sure all base group members can define each concept.

ACTIVITY 5: PLANNING YOUR HUMAN RELATIONS FUTURE

Tasks: (1) Diagnose your current level of expertise in using human relations and (2) make a plan for increasing your expertise. The diagnosis and plan must be in writing and signed by all base group members.

Procedure: Meet in your base group and work cooperatively. Ensure all members (a) have completed the above two tasks and (b) agree with each member's diagnosis and plan (noted by the signatures on each member's plan). In diagnosing where you stand in gaining expertise in human relations, study the following considerations:

1. Your ability to achieve the following long-term goals:

    a. Taking any lesson in any subject area and teaching it cooperatively
    b. Using human relations at the routine-use level
    c. Using human relations at least 60 percent of the time
    d. Joining an ongoing collegial support group

2. The amount of training you have received

3. The amount of experience you have in using human relations

4. The effectiveness of your collegial support group in encouraging and assisting members' implementation efforts

5. Your ability to experiment, take risks, and generally stay on the edge of your comfort zone to increase your expertise

6. The quality and quantity of the feedback you are receiving on your implementation efforts

7. The quality and quantity of your reflections and problem solving from the feedback received

8. Your persistence in using human relations again and again

9. Your experience in encouraging and assisting your colleagues' efforts to implement human relations

Task: Increase your expertise in implementing the eight steps of human relations.

Procedure: Develop a plan that includes the following steps:

1. List the units coming up in which human relations should be used.

2. List the human relations skills you plan to teach to your students.

3. Form and maintain a collegial support group in your school to focus on human relations.

4. Develop your own skill in working cooperatively with colleagues.

5. Plan a time schedule as to when human relations skills will be taught and perfected by your students as well as when you will provide opportunities for the use of the skills, feedback on how well each student is performing the skill, and encouragement for each student to continue practicing the skill.

6. Record the phone numbers of your base group members and the time you will call each one to report on your progress.

ACTIVITY 6: WHOLE-CLASS REVIEW BY DRAWING NAMES

Task: Provide a fun review of the course.

Procedure: The instructor asks a question and then draws a participant's name from a hat. The participant named must give an interesting and truthful answer.

ACTIVITY 7: THANKING YOUR LEARNING PARTNERS

Task: Seek out the people who have helped you learn how to implement human relations.

Procedure: Thank them.

ACTIVITY 8: ACTION PLAN

1. Your next steps:

2. Support from whom:

3. In what ways:

4. Realities to be faced:

5. Your vision of the classroom and school in which the eight steps of human relations have been implemented:

REFERENCES

Abelson, R., Dasgupta, N., Park, J., & Banaji, M. (1998). Perceptions of the collective other. *Personality and Social Psychology Review, 2*(4), 243–250.

Abrams, D., & Hogg, M. (1990). An introduction to the social identity approach. In D. Abrams & M. Hogg (Eds.), *Social identity* (pp. 1–9). New York: Springer-Verlag.

Adorno, T., Frenkel-Brunswik, E., Levinson, D., & Sanford, R. (1950). *The authoritarian personality.* New York: Harper & Row.

Agnew, C., Van Lange, P., Rusbult, C., & Langston, C. (1998). Cognitive interdependence: Commitment and the mental representation of close relationship. *Journal of Personality and Social Psychology, 74,* 939–954.

Allen, V., & Wilder, D. (1975). Categorization, belief similarity, and group discrimination. *Journal of Personality and Social Psychology, 32,* 971–977.

Allport, G. *The nature of prejudice.* Cambridge, MA: Addison-Wesley.

Allport, G., & Kramer, B. (1946). Some roots of prejudice. *Journal of Psychology, 22,* 9–39.

Altman, I. (1968). Choice points in the classification of knowledge. In B. Indik & F. Berrien (Eds.), *People, groups, and organizations* (pp. 47–72). New York: Teachers College Press.

Amir, Y. (1969). Contact hypothesis in ethnic relations. *Psychological Bulletin, 71,* 319–352.

Amir, Y. (1976). The role of intergroup contact in change in prejudice and ethnic relations. In P. Katz (Ed.), *Towards the elimination of racism* (pp. 245–308). New York: Pergamon.

Aristotle (384–322 B.C./1991). *The art of rhetoric* (H. C. Lawson-Tancred, Trans.). New York: Penguin Books.

Aron, A., & Aron, E. (1997). Self-expansion motivation and including other in the self. In S. Duck (Ed.), *Handbook of personal relationships: Theory, research, and intervention* (2nd ed., pp. 251–270). Chichester, England: Wiley.

Aronson, E. (1978). *The jigsaw classroom.* Beverly Hills, CA: Sage.

Arriaga, X., & Rusbult, C. (1998). Standing in my partner's shoes: Partner perspective taking and reactions to accommodative dilemmas. *Personality and Social Psychology Bulletin, 24*(9), 927–948.

Asch, S. (1952). *Social psychology.* Englewood Cliffs, NJ: Prentice-Hall.

Ashmore, R., & Del Boca, F. (1979). Sex stereotypes and implicit personality theory: Toward a cognitive-social psychological conceptualization. *Sex Roles, 5,* 219–248.

Astin, A. (1993). *What matters in college? Four critical years revised.* San Francisco: Jossey-Bass.

Atkinson, J. (1964). *An introduction to achievement motivation.* New York: Van Nostrand.

Axelrod, R., & Hamilton, W. (1981). The evolution of cooperation. *Science, 211,* 1390–1396.

Ayres, I., & Siegelman, P. (1995). Race and gender discrimination in bargaining for a new car. *American Economic Review, 85,* 304–321.

Babad, E. (1993). Pygmalion—25 years after interpersonal expectations in the classroom. In P. Blanck (Ed.), *Interpersonal expectations: Theory, research, and application* (pp. 125–153). Paris, France: Cambridge University Press.

Baily, K. (1994). *Typologies and taxonomies.* Belmont, CA: Sage.

Bantel, K., & Jackson, S. (1989). Top management and innovations in banking: Does the composition of the top team make a difference? *Strategic Management Journal, 10,* 107–124.

Baron, R., Albright, L., & Malloy, T. (1995). Effects of behavioral and social class information on social judgment. *Personality and Social Psychology Bulletin, 21,* 308–315.

Baron, R., Tom, D., & Cooper, H. (1985). Social class, race and teacher expectations. In J. Dusek (Ed.), *Teacher expectations* (pp. 251–270). Hillsdale, NJ: Erlbaum.

Baumeister, R., Smart, L., & Boden, J. (1996). Relation of threatened egotism to violence and aggression: The dark side of high self-esteem. *Psychological Review, 103,* 5–33.

Baumgartner, M. (1984). Social control from below. In D. Black (Ed.), *Toward a general theory of social control. Vol. 1: Fundamentals* (pp. 303–345). New York: Academic Press.

Berlyne, D. (1965). Curiosity and education. In J. Krumboltz (Ed.), *Learning and the educational process.* Chicago: Rand-McNally.

Berlyne, D. (1966). Notes on intrinsic motivation and intrinsic reward in relation to instruction. In J. Bruner (Ed.), *Learning about learning* (*Cooperative Research Monograph, No. 15*). Washington, DC: U.S. Department of Health, Education, and Welfare, Office of Education.

Bettencourt, B., Brewer, M., Croak, M., & Miller, N. (1992). Cooperation and reduction of intergroup bias: The role of reward structure and social orientation. *Journal of Experimental Social Psychology, 28,* 301–319.

Bettencourt, B., Charlton, K., & Kernahan, C. (in press). Numerical representation of groups in cooperative settings: Social orientation effects on ingroup bias. *Journal of Experimental Social Psychology.*

Bettencourt, B., & Dorr, N. (1998). Cooperative interaction and intergroup bias: Effects of numerical representation and cross-cut role assignment. *Personality and Social Psychology Bulletin, 24*(12), 1276–1293.

Blake, R., & Mouton, J. (1962). The intergroup dynamics of win-lose conflict and problem-solving collaboration in union-management relations. In M. Sherif (Ed.), *Intergroup relations and leadership* (pp. 94–140). New York: John Wiley.

Blake, R., & Mouton, J. (1983). Lateral conflict. In D. Tjosvold & D. W. Johnson (Eds.), *Productive conflict management: Perspectives for organizations.* Edina, MN: Interaction Book Company.

Blanchard, F., Crandall, C., Brigham, J., & Vaughn, L. (1994). Condemning and condoning racism: A social context approach to interracial settings. *Journal of Applied Psychology, 79,* 993–997.

Blanchard, F., Lilly, T., & Vaughn, L. (1991). Reducing the expression of racial prejudice. *Psychological Science, 2,* 101–105.

Blanchard, F., Weigal, R., & Cook, S. (1975). The effect of relative competence of group members upon interpersonal attraction in cooperating interracial groups. *Journal of Personality and Social Psychology, 32,* 519–530.

Bodenhausen, G. (1993). Emotions, arousal, and stereotypic judgments: A heuristic model of affect and stereotyping. In D. Mackie & D. Hamilton (Eds.), *Affect, cognition, and stereotyping: Interactive processes in group perception* (pp. 13–37). San Diego, CA: Academic Press.

Bond, M. (1988). Finding the universal dimensions of individual variation in multiculural studies of values: The Rokeach and Chinese value surveys. *Journal of Personality and Social Psychology, 55,* 1009–1015.

Bowen, W., & Bok, D. (1998). *The shape of the river: Long-term consequences of considering race in college and university admissions.* Princeton, NJ: Princeton University Press.

Braddock, J. (1985). School desegregation and black assimilation. *Journal of Social Issues, 41*(3), 9–22.

Braddock, J., Crain, R., & McPartland, J. (1984). A long-term view of school desegregation: Some recent studies on graduates as adults. *Phi Delta Kappan, 66,* 259–264.

Brewer, M. (1979). In-group bias in the minimal intergroup situation: A cognitive motivational analysis. *Psychological Bulletin, 86,* 307–324.

Brewer, M. (1988). A dual process model of impression formation. In T. Srull & R. Wyer, Jr. (Eds.), *Advances in social cognition* (Vol. 1, pp. 1–36). Hillsdale, NJ: Erlbaum.

Brewer, M. (1991). The social self: On being the same and different at the same time. *Personality and Social Psychology Bulletin, 17,* 475–482.

Brewer, M. (1996). Managing diversity: The role of social identities. In S. Jackson & M. Ruderman (Eds.), *Diversity in work teams* (pp. 47–68). Washington, DC: American Psychological Association.

Brewer, M. (1997). The social psychology of intergroup relations: Can research inform practice? *Journal of Social Issues, 33*(1), 197–211.

Brewer, M., Ho, H., Lee, J., & Miller, N. (1987). Social identity and social distance among Hong Kong schoolchildren. *Personality and Social Psychology Bulletin, 13,* 156–165.

Brewer, M., Manzi, K., & Shaw, J. (1993). Ingroup identification as a function of depersonalization, distinctiveness, and status. *Psychological Science, 4,* 88–92.

Brewer, M., & Miller, N. (1984). Beyond the contact hypothesis: Theoretical perspectives on desegregation. In N. Miller & M. Brewer (Eds.), *Groups in contact: The psychology of desegregation* (pp. 281–302). New York: Academic Press.

Brewer, M., & Miller, N. (1988). Contact and cooperation: When do they work? In P. Katz & D. Taylor (Eds.), *Eliminating racism: Profiles in controversy* (pp. 315–326). New York: Plenum.

Brophy, J. (1945). The luxury of anti-Negro prejudice. *Public Opinion Quarterly, 9,* 456–466.

Brophy, J. (1983). Research on the self-fulfilling prophecy and teacher expectations. *Journal of Educational Psychology, 76,* 236–247.

Brophy, J. (1985). Teacher–student interactions. In J. Dusek (Ed.), *Teacher expectations* (pp. 303–328). Hillsdale, NJ: Erlbaum.

Brullis, H. (1954). *Human relations in action.* New York: Wiley.

Bruner, J. (1961). *The process of education.* Cambridge, MA: Harvard University Press.

Buss, D. (1990). Evolutionary social psychology: Prospects and pitfalls. *Motivation and Emotion, 14,* 265–460.

Byrne, D. (1971). *The attraction paradigm.* New York: Academic Press.

Campbell, D. (1965). Variation and selective retention in socio-cultural evolution. In H. Barringer, G. Blanksten, & R. Mack (Eds.), *Social change in developing areas* (pp. 19–49). Cambridge, MA: Schenkman.

Campbell, D. (1967). Stereotypes and the perception of group differences. *American Psychologist, 22,* 817–829.

Campbell, D. (1982). Legal and primary social controls. *Journal of Social and Biological Structures, 5,* 431–438.

Carnegie Foundation. (1995). Draft: Report of the Carnegie task force on learning in the primary grades. New York: Author.

Caspi, A. (1984). Contact hypothesis and inter-age attitudes: A field study of cross-age contact. *Social Psychology Quarterly, 47,* 74–80.

Cialdini, R., Borden, R., Thorne, A., Walker, M., Freeman, S., & Sloane, L. (1976). Basking in reflected glory: Three (football) field studies. *Journal of Personality and Social Psychology, 34,* 366–375.

Cialdini, R., & Richardson, K. (1980). Two indirect tactics of image management: Basking and blasting. *Journal of Personality and Social Psychology, 39,* 406–415.

Cohen, E. (1984). Talking and working together: Status, interaction and learning. In P. Peterson, L. Wilkinson, & M. Hallinan (Eds.), *The social context of instruction: Group organization and group processes* (pp. 171–187). New York: Academic Press.

Cohen, L., & Swim, J. (1995). The differential impact of gender ratios on women and men: Tokenism, self-confidence, and expectations. *Personality and Social Psychology Bulletin, 21,* 876–884.

Coleman, J., Campbell, E., Hobson, C., McPartland, J., Mood, A., Weinfeld, F., & York, R. (1966). *Equality of educational opportunity.* Washington, DC: U.S. Government Printing Office.

Comer, J. (1980). *School power.* New York: Free Press.

Cook, S. (1957). Desegregation: A psychological analysis. *American Psychologist, 12,* 1–13.

Cook, S. (1978). Interpersonal and attitudinal outcomes in cooperating interracial groups. *Journal of Research in Developmental Education, 12,* 87–113.

Cook, S. (1985). Experimenting on social issues: The case of school desegregation. *American Psychologist, 40,* 452–460.

Cook, S., Armor, D., Crain, R., Miller, N., Stephasn, W., Walberg, H., & Wortman, P. (Eds.). (1984). *School desegregation and black achievement.* Washington, DC: National Institute of Education.

Cooley, C. (1902). *Human nature and the social order.* New York: Charles Scribner's Sons.

Cooper, H. (1993). In search of a social fact. A commentary on the study of interpersonal expectations. In P. Blanck (Ed.), *Interpersonal expectations: Theory, research, and application* (pp. 218–226). Paris: Cambridge University Press.

Cooper, L., Johnson, D. W., Johnson, R., & Wilderson, F. (1980). The effects of cooperative, competitive, and individualistic experiences on interpersonal attraction among heterogeneous peers. *Journal of Social Psychology, 111,* 243–253.

Coovert, M., & Reeder, G. (1990). Negativity effects in impression formation: The role of unit formation and schematic expectations. *Journal of Personality and Social Psychology, 26,* 49–62.

Coser, L. (1956). *The function of social conflict.* Glencoe, IL: Free Press.

Cosier, R. (1981). Dialectical inquiry in strategic planning: A case of premature acceptance? *Academy of Management Review, 6,* 643–648.

Cox, O. (1959). *Caste, class, and race: A study in social dynamics.* New York: Monthly Review Press.

Crain, R. (1984, April). *Desegregated schools and the nonacademic side of college survival.* Paper presented at the annual meeting of the American Educational Research Association, New Orleans, LA.

Crain, R., & McPartland, J. (1984). A long-term view of desegregation: Some recent studies of graduates as adults. *Phi Delta Kappan, 66,* 259–264.

Crandall, C. (1995). Do parents discriminate against their heavyweight daughters? *Personality and Social Psychology Bulletin, 21,* 724–735.

Criswell, J. (1939). Social structure revealed in a sociometric test. *Sociometry, 2,* 69–75.

Crocker, J., & Luhranen, R. (1990). Collection self-esteem and ingroup bias. *Journal of Personality and Social Psychology, 58,* 60–67.

Crocker, J., & Major, B. (1989). Social stigma and self-esteem: The self-protective properties of stigma. *Psychological Review, 96,* 608–630.

Crocker, J., Voelkl, K., Testa, M., & Major, B. (1991). Social stigma: The affective consequences of attributional complexity. *Journal of Personality and Social Psychology, 60,* 218–228.

Croizet, J., & Claire, T. (1998). Extending the concept of stereotype threat to social class: The intellectual underperformance of students from low socioeconomic backgrounds. *Personality and Social Psychology Bulletin, 24(6),* 588–594.

Davidson, O. (1996). *The best of enemies: Race and redemption in the New South.* New York: Scribner.

Dawkins, M. (1994). Long-term effects of school desegregation on African Americans: Evidence from the National Survey of Black Americans. *Negro Educational Review, 45,* 4–15.

DeCecco, J., & Richards, A. (1974). *Growing pains: Uses of school conflict.* New York: Aberdeen Press.

Deschamps, J. (1977). Effect of crossing category membership on quantitative judgment. *European Journal of Social Psychology, 22,* 189–195.

Deschamps, J., & Doise, W. (1978). Crossed category memberships in intergroup relations. In H. Tajfel (Ed.), *Differentiation between social groups: Studies in the social psychology of intergroup relations* (pp. 141–158). New York: Academic Press.

Desforges, D., Lord, C., Ramsey, S., Mason, J., Van Leeuwen, M., West, S., & Lepper, M. (1991). Effects of structured cooperative contact on changing negative attitudes toward stigmatized social groups. *Journal of Personality and Social Psychology, 60,* 531–544.

Deutsch, M. (1949). A theory of cooperation and competition. *Human Relations, 2,* 129–152.

Deutsch, M. (1962). Cooperation and trust: Some theoretical notes. In M. Jones (Ed.), *Nebraska symposium on motivation* (pp. 275–319). Lincoln: University of Nebraska Press.

Deutsch, M. (1969). Conflicts: Productive and destructive. *Journal of Social Issues, 25,* 7–43.

Deutsch, M. (1973). *The resolution of conflict.* New Haven, CT: Yale University Press.

Deutsch, M. (1985). *Distributive justice: A social psychological perspective.* New Haven, CT: Yale University Press.

Deutsch, M., Canavan, D., & Rubin, J. (1971). The effects of size of conflict and sex of experimenter upon interpersonal bargaining. *Journal of Experimental Social Psychology, 7,* 258–267.

Deutsch, M., & Collins, M. (1951). *Interracial housing: A psychological evaluation of a social experiment.* Minneapolis: University of Minnesota Press.

Deutsch, M., & Lewicki, R. (1970). "Locking in" effects during a game of chicken. *Journal of Conflict Resolution, 14,* 367–378.

Devine, P., Monteith, M., Zawerink, J., & Elliot, A. (1991). Prejudice with and without compunction. *Journal of Personality and Social Psychology, 60,* 817–830.

DeVries, D., & Edwards, K. (1973). Learning games and student teams: Their effects on classroom process. *American Educational Research Journal, 10,* 307–318.

DeVries, D., & Edwards, K. (1974, April). *Cooperation in the classroom: Towards a theory of alternative reward–task classroom structures.* Paper presented at the meeting of the American Educational Research Association, Chicago.

Dewey, J. (1934). *A common faith.* New Haven, CT: Yale University Press.

Dovidio, J., & Gaertner, S. (1991). Changes in the expression and assessment of racial prejudice. In H. Knopke, R. Norrell, & R. Rogers (Eds.), *Opening doors: Perspectives on race relations in contemporary America* (pp. 119–148). Tuscaloosa: University of Alabama Press.

DuBois, W. E. B. (1989). *The souls of Black folk.* New York: Penguin (Original work published 1903).

Duckitt, J. (1992). *The social psychology of racism.* London: Praeger.

Duval, S. (1976). Conformity on a visual task as a function of personal novelty on attitudinal dimensions and being reminded of the object status of self. *Journal of Experimental Social Psychology, 12,* 87–98.

Edelman, M. (1973). Southern school desegregation, 1954–1973: A judicial-political overview. *Annals of the American Academy of Political and Social Science, 407,* 32–42.

Elam, S., Rose, L., & Gallup, A. (1994, September). The 26th annual Gallup poll of the public's attitudes toward the public schools. *Phi Delta Kappa, 76,* 41–56.

Epstein, S., & Taylor, S. (1967). Instigation to aggression as a function of degree of defeat and perceived aggressive intent of the opponent. *Journal of Personality, 35,* 265–289.

Erikson, E. (1950). *Childhood and society.* New York: W. W. Norton.

Espenshade, T., & Calhoun, C. (1993). An analysis of public opinion toward undocumented immigration. *Population Research and Policy Review, 12,* 189–224.

Fein, S., & Spencer, S. (1997). Prejudice as self-image maintenance: Affirming the self through derogating others. *Journal of Personality and Social Psychology, 73(1),* 31–44.

Festinger, L. (1954). A theory of social comparison processes. *Human Relations, 7,* 117–140.

Fine, G. (1979). The Pinkston settlement: An historical and social psychological investigation of the contact hypothesis. *Phylon, 40,* 229–242.

Fishbein, J. (1996). *Peer prejudice and discrimination: Evolutionary, cultural, and developmental dynamics.* Boulder, CO: Westview.

Fiske, S. (1980). Attention and weight in person perception: The impact of negative and extreme behavior. *Journal of Personality and Social Psychology, 38,* 889–906.

Fiske, S. (1993). Controlling other people: The impact of power on stereotyping. *American Psychologist, 48,* 621–628.

Fiske, S., & Morling, B. (1996). Stereotyping as a function of personal control motives and capacity constraints: The odd couple of power and anxiety. In R. Sorrentino & E. Higgins (Vol. Eds.), *Handbook of motivation and cognition: Vol. 3. The interpersonal context* (pp. 322–346). New York: Guilford.

Fiske, S., & Neuberg, S. (1990). A continuum of impression formation, from category-based to individuating processes: Influences of information and motivation on attention and interpretation. In M. Zanna (Ed.), *Advances in experimental social psychology* (Vol. 23, pp. 1–74). New York: Academic Press.

Fiske, S., & Van Hendy, H. (1992). Personality feedback and situational norms can control stereotyping processes. *Journal of Personality and Social Psychology, 62,* 577–596.

Fowers, B., & Richardson, F. (1996). Why is multiculturalism good? *American Psychologist, 51,* 609–621.

Fox, R. (1992). Prejudice and the unfinished mind: A new look at an old failing. *Psychological Inquiry, 3,* 137–152.

Froming, W., Nasby, W., & McManus, J. (1998). Prosocial self-schemas, self-awareness, and children's prosocial behavior. *Journal of Personality and Social Psychology, 75*(3), 766–777.

Gaertner, S., & Dovidio, J. (1986). The aversive form of racism. In J. Dovidio & S. Gaertner (Eds.), *Prejudice, discrimination, and racism* (pp. 61–89). New York: Academic Press.

Gaertner, S., Dovidio, J., Anastasio, P., Bachman, B., & Rust, M. (1993). The common ingroup identity model: Recategorization and the reduction of intergroup bias. In W. Stroebe & M. Hewstone (Eds.), *European review of social psychology* (Vol. 4, pp. 1–26). Chichester, England: Wiley.

Georgesen, J., & Harris, M. (1998). Why's my boss always holding me down? A meta-analysis of power effects on performance evaluations. *Personality and Social Psychology Review, 2*(3), 184–195.

Gerard, H., & Hoyt, M. (1974). Distinctiveness of social categorization and attitude toward ingroup members. *Journal of Personality and Social Psychology, 27,* 836–842.

Gerard, H., & Miller, N. (1975). *School desegregation.* New York: Plenum Press.

Gilbert, P. (1992). *Depression: The evolution of powerlessness.* New York: Guilford.

Giles, M., & Hertz, K. (1994). Racial threat and partisan identification. *American Political Science Review, 88,* 317–326.

Glasser, W. (1984). *Control theory.* New York: Harper & Row.

Goffman, E. (1993). *Stigma: Notes on the management of spoiled identity.* Englewood Cliffs, NJ: Prentice-Hall.

Graham, S. (1991). A review of attribution theory in achievement contexts. *Educational Psychology Review, 3,* 5–39.

Gray, J., & Thompson, A. (1953). The ethnic prejudices of white and Negro college students. *Journal of Abnormal and Social Psychology, 48,* 311–313.

Greenberg, J., & Pyszczynski, T. (1986). Persistent high self-focus after failure and low self-focus after success: The depressive self-focusing style. *Journal of Personality and Social Psychology, 50,* 1039–1044.

Gundlach, R. (1950). The effect of on-the-job experience with Negroes upon social attitudes of white workers in union shops. *American Psychologist, 5,* 300.

Hamilton, D. (1979). A cognitive-attributional analysis of stereotyping. In L. Berkowitz (Ed.), *Advances in experimental social psychology* (Vol. 12, pp. 53–84). New York: Academic Press.

Hamilton, D., & Sherman, J. (1994). Stereotypes. In R. Wyer, Jr. & T. Srull (Eds.), *Handbook of social cognition* (2nd ed., Vol. 2, pp. 1–68). Hillsdale, NJ: Erlbaum.

Hamilton, D., & Sherman, J. (1996). Perceiving person and groups. *Psychological Review, 103,* 336–355.

Hamilton, D., Sherman, S., & Ruvolo, C. (1990). Stereotype-based expectancies: Effects on information processing and social behavior. *Journal of Personality and Social Psychology, 46,* 35–60.

Hamilton, W. (1964). The genetical evolution of social behavior. *Journal of Theoretical Biology, 7,* 1–32.

Hammond, K. (1965). New directions in research on conflict resolution. *Journal of Social Issues, 11,* 44–66.

Hardin, C., & Higgins, E. (1996). Shared reality: How social verification makes the subjective objective. In R. Sorrentino & E. Higgins (Eds.), *Handbook of motivation and cognition: The interpersonal context* (Vol. 3, pp. 28–84). New York: Guilford.

Harding, J., & Hogerge, R. (1952). Attitudes of white department store employees toward Negro co-workers. *Journal of Social Issues, 8,* 18–28.

Harlan, H. (1942). Some factors affecting attitude toward Jews. *American Sociological Review, 7,* 816–827.

Harris, M. (1993). Issues in studying the mediation of expectancy effects: A taxonomy of expectancy situations. In P. Blanck (Ed.), *Interpersonal expectations: Theory, research, and application* (pp. 350–378). Paris: Cambridge University Press.

Harris, M., & Rosenthal, R. (1985). Mediation of the interpersonal expectancy effect: 31 meta-analyses. *Psychological Bulletin, 97,* 363–386.

Harris, M., & Rosenthal, R. (1986). Four factors in the mediation of teacher expectancy effects. In R. Feldman (Ed.), *The social psychology of education: Currrent research and theory* (pp. 91–131). New York: Cambridge University Press.

Harris, M., & Schaubroeck. J. (1988). A meta-analysis of self-supervisor, self-peer, and peer-supervisor ratings. *Personnel Psychology, 41,* 43–62.

Hastorf, A., Northcraft, G., & Picciotot, S. (1979). Helping the handicapped: How realistic is the performance feedback? *Personality and Social Psychology Bulletin, 5,* 373–376.

Haunschild, P., Moreland, R., & Murrell, A. (1994). Sources of resistance to mergers between groups. *Journal of Applied Social Psychology, 24,* 1150–1178.

Heider, F. (1958). *The psychology of interpersonal relations.* New York: Wiley.

Herek, G., & Capitanio, J. (1996). "Some of my best friends": Intergroup contact, concealable stigma, and heterosexuals' attitudes toward gay men and lesbians. *Personality and Social Psychology Bulletin, 22,* 412–424.

Hesse, B., Werner, C., & Altman, I. (1988). Temporal aspects of computer-mediated communication. *Computers in Human Relations, 4,* 147–165.

Hewstone, M., & Brown, R. (Eds.). (1986). *Contact and conflict in intergroup relations.* Oxford, England: Basil Blackwell.

Hewstone, M., & Brown, R. (1986). Contact is not enough: An intergroup perspective on the "contact hypothesis." In M. Hewstone & R. Brown (Eds.), *Contact and conflict in intergroup encounters* (pp. 1–44). Oxford, England: Basil Blackwell.

Hoffman, L., Harburg, E., & Maier, N. (1962). Differences in disagreements as factors in creative problem solving. *Journal of Abnormal and Social Psychology, 64,* 206–214.

Hofstede, G. (1980). *Culture's consequences.* Beverly Hills, CA: Sage.

Hogg, M., & Abrams, D. (1993). Towards a single process uncertainty–reduction model of social motivation in groups. In M. Hogg & D. Abrams (Eds.), *Group motivation* (pp. 173–190). New York: Harvester Wheatsheaf.

Hong, O., & Harrod, W. (1988). The role of reasons in the ingroup bias phenomenon. *European Journal of Social Psychology, 18,* 537–545.

Hornstein, H., & Johnson, D. W. (1966). The effects of process analysis and ties to his group upon the negotiator's attitudes toward the outcomes of negotiations. *Journal of Applied Behavioral Science, 2,* 449–465.

Horowitz, E. (1936). The development of attitude toward the Negro. *Archives of Psychology,* (Monograph No. 194).

Hovland, C., & Sears, R. (1940). Minor studies of aggression: Correlation of lynchings with economic indices. *Journal of Psychology, 9,* 301–310.

Howard, J., & Rothbart, M. (1980). Social categorization and memory for in-group and out-group behavior. *Journal of Personality and Social Psychology, 38,* 301–310.

Hunt, J. (1964). Introduction: Revisiting Montessori. In M. Montessori (Ed.), *The Montessori method* (pp. i–viii). New York: Shocken Books.

Hunter, J., Platow, M., Howard, M., & Stringer, M. (1996). Social identity and intergroup evaluation bias: Realistic categories and domain-specific self-esteem in a conflict setting. *European Journal of Social Psychology, 26,* 631–647.

Irish, D. (1952). Reactions of Caucasian residents to Japanese-American neighbors. *Journal of Social Issues, 8,* 10–17.

Islam, M., & Hewstone, M. (1993). Intergroup attributions and affective consequences in majority and minority groups. *Journal of Personality and Social Psychology, 64,* 936–950.

Jackman, M., & Crane, M. (1986). "Some of my best friends are black…" Interracial friendship and whites' racial attitudes. *Public Opinion Quarterly, 50,* 459–486.

Jackson, S. (1992). Team composition in organizational settings: Issues in managing an increasingly diverse work force. In S. Worchel, W. Wood, & J. Simpson (Eds.), *Group process and productivity* (pp. 138–173). Newbury Park, CA: Sage.

Jackson, S., Brett, J., Sessa, V., Cooper, D., Julin, J., & Peyronnin, K. (1991). Some differences make a difference: Interpersonal dissimilarity and group heterogeneity as correlates of recruitment, promotion, and turnover. *Journal of Applied Psychology, 76,* 675–689.

Jahoda, M., & West, P. (1951). Race relations in public housing. *Journal of Social Issues, 7,* 132–139.

James, W. (1981). *Principles of behavior* (Vol. 1). New York: Dover. (Original work published 1890).

Janis, I. (1982). *Groupthink: Psychological studies of policy decisions and fiascoes.* Boston: Houghton-Mifflin.

Janis, I., & Mann, L. (1965). Effectiveness of emotional role-playing in modifying smoking habits and attitudes. *Journal of Experimental Research in Personality, 1,* 84–90.

Janz, T., & Tjosvold, D. (1985). Cost effective vs. ineffective work relationships. *Canadian Journal of Administrative Sciences, 2,* 43–51.

Jefferson, T. (1818). Letter to Thomas Cooper.

Johnson, D., & Rusbult, C. (1989). Resisting temptation: Devaluation of alternative partners as a means of maintaining commitment in close relationships. *Journal of Personality and Social Psychology, 57,* 967–980.

Johnson, D. W. (1966a). Freedom school effectiveness: Changes in attitudes of Negro children. *Journal of Applied Behavioral Science, 2,* 325–331.

Johnson, D. W. (1966b). Racial attitudes of Negro Freedom School participants and Negro and white civil rights participants. *Social Forces, 45,* 266–274.

Johnson, D. W. (1966c). The use of role reversal in intergroup competition. *Dissertation Abstracts, 27*(9-A), 3121.

Johnson, D. W. (1967). Use of role reversal in intergroup competition. *Journal of Personality and Social Psychology, 7,* 135–141.

Johnson, D. W. (1970). *The social psychology of education.* New York: Holt, Rinehart & Winston.

Johnson, D. W. (1971). Role reversal: A summary and review of the research. *International Journal of Group Tensions, 1,* 318–334.

Johnson, D. W. (1972). *Reaching out.* Boston: Allyn & Bacon.

Johnson, D. W. (1974). Communication and the inducement of cooperative behavior in conflicts. *Speech Monographs, 41,* 64–78.

Johnson, D. W. (1979). *Educational psychology.* Englewood Cliffs, NJ: Prentice-Hall.

Johnson, D. W. (1980a). Group processes: Influences of student–student interactions on school outcomes. In J. McMillan (Ed.), *Social psychology of school learning.* New York: Academic Press.

Johnson, D. W. (1980b). Constructive peer relationships, social development, and cooperative learning experiences: Implications for the prevention of drug abuse. *Journal of Drug Education, 10,* 7–24.

Johnson, D. W. (2000). *Reaching out: Interpersonal effectiveness and self-acutalization* (6th ed.). Englewood Cliffs, NJ: Prentice-Hall.

Johnson, D. W., & Allen, S. (1972). Deviation from organizational norms concerning the relations between status and power. *Sociological Quarterly, 13,* 174–182.

Johnson, D. W., & Johnson, F. (1975). *Joining Together.* Boston: Allyn & Bacon.

Johnson D. W., & Johnson, F. (2000). *Joining together: Group theory and group skills* (6th ed.). Englewood Cliffs, NJ: Prentice-Hall.

Johnson, D. W., Johnson, F., & Johnson, R. (1976). Promoting constructive conflict in the classroom. *Notre Dame Journal of Education, 7,* 163–168.

Johnson, D. W., & Johnson, R. (1979). Conflict in the classroom: Controversy and learning. *Review of Educational Research, 49,* 51–61.

Johnson, D. W., & Johnson, R. (1980). Integrating handicapped students into the mainstream. *Exceptional Children, 46,* 89–98.

Johnson, D. W., & Johnson, R. (1981). Effects of cooperative and individualistic learning experiences on interethnic interaction. *Journal of Educational Psychology, 73,* 454–459.

Johnson, D. W., & Johnson, R. (1982). Effects of cooperative, competitive, and individualistic learning experiences on cross-ethnic interaction and friendships. *Journal of Social Psychology, 118,* 47–58.

Johnson, D. W., & Johnson, R. (1985). Relationships between black and white students in intergroup cooperation and competition. *Journal of Social Psychology, 125,* 421–428.

Johnson, D. W., & Johnson, R. (1989). *Cooperation and competition: Theory and research*. Edina, MN: Interaction Book Company.

Johnson, D. W., & Johnson, R. (1992). Positive interdependence: Key to effective cooperation. In R. Hertz-Lazarowitz & N. Miller (Ed.), *Interaction in cooperative groups: The theoretical anatomy of group learning* (pp. 174–199). Cambridge, England: Cambridge University Press.

Johnson, D. W., & Johnson, R. (1992). Cooperative learning in the culturally diverse classroom. In R. DeVillar, C. Faltis, & J. Cummins (Eds.), *Successful cultural diversity: Classroom practices for the 21st century* (pp. 57–73). Albany: State University of New York Press.

Johnson, D. W., & Johnson, R. (1994a). *Leading the cooperative school* (2nd ed.). Edina, MN: Interaction Book Company.

Johnson, D. W., & Johnson, R. (1994b). Cooperative learning and American values. *The Cooperative Link, 9*(3), 3–4.

Johnson, D. W., & Johnson, R. (1995a). *Teaching students to be peacemakers*. Edina, MN: Interaction Book Company.

Johnson, D. W., & Johnson, R. (1995b). *My mediation notebook* (3rd ed.). Edina, MN: Interaction Book Company.

Johnson, D. W., & Johnson, R. (1995c). *Creative controversy: Intellectual challenge in the classroom*. Edina, MN: Interaction Book Company.

Johnson, D. W., & Johnson, R. (1995d). Teaching students to be peacemakers: Results of five years of research. *Peace and Conflict: Journal of Peace Psychology, 1*(4), 417–438.

Johnson, D. W., & Johnson, R. (1996a). Conflict resolution and peer mediation programs in elementary and secondary schools: A review of the research. *Review of Educational Research, 66*(4), 459–506.

Johnson, D. W., & Johnson, R. (1996b). Cooperative learning and traditional American values. *NASSP Bulletin, 80*(579), 11–18.

Johnson, D. W., & Johnson, R. (1996c). *Meaningful and manageable assessment through cooperative learning*. Edina, MN: Interaction Book Company.

Johnson, D. W., & Johnson, R. (1997). *Learning to lead teams: Developing leadership skills*. Edina, MN: Interaction Book Company.

Johnson, D. W., & Johnson, R. (1999). The three Cs of school and classroom management. In H. Freiberg (Ed.), *Beyond behaviorism: Changing the classroom management paradigm* (pp. 119–144). Boston: Allyn & Bacon.

Johnson, D. W., & Johnson, R. (2000). Cooperative learning, values, and culturally plural classrooms. In M. Leicester, C. Modgill, & S. Modgil (Eds.). *Values, the classroom, and cultural diversity* (pp. 89–110). London: Cassell PLC.

Johnson, D. W., & Johnson, R. (2000, June). *Teaching students to be peacemakers: A meta-analysis*. Paper presented at the Society for Psychological Study of Social Issues Convention, Minneapolis

Johnson, D. W., Johnson, R., & Holubec, E. (1994). *The nuts and bolts of cooperative learning*. Edina, MN: Interaction Book Company.

Johnson, D. W., Johnson, R., & Holubec, E. (1998a). *Cooperation in the classroom* (6th ed.). Edina, MN: Interaction Book Company.

Johnson, D. W., Johnson, R., & Holubec, E. (1998b). *Advanced cooperative learning* (3rd ed.). Edina, MN: Interaction Book Company.

Johnson, D. W., Johnson, R., & Maruyama, G. (1983). Interdependence and interpersonal attraction among heterogeneous and homogeneous individuals: A theoretical formulation and a meta-analysis of the research. *Review of Educational Research, 53*, 5–54.

Johnson, D. W., Johnson, R., & Maruyama, G. (1984). Goal interdependence and interpersonal attraction among members of different ethnic groups and between handicapped and nonhandicapped individuals: A meta-analysis. In N. Miller & M. Brewer (Eds.), *Groups in contact: The psychology of desegregation* (pp. 187–212). New York: Academic Press.

Johnson, D. W., Johnson, R., & Smith, K. (1986). Academic conflict among students: Controversy and learning. In R. Feldman (Ed.), *Social psychological applications to education* (pp. 199–231). Cambridge, England: Cambridge University Press.

Johnson, D. W., Johnson, R., & Smith, K. (1989). Controversy within decision-making situations. In M. Rahim (Ed.), *Managing conflict: An interdisciplinary approach* (pp. 251–264). New York: Praeger.

Johnson, D. W., Johnson, R., & Smith, K. (1998). *Active learning: Cooperation in the college classroom* (2nd ed.). Edina, MN: Interaction Book Company.

Johnson, D. W., Johnson, R., Smith, K., & Tjosvold, D. (1990). Pro, con, and synthesis: Training managers to engage in constructive controversy. In B. Sheppard, M. Bazerman, & R. Lewicki, (Eds.), *Research on negotiation in organizations* (Vol. 2, pp. 135–170). Greenwich, CT: JAI Press.

Johnson, D. W., Johnson, R., & Tiffany, M. (1984). Structuring academic conflicts between majority and minority students: Hindrance or help to integration. *Contemporary Educational Psychology, 9*, 61–73.

Johnson, D. W., Johnson, R., Tiffany, M., & Zaidman, B. (1983). Are low achievers disliked in a cooperative situation? A test of rival theories in a mixed ethnic situation. *Contemporary Educational Psychology, 8*, 189–200.

Johnson, D. W., Johnson, R., Tiffany, M., & Zaidman, B. (1984). Cross-ethnic relationships: The impact of intergroup cooperation and intergroup competition. *Journal of Educational Research, 78*, 75–79.

Johnson, D. W., & Johnson, S. (1972). The effects of attitude similarity, expectation of goal facilitation, and actual goal facilitation on interpersonal attraction. *Journal of Experimental Social Psychology, 8*, 197–206.

Johnson, D. W., Maruyama, G., Johnson, R., Nelson, D., & Skon, L. (1981). Effects of cooperative, competitive, and individualistic goal structures on achievement: A meta-analysis. *Psychological Bulletin, 89*, 47–62.

Johnson, R., & Johnson, D. W. (1980). The social integration of handicapped students into the mainstream. In M. Reynolds (Ed.), *Social environment of the schools* (pp. 9–38). Reston, VA: Council for Exceptional Children.

Johnson, R., & Johnson, D. W. (1990). *Cooperative learning: Warm-ups, grouping strategies and group activities* (2nd ed.). Edina, MN: Interaction Book Company.

Johnson, S., & Johnson, D. W. (1972). The effects of other's actions, attitude similarity, and race on attraction towards the other. *Human Relations, 25*, 121–130.

Jones, E. (1990). *Interpersonal perception*. New York: Freeman.

Jones, E., & Gerard, H. (1967). *Foundations of social psychology*. New York: Wiley.

Jones, R. (1970). Learning and association in the presence of the blind. *The New Outlook*, 317–329.

Jussim, L. (1993). Accuracy of interpersonal expectations: A reflection–construction analysis of current and classic research. *Journal of Personality, 61*, 637–668.

Katz, D., & Braly, K. (1933). Racial stereotypes of 100 college students. *Journal of Abnormal and Social Psychology, 28,* 280–290.

Katz, I., & Hass, R. (1988). Racial ambivalence and American value conflict: Correlational and priming studies of dual cognitive structures. *Journal of Personality and Social Psychology, 55,* 893–905.

Katz, I., Wachenhut, J., & Hass, R. (1986). Racial ambivalence, value duality, and behavior. In J. Dovidio & S. Gaertner (Eds.), *Prejudice, discrimination, and racism* (pp. 35–60). New York: Academic Press.

Kelley, G. (1955). *The psychology of personal constructs.* New York: Norton.

Kelley, H. (1979). *Personal relationships: Their structures and processes.* Hillsdale, NJ: Erlbaum.

Kelley, J. (1955). Salience of membership and resistance to change of group-anchored attitudes. *Human Relations, 8,* 275–289.

Key, V. (1949). *Southern politics in state and nation.* New York: Knopf.

Kiesler, S., Siegel, J., & McGuire, T. (1984). Social psychological aspects of computer-mediated communication. *American Psychologist, 39,* 1123–1134.

Kihlstrom, J., & Klein, S. (1994). The self as a knowledge structure. In R. Wyer & T. Srull (Eds.), *Handbook of social cognition* (Vol. 1, pp. 153–208). Hillsdale, NJ: Jossey-Bass.

Kim, S., Smith, R., & Brigham, N. (1998). Effects of power imbalance and the presence of third parties on reactions to harm: Upward and downward revenge. *Personality and Social Psychology Bulletin, 24*(4), 353–361.

Kinder, D., & Mendelberg, T. (1995). Cracks in American apartheid: The political impact of prejudice among desegregated whites. *The Journal of Politics, 57,* 402–424.

Kipnis, D. (1972). Does power corrupt? *Journal of Personality and Social Psychology, 24,* 33–41.

Kipnis, D. (1994). Accounting for the use of behavior technologies in social psychology. *American Psychologist, 49,* 165–172.

Kipnis, D. (1997). Ghosts, taxonomies, and social psychology. *American Psychologist, 52*(3), 205–211.

Kipnis, D., Castell, P., Gergen, M., & Mauch, D. (1976). Metamorphic effects of power. *Journal of Applied Psychology, 61,* 127–135.

Kipnis, D., Schmidt, S., Prince K., & Stitt, C. (1981). Why do I like thee: Is it your performance or my orders? *Journal of Applied Psychology, 66,* 324–328.

Kleck, R. (1966). Emotional arousal in interaction with stigmatized persons. *Psychological Reports, 19,* 1226.

Kohlberg, L. (1969). Stage and sequence: The cognitive-developmental approach to socialization. In D. Goslin (Ed.), *Handbook of socialization theory and research* (pp. 347–480). Chicago: Rand McNally.

Kohn, A. (1997, February). How not to teach values. *Phi Delta Kappan,* 429–440.

Kouzes, J., & Posner, B. (1987). *The leadership challenge.* San Francisco: Jossey-Bass.

Kramer, G. (1951). *Residential contact as a determinant of attitudes toward Negroes.* Unpublished doctoral dissertation, Harvard University.

Kramer, R. (1996). Divergent realities and convergent disappointments in the hierarchic relation: Trust and the intuitive auditor at work. In R. Kramer & T. Tyler (Eds.), *Trust in organizations: Frontiers of theory and research* (pp. 216–245). Thousand Oaks, CA: Sage.

LaFromboise, T., Coleman, H., & Gerton, J. (1993). Psychological impact of biculturalism: Evidence and theory. *Psychological Bulletin, 114,* 395–412.

Lawler, E., & Yoon, J. (1993). Power and the emergence of commitment behavior in negotiated exchange. *American Sociological Review, 58,* 465–481.

Lemyre, L., & Smith, P. (1985). Intergroup discrimination and self-esteem in the minimal group paradigm. *Journal of Personality and Social Psychology, 49,* 660–670.

Lewin, K. (1947). Group decision and social change. In T. Newcomb & E. Hartley (Eds.), *Readings in social psychology* (pp. 330–344). New York: Holt.

Lindskold, S., & Aronoff, J. (1980). Conciliatory strategies and relative power. *Journal of Experimental Social Psychology, 16,* 187–196.

Lippmann, W. (1922). *Public opinion.* New York: Harcourt, Brace, Javanovich.

Lord, C., & Saenz, D. (1985). Memory deficits and memory surfeits: Differential cognitive consequences of tokenism for tokens and observers. *Journal of Personality and Social Psychology, 49,* 918–926.

Luft, J. (1969). *Of human interaction.* Palo Alto, CA: National Press.

MacKenzie, B. (1948). The importance of contact in determining attitudes toward Negroes. *Journal of Abnormal and Social Psychology, 43,* 417–441.

Madon, S., Jussim, L., Keiper, S., Eccles, J., Smith, A., & Palumbo, P. (1998). The accuracy and power of sex, social class, and ethnic stereotypes: A naturalistic study in person perception. *Personality and Social Psychology Bulletin, 24,* 1304–1318.

Maier, N. (1970). *Problem-solving and creativity in individuals and group.* Belmont, CA: Brooks/Cole.

Major, B., & Crocker, J. (1993). Social stigma: The affective consequences of attributional ambiguity. In D. Mackie & D. Hamilton (Eds.), *Affect, cognition, and stereotyping: Interactive processes in intergroup perception* (pp. 345–370). New York: Academic Press.

Major, B., Spencer, S., Schmader, T., Wolfe, C., & Crocker, J. (1998). Coping with negative stereotypes about intellectual performance: The role of psychological disengagement. *Personality and Social Psychology Bulletin, 24,* 34–50.

Mannheimer, D., & Williams, R. (1949). A note on Negro troops in combat. In S. Stouffer, E. Suchman, L. DeVinney, S. Star, & R. Williams (Eds.), *The American Soldier* (Vol. 1). Princeton, NJ: Princeton University Press.

Marcus-Newhall, A., Miller, N., Holtz, R., & Brewer, M. (1993). Cross-cutting category membership with role assignment: A means of reducing intergroup bias. *British Journal of Social Psychology, 32,* 124–146.

Markus, H., & Kitayama, S. (1991). Culture and the self: Implications for cognition, emotion, and motivation. *Psychological Review, 98,* 224–253.

Maruyama, G., Miller, N., & Holtz, R. (1986). The relation between popularity and achievement: A longitudinal test of the lateral transmission of value hypothesis. *Journal of Personality and Social Psychology, 51,* 730–741.

Marwell, G., & Schmidt, D. (1975). *Cooperation: An experimental analysis.* New York: Academic Press.

McCain, B., O'Reilly, C., & Pfeffer, J. (1983). The effects of departmental demography on turnover. *Academy of Management Journal, 26,* 626–641.

McClelland, D. (1961). *The achieving society.* Princeton, NJ: Van Nostrand.

McConahay, J. (1986). Modern racism, ambivalence, and the modern racism scale. In J. Dovidio & S. Gaertner (Eds.), *Prejudice, discrimination, and racism* (pp. 91–125). New York: Academic Press.

McConnell, A., Sherman, S., & Hamilton, D. (1994a). Illusory correlation in the perception of groups: An extension of the distinctiveness-based account. *Journal of Personality and Social Psychology, 67,* 414–429.

McConnell, A., Sherman, S., & Hamilton, D. (1994b). On-line and memory-based aspects of individual and group target judgments. *Journal of Personality and Social Psychology, 67,* 173–185.

McGrath, J. (1984). *Groups: Interaction and performance.* Englewood Cliffs, NJ: Prentice-Hall.

McGuire, W., McGuire, C., Child, P., & Fujioka, P. (1978). Salience of ethnicity in the spontaneous self-concept as a function of one's ethnic distinctiveness in the social environment. *Journal of Personality and Social Psychology, 36,* 511–520.

McGuire, W., McGuire, C., & Winton, W. (1979). Effects of household sex composition on the salience of one's gender in the spontaneous self-concept. *Journal of Experimental Social Psychology, 15,* 77–90.

McPartland, J. (1969). The relative influence of school and of classroom desegregation on the academic achievement of ninth grade Negro students. *Journal of Social Issues, 25,* 93–102.

Mead, G. (1934). *Mind, self, and society.* Chicago: University of Chicago Press.

Medin, D. (1988). Social categorization: Structures, processes, and purposes. In R. Wyer, Jr. & T. Srull (Eds.), *Handbook of social cognition* (2nd ed., Vol. 2, pp. 1–68). Hillsdale, NJ: Erlbaum.

Meer, B., & Freedman, E. (1966). The impact of Negro neighbors on White house owners. *Social Forces, 45,* 11–19.

Merton, R. (1948). The self-filling prophecy. *Antioch Review, 8,* 193–210.

Messe, L., Kerr, N., & Sattler, D. (1992). "But some animals are more equal than others": The supervisor as a privileged status in group contexts. In S. Worchel, W. Wood, & J. Simpson (Eds.), *Group process and productivity* (pp. 203–223). Newburn Park, CA: Sage.

Miller, G. (1988). *The meaning of general education.* New York: Wiley.

Miller, N., & Brewer, M. (Ed.). (1984). *Groups in contact: The psychology of desegregation.* New York: Academic Press.

Miller, N., Brewer, M., & Edwards, K. (1985). Cooperative interaction in desegregated settings: A laboratory analogue. *Journal of Social Issues, 41*(3), 63–79.

Miller, N., & Davidson-Podgorny, G. (1987). Theoretical models of intergroup relations and the use of cooperative teams as an intervention for desegregated settings. In C. Hendrick (Ed.), *Annual review of personality and social psychology: Group processes and intergroup relations* (Vol. 9, pp. 23–39). Newbury Park, CA: Sage.

Minard, R. (1952). Race relationships in the Pocahontas coal field. *Journal of Social Issues, 8,* 29–44.

Monteith, M. (1996a). Affective reactions to prejudice-related discrepant responses: The impact of standard salience. *Personality and Social Psychology Bulletin, 22,* 48–59.

Monteith, M. (1996b). Contemporary forms of prejudice-related conflict: In search of a nutshell. *Personality and Social Psychology Bulletin, 22,* 461–473.

Monteith, M., Devine, P., & Zuwerink, J. (1993). Self-directed versus other-directed affect as a consequence of prejudice-related discrepancies. *Journal of Personality and Social Psychology, 64,* 198–210.

Monteith, M., & Walters, G. (1998). Egalitarianism, moral obligation, and prejudice-related personal standards. *Personality and Social Psychology Bulletin, 24*(2), 186–199.

Montesquieu, C. (1748). *The spirit of laws.*

Moreno, J. (1953). *Who shall survive?* (2nd ed.). New York: Beacon House.

Moscovici, S. (1980). Toward a theory of conversion behavior. In L. Berkowitz (Ed.), *Advances in experimental social psychology* (Vol. 15, pp. 209–239). New York: Academic Press.

Moscovici, S. (1985a). Innovation and minority influence. In S. Moscovici, G. Mugny, & E. Van Avermaet (Eds.), *Perspectives on minority influence* (pp. 9–51). Cambridge, England: Cambridge University Press.

Moscovici, S. (1985b). Social influence and conformity. In G. Lindzey & E. Aronson, (Eds.), *The Handbook of Social Psychology* (3rd ed., Vol. 2, pp. 347–412). New York: Random House.

Mullen, B. (1983). Operationalizing the effect of the group on the individual: A self-attention perspective. *Journal of Experimental Social Psychology, 19,* 295–322.

Mullen, B., Brown, R., & Smith, C. (1992). Ingroup bias as a function of salience, relevance, and status: An integration. *European Journal of Social Psychology, 22,* 103–122.

Murnighan, J., & Pillutla, M. (1995). Fairness versus self-interest: Asymmetric moral imperatives in ultimatum bargaining. In R. Kramer & D. Messick (Eds.), *Negotiation as a social process* (pp. 240–267). Thousand Oaks, CA: Sage.

Mussen, P. (1953). Differences between the TAT responses of Negro and white boys. *Journal of Consulting Psychology, 17,* 373–376.

Myrdal, G. (1944). *An American dilemma.* New York: Harper & Row.

Nadler, D., Hackman, J., & Lawler, E. (1979). *Managing organizational behavior.* Boston: Little, Brown.

Neuberg, S., Smith, D., Hoffman, J., & Russell, F. (1994). When we observe stigmatized and "normal" individuals interacting: Stigma by association. *Personality and Social Psychology Bulletin, 20,* 196–209.

Newcomb, T. (1956). The prediction of interpersonal attraction. *American Psychologist, 11,* 575–586.

Newcomb, T. (1961). *The acquaintance process.* New York: Holt, Rinehart, & Winston.

Nijhof, W., & Kommers, P. (1982, July). *Analysis of cooperation in relation to cognitive controversy.* Paper presented at International Conference on Cooperation in Education, Provo, UT.

Noel, J., Wann, D., & Branscombe, N. (1995). Peripheral ingroup membership status and public negativity toward outgroups. *Journal of Personality and Social Psychology, 68,* 127–137.

Oakes, P. (1987). The salience of social categories. In J. Turner, M. Hogg, P. Oakes, S. Reicher, & M. Wetherell (Eds.), *Rediscovering the social group: A self-categorization theory* (pp. 117–141). Oxford, England: Basil Blackwell.

Oakes, P., & Turner, J. (1980). Social categorization and intergroup behavior: Does minimal intergroup discrimination make social identity more positive? *European Journal of Social Psychology, 10,* 295–301.

Oakes, P., & Turner, J. (1986). Distinctiveness and the salience of social category memberships: Is there an automatic perceptual bias toward novelty? *European Journal of Social Psychology, 16,* 325–344.

Oakes, P., Turner, J., & Haslam, S. (1991). Perceiving people as group members: The role of fit in the salience of social categorizations. *British Journal of Social Psychology, 30,* 125–144.

Ohbuchi, K., & Saito, M. (1986). Power imbalance, its legitimacy, and aggression. *Aggressive Behavior, 12,* 33–40.

O'Reilly, C., Caldwell, D., & Barnett, W. (1989). Work group demography, social integration, and turnover. *Administrative Science Quarterly, 34,* 21–37.

Osborne, J. (1995). Academics, self-esteem, and race: A look at the underlying assumptions of the disidentification hypothesis. *Personality and Social Psychology Bulletin, 21,* 449–455.

Oyserman, D. (1993). The lens of personhood: Viewing the self and others in a multiculural society. *Journal of Personality and Social Psychology, 65,* 993–1009.

Padilla, A. (1994). Bicultural development: A theoretical and empirical examination. In R. Malgady & O. Rodriguez (Eds.), *Theoretical and conceptual issues in Hispanic mental health* (pp. 20–51). Malabar, FL: Krieger.

Palmer, P. (1990). Good teaching: A matter of living the mystery. *Change, 22* (1, January/February), 11–16.

Palmer, P. (1991). The courage to teach. *National Teaching and Learning Forum, 1*(2), 1–3.

Palmer, P. (1992). Divided no more. *Change* (March/April), 11–17.

Pascarella, E., Smart, J., Ethington, C., & Nettles, M. (1987). The influence of college on self-concept: A consideration of race and gender differences. *American Educational Research Journal, 24,* 49–77.

Pearce, D., Crain, R., & Farley, R. (1984, April). *Lessons not lost: The effect of school desegregation on the role of residential desegregation in large center cities.* Paper presented at the annual meeting of the American Educational Research Association, New Orleans, LA.

Perdue, C., Dovidio. J., Gurtman, M., & Tyler, R. (1990). Us and them: Social categorization and the process of intergroup bias. *Journal of Personality and Social Psychology, 59,* 475–486.

Perls, F. (1973). *The Gestalt approach and eyewitness to therapy.* Ben Lomond, CA: Science and Behavior Books.

Peterson, B., Doty, R., & Winter, D. (1993). Authoritarianism and attitudes toward contemporary social issues. *Personality and Social Psychology Bulletin, 19,* 174–184.

Pettigrew, T. (1958). Personality and sociocultural factors in intergroup attitudes: A cross-national comparison. *Conflict Resolution, 2,* 29–42.

Pettigrew, T. (1969). Gordon Willard Allport: 1897–1967. *Journal of Personality and Social Psychology, 12,* 1–5.

Pettigrew, T. (1973). Racism and the mental health of white Americans: A social psychological view. In C. Willie, B. Kramer, & B. Brown (Eds.), *Racism and mental health* (pp. 269–298). Pittsburgh: University of Pittsburgh Press.

Pettigrew, T. (1975). The racial integration of the schools. In T. Pettigrew (Ed.), *Racial discrimination of the United States* (pp. 224–239). New York: Harper & Row.

Pettigrew, T. (1979). The ultimate attribution error: Extending Allport's cognitive analysis of prejudice. *Personality and Social Psychology Bulletin, 5,* 461–476.

Pettigrew, T. (1997). Generalized intergroup contact effects on prejudice. *Personality and Social Psychology Bulletin, 23*(2), 173–185.

Pettigrew, T. (1998). Intergroup contact theory. *Annual Review of Psychology, 49,* 65–85.

Pettigrew, T., & Meertens, R. (1995). Subtle and blatant prejudice in Western Europe. *European Journal of Social Psychology, 25,* 57–75.

Phinney, J., & Devich-Navarro, M. (1997). Variations in bicultural identification among African American and Mexican American adolescents. *Journal of Research on Adolescence, 7,* 3–32.

Piaget, J. (1948). *The moral judgment of the child* (2nd ed.). Glencoe, IL: Free Press.

Piaget, J. (1950). *The psychology of intelligence.* New York: Harcourt.

Pratto, F., & John, O. (1991). Automatic vigilance: The attention-grabbing power of negative social information. *Journal of Personality and Social Psychology, 61,* 380–391.

Pruitt, D. (1981). *Negotiation behavior.* New York: Academic Press.

Rawls, J. (1971). *A theory of justice.* Cambridge, MA: Harvard University Press.

Reed, B. (1947). Accommodation between Negro and white employees in a west coast aircraft industry, 1942–1944. *Social Forces, 26,* 76–84.

Reich, M. (1971). The economics of racism. In D. Gordon (Ed.), *Problems in political economy* (pp. 107–113). Lexington, MA: Heath.

Riesman, D. (1950). *The lonely crowd.* New Haven, CT: Yale University Press.

Rogers, M., Hennigan, K., Bosman, C., & Miller, N. (1984). Intergroup acceptance in classroom and playground settings. In N. Miller & M. Brewer (Eds.), *Groups in contact: The psychology of desegregation* (pp. 187–212). Orlando, FL: Academic Press.

Rokeach, M. (1960). *The open and closed mind.* New York: Basic Books.

Rose, A. (1948). Race relations in a Chicago industry. In M. Rose (Ed.), *Studies in the reduction of prejudice.* Chicago: American Council on Race Relations.

Rosenberg, N., & Simmons, R. (1971). *Black and white self-esteem: The urban school child.* Washington, DC: American Sociological Associations.

Rosenblith, J. (1949). A replication of "some roots of prejudice." *Journal of Abnormal and Social Psychology, 44,* 470–489.

Rosenthal, R. (1973). The mediation of Pygmalion effects: A four factor theory. *Papua New Guinea Journal of Education, 9,* 1–12.

Rosenthal, R., & Jacobson, D. (1968). *Pygmalion in the classroom.* New York: Holt, Rinehart, & Winston.

Rosenthal, R., & Rubin, D. (1978). Interpersonal expectancy effects: The first 345 studies. *Behavioral and Brain Sciences, 1,* 377–415.

Rossell, C. (1990). *The carrot or the stick for school desegregation policy: Magnet schools or forced busing.* Philadelphia: Temple University Press.

Rothbart, M., Evans, M., & Fulero, S. (1979). Recall for confirming events: Memory processes and the maintenance of social stereotypes. *Journal of Experimental Social Psychology, 15,* 343–355.

Rusbult, C. (1980). Commitment and satisfaction in romantic associations: A test of the investment model. *Journal of Experimental Social Psychology, 16,* 172–186.

Rusbult, C. (1983). A longitudinal test of the investment model: The development (and deterioration) of satisfaction and commitment in heterosexual involvements. *Journal of Personality and Social Psychology, 45,* 101–117.

Rusbult, C., Bissonnette, V., Arriaga, X., & Cox, C. (in press). Accommodation processes during the early years of marriage. In T. Bradbury (Ed.), *The developmental course of marital dysfunction.* New York: Cambridge University Press.

Rusbult, C., & Buunk, B. (1993). Commitment processes in close relationships: An interdependence analysis. *Journal of Social and Personal Relationships, 10,* 175–204.

Rusbult, C., Johnson, D., & Morrow, G. (1986). Impact of couple patterns of problem solving on distress and nondistress in dating relationships. *Journal of Personality and Social Psychology, 50,* 744–753.

Rusbult, C., Van Lange, P., Berette, J., Yovetich, N., & Wildschut, K. (1997). *A functional analysis of perceived superiority in close relationships.* Unpublished manuscript, University of North Carolina at Chapel Hill.

Rusbult, C., Verette, J., Whitney, G., Slovik, L., & Lipkus, I. (1991). Accommodation processes in close relationships: Theory and preliminary empirical evidence. *Journal of Personality and Social Psychology, 60,* 53–78.

Rusbult, C., Yovetich, N., & Verette, J. (1996). An interdependence analysis of accommodation processes. In G. Fletcher & J. Fitness (Eds.), *Knowledge structures in close relationships: A social psychological approach* (pp. 63–90). Mahwah, NJ: Erlbaum.

Ryan, K. (1988). Teacher education and moral education. *Journal of Teacher Education, 39*(4), 18–23.

Sachdev, I., & Bourhis, R. (1984). Minimal majorities and minorities. *European Journal of Social Psychology, 14,* 35–52.

Sachdev, I., & Bourhis, R. (1991). Power and status differentials in minority and majority group relations. *European Journal of Social Psychology, 21,* 1–24.

Saenz, D. (1994). Token status and problem-solving deficits: Detrimental effects of distinctiveness and performance monitoring. *Social Cognition, 12,* 61–74.

St. John, N. (1975). *School desegregation.* New York: Wiley.

Schmidt, W. (1974). Conflict: A powerful process for (good and bad) change. *Management Review, 63,* 4–10.

Schneider, J. (1990). Research, meta-analysis, and desegregation policy. In K. Wachter & M. Straf (Eds.), *The future of meta-analysis* (pp. 55–60). New York: Russell Sage Foundation.

Schofield, J. (1978). School desegregation and intergroup relations. In D. Bar-Tal & L. Saxe (Eds.), *Social psychology of education: Theory and research.* New York: Wiley.

Schofield, J. (1986). *Black-White contact in desegregated schools.* Pittsburgh: University of Pittsburgh, Learning Research and Development Center.

Schofeld, J. (1997). School desegregation 40 years after *Brown v. Board of Education:* Looking forward and looking backward. In D. Johnson (Ed.), *Minorities and girls in school: Effects on achievement and performance* (pp. 1–36). Thousand Oaks, CA: Sage.

Schofield, J., & Sagar, H. (1977). Peer interaction patterns in an integrated middle school. *Sociometry, 40*(2), 130–138.

Schopler, J., & Insko, C. (1992). The discontinuity effect in interpersonal and intergroup relations: Generality and mediation. In W. Stoebe & M. Mewstone (Eds.), *European review of social psychology* (Vol. 3, pp. 121–151). Chichester, England: Wiley.

Schweiger, D., Sandberg, W., & Rechner, P. (1989). Experiential effects of dialectical inquiry, devil's advocacy, and consensus approaches to strategic decision making. *Academy of Management Journal, 32,* 722–745.

Schwenk, C. (1983). Laboratory research on ill-structured decision aids: The case of dialectical inquiry. *Decision Sciences, 14,* 140–144.

Scott, R. (1979, July). *National comparisons of racial attitudes of segregated and desegregated students.* Johns Hopkins University, Center for Social Organizations of Schools, Report #279.

Sears, D. (1983). The person–positivity bias. *Journal of Personality and Social Psychology, 44,* 233–250.

Seelye, H., & Wasilewski, J. (1996). *Between cultures: Developing self-identity in a world of diversity.* Lincolnwood, IL: NTC Publishing.

Seligman, M. (1975). *On depression, development, and death.* San Francisco: Freeman.

Sells, S. (1964). Towards a taxonomy of organizations. In W. Leavitt & M. Shelley (Eds.), *New perspectives in organizational research* (pp. 515–532). New York: Wiley.

Shah, J., Kruglanski, A., & Thompson, E. (1998). Membership has its (epistemic) rewards: Need for closure effects on in-group bias. *Journal of Personality and Social Psychology, 75*(2), 383–393.

Shaw, M. (1973). Changes in sociometric choices following forced integration of an elementary school. *Journal of Social Issues, 29,* 143–159.

Sheets, T., & Bushardt, S. (1994). Effects of the applicant's gender appropriateness and qualifications and rater self-monitoring propensities on hiring decisions. *Public Personnel Management, 23,* 373–382.

Sherif, M. (1936). *The psychology of social norms.* New York: Harper.

Sherif, M. (1966). *In common predicament.* Boston: Houghton Mifflin.

Sherif, M., Harvey, O., White, J., Hood, W., & Sherif, C. (1961). *Intergroup conflict and cooperation: The robbers cave experiment.* Norman: University of Oklahoma Institute of Intergroup Relations.

Sherman, J. (1996). Development and mental representation of stereotypes. *Journal of Personality and Social Psychology, 70,* 1126–1141.

Sherman, J., Lee, A., Bessenoff, G., & Frost, L. (1998). Stereotype efficiency reconsidered: Encoding flexibility under cognitive load. *Journal of Personality and Social Psychology, 75*(3), 589–606.

Shinagawa, L. (1997). *Atlas of American diversity.* Thousand Oaks, CA: Sage.

Shore, B. (1996). *Culture in mind: Cognition, culture, and the problem of meaning.* New York: Oxford University Press.

Sidanius, J. (1993). The psychology of group conflict and dynamics of oppression: A social dominance perspective. In S. Iyengar & W. McGuire (Eds.), *Explorations in political psychology* (pp. 183–219). Durham, NC: Duke University Press.

Sigelman, C., Howell, J., Cornell, D., Cutright, J., & Dewey, J. (1991). Courtesy stigma: The social implications of associating with a gay person. *Journal of Social Psychology, 131,* 45–56.

Sigelman, L., & Welch, S. (1993). The contact hypothesis revisited: Black–White interaction and positive racial attitudes. *Social Forces, 71,* 781–795.

Simmel, G. (1955). *Conflict.* New York: Free Press.

Singelis, T. (1994). The measurement of independent and interdependent self-construals. *Personality and Social Psychology Bulletin, 20,* 580–591.

Singh, R., Choo, W., & Poh, L. (1998). In-group bias and fair-mindedness as strategies of self-presentation in intergroup perception. *Personality and Social Psychology Bulletin, 24*(2), 147–162.

Singleton, L. (1974). *The effects of sex and race in children's sociometric choices for play and work.* Urbana: University of Illinois. (ERIC Document Reproduction No. ED 100 520).

Sirota, A., Alpher, S., & Pfau, S. (1989). *Report to respondents: Survey of views toward human resources policies and practices.* New York: Author.

Smith, F. (1943). *An experiment in modifying attitudes toward the Negro* (Teachers College Contributions to Education, 887). New York: Columbia University.

Smith, P., & Bond, M. (1993). *Social psychology across cultures.* Boston: Allyn & Bacon.

Sniderman, P., & Piazza, T. (1993). *The scar of race.* Cambridge, MA: Harvard University Press.

Snow, M. (1997, March 6). Mindworks: Disbehavior. *Minneapolis Tribune,* Section E, 1–2, 14.

Snyder, C., Lassegard, M., & Ford, C. (1986). Distancing after group success and failure: Basking in reflected glory and cutting off reflected failure. *Journal of Personality and Social Psychology, 51,* 382–388.

Snyder, M. (1974). Self-monitoring of expressive behavior. *Journal of Personality and Social Psychology, 30,* 526–537.

Spencer, S., Fein, S., Wolfe, C., Fong, C., & Dunn, M. (1998). Automatic activation of stereotypes: The role of self-image threat. *Personality and Social Psychology Bulletin, 24*(11), 1139–1152.

Spencer, S., Steele, C., & Quinn, D. (in press). Stereotype threat and women's math performance. *Journal of Experimental Social Psychology.*

Star, S., Williams, R., & Stouffer, S. (1965). Negro infantry platoons in white companies. In H. Proshansky & B. Seidenberg (Eds.), *Basic studies in social psychology.* New York: Holt, Rinehart & Winston.

Steeh, C., & Schuman, H. (1991). Changes in racial attitudes among young white adults, 1984–1990. *American Journal of Sociology, 96,* 340–367.

Steele, C. (1992, April). Race and the schooling of Black Americans. *The Atlantic Monthly,* 68–78.

Steele, C., & Aronson, J. (1995). Stereotype threat and the intellectual test performance of African Americans. *Journal of Personality and Social Psychology, 69,* 797–811.

Stephan, W. (1978). School desegregation: An evaluation of predictions made in *Brown v. Board of Education. Psychological Bulletin, 85,* 217–238.

Stephan, W. (1986). The effects of school desegregation: An evaluation 30 years after *Brown.* In M. Saks & L. Saxe (Eds.), *Advances in applied social psychology* (Vol. 3, pp. 181–206). Hillsdale, NJ: Erlbaum.

Stephan, W. (1987). The contact hypothesis in intergroup relations. In C. Hendrick (Ed.), *Group processes and intergroup relations* (pp. 13–40). Beverly Hills, CA: Sage.

Stephan, W. (1991). School desegregation: Short-term and long-term effects. In H. Knopke, R. Norrell, & R. Rogers (Eds.), *Opening doors: Perspectives on race relations in contemporary America* (pp. 100–118). Tuscaloosa: University of Alabama Press.

Stephan, W. (1999). *Reducing prejudice and stereotyping in schools.* New York: Teachers College Press.

Stephan, W., & Rosenfield, D. (1978a). Effects of desegregation on racial attitudes. *Journal of Personality and Social Psychology, 36,* 795–804.

Stephan, W., & Rosenfield, D. (1978b). The effects of desegregation on racial relations and self-esteem. *Journal of Educational Psychology, 70,* 670–679.

Stephan, W., & Rosenfield, D. (1980). Racial and ethnic stereotypes. In A. Miller (Ed.), *In the eye of the beholder: Contemporary issues in stereotyping.* New York: Holt, Rinehart & Winston.

Stephan, W., & Stephan, C. (1985). Intergroup anxiety. *Journal of Social Issues, 41,* 157–176.

Stephan, W., & Stephan, C. (1996). *Intergroup relations.* Boulder, CO: Westview.

Stone, W. (1993). Psychodynamics, cognitive functioning, or group orientation: Research and theory in the 1980s. In W. Stone, G. Lederer, & R. Christie (Eds.), *Strength and weakness: The authoritarian personality today* (pp. 159–181). New York: Springer-Verlag.

Stotle, J. (1978). Power structure and personal competence. *Journal of Social Psychology, 38,* 72–83.

Stroh, L., Brett, J., & Reilly, A. (1992). All the right stuff: A comparison of female and male managers' career progression. *Journal of Applied Psychology, 77,* 251–260.

Sumner, W. (1906). *Folkways.* New York: Ginn.

Sutton-Smith, B. (1986). *Toys as culture.* New York: Gardner Press.

Swann, W. (1984). Quest for accuracy in person perception: A matter of pragmatics. *Psychological Review, 91,* 457–477.

Swim, K., Aikin, K., Hall, W., & Hunter, B. (1995). Sexism and racism: Old-fashioned and modern prejudices. *Journal of Personality and Social Psychology, 68,* 199–214.

Swim, K., Ferguson, M., & Hyers, L. (in press). Avoiding stigma by association: Subtle prejudice against lesbians in the form of social distancing. *Basic and Applied Social Psychology.*

Tajfel, H. (1969). Cognitive aspects of prejudice. *Journal of Social Issues, 25,* 79–87.

Tajfel, H. (1978). Social categorization, social identity, and social comparison. In H. Tajfel (Ed.), *Differentiation between social groups* (pp. 61–76). London: Academic Press.

Tajfel, H. (Ed.). (1982). *Social identity and intergroup relations.* Cambridge, England: Cambridge University Press.

Tajfel, H., Billig, M., Bundy, R., & Flament, C. (1971). Social categorization and intergroup behavior. *European Journal of Social Psychology, 1,* 149–178.

Tajfel, H., & Turner, J. (1979). *An integrative theory of intergroup conflict.* Monterey, CA: Brooks/Cole.

Tajfel, H., & Turner, J. (1986). The social identity theory of intergroup relation. In S. Worchel & W. Austin (Eds.), *Psychology of intergroup relations* (pp. 7–24). Chicago: Nelson-Hall.

Taylor, D. (1991). The social psychology of racial and cultural diversity: Issues of assimilation and multiculturalism. In A. Reynolds (Ed.), *Bilingualism, multiculturalism, and second language learning* (pp. 1–19). Hillsdale, NJ: Lawrence Erlbaum.

Taylor, D., & McKirnan, D. (1984). A five-stage model of intergroup relations. *British Journal of Social Psychology, 23,* 291–300.

Taylor, D., & Moghaddam, F. (1994). *Theories of intergroup relations: International social psychological perspectives* (2nd ed.). Westport, CT: Praeger.

Taylor, S. (1991). Asymmetrical effects of positive and negative events: The mobilization–minimization hypothesis. *Psychological Bulletin, 110,* 67–85.

Terborg, J., Castore, C., & DeNinno, J. (1976). A longitudinal field investigation of the impact of group composition on group performance and cohesion. *Journal of Personality and Social Psychology, 34,* 782–790.

Thomas, K., & Schmidt, W. (1976). A survey of managerial interests with respect to conflict. *Academy of Management Journal, 19,* 315–318.

Tjosvold, D. (1978). Alternative organizations for schools and classrooms. In D. Bar-Tal & L. Saxe (Eds.), *Social psychology of education: Theory & research* (pp. 275–298). Washington, DC: Hemisphere.

Tjosvold, D. (1986). *Working together to get things done.* Lexington, MA: D. C. Heath.

Tjosvold, D. (1991). *The conflict positive organization.* Reading, MA: Addison-Wesley.

Tjosvold, D., & Johnson, D. W. (Eds.). (1983). *Productive conflict management.* New York: Irvington.

Tjosvold, D., & Sagaria, D. (1978). Effects of relative power of cognitive perspective-taking. *Personality and Social Psychology Bulletin, 4,* 256–259.

Tocqueville, A. (1945). *Democracy in America* (Vol. 2). New York: Knopf.

Triandis, H. (1989). The self and social behavior in different cultural contexts. *Psychological Review, 96,* 506–520.

Triandis, H. (1994). *Culture and social behavior.* New York: McGraw-Hill.

Triplett, N. (1898). The dynamogenic factors in peacemaking and competition. *American Journal of Psychology, 9,* 507–533.

Trivers, R. (1971). The evolution of reciprocal altruism. *Quarterly Review of Biology, 46,* 35–57.

Trosset, C. (1998). Obstacles to open discussion and critical thinking: The Grinnel College study. *Change, 30*(5), 44–49.

Turner, J. (1982). Toward a cognitive redefinition of the social group. In H. Tajfel (Ed.), *Social identity and intergroup relations* (pp. 15–40). Cambridge, England: Cambridge University Press.

Turner, J. (1985). Social categorization and the self-concept: A social cognitive theory of group behavior. In E. Lawler (Ed.), *Advances in group processes* (Vol. 2, pp. 77–122). Greenwich, CT: JAI Press.

Turner, J. (1987). *Rediscovering the social group: A self-categorization theory.* Oxford, England: Basil Blackwell.

Turner, J., & Oakes, P. (1989). Self-categorization theory and social influence. In P. Paulus (Ed.), *Psychology of group influence* (2nd ed., pp. 233–275). Hillsdale, NJ: Erlbaum.

Turner, J., Sacdev, I., & Hogg, M. (1983). Social categorization, interpersonal attraction and group formation. *British Journal of Social Psychology, 22,* 227–239.

Turner, M., Pratkanis, A., Probasco, P., & Leve, C. (1992). Threat, cohesion, and group effectiveness: Testing a social identity maintenance perspective on groupthink. *Journal of Personality and Social Psychology, 63,* 781–796.

Tyler, T., Lind, E., Ohbuchi, K., Sugawara, I., & Huo, Y. (1998). Conflict with outsiders: Disputing within and across cultural boundaries. *Personality and Social Psychology Bulletin, 24*(2), 137–146.

Urban, L., & Miller, N. (in press). *A theoretical analysis of crossed categorization effects: A meta-analysis.* Manuscript submitted for publication.

Vanbeselaere, N. (1987). The effects of dichotomous and crossed social categorizations upon intergroup discrimination. *European Journal of Social Psychology, 17,* 143–156.

Vanbeselaere, N. (1991). The different effects of simple and crossed categorization: A result of the category differentiation process or of differential category salience? In W. Stroebe & M. Hewstone (Eds.), *European review of social psychology* (Vol. 2, pp. 143–156). Chichester, England: Wiley.

Van Lange, P., Rusbult, C., Drigotas, S., Arriaga, X., Witcher, B., & Cox, C. (1997). Willingness to sacrifice in close relationships. *Journal of Personality and Social Psychology, 72,* 1373–1395.

Vonk, R. (1993). The negativity effect in trait ratings and in open-ended descriptions of persons. *Personality and Social Psychology Bulletin, 19,* 269–278.

Wagner, U., Hewstone, M., & Machleit, U. (1989). Contact and prejudice between Germans and Turks. *Human Relations, 42,* 561–574.

Warring, D., Johnson, D. W., Maruyama, G., & Johnson, R. (1985). Impact of different types of cooperative learning on cross-ethnic and cross-sex relationships. *Journal of Educational Psychology, 77,* 53–59.

Watson, G. (1925). *The measurement of fair-mindedness.* New York: Teachers College, Columbia University, Bureau of Publications.

Watson, G. (1947). *Action for unity.* New York: Harper.

Watson, G., & Johnson, D. W. (1972). *Social psychology: Issues and insights* (2nd ed.). Philadelphia: Lippincott.

Weigel, R., & Howes, P. (1985). Conceptions of racial prejudice. *Journal of Social Issues, 41*(3), 117–138.

Weinstein, R., Soule, C., Collins, F., Cone, J., Melhorn, M., & Simantocci, K. (1991). Expectations and high school change: Teacher–researcher collaboration to prevent school failure. *American Journal of Community Psychology, 19,* 333–402.

Welch, F., & Light, A. (1987). *New evidence on school desegregation.* Washington, DC: U.S. Commission on Civil Rights.

Wells, A., & Crain, R. (1994). Perpetuation theory and the long-term effects of desegregation. *Review of Educational Research, 64,* 531–555.

Wilder, D. (1977). Perception of group, size of opposition, and social influence. *Journal of Experimental Social Psychology, 13,* 253–268.

Wilder, D. (1978a). Perceiving persons as a group: Effects on attributions of causality and beliefs. *Social Psychology, 41,* 13–3

Wilder, D. (1978b). Reduction of intergroup discrimination through individuation of the out-group. *Journal of Personality and Social Psychology, 36,* 1361–1374.

Wilder, D. (1984). Intergroup contact: The typical member and exception to the rule. *Journal of Experimental Social Psychology, 20,* 177–194.

Wilder, D. (1993). Freezing intergroup evaluations: Anxiety and resistance to counterstereotypic information. In M. Hogg & D. Abrams (Eds.), *Group motivation: Social psychological perspectives* (pp. 68–86). London: Harvester Wheatsheaf.

Wilder, D., & Shapiro, P. (1989a). Effects of anxiety on impression formation in a group context: An anxiety–assimilation hypothesis. *Journal of Experimental Social Psychology, 25,* 481–499.

Wilder, D., & Shapiro, P. (1989b). Role of competition-induced anxiety in limiting the beneficial impact of positive behavior by an out-group member. *Journal of Personality and Social Psychology, 56,* 60–69.

Wilder, D., & Shapiro, P. (1991). Facilitation of outgroup stereotypes by enhanced ingroup identity. *Journal of Experimental Social Psychology, 27,* 431–452.

Wilkinson, I., & Kipnis, D. (1978). Interfirm use of power. *Journal of Applied Psychology, 63,* 315–320.

Williams, J. (1987). Eyes on the prize: America's civil rights years: 1954–1965. New York: Viking Penguin.

Williams, R. (1947). *The reduction of intergroup tensions.* New York: Social Science Research Council.

Williams, R. (1948). The effects of an interracial project upon the attitudes of Negro and white girls within the YWCA. In A. Rose (Ed.), *Studies in the reduction of prejudice.* Chicago: American Council of Race Relations.

Williams, R., & Ryan, M. (Eds.). (1954). *Schools of transition: Community experiences in desegregation.* Chapel Hill: University of North Carolina Press.

Wilner, D., Walkley, R., & Cook, S. (1952). Residential proximity and intergroup relations in public housing projects. *Journal of Social Issues, 8,* 45–69.

Winder, A. (1952). White attitudes toward Negro-white interaction in an area of changing racial composition. *American Psychologist, 7,* 330–331.

Wood, P., & Sonleitner, N. (1996). The effect of children interracial contact on adult antiblack prejudice. *International Journal of Intercultural Relations, 20,* 1–7.

Woodward, C. (1966). *The strange career of Jim Crow.* New York: Oxford University Press.

Worchel, S., Andreoli, V., & Folger, R. (1977). Intergroup cooperation and intergroup attraction: The effect of previous interaction and outcome on combined effort. *Journal of Experimental Social Psychology, 13,* 131–140.

Wright, S., Aron, A., McLaughlin-Volpe, T., & Ropp, S. (1997). The extended contact effect: Knowledge of cross-group friendships and prejudice. *Journal of Personality and Social Psychology, 73*(1), 73–90.

Yarrow, M., Campbell, J., & Yarrow, L. (1958). Interpersonal dynamics in racial integration. In E. Maccoby, T. Newcomb, & E. Hartley (Eds.), *Readings in social psychology.* New York: Holt, Rinehart, & Winston.

Yinger, J. (1995). *Closed doors, opportunities lost: The continuing costs of housing discrimination.* New York: Russell Sage Foundation.

Young, D. (1932). *American minority people: A study in racial and cultural conflicts in the United States.* New York: Harper.

Zuwerink, J., Monteith, M., Devine, P., & Cook, D. (1996). Prejudice towards Blacks: With and without compunction? *Basic and Applied Social Psychology, 18,* 131–150.